Sophie Hohmann holds a PhD in social sciences and demography from the EHESS (School of Advanced Studies in Social Sciences) in Paris.

Claire Mouradian is senior research fellow at the CNRS (National Centre for Scientific Research) and coordinates Caucasian studies at the CERCEC (Centre for Russian, Caucasian and East-European Studies).

Silvia Serrano is maître de conférences (associated professor) in political science at the Universite d'Auvergne in Clermont-Ferrand and is a research fellow at the CERCEC, EHESS/CNRS.

Julien Thorez is research fellow at the CNRS in Paris and member of the unit 'Iranian and Indian Worlds' composed of researchers from the CNRS, EPHE (Practical School of Advanced Studies), Sorbonne Nouvelle and INALCO (National Institute for Oriental Languages and Civilisations).

DEVELOPMENT IN CENTRAL ASIA AND THE CAUCASUS

Migration, Democratisation and Inequality in the Post-Soviet Era

Edited by

Sophie Hohmann, Claire Mouradian, Silvia Serrano and Julien Thorez

I.B. TAURIS
LONDON · NEW YORK

Published in 2014 by I.B.Tauris & Co Ltd
6 Salem Road, London W2 4BU
175 Fifth Avenue, New York NY 10010
www.ibtauris.com

Distributed in the United States and Canada
Exclusively by Palgrave Macmillan
175 Fifth Avenue, New York NY 10010

Library of International Relations 70

ISBN: 978 1 78076 579 2

A full CIP record for this book is available from the British Library
A full CIP record is available from the Library of Congress

Library of Congress Catalog Card Number: available

Typeset in Garamond Three by OKS Prepress Services, Chennai, India
Printed and bound by CPI Group (UK) Ltd, Croydon, CR0 4YY

CONTENTS

LIST OF FIGURES

LIST OF TABLES

LIST OF MAPS

the thought process and institutional development inside the academic world is in tune with geopolitical tendencies. This work is the result of a call for contributions to promote the analysis of the 'Global South',[4] and this framework has without doubt influenced the research questions raised by the contributing authors.

Authors responded to a call for project made by the IRD (Institut de Recherche pour le Développement), an institution founded on the desire of the French state to arm itself with the necessary tools to maintain its colonial empire and ensure cooperation with developing countries after decolonization. The call for project was made in the context of academic and ideological traditions anchored in French colonial history. As such, applying the term 'South' to the republics of Central Asia and the Caucasus raised questions regarding the notion itself and the role of these regions in the world. The project 'The post-Soviet Caucasus and Central Asia: another South?' was carried out between 2007 and 2011 by a French team of researchers from several social science fields: historians, sociologists, political scientists, geographers, anthropologists. The team worked with authors from both the Western world and the concerned countries of the South. This book presents the results of field work and the consecutive discussions held at the closing conference in Almaty, Kazakstan in 2011.[5]

From where we write in France, the established West with its specific view of the world, we analyse the 'South' from a critical standpoint with the aim of 1) re-examining the position of the Caucasus and Central Asian republics of the USSR as regards Moscow by considering them within the context of recent debates on empires and post-colonialism; 2) opening up the post-Soviet space in connection with the analysis of globalization and the global balance of power since the disintegration of the USSR. Use of the term 'South' allows us to analyse the notion of domination within the current global world. It shows the states of the Caucasus and Central Asia as new areas of influence for the great powers, both global and regional. Stéphane de Tapia invites us to take a close look at the strategies of medium-sized powers in the region, such as Turkey, and to consider the various political, economic and cultural policies of the Turkish presence in Central Asia.

On a wider note, this book considers positioning within the 'World-Economy', to quote I. Wallerstein, to be a determining factor for post-Soviet trajectories. The latter cannot be fully understood from a state-centred approach alone but should be considered in a global context and coupled with the evolution of a 'World-System'. In this system of domination, Central Asian states and the Caucasus are a 'periphery', a divergent one as George Tarkhan-Mouravi points out. They are a 'South' whose 'North', Russia, went through similar economic, social and political changes.

Disparity, Crisis, Poverty: the Passage South

The years following the disintegration of the USSR correspond to a general collapse of the economy, reflected by a spectacular drop in the GDP of all former Soviet Union countries. From 1990 to 1995, the GDP per capita for Armenia was halved, divided in three in the case of Georgia and Tajikistan and even the better fairing countries faced considerable declines.[6]

The change from an essentially self-sustained and closed system to a system open to the liberal world economy, along with the disorganization of Soviet economic relations, created inequalities only intensified by the imposition of neoliberal 'solutions' (budget balancing, ending of exchange control, opening of borders, privatizations, liberalization of prices, etc.). Added to this were the economic consequences of the conflicts affecting many of these republics including destruction, refugees and the consequences of military investments.

The general impoverishment of those states once belonging to one of the world's superpowers is the first reason for using of the term 'South.' Despite resumed growth at the end of the 1990s, with growth rates exceeding 10 per cent at the beginning of the 2000s for many countries, the GDP per capita can still be compared to states normally classed as 'South'. For example, in 2010 the GDP per capita[7] for Tajikistan ($1,940) was below that of Cambodia ($1,968), the GDP for Kyrgyzstan ($2,039) was between that of Sudan ($2,023) and Cameroon ($2,058), and Georgia ($4,551) only just exceeded that of Bolivia ($4,350). Renewed growth was accompanied by a change in the GDP make-up of these countries where the exportation of raw materials, agricultural products and workers occupied an ever-increasing place alongside services, to the detriment of industries inherited from the Soviet era.

The hardship faced by these countries is as disparate as their integration into the world economy. Recourse to solutions provided by international financial institutions varies depending on the state, the strategies adopted by leaders and the capacity of the republics to use their own resources. Kyrgyzstan was the first former USSR country to enter the WTO in 1998, in stark contrast to neighbouring Uzbekistan which continues to control prices, exchanges and international trading of cotton. As they take up their places in the world market, countries rich in natural resources, oil and gas, benefit from high prices on the hydrocarbons market. This goes a long way to explaining the varying recovery and growth rates. The GDP of Azerbaijan in 2010 reached almost two and a half times that of 1990, whereas Tajikistan had still not returned to 1990 figures. A North/South divide is thus apparent within the Central Asia and Caucasus region, as pointed out by Julien Thorez.

Even those countries with rapid economic growth during the 2000s experienced social and even demographic repercussions from these economic changes. Reduced investment in education, 'deindustrialization' and increased inequalities all had consequences on education and training, as highlighted by Saodat Olimova and Muzaffar Olimov when they refer to 'human capital'. In most of these countries, life expectancy at birth dropped between 1990 and 1995 and death rates exceeded birth rates in the three countries of the Caucasus. This can be linked to the collapse of the Soviet health system as health expenditure per inhabitant per annum (in current $ per annum) in 2009 aligned Uzbekistan ($62) with Senegal ($59) and placed Georgia ($256) alongside Gabon ($266).

Although comparisons and statistics are a means to draw parallels, sometimes unexpected and thus leading to occasional disapproval at local level, their role is limited due to the use of various indicators. Cécile Lefèvre and Sophie Hohmann reiterate how the choice of a development indicator, such as the HDI which includes literacy levels, ranks countries at the high end of the scale due to successful schooling levels inherited from the Soviet era.

However, these figures do not take the perceived measure of poverty into consideration. Inflation, non-payment of salaries and collapse of the social security system all affected individual situations but were also seen by the citizens of the ex-USSR as signs of the state collapsing. In many countries, perceived poverty led to a sentiment of downgrading and state abandon, coupled with a feeling of loss of power in the aftermath of the disintegration of the USSR.[8] This feeling of collapse predominated and, as such, Central Asian NGOs only recently applied the term 'South' to affirm their position in a 'Global South' with common challenges and wealth.[9]

The diverse evolutions of the ex-USSR countries, and the 'passage South' for some of them, can also be viewed in the context of labour migration developments since the beginning of the 2000s. According to the World Bank, Russia is now home to the second largest number of migrants in the world.[10] Central Asian countries, influenced by international organizations, tend to model migration policies on those developed by other Asian countries.[11]

These migrations are perceived as the movement of a less developed South towards a more developed North, reflecting stereotypes of an underdeveloped Central Asia and Caucasus. Claire Mouradian illustrates this as a continuation of the opinions and management methods of the Russian Empire that existed throughout the Soviet era. They are also a result of the Soviet management of diasporas and vision of migrants as a necessary but poorly qualified workforce, bringing with them certain sanitation risks as mentioned by Anne Le Huérou. The new diasporas of Europe and the United States highlight the desire of certain states to reinforce their presence abroad and are, as such, used as a foreign policy tool, as Sergey Rumyantsev highlights regarding Azerbaijan.

On the basis of demand for workers, migration had become a fundamental question in Russia by the end of the 2000s, both politically and academically. Most research institutes of the Academy of Science of the Russian Federation have broached the question, with studies often financed by international organizations working with researchers from Central Asia and the Caucasus. Natalya Zotova's article is a particularly interesting reflection on these practices and related research conditions.

Methods of Governance and Political Construction

'Transitology' was one of the lasting analytical theories used to conceptualize the post-Soviet period.[12] Based on the idea of rational choice, this paradigm concentrated on agents, prioritized politics over structures and the economy and tended to focus on state level, overlooking international factors influencing change. The theory was also highly ambitious believing in the creation of programmes to export/diffuse democracy and that lessons learnt from prior transitions would form a basis for assisting transition policies, including institutional reforms and privatization programmes.[13] The transitional paradigm formatted the cognitive frameworks of elites of certain states of the Caucasus and Central Asia, on the basis of which policies were established. In the case of post-Soviet states, the move away from an authoritarian regime and the planned economy were brought to the fore, as opposed to the move away from colonial or imperial rule.

Only recently have case studies on the region appeared in collective works, for example alongside publications on the state or political regimes in Africa.[14] Irrespective of the comparative nature of these works, there is a shift in political studies concerning the region which also results from new academic approaches.

The 2000s brought with it disappointment as to the slow arrival of democracy. Publications focused more on the numerous post-Soviet trajectories[15] and the diverse and hybrid nature of regimes.[16] Questions arose concerning the obstacles preventing transition or democratic consolidation at development, institutional inheritance or cultural and geopolitical level. Indeed, the evolution of post-Soviet regimes dampened hopes of a democratic transition, failures[17] and delays[18] are highlighted. General consensus was that the arrival of a market economy came hand in hand with democracy. However, in most cases this correlation was not confirmed. This is further marked by the reinforcement of semi-authoritarian regimes,[19] with the formal characteristics of democracy but without the risk of the ruling class losing power.

For hydrocarbon-rich states such as Kazakhstan, Turkmenistan or Azerbaijan, revenues provide the elite with an opportunity to benefit from privatizations and cash on resources and capital and, via new clients, consolidate their domination through both strong bureaucracy–inherited from the USSR and/or (re)produced by ad hoc policies–and non-official networks. As Hélène Rousselot points out with regards to Kazakhstan and Turkmenistan, the question of income-sharing and possible modalities of participation arises. The neopatrimonal regimes that appeared in Uzbekistan,[20] Kazakhstan[21] and Azerbaijan[22] combined legal-rational authority with, at times, exorbitant personal power. In these cases, transition was from one form of authoritarianism to another.

On the other hand, states with few resources, such as Georgia or Kyrgyzstan, have depended more on international aid programmes. They played the democracy card to secure aid, but democracy from above, powered by donors and foreign 'partners'. Elites with limited means to consolidate their power saw this aid as an opportunity to reinforce credibility, although with no guarantee of stability. This can be seen with the various 'revolutions' that occurred in some of these countries (2003 Rose Revolution in Georgia, 2005 Tulip Revolution in Kyrgyzstan) and the following political upheavals (Russian-Georgian war of August 2008, inter-ethnic clashes in Osh, Kyrgyzstan in 2010).

A strong regime does not necessarily mean a strong state. Some states succeeded in consolidating without democratizing under a neo-patrimonial regime that does not exclude a certain level of redistribution and increased state capacity, as seen with Kazakhstan. However, the appropriation of riches by the elite in power, as in Uzbekistan[23] or Azerbaijan, can affect the development potential of a country. In the last case, and as a result of the lack of resolution in the

Nagorno-Karabagh conflict, state means were allocated to reinforcing coercive capacity,[24] sometimes to the detriment of the social sector.

Some countries were incapacitated to the extent that they were described as weak or 'failed' states. This labelling by think tanks, based on a univocal analysis of the situation, justifies international guardianship.[25] Labelling Georgia as a failed state in 2002 legitimized sending US military instructors in the framework of the Equip and Train programme. For Russian ideologist A. Dugin, it was also justification for the assault of the Russian army in August 2008. A poorly centralized coercive apparatus, an inability to control borders, often coupled with the tricky task of redefining borders with neighbours, and a labour flow onto the territory are all taken as signs of a failed state, more so than the low level of tax collection, lack of redistribution and collapse of the tools of the welfare state.

These so-called 'failed' periphery states are under more pressure than others to redefine their public policies on the basis of neo-liberal governance. As with other 'Souths' in the past, external aid depended on 'structural reforms', which meant the privatization of public services. States are not entirely powerless in the face of these paradoxes of good governance, as Mana Farooghi points out for Tajikistan, although their room for manoeuvre is reduced. States now compete at global level, rewarded by international organizations as they climb the ratings based on benchmarks which supposedly reflect the success of reforms. These ratings in turn become a criterion for investors and public authorities keen to be perceived as 'good students' and model new policies on this basis.

Following neo-liberal doctrine, reducing state perimeters increases efficiency and part of the prerogatives formerly vested in the welfare state are carried out by independent agencies, foreign foundations and NGOs, for example in the social, health or education sectors.[26] The flip-side of this self-divestiture is the fragmentation of the public action, becoming less coherent as reforms are implemented on the basis of different market models.[27] This division of common goods and services formerly provided by the state reinforces social and territorial inequalities.

State privatization can sometimes lead to core state prerogatives passing into the hands of private enterprises. In the context of negotiations for Russian membership to the WTO, Georgia privatized customs control. In Azerbaijan, the desire to overcome obstacles linked to the competition of patronage networks at the head of the state gave rise to a 'doubling-up' of structures responsible for external politics. Consequently, in some countries, oil companies *de facto* represent the state of Azerbaijan, with embassies playing a secondary role.

Externalizing state governance also has implications on the construction of politics. The promotion of democracy brings with it an invitation to build a civil society to complement state structures. Lobbying, as opposed to competition and political impulsion, is encouraged with political institutions being delegitimized to the benefit of associations as participation becomes less political. 'Vivid' civil society runs parallel to weak parties and ideological polarizations. Opposition is thus often outside party politics, as seen with the increasing predominance of religious actors.

This book aims to analyze the post-Soviet trajectory of Central Asia and the Caucasus and to develop methodology based on case studies. It reflects a multidisciplinary approach including as many processes as there are authors and social sciences. It is based on data collected during field trips, in particular interviews, observations, and the analysis of information provided by local administrations and archives. All contributing sociologists, political scientists, anthropologists, historians, and geographers, originating from Central Asia, the Caucasus, Russia, Japan and Europe, promote field work and provide studies based on an empirical method with the reactions, habits, customs, views and actions of relevant actors at the centre of the analysis of the socio-political changes experienced by the Caucasus and Central Asian republics since the collapse of the USSR.

This book is composed of four parts, respectively addressing the imperial and post-colonial issue, the question of development, migrations and external influences linked to globalization. Each chapter highlights the complex factors that have influenced trajectories since the end of the Soviet system.

To help understand the diverse nature of countries of Central Asia and the Caucasus, the first part considers the most appropriate analytical perspective: post-colonial or post-Soviet? It first looks at practices under the Russian Empire, later used by the Bolsheviks (chapter 1), reconsiders management policies under Brejnev (chapter 2), discusses the articulation between these categories and that of Nation within Central Asia (chapter 3) and finally highlights the areas of tension and clusters formed by post-Soviet countries (chapter 4).

The second part considers development, inequality and poverty, three notions that are at the heart of the definition of 'South', in their economical through to social contexts. After examining the effects of the resources based economy in Kazakstan and Turkmenistan (chapter 5), the roles played by the notion of Human Capital in Tajikistan (chapter 6), poverty measures in Central Asia and the Caucasus are considered (chapter 7).

The third part looks at labour migration and what this reveals about new North–South relations. An initial chapter covers the correlation between the development of regional inequalities and that of migrations and migration routes (chapter 8), followed by an anthropological approach in a study on female migrations made by women migrants (chapter 9). Labour migrations in the town of Omsk are then analysed by looking at management practices and the creation of new social relations (chapter 10).

Finally, the fourth part considers this region in a global context, where state strategies and actions of international organizations are played out. State practices are considered via the policies of the creation of a diaspora in Azerbaijan (chapter 11), Turkish foreign policy in Central Asia (chapter 12) and finally with the example of Tajikistan and the effect of geopolitical externalities on state agendas (chapter 13).

Complex factors have thus influenced trajectories since the end of the Soviet era. Amongst others, state resources and becoming part of the global economy go a long way to explaining the differences observed between states. As such, developments in Central Asia and the Caucuses cannot be analysed without taking into account the balance of power at global level. At the heart of this book is the analysis of domination, its social and spatial geography and an examination of the economic, political and discursive tools which enable domination to take place. This book also focuses on the strategies and room for manoeuvre of agents (states, international organisations, enterprises, associations, individuals) involved in new North/South relationships within the post-Soviet sphere.

Notes

1 In particular, the analysis of indicators and infant mortality rates (see Blum, A., *Naître, vivre et mourir en URSS*, Paris: Payot, 2004, p. 315, and Hohmann, S., *La mortalité infantile et juvénile en Ouzbékistan*, Sarrebruck: Editions Universitaires Européennes, 2010).

2 Burbank, J., Cooper, F., *Empires in World History: Power and the Politics of Difference,* Princeton, NJ: Princeton University Press, 2009.

3 Adams, L., 'Can We Apply a Post-colonial Theory to Central Asia?', *Central Eurasia Studies Review,* 2008, vol. 7/1, pp. 2–8; Reeves, M., 'Locating danger: *konfliktologiia* and the search for fixity in the Ferghana Valley borderlands', *Central Asian Survey*, 2005, vol. 24/1, pp. 67–81.

4 The programme '*Suds*' of the *Agence nationale de la recherche* (France) was launched jointly with the *IRD* (*Institut de Recherche pour le Développement*, France) in 2007 as a call for projects.

5 'The Caucasus and Central Asia Twenty Years after Independence: Questioning the notion of "South countries"' organized in collaboration with the Institute for Oriental Studies Suleymenov, Kazakhstan, August 25–27, 2011.

6 Unless otherwise stated, all figures provided herein come from statistics of the project *'Perspective monde'* of the University of Sherbrooke, itself based on data from the World Bank (http://perspective.usherbrooke.ca). Although statistics provided by the Statistical Committee of the Soviet Union *(Goskomstat)* and the CIS states differ, the general evolution and quantification of changes of these figures are comparable (see for example the analyses of Radvanyi, J., *Les Etats post-soviétiques. Identités en construction, transformations politiques, trajectoires économiques,* Paris: Armand Colin, 3rd edn, 2011).

7 GDP per inhabitant in purchasing power parity and constant 2000 international dollars.

8 Hours, B., Sélim, M., 'La pauvreté à l'épreuve de l'Ouzbékistan', *Homme et la société*, 2006, vol. 2/3, n°160–161, pp. 221–38.

9 Moldosheva, A., 'Gender in Development: Who Are the Winners and Losers?' in *The Caucasus and Central Asia Twenty Years after the Independence: Rethinking the Notion of South Countries*, Almaty, August 2011, Conference Proceedings, Paris,

Almaty: CERCEC and Institute of Oriental Studies, 2011, pp. 182–6 (http://lodel.ehess.fr/cercec/docannexe.php?id=1705).

10 World Bank, *Migration and Remittances Factbook 2011* (http://siteresources.worldbank.org/INTPROSPECTS/Resources/334934-1199807908806/Top10.pdf).

11 Regamey, A., 'Importing the Filipino Model of Migration Management in Tajikistan', in *The Caucasus and Central Asia Twenty Years after the Independence: Rethinking the Notion of South Countries*, Almaty, August 2011, Conference Proceedings, Paris, Almaty: CERCEC and Institute of Oriental Studies, 2011, pp. 76–81.

12 Linz, J.J., Stepan, A.C., *Problems of Democratic Transition and Consolidation: Southern Europe, South America, and Post-Communist Europe*, Washington D.C.: Johns Hopkins University Press, 1996; O'Donnell, G., Schmitter, P., Whitehead, L., *Transitions from Authoritarian Rule: Tentative Conclusions About Uncertain Democracies*, Washington D.C.: Johns Hopkins University Press, 1986.

13 Nodia, G., 'The democratic path', *Journal of Democracy*, 2002, vol. 13/3.

14 See for instance Bessinger, M., Young, C. (eds), *Beyond State Crisis? Post-Colonial Africa and Post-Soviet Eurasia in Comparative Perspective*, Washington D.C.: Woodrow Wilson Center Press, 2002; Bach, D., Gazibo, M. (eds), *Neopatrimonialism in Africa and Beyond*, London & New York, Routledge, 2012.

15 Carothers, T., 'The end of the transition paradigm', *Journal of Democracy*, 2002, vol. 13/1.

16 Diamond, 2002.

17 Jones, S.F., 'Georgia: A Failed Democratic Transition', in Bremmer, I, Taras, R. (eds), *Nations and Politics in the Soviet Successor States*, New York: Cambridge University Press, 1993.

18 Wheatley, J., *Georgia from National Awakening to Rose Revolution: Delayed Transition in the Former Soviet Union*, Aldershot (UK) & Burlington, Vt, Ashgate, 2005.

19 Ottaway, M., *Democracy Challenged: The Rise of Semi-Authoritarianism*, Washington D.C.: Carnegie Endowment for International Peace, 2003.

20 Ikhamov, A., 'Neopatrimonialism, Patronage and Factionalism in Post-Soviet Uzbekistan', in Bach, D., Gazibo, M., *Neopatrimonialism in Africa and Beyond*, Routledge, 2012, pp. 186–96.

21 Dumoulin, M., 'Générations et profils de carrière au sein de l'élite politique kazakhstanaise', *Revue d'études comparatives Est-Ouest*, 2012, vol. 43/1–2.

22 Lussac, S., *L'Azerbaïdjan, les hydrocarbures et les pipelines. Réseaux sociotechniques et régionalisation*, PhD thesis under the direction of Daniel Compagnon, Bordeaux: Institut of Political Studies, 2011.

23 On the wealth of the daughter of the Uzbek President, Gulnara Karimova, see for example 'De Tachkent à Cologny. La saga des sœurs Karimova', *L'Hebdo*, 22 December 2010 (http://www.hebdo.ch/la_saga_des_karimova_77690_.html).

24 With an 89 per cent increment in 2011, Azerbaijan increased its military spending more than any other country worldwide (see data of SIPRI on http://www.sipri.org/research/armaments/milex).

25 For example, the classification of the Fund for Peace and Foreign Policy, that places Turkey and the states of the Caucasus and Central Asia in the same region: http://www.fundforpeace.org/global/?q=states-region-centralasia.

26 Baumann, E., 'Social Protection in the South: Georgia and Senegal. To compare the Incomparable?' in *The Caucasus and Central Asia Twenty Years after the Independence: Rethinking the Notion of South Countries*, Almaty, August 2011, Conference Proceedings, Paris, Almaty: CERCEC and Institute of Oriental Studies, 2011.

27 Closson, S., 'State Weakness in Perspective: Strong Politico-Economic Networks in Georgia's Energy Sector', *Europe-Asia Studies*, 2009, vol. 61/5, pp. 759–78; Christophe, B., 'From Hybrid Regime to Hybrid Capitalism? The Political Economy of Georgia under Eduard Shevardnadze', in Koehler, J., Zürcher, C. (eds), *Potentials of Disorder*, Manchester: Manchester University Press, 2003.

PART 1

POST-SOVIET REGION OR POST-COLONIAL COUNTRIES?

CHAPTER 1

THE ORIGINS OF A COLONIAL VISION OF SOUTHERN RUSSIA FROM THE TSARS TO THE SOVIETS: ABOUT SOME IMPERIAL PRACTICES IN THE CAUCASUS

Claire Mouradian
(CNRS & EHESS—School of Advanced Studies in Social Sciences, Paris)

> We know that the working masses of the East are in some places, through no fault of their own, very backward: illiterate, ignorant, they are sunk in superstition and believe in spirits, they are unable to read newspapers, they do not know what is going on in the world at large, they do not understand the most elementary principles of hygiene . . . that is their misfortune . . . The task of the more civilized, more literate, more organized workers of Europe and America is to help the backward toilers of the East. Not to mock them, not to put on airs, not to swank about their superiority over the backward Eastern peasants, but to be concerned about the ignorance and backwardness of the latter, to extend the hand of aid to them, and to help them.[1]

In the early days of the new Soviet regime, Zinoviev, chairman of the Komintern, used these condescending clichés in his inaugural speech to the Congress of the Peoples of the East in Baku, when summoning colonized peoples to 'a Holy War ... against British imperialism' and arguing for a break with Tsarist colonial policy. For the 50th anniversary of the USSR, one of the many official commemorative texts boasted of the achievements of this 'Russian helping hand', repeating the standard refrain of colonial empires' civilizing mission:

> For the peoples of the Caucasus, Central Asia, Kazakhstan and other nationalities, annexation to Russia preserved them from absorption by even less advanced neighbouring powers, ended their devastating internal wars and then brought them into the general system of capital-intensive development and associated them with the highly developed democratic culture of the Russian people.[2]

When the USSR collapsed, the so-called 'inter-ethnic' conflicts, in fact post-colonial, that erupted in these regions were often ascribed to the failure–and not to the principle–of this civilizing mission, seen in Soviet times in terms of economic modernization, a failure caused by the immensity of the task.[3]

From the Tsars to the Soviets, the viewpoint of the central Russian state on the management of the Southern edge of its area of domination was indissociable from two recurring and related debates that emerged from the 18th century onwards both inside and outside the country: Russian identity[4]–European? Asian? Eurasian?–and the nature of the Empire and the purpose of its expansion–defensive or colonial? To this were added in Soviet times the controversies about the character of the new federal state, an empire inheriting and continuing the tsarist 'prison of peoples' under another form in which the Russians would remain 'more equal than others', the very model of the radiant city of 'friendship between peoples' or 'incubator of nations' (not necessarily a contradiction). At present, there is the question of this inheritance in terms of mental representation, the status of the successor states and the factors determining their post-Soviet paths.

Since not all these questions can be addressed here, except by implication, it seems worth to replace the steps leading to the emergence of the new independent states of the region in a *longue durée* historical perspective and to confort the issue of the colonial legacy of Russian and Soviet regimes. I intend in this chapter to look at the origins of the imperial vision and economic and administrative policies for the South of the Empire, using the Caucasus as a case study. From its earliest conquest to the end of the Soviet period, despite the formal disappearance of the inequality between the 'rulers' and 'ruled' after 1917, a number of obvious elements of continuity can be seen in the conception of a centralized state drawing its power from the dominant role of 'elder brother', imposing its culture and vision of the world, directly or indirectly, be it in the name of nationalism or internationalism, but always with the conviction of belonging to a superior civilization.[5]

An 'Atypical' Colonial Empire?

As Dominic Lieven points out,[6] the word empire did not always have the negative connotation it took on under the Marxist definition of a political, cultural and economically exploitative domination by a national metropolis of its colonial periphery, supposedly applicable only to the modern maritime empires of Western Europe.[7] As a specialist in the Tsarist governing elite from which he himself 'descends',[8] Lieven still hesitates to call the Russian Empire colonial, a step that other historians of Russia, particularly of its Southern possessions, find it much easier to take.[9]

With the short-lived exception after October 1917 of the school of the orthodox Marxist Pokrovsky,[10] Soviet historiography not only promoted the image of the USSR as a champion of anti-colonial struggle but also provided it with a genealogy by rehabilitating the Tsarist Empire as a 'lesser evil', and then under Stalin as an 'absolute good': had it not snatched from the grasp of neighbouring 'Oriental despotisms' peoples who were thus able to enjoy 'enlightened' administration and then, the 'radiant future' of Communism thanks to its Revolutionary vanguard? Not the least of the fictions created was that of the colonizing nation as 'victim', devoting itself at the cost of its own interests to the progress of the colonized. The 50th anniversary of the USSR was one of the emblematic opportunities to express this:

> Within the bosom of the united family of Soviet peoples, it was easier for the developed regions and primarily the Russian people and working class to help the workers of the former national periphery in economic and cultural terms. This aid, said Leonid [Brejnev], this readiness to make enormous efforts and, to put it frankly, sacrifices to overcome the backwardness of the national peripheral regions and ensure their accelerated development, was recommended to the Russian proletariat by Lenin as an internationalist duty of the highest importance. And the Russian working class, the Russian people have carried out this task with honour.[11]

Is there not here a distant echo of Kipling's 'white man's burden'? Traces of it can still be found in the bitter remarks of some Russian politicians, whether nationalist or liberal, among the Neo-Eurasianists and certain post-Soviet scholars,[12] who attribute the misfortunes of their country to the 'sacrifices' made by the imperial centre.

One specific characteristic of the Russian Empire, straddling Europe and Asia, is the continental manner of its expansion, the ambivalent and pragmatic forms of its domination, sometimes flexible, sometimes less so, over the vast time and space of its conquest. And also the status of the conquered territories, the marches of other empires, the political entities of varying structure and autonomy, whose elites sometimes sought the support of the Russians, as of other conquerors before them, to free themselves from their masters of the moment or to settle their internal disputes and dynastic quarrels. This gave rise to the myth of 'voluntary union' with Russia, extending the theme of the 'gathering of Russian lands', apparently supported by the earlier feudal practice[13] of co-opting loyal elites in conquered areas. Examples were the Tatar, Baltic and Georgian nobilities, integrated into the Tsarist army and state apparatus. Another feature that differs from the other European powers: the comparison of the level of political and cultural development and economic and social conditions of the 'natives', with their strong identities and a past that could have been glorious and prosperous, did not always favour a colonizer whose peasants were serfs and whose nobility was subjugated by the sovereign. This was blatantly clear in the European part of the Empire (Poland, Baltic States) and even in the Caucasus and Central Asia, a crossroads of ancient civilizations and major trade routes between East and West, such as the Silk Road. The image of a crude, poor Russia was often unimpressive for the colonized peoples, even when that country had numerical and military superiority. The authorities would do their best to reverse this image.

In the long history of the formation of the Empire,[14] the difficult conquest of the Caucasus and Central Asia, although it may have been defined as 'defensive imperialism',[15] appears on the face of it more similar to the European colonial adventure. No doubt because of the 'exotic' nature of these peoples, enabling the Russians to escape from their complex of being thought 'Asian' in Paris and London, at least until Peter the Great. The conquest of Ukraine, Poland and the Baltic countries had already brought them geographically closer to Western Europe. Their drive to the 'South' and East, while establishing them in Asia, confirmed their 'Europeanness' by enabling them to project every Orientalist stereotype they have suffered onto the real 'Orientals' on their periphery, leading to the inferiorization of this 'barbarous' and 'backward' Other: the conquest was legitimized not only by the need to open up sea trade routes and acquire new resources, but also by the civilizing mission of a modernized state, indeed the protective mission of the 'Third Rome' towards Christians ill-treated by 'Oriental despotisms', enshrined in the Treaty of Küçük Kaynarca (1774) that initiated the Eastern Question,[16] and the right to defend oneself by exterminating, if necessary, the 'savage' 'mountaineer' and 'nomad'.

In 1776, General Jacobi, Governor of Astrakhan charged with studying the plans for the Caucasus Line, produced a report that already contains elements of this discourse, defining the network of military fortifications along the rivers to consolidate the Russian advance as the border between civilization and barbarity, order and disorder, a border protecting the proper order and economic development of a modern state:

> This line protects from neighbours' raids the border between Astrakhan and the Don and the lands of our Kalmyks and Tatars, giving them the means to spread out all the way to *Temnoi Les* (Dark Wood) and the Egorlyk and thus access to better means of subsistence, and separating the various mountain peoples for grazing cattle and herds of horses from the regions that are for the profit of our subjects; it is so placed as to make it possible to build mills to produce wine, silk and paper, develop cattle raising, horse breeding, gardens and arable land . . . During any war with neighbouring peoples, it can stop their raids on our lands, support the operations of our troops in Crimea and other places; furthermore, it opens up a way to enter the mountains and the lands of the Ossetians, and in time, to exploit their mines and ores; it will prevent the smuggling of prohibited goods into Russia, thus increasing the customs revenues that are at present insignificant because of the many open roads across the steppe.[17]

'Enlightened' Conquest and 'Holy War'

During the Russo–Turkish war of 1787–1791, a mysterious Sheikh Mansur[18] preached a 'holy war' (*gazavat*) to the Circassians (Adyghe) who had only recently become Muslims. They were motivated actually much more by the rejection of all domination and growing hostility towards the colonists settling in the piedmont with the support of the army. Their resistance might be legitimate but it was an unbearable affront to the advance of Enlightenment that Catherine II so prized:

> The anarchy that is at the root of the disorder, insolence and pillage in Greater and Lesser Kabarda is the reason why this people that is subject to Us has not so far been able to be of use to Our Empire, creating by its violence many a trouble and concern; but We are convinced that it is easy to tame this people's fierce manners by following the rules that conform to Our known humanitarian feelings and Our concern for the welfare of all. The peoples living in the inaccessible mountains where they have safe shelter against Our troops must not be driven by the force of arms, but their trust must be gained by justice and fairness, their manner softened by mercy, their hearts won over and accustomed to dealings with the Russians.[19]

The Westward expansion after the three Partitions of Poland with Austria and Prussia (1772, 1793, 1795), victories over the Turks and Persians, the cultural and political role of Germans at court and in the exploration of the Caucasus,[20] the influence of the Enlightenment, in particular the 'theory of climates', all encouraged a growing Eurocentrism and a new feeling of superiority over the East. After religion (Christianity, Islam and animism), way of life (sedentary or nomadic) also became a criterion for ranking humankind, supposed to have regularly evolved from hunting and gathering to nomadic animal husbandry and finally to sedentarization. The nomad and his Caucasian variant–the mountaineer–became synonyms for backwardness and then moral inferiority. The break occurred in 1767, when nomads were excluded from the Legislative Commission, although sedentary Muslims and Animists were accepted. The nomads were explicitly designated to be second-class subjects and placed under specific legislation.

Any resistance to such an 'enlightened' state could only provide evidence of the 'fierce manners' of these local 'savages'–the mountaineers–who were to be 'tamed' by force (military operations, population transfer to the piedmont for better control), by coaxing (offers of service in the Russian army, awards of ranks and money, of trinkets for women), the presence of civilizing settlers and missionaries, and the introduction of 'enlightened' law and order, such as elected 'tribal courts'. Unfortunately, the 'savages' were not always amenable to the 'benefits' brought by the army and the Cossacks. There began a spiral descent into guerrilla and punitive expeditions. The 1830 memorandum from the Russian Chief of Staff and future War minister Aleksandr Chernichev (1785–1857), offering France the benefit of Russian experience in the wars in the Caucasus as it prepared to conquer Kabylia in Algeria, is fairly typical of the feeling of superiority based on 'European discipline' that would crush 'the barbarians' intemperate passion'.[21]

At the same period, Platon Pavlovich Zubov, chief of the medical corps of Ermolov's army in the Caucasus, deplored the fact that this Transcaucasian Eldorado was spoilt by a lazy population intellectually stunted by long submission to the Turks and Persians and the menace of the savage mountaineers. To pacify them he suggested tempting the women with luxury products offered by missionaries who would combine trade and preaching, moving the mountaineers to central Russia and replacing them with Russian peasants, educating the children of the co-opted nobility in schools in St Petersburg and then, in a second stage, religious conversion, since the subtleties of the Christian faith were too difficult for them.[22] Ermolov,[23] for whom the Caucasians could be divided into 'pacifiable' and 'non-pacifiable', only envisaged extreme brutality for the latter:

> I desire that the terror of my name should guard our frontiers more potently than chains or fortresses, that my word should be for the natives a law more inevitable than death. Condescension in the eyes of Asiatics is a sign of weakness, and out of pure humanity I am inexorably severe. One execution saves hundreds of Russians from destruction, and thousands of Muslims from treason.[24]

Russia's sense of humiliation at being thwarted by a handful of 'backward' mountaineers often led to military escalation and then a war of extermination. This sometimes prompted feelings of guilt in liberal circles, where conviction of the legitimacy of civilizing conquest went with criticism of the atrocities it involved. The great figures of Romantic literature describe this development,[25] with the ambiguous figure of the mountaineer, a symbol of liberty like the wild and sublime nature where he lived, and also the 'fierce' and 'primitive' Oriental whose 'manners must be softened'. Pushkin did agree that the Circassians had reasons to hate the Russians–'We have driven them from their rich pastures, their *auls* have been razed to the ground and entire tribes annihilated'–but he also thought that to 'calm down' 'such a people' for whom murder was a 'simple corporal exercise' and whose children learnt to handle the sword and the dagger 'even before they learnt to speak', needed a combination of the sword, the samovar and the Gospel.[26]

In November 1864, as the conquest of the Caucasus had come to an end and that of Central Asia was entering its most active phase, the Foreign minister, Aleksandr Gorchakov, in a circular to his diplomats, confirmed the continuity of the 'defensive' and 'civilizing' principles of Russian expansion with now explicit reference to the competing European colonial powers:

> The situation of Russia in Central Asia is similar to that of all civilized states that come into contact with half-savage nomadic tribes without a firm social organization. In such cases, the interests of border security and trade relations always require that the more civilized state have a certain authority over its neighbors, whose wild and unruly customs render them very troublesome. It begins first by curbing raids and pillaging. To put an end to these, it is often compelled to reduce the neighboring tribes to some degree of close subordination. Once this result has been achieved, the latter take on more peaceful habits, but in their turn they are exposed to the attack of tribes living farther off ... The state therefore must make a choice: either to give up this continuous effort and doom its borders to

constant unrest, which would make prosperity, safety, and cultural progress impossible here, or else to advance farther and farther into the heart of the savage lands, where the vast distances, with every step forward, increase the difficulties and hardships it incurs. Such has been the fate of all states placed in a similar situation. The USA, France in Africa, Holland in its colonies, England in the East Indies—they all were inevitably driven to choose the path of onward movement, not so much from ambition as from dire necessity, where the greatest difficulty lies in being able to stop.[27]

Consolidating the Conquest of the South: A Constant Objective but Varying Administrative Practices

Administrative organization was intended to cement the Empire together just as the rationalization of the state, beginning in the 18th century, strengthened the legitimacy of its domination.[28] Without waiting for the din of war to cease, the earliest representatives of government were appointed, with the dual task of colonizing the territory and binding it to Russia.

For half a century the military dimension dominated all other considerations. A line of fortresses was built and secured along a moving and contested border, garrisons were established in urban centres. Civilian organization made use of the first population surveys into the number and social and national composition of hearths (households) in these new, as yet undiscovered provinces[29] whose population was to be categorized by Russian standards.

Devising a form of governance for the Caucasus was quickly seen to be a conundrum: on top of the extreme ethnic and religious diversity there was the century already spent on incorporating these lands, leading to an overlapping of highly varying practices as the region served as a laboratory, which caused many controversies of interpretation. Depending on the degree of resistance, experience acquired elsewhere in the Empire or observed in others, the methods of policy changed, even if its principles did not. Pragmatism was always applied to objectives–security along the new borders, abolition of previous structures, neutralization of focuses of separatism and administrative uniformity–that remained constant. According to the personality of the Tsar and, not least, his local representative, courtier or man of action, two opposing schools of thought alternated: rigid Russifying centralism or flexible regionalism allowing for local specific features. The Tsarist conception continually wavered between direct and indirect rule. These hesitations about tactics can, it is true, also be found in the more Northern 'European' parts of the Empire, such as Poland and Finland. But in the Caucasus, and a little later in Central Asia, the question arises whether there was a link between the more frequent brutality of Tsarist practice and the conceptualization of these regions as lands to be 'civilized'. The barons from the Baltic, over-represented in government, were often particularly arrogant.

In the first ten years of its annexation, Georgia served as an administrative laboratory. The 'Constitution of the internal organization of the administration of Georgia', promulgated on 12 September 1801 along with the Manifesto of Annexation, divided the former kingdom of Kartli-Kakheti into five *uyezds* under the authority of a military governor who, for nearly 50 years, would also be commander-in-chief of the Caucasus Line. In the four districts set up, 'state' powers (executive, economy and budget, criminal justice) belonged to the conqueror, who might or might not be assisted by local advisors, and civil affairs alone were left to a loyal Georgian.[30] One sign of state long-term thinking was the creation of an archive department in the Governor's chancellery, the embryo of the future central archives of the Caucasus.

When the highly centralizing approach of the first governor, General Knorring, a Baltic German, caused riots, St Petersburg sent for a Russo-Georgian prince Pavel Dmitriyevich Tsitsianov (Paata Tsitsishvili). He came from one of the aristocratic families of the court of King Vakhtang VI forced to seek refuge in Russia for having taken Peter I's side against Persia, and who had entered the Tsar's service.[31] Although Tsitsianov unceremoniously exiled the last representatives of the royal family, he also sought to reduce tensions:

recognition of nobles' privileges, offer of estates confiscated to the Crown and senior posts to collaborators, restitution of the Cross of Saint Nino, evangelizer of Georgia, subsidies for the restoration of Sioni Cathedral, translation into Russian of Vakhtang VI's *Code*, the collection of the country's canon and customary laws. He worked for the reunification of the Georgian principalities, even under the Tsar's authority, while fostering rivalry among the sovereigns in order to strengthen the control of the Empire, which became the arbiter between them.[32]

Tsitsianov also continued the war against the Khans of Dagestan and Azerbaijan, using diplomacy and terror to gain their allegiance and the signature of treaties of protectorate, a prelude to annexation. This became clear after the fall of Ganja (January 1804), renamed Yelizavetpol in honour of the Tsarina, a sign of the irreversible nature of the conquest. After he was killed during the siege of Baku (February 1806), policy returned to more direct methods of integration.

Tsitsianov's 'reign' did, however, establish a certain model for relations between the local and central authorities. Although the Tsar was highly jealous of his prerogatives in foreign policy, as can be seen from the frequent changes of ministers of Foreign Affairs, the chief of the Caucasus army enjoyed a *de facto* power of initiative, if only because of the slowness of communications, even though his action involved engagement with neighbouring states. This initiative also affected the social foundations of the conquered peoples: justice, land ownership, relations between nobles and peasants, religious institutions. Not without some resistance from the local population. This occurred when the venerable national Orthodox Church–Georgia's conversion (AD 321) was over six centuries older than Russia's–was brought to heel, its autocephaly abrogated (11 July 1811)[33] and the Catholicos (Antonius II, youngest son of King Erekle II) cloistered away in Russia until his death in 1828. Antonius was quickly replaced by a Russian bishop, Church Slavonic imposed in the liturgy, dioceses reorganized, Russian priests appointed to replace Georgians, church property and income taken under administration. Revolts, put down by the Tsar's troops, were numerous until the early 1840s.[34]

When the reaction was too violent and the balance of forces threatened to be reversed, administrative practice became more flexible, even under Ermolov, who combined the qualities of an administrator sensitive to grassroots reality and the wise counsels of Caucasian subordinates with a pitiless determination to 'pacify' the mountaineers. He showed this in the names he gave the fortresses along the River Sunzha: Grozny (terrible), Burnaya (turbulent), Vnezapnaya (sudden [attack]). His successor and sworn enemy Ivan Paskevich,[35] a brilliant officer who completed the conquest of Transcaucasia, and also a courtier close to Nicholas I and member of the special court that tried the Decembrists, under a more civilian guise, chose a much less subtle policy, as he pointed out in a report to the Tsar in 1833:

> The whole of the Caucasus must be attached to Russia so as to form henceforth a single body, by political and civil bonds, and its population must be forced to speak, think and feel in Russian.[36]

The task was given first to the 'Interministerial Committee for the Organization of the Territory of the Transcaucasus' or 'Caucasus Committee'.[37] This was created in 1833, reshuffled a number of times and abolished in 1882. It was chaired from 1840 by the minister of War, and comprised representatives from the ministries of War, Finance, Interior, Justice and Imperial Domains. In 1837, it was joined by a Special Commission to prepare a status for the region, in the manner of Speransky,[38] who recommended for the 'aliens' (*inorodtsy*)[39] of Siberia autonomy under the protection of the state. In October 1842, the Committee was placed under the supervision of the Tsar's Own Chancellery, Sixth Section.

Under the chairmanship of von Hahn,[40] the plan was to align civil and judicial administration on that of the Russian provinces, abolishing the last vestiges of national entities (Georgia governorate, Armenian province) in 1838 and 1840. Not without some dispute, von Hahn was relieved of his post. The Caucasus then wore out another two governors (Golovin and Neidgardt) in two years, before being entrusted to a personality of quite a different stamp, from the highest reaches of the nobility, Mikhail Vorontsov.[41]

He had been a member of the circle of liberal young aristocrats around Alexander I, was educated in England, where his father was ambassador, and had spent a couple of successful decades in the administration of New Russia (1823–1844), when Nicholas I appointed him Viceroy (*namestnik*) of the Caucasus with plenipotentiary powers, reporting solely to the Tsar (November 1844). The Caucasus Committee was reduced to being the Viceroy's office in St Petersburg. This marked a return to the pre-Petrovian system of regional *prikazy*, the reverse of specialized modern ministries. Like its precedents in Poland and Bessarabia, the viceroyalty was an extraordinary direct administration, whose character depended on the man at the top. Vorontsov's more flexible and 'enlightened' approach did not prevent him continuing the war. But rather than engage in expensive and ineffective broad offensives, Vorontsov preferred the tactic of strangling the mountaineers with a *cordon sanitaire* and dividing those who resisted. In this way he rallied the tribal chiefs of Dagestan by restoring their traditional rights, which had been abolished by the Murids of Imam Shamil. Although final victory and Shamil's surrender only occurred under his successor, Baryatinsky,[42] a former subaltern of Ermolov's, it was Volontsov's cunning policy that prepared them.

Territorial division were revised along lines closer to the ancient entities. The governorates of Tiflis and Kutaisi more or less corresponded to the kingdoms of Kartli-Kakheti and Imereti respectively. Similarly, the province of the Caspian was split into three governorates: Derbent (Dagestan), Shemakha (Azerbaijan) and Erivan (Armenia), which tended to reduce the tensions that came from bringing hostile groups together, and also subtly advanced the process of absorption; administrative units were no longer named ethnically but toponymically, in this case by their main town, like French *départements* by geographical features since the Revolution. The Viceroy's Council and Chancellery, made up of Russians and

Caucasians, bound together the new system, combining direct government with decentralized administration. Tiflis (Tbilisi) became the capital of the Caucasus. One of the Caucasians' main demands, to be tried under their own laws, was met in part. Vorontsov commissioned a new translation of Vakhtang's *Code*. In fact, of several hundred rules, only 20 were included in the tenth volume of the *Collection of Laws of the Russian Empire,* applicable in the Georgian provinces.

Access to senior administrative and military posts was opened up to the local elites, not without some discrimination. Vorontsov preferred to employ Christians, particularly Georgians, whose historic nobility was better preserved than that of the Armenians deprived earlier of their state. The Viceroy judged the Georgians better fitted by social and religious affinity to seize the advantages of Russian 'civilization'. Rather like the indigenous schools in the French colonies, an educational network was set up, first with a special status (1848), and then integrated into the imperial system (1853). It quickly grew. One hundred and sixty government scholarships a year for studies in Russia crowned this project of assimilation by education. Vorontsov also encouraged intellectual life (press, printing houses, bookshops, drama troupes in local languages, Caucasus branch of the Imperial Russian Geographical Society, etc.). Ironically, as in other empires, all this laid the foundations for the rise of a movement of national opposition.

The Viceroy did not neglect the economy: he ordered steamships from England to improve communications on the Black Sea and the Caspian, widened roads, built new towns, supported markets and fairs, exempted transit trade from duties. The benefits of being integrated into the Empire could thus be seen in material terms. From 1846 to 1916, the *Kavkazskii Kalendar,* the official almanac of the Viceregal Chancellery, recorded them. Similarly, the 12-volume collection (1866–1904) of archival documents concerning the conquest and the measures taken by the region's governors, published by the Caucasus Archaeographic Commission[43] and edited by a former colleague of Vorontsov's, A.P. Bergé, contributed to the glorification of the Empire's achievements.

Vorontsov's policy of using local practices as a way of gaining loyalty to some extent foreshadows the Soviet policy of *korenizatsiya* (putting down roots) adopted in the period of 'national Communism', Lenin's 'one step forward, two steps back' intended to pacify population groups exasperated by the early days of Bolshevik 'war Communism'. Stalin later theorized it as 'national in form, Socialist in content'.

The viceroyalty was abolished in 1883, during the period of reaction that followed Alexander II's assassination, when Russification became more aggressive. The new 'civil administration of the Caucasus', headed by a governor-general, as for other Russian provinces, was evidence of this desire for 'normalization'. The Caucasus remained, however, extraordinary in its government: the reform of the *zemstvos*, the representative provincial assemblies set up by Alexander II, was never applied here, even after the 1905 Revolution. Nevertheless, in the municipal *zemstvos*, the only ones allowed, a number of senior administrators were trained who headed the future independent republics of 1918–1920.[44]

Increasing restrictions were placed on the national schools, where Russian soon became the sole national language, and right up to the end of the Empire, the central government opposed the creation of universities, those nests of revolutionaries. All to no avail. In the first revolutionary fervour of 1905, the Caucasus saw a wave of terrorism and inter-ethnic violence, which opponents claimed were police provocation.[45] The viceroyalty was restored. The task of pacifying the tensions fell to a relative of Mikhail Vorontsov's, Illarion Vorontsov-Dashkov.[46] The last viceroy of all, Grand Duke Nicholas (1915–1917), could only look on impotently as the forces of independentism rose and the imperial superstructure collapsed.

The consolidation of the Empire's borders, achieved by the foreign policy instruments of diplomacy and war, as much as by infrastructure, did not survive the country's defeat. The successive reorganizations and new divisions of the annexed provinces, intended to dilute nationalism and reduce the risk of secession by erasing all trace of the old national entities, only aroused fierce fighting when independence dawned. In 1918–1921, as the Tsars' empire collapsed, just as when the USSR collapsed, and also as in other post-colonial situations in Africa or Asia, the nations tore each other apart to redefine the borders of their sovereignty within a region where each of the empires that had ruled over them, Russian, Persian and Ottoman, had deliberately shuffled the cards: from 1775 to 1880, the Tsars carried out eight major reorganizations of the Caucasus.[47]

The Soviets were no different, even though their stated principle of administrative rationality sought to make the ethnic and administrative maps coincide, to erase regional differences by mutual aid to promote the harmonious development and friendship of equal peoples. Not unlike the former regime,[48] they advanced by trial and error between centralism (in principle) and compromise (in tactics) in handling national aspirations to autonomy. It depended on the balance of power and also an implicit ranking of nations inherited from the Empire. Language now became the basis for an unstated racial classification. Having an alphabet or not, a literature that was written or only oral, made a people's language an indicator of what stage they had reached on the way to nationhood, their level of development,[49] and consequently the entitlement of its speakers to a given rank of administrative unit in the Soviet system–federative or autonomous republic, territory, province or district. Successive constitutions restricted local powers in favour of central government, all closely supervised by the Communist Party, and restored a sort of equality: whatever their apparent ranking, all these entities were empty shells and any stated sovereignty a pure fiction.[50]

The terminology for measuring the degree of attachment changed: no longer the military connotations of 'pacifiable' and 'non-pacifiable', but rather an apparently socio-cultural distinction between 'progressive' and 'backward'. In 1932, the People's Commissariat of Nationalities defined the five characteristics of 'culturally backward' nations: 1) low adult literacy; 2) low school enrolment; 3) absence of an alphabet or written literature; 4) 'social vestiges' such as the oppression of women, religious fanaticism, nomadism, racial hostility, clan vengeance, etc.; 5) absence of national cadres in the various fields of Soviet construction. And apart from the Armenians and Georgians, the official list of 97 'culturally backward' peoples included almost all in the Caucasus and Central Asia,[51] even the Greeks, Bulgarians and Chinese.

The civilizing mission by both Tsars and Soviets made them so proud of economic development for the good of the 'backward' peoples and, not least, the Empire.

Develop the South or Digest It?

The strategic and political goals of conquering the Caucasus were often presented as being the most important. Economic goals–trade routes to the East, markets for furs and the products of Russia's infant industry, natural resources–were also essential and stated to be so. These were the same ingredients of standard colonial policy in addition to settling the new lands. The Black Sea and the Caspian had to become Russian lakes. Control of natural resources was no less important, as evidenced by the creation of the *Gornyi Zhurnal* (Mining Journal) in 1825.

When Peter the Great's expedition reached Baku in 1722, petroleum was of little interest. An increasing number of exploratory geological missions were sent out in the 18th century. Worthy of particular note are those of the naturalist Kerkh (1745), Pallas (1770) and Gmelin (1768–1774).[52] Potemkin used the Caucasus's mineral resources[53] as an argument for conquest. Mining administrators took part in the negotiations for the Treaty of Georgievsk (1783) with Erekle II: the Georgian king offered concessions in exchange for the protectorate. Members of the imperial court, particularly those who intended to trade in the region,[54] began to acquire estates and villages. The chemist Count Apollo Musin-Pushkin, in a report in 1800, pointed out the benefits that could be drawn from Georgia's mineral resources, which should not be left within the sphere of the Persians or Ottomans. He was appointed Commissioner of Mines in 1801, after annexation, and began the exploitation of the copper mines at Alaverdi and Akhalkalaki, using the forced labour of Armenian refugees who had fled the combat zones of the Russo-Persian wars in Karabakh and Ganja. They had been freeborn peasants, but their protests to Tsitsianov went unheard. After the victory over the Turks in 1829, Pontic Greeks were employed.[55]

Inspired by Jean Bodin's mercantilism, opposed to any local industry, the mining was purely extractive. An 1826 report from the Minister of Finance, Kankrin,[56] considered that there was no point in establishing industries in the Caucasus because Russia's contribution of order and security was a sufficient factor of 'civilization' and development. Local industry only began at the turn of the 20th century with the Baku oil boom. Russian and foreign engineers provided virtually all the senior managers, despite increasing competition from local engineers, especially Armenians and Georgians, trained at universities in Russia and Western Europe, since there were none at home.[57]

The Caucasus was also considered to be a colony for settlement, despite the lack, unlike Siberia and Central Asia, of vast 'virgin' expanses that were 'empty' or claimed to be. After the army there arrived various sorts of settlers: peasant-soldiers like the Cossacks, other Slavonic peasants, Russians and Ukrainians, sect-members (Doukhobors, Molokans), German Mennonites, Pontic Greeks specializing in particular crops or mining, Jews displaced South of the Pale of Settlement.[58]

Colonization followed a number of simultaneous or successive goals: economic (farming fertile land, developing southern crops (vines, orchards)) and, not least, industrial ones (silk, tea, tobacco, etc.); political (removal of suspect or rebellious groups (sect-members, Old Believers), Decembrists and Polish insurgents sent to the front); administrative (civil servants, garrisons). Another determining purpose was to use a human shield to consolidate a new border, seen in the massive displacement of people to replace doubtful elements by more reliable ones: a common Christianity was not the criterion for reliability, as when, in 1778–1779, Crimean Greeks and Armenians were transferred to be replaced by Cossacks and Russians. This forced displacement drained the Khan's finances and prestige. It also ruined those displaced, if it had not killed them on the journey.[59] No housing on arrival in the lands to be opened up, quickly forgotten promises from Catherine of tax exemption and community autonomy. After Crimea was annexed (July 1783), and the Treaty of Küçük Kaynarca was breached on the pretext of the military and financial cost of maintaining independence and the pro-Russian Khan, it was the turn of the Tatars to leave. Despite promises of protection for their persons, property and faith and the guarantee of equal rights with the Tsarina's 'natural subjects', nearly 100,000 of them preferred to emigrate to the Ottoman Empire.[60] This massive exodus, foreshadowing that of the defeated Muslim mountaineers from the Caucasus in the following century and the deportation of 'punished peoples' during the Second World War, helped to realign ethnic borders as well as administrative ones.

During the 1760s, various decrees encouraged colonization and farming in the border provinces along the fortified line,[61] the edge of historical Muscovy, in the steppe area of Kuban and Terek occupied by Nogai and Kalmyk nomads. The aim was to establish a rear base for the conquest. But transferring serfs to the vast estates allocated to favourites (more than 600,000 *dessiatins*[62] in 1803) was no easy task. Nor was settlement by free peasants, which aroused little enthusiasm: 4,000 men from 1791 to 1801. Faced with marshland, malaria and wolves, with no fuel, building materials, tools or seeds, and no help, the settlers came home at the least poor harvest. Spontaneous colonization, harder to estimate (perhaps 25,000 peasants from Central Russia by 1790) only involved the region between Stavropol and Mozdok, which was then laid waste during the Russo-Turkish war of 1787–91. The Peace of Jassy (1792) started migration again: by 1804 the region, now a governorate, had a population of 100,000, of whom 24,000 were city dwellers. Former Georgian and Armenian refugees (some 7,000 in 1804), who had fled to Russia to escape the rampages of the Persian and Ottoman armies after Peter the Great's expedition (1722), also helped settle the piedmont, as did German colonists invited in by Catherine II.

Systematic colonization became official policy after 1805. In the Northern Caucasus, the settlers were Cossacks, tending to confirm the perception of the border as a front for expansion. In 1859, they were more than half the highly dispersed population of the pre-Caucasian region (432,000 of 740,000). By the 1897 census,

Russians had become the major element in North Caucasus (approx. 1,600,000, or 42 per cent of the 3,784,000 population), concentrated in the piedmont, but few in the interior, despite the massive exodus of defeated Muslim mountaineers to the Ottoman Empire. By 1915, Russians were only 0.3 to 3.2 per cent of the population in the districts of Vladikavkaz, Grozny, Vedeno and Nazran, 16 to 20 per cent in those of Khasavyurt and Nalchik.[63] It is true that throughout the conquest, official discourse and literature gave an unattractive picture of a savage, inhospitable Caucasus inhabited by bandits. South of the mountain range, the Russian presence was even sparser, limited by the lack of vacant land and a higher density of locals. These frontier areas along unstabilized borders became more a place of exile than of real farm settlement. An Act in 1830 sent there 'the most pernicious' members of sects–Doukhobors, Molokans, Subotniks–so as to isolate their 'heretical infection'.[64] On 1 January 1849, the newspaper *Kavkaz* reported 3,259 families, or 19,341 individuals, in the whole of Transcaucasia. By the end of the century, they were most of the Russians (235,000 in the 1897 census). On top of the legal requirements came millenarianist claims placing the 'new Jerusalem' near Mount Ararat. The sect members' former villages can still be recognized by their Russian names. Suspect in the eyes of the state, poorly received by local peasants who envied their larger land allocations, they still contributed to the Empire's reach by succeeding economically in farming and transport. Their strong four-wheelers could carry more than the local two-wheel *arabas* and were of great use to the tsar's armies during the Crimean War and the Russo-Turkish war of 1877–78, not to mention their care for the wounded. As a reward they were given the best lands in the recently annexed province of Kars. Others encouraged to settle here were German colonists (some 500 families) and Greeks (400 in 1817 and more than 40,000 by 1897[65]).

In Georgia, where more than half the land that had belonged to the King or the Church was confiscated for the Russian Crown, settlers were more numerous than in Armenia, which had less arable land. There other Armenians were encouraged to immigrate from the border provinces of Iran and the Ottoman Empire. A 'Committee for the transfer of Christians from Turkey to the Caucasus' was set up in Tbilisi in 1810 and such action was stipulated in the treaties with the defeated Persian and Ottoman empires. Each war with the other empires led to cross-migration of Muslim and Christian refugees, in the South and North and along the Black Sea coast. Pontic Greeks and Armenians turned up in Abkhazia, where they helped with the development of tobacco farming. Under Abdülhamid II (1876–1909) and later the Young Turks, massacres and the genocide of the Armenians and Pontic Greeks sent escapees into the Russian Caucasus.

Apart from the ports and industrial cities (such as Baku), although the state was the main landowner,[66] the Russian presence South of the mountain range remained limited, to the disappointment of a representative of the ministry of Agriculture and Imperial Domains in Georgia in 1894:

> Throughout their long, hard history, the Russian people have wept for their dead, and turned to the South, to sunny skies and the warm sea. And finally they seized those skies and that sea. Here in the Caucasus was founded for eternity the stability of Russia. Here flies the Russian flag, here soars the Russian eagle ... Why does the Russian not feel comfortable here, because here he feels hemmed in, ill at ease along this warm coast under this burning sun? The reason is that on these lands once conquered at the cost of Russian blood all sorts of peoples are assembled who have taken the best land and not only encircle the Russian, but mock him and despise him. However, that will not last long. Our national interests require this region to become Russian, not only in name but in fact, so that the Russian may be supported and strengthened in his hopes. We wish, therefore, Gentlemen, that this should happen as soon as possible, so that all this mass of varied races and languages is digested by the Russian stomach and this sea and sky become really Russian.'[67]

The perception of the Caucasus as a colony for exploitation and settlement, with the aim of 'commandeering the natural and human resources of the conquered territories for the benefit of the Motherland',[68] combined with that of a 'South: undefined area associating ideas of heat and under-development, given the economic domination of the Northern hemisphere',[69] appears here in its bluntest imperialist expression. Space does not permit citation of the contribution to this perception of literature, ethnographic and geographical research,[70] the historiography and iconography of conquest, the emergence of a colonial society, etc.

Twenty-five years later, in order to persuade the 'insurgent peoples of the East' to ally themselves to a 'Sovietist Russia' that had broken with imperialism, Radek's 'rational arguments' were that

> Soviet Russia arose in order that there might be no more slaves and masters, no more rich and poor. Soviet Russia is a huge, well-endowed country, which can feed itself, now that it has thrown out the lice, parasites and vampires that sucked the blood of Russian peasants and workers ... The Russian peasant and the Russian workers do not need to seek bread in other lands, for their own produces enough of it, they do not need to go in search of metals, for in the depths of their own land there is an unheard-of treasure-house of these ... And whoever says that this is Bolshevik 'imperialism,' that we are going to the East for purposes of conquest and to get food for our army, is consciously spreading lies between the workers and peasants, so as to divide them, in order that the lords of the world may crush them separately.[71]

And yet, according to Lenin himself, the interests of Soviet Russia required putting the wheat of Kuban and the oil of Baku at the service of the Revolution,[72] whose vanguard could only be the Russian proletariat, and thus taking back the control of Ukraine, the Caucasus and Central Asia.

This ambiguity would last throughout the Soviet period, whatever the variations in nationality policy over time. The domination of a

Russia although now internationalist and proletarian, 'marching towards Communism', 'the highest stage of human evolution', was always justified by its support for development, 'the higher stage of growth', defined solely in quantitative terms, granted to 'countries lagging behind on the road already taken by the developed countries, implicitly the only road possible'.[73] It can even be found in the national anthems of the republics composed after the Second World War. With the notable exceptions of Estonia and Georgia,[74] they all, from North to South of the Soviet Union, paid homage to Russia's brotherly aid and guiding role. Some peoples, however, appeared to owe less than others to Russian efforts: in this mirror of society and its stereotypes held up by satirical cartoons, 'under-development' in technology, culture, the status of women, 'traditional' crimes, parallel economy, corruption, superstition, etc., is seen to apply exclusively to the Caucasian and Central Asian South.[75]

Notes

1 *Congress of the Peoples of the East. Baku, September 1920. Stenographic Report*, London: New Park Publications, 1977 (http://www.marxists.org/history/international/comintern/baku/ch01.htm).

2 Koulitchenko *et al.*, *L'Etat soviétique multinational*, Moscow: Editions du Progrès, 1972, p. 130.

3 See some of the contributions to the work edited by Buttino, M. (eds), *In a Collapsing Empire. Underdevelopment, Ethnic Conflicts and Nationalisms in the Soviet Union*, Milan: Feltrinelli, 1992.

4 Laruelle, M., *Le nouveau nationalisme russe: des repères pour comprendre*, Paris: Editions de l'Oeuvre, 2010.

5 On the political and ethnic dimension of a Russo-centric project for Soviet modernity, see Bonnet, A., 'Communists Like Us. Ethnicized Modernity and the Idea of "The West" in the Soviet Union', *Ethnicities*, 2002, vol. 2/4, pp. 435–67.

6 Lieven, D., *Empire. The Russian Empire and Its Rivals*, New Haven & London: Yale University Press, 2000.

7 This holds for standard historiography (Guillaume, P., *Le monde colonial, XIX*[e]*-XX*[e] *siècles*, Paris: Armand Colin, 1994).

8 The Lievens are one of the oldest and noblest families of Baltic Germans; they were major landowners, close to the Romanovs, and were given senior positions in the tsarist administration and army.

9 See for example Khodarkovsky, M., *Russia's Steppe Frontier. The Making of a Colonial Empire, 1500–1800*, Bloomington: Indiana University press, 2001, and

Mouradian, C., 'Les Russes au Caucase', in Ferro, M. (ed.), *Le Livre noir du colonialisme*, Paris: Robert Laffont, 2003, pp. 392–406.

10 Mikhail Nikolayevich Pokrovsky (1868–1932) was condemned in the 1930s for his 'negative' vision of Russian Imperial history (Cf. his *History of Russia, From the Earliest Times to the Rise of Commercial Capitalism* (transl. and ed. by Clarkson, J.D., Griffiths, M.R.), Bloomington: Indiana University Press, 1966 (reedition.), and *Russia in World History, Selected Essays* (transl. by R. and M.A. Szporluk), Ann Arbor: University of Michigan Press, 1970.

11 Koulitchenko *et al., op. cit.*, p. 132.

12 For an analysis of recent research, see Morrison, A., 'What is "Colonisation"? An Alternative View of *Taming the Wild Fields*', *Forum for Anthropology and Culture*, 2007, vol. 4, pp. 402–15.

13 Berelowitch, A., *La Hiérarchie des égaux. La noblesse russe d'Ancien Régime (XVI*[e]*-XVII*[e] *siècles),* Paris: Seuil, 2001.

14 Nolde, B., *La Formation de l'Empire russe*, Paris: Institut d'Etudes Slaves, 1952–1953 (2 volumes), and Kappeler, A., *The Russian Empire: A Multi-Ethnic History*, London: Longman, 2001.

15 Raeff, M., *Comprendre l'Ancien Régime russe. État et société en Russie impériale, essai d'interprétation*, Paris: Le Seuil, 1982.

16 In addition to part of Crimea, the control of the Eastern shores of the Black Sea, free navigation in that sea and the right for the Russian merchant fleet to pass through the Dardanelles, the Treaty contained clauses protecting the Orthodox faithful in the Ottoman Empire, providing Russia with an instrument of interference, like the Capitulations that enabled Western powers to protect Catholics.

17 Nolde, B., *op. cit.*, p. 347.

18 According to J.F. Baddeley, he was an Italian renegade and Ottoman agent: *The Russian Conquest of the Caucasus*, London: Longman, Green & Co, 1908, p. 48.

19 Nolde, B., *op. cit.*, p. 350. This *ukaz* of 28 February 1792 followed the Peace of Jassy (January 1792) after the victory over the Turks.

20 The first travellers, 'scouts' for the conquest, sent out by the Russian state were Germans: Guldenstadt, Jacob Reineggs, Julius von Klaproth. See among others Hewitt, G., *The Russian Imperial Academy and Western Transcaucasia (late 18th century to the 1850s)* (http://www.circassianworld.com/Hewitt_Kymenlaakso.pdf)

21 Haule, S., 'Us et coutumes adoptées dans nos guerres d'Orient. L'expérience coloniale russe et l'expédition française d'Alger', *Cahiers du Monde russe*, 2004, vol. 45/1–2, pp. 293–320.

22 *Kartina Kavkazskaya Kraia punadlezhashcheo Rossii i sopredel'nykh emu zemel'*, St Petersburg: A. Vingeber, 1834–35 (2 volumes) quoted vol. 1, p. 87 in Bennigsen-Broxup, M. (ed.), *The North Caucasus Barrier. The Russian Advance Toward the Muslim World,* London: Hurst, 1992, p. 10. Zubov (not to be confused with Platon Alexandrovich, Catherine II's favourite) was also the author of a number of books and historical novels about the wars in the Caucasus.

23 On Alexander Ermolov (1777–1861), who ruled the Caucasus with an iron fist from 1816 to 1827, while being considered in Russia to be a liberal close to the Decembrists, see Whittock, M., 'Ermolov–Proconsul of the Caucasus', *Russian Review*, 1959, vol. 18/1, pp. 53–60.

24 Baddeley, J.F., *op. cit.*, p. 97.

25 Layton, S., *Russian Literature and Empire. The Conquest of the Caucasus from Pushkin to Tolstoy*, Cambridge: Cambridge University Press, 1994; Ram, H., *Prisoners of the Caucasus: Literary Myths and Media Representations of the Chechen Conflict*, 1999 (http://socrates.berkeley.edu/~bsp/publications.htm).

26 Extract from 'Voyage à Erzeroum', in Griboiedov, Pouchkine, Lermontov, *Œuvres*, Paris: Gallimard, La Pleïade, pp. 484–5.

27 Quoted by Kappeler, A., *op. cit.*

28 See Raeff, M., *op. cit.*, and LeDonne, J.P., 'Russian Governors General, 1775–1825. Territorial or functional administration?', in *Cahiers du Monde russe*, 2001, vol. 42/1, pp. 5–30 and 'Administrative regionalization in the Russian empire, 1802–1826', *ibid.*, 2002, vol. 43/1, pp. 5–34.

29 See the list of general censuses of Transcaucasia (four from 1803 to 1843) in Bournoutian, G. (ed), *Russia and the Armenians of Transcaucasia, 1797–1889. A Documentary Record*, Costa Mesa: Mazda Publ., 1998, pp. 386–7, and Bournoutian, G. (ed.), *1823 Russian Survey of the Karabagh Province*, Costa Mesa: Mazda Publ., 2011.

30 Rhinelander, A., 'Russia's Imperial Policy: The Administration of the Caucasus in the First Half of the Nineteenth Century', in *Canadian Slavonic Papers*, 1975, vol. 17, pp. 218–35; Rhinelander, A., *Prince Michael Vorontsov, Viceroy to the Tsar*, Montréal & Kingston, London, Buffalo: McGill-Queen's University Press, 1990.

31 His grandfather died fighting in the war against Sweden, his father, Dimitri, who married a Russian princess, headed the Moscow nobility's delegation to the 1767 Legislative Commission. Pavel Tsitsianov (1754–1806), born in Moscow, took part in the Russo–Turkish War of 1787–91, the repression of Polish revolts at the Second Partition (1793), and Zubov's expedition to the Caucasus in 1796. In disgrace under Paul I, he was recalled by Alexander I. (Rhinelander, A., *ibid.*).

32 Such as the rivalries beween the sovereigns of Imereti and Mingrelia, the latter favoured by their early alliance with Russia in exchange for the preservation of their dynasty, which ruled until 1857, and expansion into Svaneti and Abkhazia. King Solomon of Imereti was forced to sign a similar treaty of protectorate and was finally deposed in 1810, after attempting an alliance with the Ottomans, and his kingdom annexed (Gvosdev, N., *Imperial Policies and Perspectives Towards Georgia: 1760–1819*, Basingstoke: Macmillan, 2000).

33 Autocephaly was re-established after the February 1917 revolution but only reconfirmed at the end of the Soviet period (Jones, S., 'The Georgian Orthodox Church', in Ramet, P. (ed.), *Eastern Christianity and Politics in the Twentieth Century*, Durham: Duke University Press, 1988, pp. 286–308).

34 The plan to assassinate Russian administrators at a ball intended to launch an insurrection allied to that of the Poles to recover independence. The plot was discovered, 145 suspects were arrested, a dozen sentenced to death and finally exiled to Siberia (Jones, S., 'Russian Imperial Administration and the Georgian Nobility: the Georgian Conspiracy of 1832', *Slavonic and East European Review*, 1987, vol. 65/1, pp. 53–76).

35 Ivan Paskevich (1782–1856), known as Erivanski-Varshavski after his seizure of the fortress of Erivan (1827) and his suppression of the Warsaw revolt (1831), was aide-de-camp to Paul I. Falling into disfavour under Alexander I, his appointment to the Caucasus rewarded his loyalty to Nicholas I, whom he had accompanied on journeys in his youth. As Viceroy of Poland after 1831 he supervised the area's 'pacification' (see his biography by Rhinelander, A., in Wieczysnki, J.L. (ed.), *The Modern Encyclopedia of Russian and Soviet History*, vol. 27, pp. 45–8.

36 Quoted in Kappeler, A., *op. cit.*, pp. 155–6.

37 Lisitsyna, G., Gordin, Ia (eds), *Rossiia i Kavkaz skvoz' dva stoletiia*, Saint Petersburg: Svezda, 2001, pp. 154–68.

38 Mikhail Speransky (1772–1839), considered to be one of the founders of Russian constitutionalism for his 1809 proposal, inspired by Napoleon, to have representative assemblies (*zemstvo*), elected by property-based suffrage with a dose of decentralization, reorganize ministries, promote by merit and tax the nobility. Accused of treason on behalf of France, he was exiled (1812), then returned to grace and was appointed Governor of Penza (1816) and Siberia (1819–21). This experience inspired his 'aliens' (or 'allogeneous') status of 1822. Divided into three categories by level of 'civilization' (fishermen-hunters, nomads, sedentary peasants), they were to enjoy privileges and protection in order gradually to rise to the higher level of full subjects. In fact, they remained second-category subjects. Nicholas I entrusted Speransky with the codification of laws, which he published as the *Collection of Laws of the Russian Empire*, 45 volumes from 1832, with an abridged version in 1835.

39 The term *inorodtsy* (literally meaning of different kin, origin) appeared in the Legislative Commission's 1798 plan for nomads. It gradually replaced *inoversty* (of different faith) and was eventually applied to all non-Russian peoples.

40 Born in Courland (Latvia), Paul Theodor von Hahn (1793–1862) fought in his youth against Napoleon. He spent some time as a diplomat, then, unhappily, as a civil governor in the Baltic countries, and travelled in Europe before taking up service again in 1836 in the ministry of the Interior, was made a senator and in 1837 was appointed to head the Commission to examine better organization for Transcaucasia.

41 Rhinelander, A., *Prince Mikhail Vorontsov*, *op. cit.*, and his biography in Wieczysnki, J.L. (ed.), *op. cit.*, vol. 43, pp. 50–5. Mikhail Semyonovich Vorontsov (1782–1856) fought in the Caucasus under Tsitsianov and against Napoleon. After Waterloo he commanded the Russian occupation forces in

France (1815–18), creating the first army postal service and schools. Viceroy of the Caucasus from 1844 to 1854.

42 Vorontsov's Chief of Staff, Alexander Baryatinsky (1815–69), a young friend of Alexander II, was promoted to Viceroy when Alexander succeeded to the throne (July 1856). With the help of Dmitry Milyutin, the future Minister of War and reformer of the army, Baryatinsky won the final battle after reorganizing and expanding the Caucasus army (over 300,000 men in 1858–59, taken from the war troops in the Crimea). He was in favour of expansion in Asia and a liberal who freed his serfs as early as 1835, argued for the economic and cultural development of the conquered territories and greater autonomy for Poland (see his biography by Brooks, E.W., in Wieczysnki, J.L. (ed.), *op.cit.*, vol. 3, pp. 115–8.

43 *Akty sobrannye Kavkazskoj arkheographitcheskoï Kommissieï*, Tiflis, 1866–1904. These collections, organized chronologically by the 'reign' of successive governors, are a mine of information.

44 Such as Alexander Khatissian, mayor of Tiflis from 1907 to 1917, later Minister of Foreign Affairs and Prime Minister of the first independent republic of Armenia.

45 Aknouni, E., *Les plaies du Caucase*, Geneva, Drochak: Armenian Revolutionary Federation, 1905 (preface by Francis de Pressensé and introduction by Pierre Quillard).

46 Illarion Vorontsov-Dashkov (1837–1916), descended from two of the oldest and most eminent noble lineages close to the Imperial family, served in the Caucasus and Turkestan, and took part in the Russo–Turkish War of 1877–78. As Minister of the Imperial Domains under Alexander III, he favoured strengthening the autocracy and expansion in Asia and the Near East. He chaired the Russian Red Cross during the war with Japan, and was then Viceroy of the Caucasus (1905–15) where he restored order (see his biography by Heilbronner, H., in Wieczysnki, J.L. (ed.), *op.cit.*, vol. 43, pp. 63–7.

47 1775–85 (lieutenancy then *oblast* of the Caucasus in the governorate of Astrakhan), 1802 (governorate of the Caucasus /*oblasts* of Kuban and Terek), 1806–1827 (Eastern Georgia, Western Georgia, Muslim provinces, Dagestan), 1828–1840 (Western Transcaucasie, Eastern Transcaucasie, Armenian province, Dagestan and khanate of Baku), 1840–45 (province of Georgia-Iméréti, province of the Caspian, Dagestan), 1845–68 (governorates of Tiflis, Kutaisi, Shemakha, Derbent, Erivan), 1868 (governorates of Dagestan, Baku, Yelizavetpol), 1878 (annexation of Kars and Batumi), 1880 (five governorates: Tiflis, Kutaisi, Erivan, Yelizavetpol, Baku; three provinces (*oblast*): Batum, Kars, Dagestan; 1 territory (*okrug*): Zakataly.

48 Saparov, A., 'Why autonomy? The Making of Nagorno-Karabagh Autonomous Region, 1918–1925', *Europe-Asia Studies*, 2012, vol. 64/2, pp. 281–323.

49 Charachidzé, G., 'L'empire et Babel. Les minorités dans la perestroika', *Le Genre humain*, 1989, vol. 20, pp. 9–36.

50 Mouradian, C., 'Souveraineté des nations', in Afanassiev, Y., Ferro, M. (eds), *50 idées qui ébranlent le monde. Dictionnaire de la Glasnost*, Paris: Payot, 1989, pp. 473–7.

51 Martin, T., *The Affirmative Action Empire: Nations and Nationalism in the Soviet Union 1923–1939*, Ithaca: Cornell University Press, 2001, pp. 166–7.

52 Pallas, P.S., *Travels Through the Southern Provinces of the Russian Empire* (transl. from German), London, 1802 (2 volumes). The academician Gmelin was captured in Dagestan on his return from a field trip to Persia and died in captivity. Tsarina Catherine ordered the Governor of Kizlyar to take reprisals (Nolde, B., *op. cit.*, p. 356).

53 Manganese at Chiatura in Georgia, coal at Tkibuli, copper at Alaverdi and the Zangezur, silver and gold. An 1837 issue of the *Mining Journal* contains an inventory of the first mineral explorations.

54 Gvosdev, N., *op. cit.*, p 4.

55 Bruneau, M. (ed.), *Les Grecs pontiques. Diaspora, identité, territoires*, Paris: CNRS Éditions, 1998.

56 Yegor Kankrin (born Cancrin (latinized Krebs) in Germany, 1774–1844) entered the service of Russia, like his father before him, in 1797. He was Intendant-General of the army during the Napoleonic Wars, member of the Council of State (1821), then Minister of Finance (1823–44). He was a protectionist, opposed to the luxury imports desired by the nobility, and a supporter of developing national industry. He set up a Manufacturing Council (1828) with sections in Moscow and the provinces (Riga, Arkhangelsk, Odessa, Taganrog) and a technical institute in St Petersburg (1825), reorganized the Forestry Institute and the School of Mines, and encouraged geological exploration.

57 Mouradian, C., Urjewicz, C., Weill, C., 'Les étudiants du Caucase en Allemagne, 1900–1914', in *Russes, Slaves, Soviétiques, Etudes d'histoire offertes à Roger Portal*, Paris: Institut d'Etudes slaves, 1992, p. 369–92.

58 The Pale was established in 1791 after the Partitions of Poland, from Lithuania to the Black Sea. Its borders and the restrictions imposed on the Jews were modified several times. Jewish communities were displaced to colonize the new lands taken from the Turks in Crimea. In 1835, the provinces of Astrakhan and North Caucasus were removed from the Pale.

59 Twelve thousand victims according to the *Events in Crimea* by Rabbi Azaria, mentioned in Nolde, R., *op. cit.*, p. 148.

60 *Ibid.*, pp. 194–5. See also Fisher, A.W., *The Crimean Tatars*, Stanford: Hoover Institution Press, 1991, and Dufaut, G., *Les Tatars de Crimée et la politique soviétique des nationalités*, Paris: Non Lieu, 2011.

61 Sunderland, W., 'Peasants on the Move: State Peasant Resettlement in Imperial Russia, 1805–1830s', in *Russia Review*, 1993, vol. 52/4, pp. 472–85; Moon, D., 'Peasant Migration and the Settlement of Russia's frontiers, 1550–1897', in *The Historical Journal*, 1997, vol. 40/4, pp. 859–93.

62 One *dessiatin* = 1.09 hectares, or 2.702 acres.

63 Quoted by Tsutsiev, *Severnij Kavkaz. Istoria i Granitsa, 1780–1995* [*North Caucasus, History and Borders, 1780–1995*], Vladikavkaz, 1997, p. 11, from the *Terskii Kalendar* [*Terek Almanac*] for 1915.

64 Breyfogle, N.B., *Heretics and Colonizers. Forging Russia's Empire in the South Caucasus,* Ithaca: Cornell University Press, 2005; Breyfogle, N.B., 'Caught in the Crossfire? Russian Sectarians in the Caucasus Theater of War, 1853–56 and 1877–78', in *Kritika: Explorations in Russian and Eurasian History*, 2001, vol. 2/4, pp. 713–50. The author thanks Estelle Amy de la Bretèque for the data from her supplementary diploma memorandum on 'The Molokans of Transcaucasia' (June 2003).

65 Charatsidis, E., 'Les Grecs d'Arménie et de Kars aux XIXe et XXe siècles', in Bruneau, M. (ed.), *op. cit.*, pp. 143–56.

66 Six million *dessiatins* were confiscated during the conquest, according to the 1854 report of the Commission of Imperial Domains, which also gives the number of peasant households by religion and province (Bournoutian, G. (ed.), *op. cit.*, pp. 401–2).

67 Quoted by Tsatsanides, P., 'Les communautés grecques et leurs territoires en Géorgie, XIXe-XXe siècles', in Bruneau, M., *op. cit.*, p. 132.

68 See the headword '*colonie*' in Brunet, R., Ferras, R., Théry, H., *Les mots de la géographie, dictionnaire critique,* Montpellier-Paris: Reclus-La Documentation française, 1992, p. 107.

69 *Ibid.,* headword 'Sud', p. 424.

70 On this last point, see Alex Marshall, *The Russian General Staff and Asia, 1800–1917*, London: Routledge, 2006.

71 *Congress of the Peoples of the East. Baku Congress of the Peoples of the East*, *op. cit.* (http://www.marxists.org/history/international/comintern/baku/ch02.htm).

72 See his speech of 29 January 1920 to the All-Russian Congress, published in *Pravda* of 30 April 1920 in *Lenin, Collected Works*, Moscow: Progress Publ., 1965, vol. 31, pp. 119–22.

73 Headword 'développement' in Brunet, R., *et al.*, *op. cit.*, p. 145.

74 The Estonian anthem only mentions 'Lenin's standard' and Soviet symbols. Georgia's rejoices at having 'given the world great Stalin who abolished the slavery of nations' and the light that Lenin brought to its 'ancient mountains'. The word 'Russia' remains unsaid.

75 Mouradian, C., 'Les peuples de l'empire russe et soviétique à travers les caricatures: des nations en quête d'images', in Godet M. (ed.), *De Russie et d'ailleurs, Feux croisés sur l'histoire, Mélanges offerts à Marc Ferro*, Paris: Institut d'études slaves, 1995, pp. 83–95.

CHAPTER 2

'TRUST IN CADRES' AND THE PARTY-BASED CONTROL IN CENTRAL ASIA DURING THE BREJNEV ERA

Tetsuro Chida
(Slavic Research Centre, Hokkaido University)

The Soviet Union was a multiethnic empire with a nested structure of national autonomous bodies. As Yuri Slezkine well portrays, Bolsheviks took a 'particularistic' approach to Soviet state-building from the residuum of the Russian Empire, creating national territories, languages, cultures and cadres.[1] In particular, most of the non-European ethnic groups were categorized as 'backward' nations, including all of the Central Asian natives, for whom Bolsheviks took 'affirmative action' measures, as Terry Martin called, and gave preferential treatment in jobs and learning opportunities.[2] The official policy of indigenization was called '*korenizatsiia*' (literally, 'taking root'), which fostered the elevation of local national executive officers in newly created national-administrative units.

Collectivization and sedentarization did result in the loss of certain 'traditional' functions of tribal and lineage groupings among nomadic people, such as the division of pasture lands and annual migration routes. Bolsheviks made vehement efforts to disrupt the tribal structure and identity of nomads and to replace it by class. The Great Terror in national republics replaced the old Bolsheviks and national intellectuals with newly trained national communists, who either received higher education in the Soviet centre (constituted still minority) or received practical job experiences from entry level inside autonomous territories. These 'socialistic fresh bloods', irrespective of their career backgrounds, at least assumed the existence of 'pseudo' federative structure of the Soviet Union and 'pseudo' nation states, which were officially called the 'national' or 'Union' republics.

Nikita Khrushchev's 'de-Stalinization' did not cease the top-down control of regional affairs. On the contrary, as Seweryn Bialar characterizes, 'the need for greater economic effectiveness generates pressures for decentralization which in turn excites fears that the party will lose political control'.[3] This sort of dilemma became a source of constant anxiety for the Khrushchev regime. Moscow was compelled to intervene in regional economic and political affairs in an *ad hoc* manner.[4] Local elites were often accused of 'localism' (*mestnichestvo*), and were disconcerted by Moscow's incoherent and inconsistent interference in locality as well as the frequent administrative-institutional reforms. Many top elites in national republics were ousted from line posts, although they had rescued Khrushchev at the time of the anti-party group rebellion in 1957. The centre–periphery relations became increasingly tense during the second half of the Khrushchev era, which, in turn, influenced the intra-elite relations in the national republics. Newly appointed leaders of national republics had to stabilize the internal political situation as well as accomplish reckless planned goal of production. As Oleg Khlevniuk describes, until the end of the Khrushchev era, all around the Soviet Union prevailed those 'strong' regional party first secretaries, who could coordinate various interests in their administrative units and bargain them to and with the centre.[5] However, as will be demonstrated in this chapter, this pattern was not entirely applicable to the leaders of Central Asian republics.

Leonid Brejnev well understood that the cohesion of regional leaders could potentially lead to regime crisis. Therefore, Brejnev implemented the policy of 'the stability of cadres', which at last led to 'the growth in the autonomy of republican party leaderships with a decline in effective control from the centre'.[6] At the same time, however, 'Brejnev was a firm believer in traditional party-based controls'.[7] He realized that top-down control was necessary, but local cadres should also be 'trusted' at the same time. Thus, the following questions may arise: how did party-based control from above function? What consequences did cadre policy bring into national republics? What did 'trust in cadres' mean in national republics? This chapter will attempt to answer these questions in the case of Central Asia, which also illustrates the actual situation of the centre-republican and the intra-elite relations during the Brejnev era.

Various scholarly endeavours have been made to explain specificities of the regional (or republican) cadre policy, the approaches of which could be typologically divided into three kinds. First is the traditional 'kremlinological' approach, which treats Soviet elites as a whole in a uniformed manner without taking into consideration the regional or national specificities and characteristics. This approach concentrates on the analysis of educational and career backgrounds or generational gaps among regional elites to account for Moscow's priority in regional management.[8] The second approach refers to the ethnic composition of various kinds of posts for the measurement of the level of autonomy of national republics. This argument quite often draws the conclusion that Russian vice-heads of all levels in national republics, especially in Central Asia, were only 'watchdogs' of the centre.[9] The third approach focuses on the intra-republican elite competition and patron–client relations, dealing with clan politics or regionalism among indigenous elites in Central Asian republics.[10]

Some of the works included in the third approach address the patron–client relations on the basis of 'tribalism' in Kazakhstan, Kyrgyzstan and Turkmenistan. However, most of them do not distinguish between faction building on the basis of the largest subsets of the genealogical category of their indigenous nations, lineage groupings of smaller tribal subdivisions and kinship relations. The latter two are more meaningful units in their ordinary life.[11] Actually, Ludmila Chvyr's assertion about multiple identities of sedentary Tajiks can be applied more or less to former nomadic people in Central Asia: 'depending on how he assesses the status of their interlocutor, he sees himself as belonging to one community or another'.[12] Therefore, the tree-form structure of their lineage identifications serves as a measure for them to grasp the distance between two persons of the same nation. Today, tribal and genealogical identity among them is quite abstract as well as obscure.[13] However, we find it impossible to discount tribal factors in personnel matters altogether even during the Brejnev era, as will be shown below.

Most of the above-mentioned studies utilize the biographical data of the republican elites and Soviet periodicals as primary sources. There are only few works written about the regional cadre policy and the control via the party line over local personnel affairs during the Brejnev era, which is based upon archival materials. Oleg Khlevniuk's and Yoram Gorlizki's works are two exceptions, but they only touched upon the Russian Federation.[14] This chapter will examine the republican cadre policy, the centre–periphery and the intra-elite relations in the Soviet Central Asia through the analysis of the archival documents at the Department for Organizational-Party Work (i.e. cadres department) of the Central Committee (CC) of the Communist Party of the Soviet Union (CPSU) from the Russian State Archive of Contemporary History (RGANI). This study is based on all the archival materials of the department's sub-section for Central Asian republics and Kazakhstan from 1966–81. Before moving on to the Brejnev era, this chapter will start off by examining one case-study about the party control under the Khrushchev regime.

Party Control During the Khrushchev Era: A Case Study about Karakalpakstan

The focus of this section is one case in Karakalpakstan, but this kind of incident was widespread all around Central Asia after 1959. In October 1959, the General Department of the CC of the CPSU received an information letter to Khrushchev from three workers of Amu-Darya District in Karakalpak Autonomous Republic. They blew a whistle at Moscow about the padding of cotton production by Sovkhoz 'Mangit', the director of which was a kin of the first secretary of Amu-Darya District Party Committee (*raikom*), S. Turemuratov.[15] This letter was neglected by Moscow at the time. Moreover, Sovkhoz 'Mangit' was highly praised in the all-Union journal '*Khlopkovotstvo*' (Cotton Growing) for accomplishing the cotton production plan up to 1965 by the end of 1959.[16] However, Moscow once again received a written accusation in March 1960. This letter informed that the production volume of cotton in the district was repeatedly padded in 1958–59 by Turemuratov's initiative; a huge amount of money was collected from workers of Sovkhoz 'Mangit' for the purchase of cottons from other districts to camouflage the over-fulfillment of the annual production plan; he illegally owned several luxurious mansions among other things. Even more critical was the alleged reports on Turemuratov operating under the auspices of Nasyr Makhmudov (the first secretary of Karakalpak Provincial Committee (*obkom*) of the Republican Communist Party) and officials of the CC of the Communist Party of Uzbekistan (CPUz).[17] Officials of the General Department of the CC of the CPSU had an interview with the writer in Moscow, and came to the conclusion that a detailed investigation was necessary. Then, the Department for Party Organs of the Union republics (later the Department for Organizational-Party Work) sent an instructor of the department to Karakalpakstan. As a result of his on-site investigation, the Bureau of the Republican CC was obliged to adopt a resolution in May 1960 that criticized Turemuratov of his mismanagement in personnel affairs and abuses of his office which was under his supervision, but he was not severely accused of organized padding in the district. Thus, Turemuratov was not ousted from the post, but just received a 'severe reprimand'. Moscow also agreed to the measures taken by Uzbekistan.

However, this was not the end. In January 1961, D. Seitniiazov, the secretary of Karakalpak *obkom*, alerted Moscow on Makhmudov's defects of his service. He suspected that Sharaf Rashidov, the Republican Party head, afforded protection for him. Actually, Makhmudov was the immediate superior of Rashidov, when he served as the first secretary of Samarkand *obkom* from 1943–48

(Rashidov was the *obkom* secretary on ideology from 1944–47). Seitniiazov avowedly criticized Makhmudov at the *obkom* plenum in November 1960, but Makhmudov disregarded the accusations. According to the dispraise by Seitniiazov, Makhmudov took no measures to the alleged massive padding and fraudulence in the autonomous republic including Amu-Darya District, although he was well aware of these facts.[18] The centre again decided to send two party officials to Karakalpakstan and ordered them to conduct a detailed inspection jointly with the CC of the CPUz. As a result of the on-site investigation, organized from above, the Bureau of the CC of the CPUz was obliged to adopt a special party resolution, which eventually dismissed Turemuratov and some other *raikom* first secretaries with harsh punishments including expulsion from the Communist Party.[19] The resolution accused Karakalpak *obkom* of its 'intolerable liberalism' in relation to leading officials and direct organizers of massive padding, whilst concrete executants alone were subjected to punishment.[20] Meanwhile, Makhmudov and other leading officials of Karakalpakstan received only a 'severe reprimand', thus succeeding in clinging onto their posts.[21] It is quite interesting to note that inspectors from the centre also accused Seitniiazov of not raising promptly these problems.[22] Subsequently, Makhmudov served as the first secretary of Karakalpak *obkom* until 1963, and successively held the leading posts in the republic: the first secretary of Ferghana *obkom* (1963–69) and the chairman of the Committee of People's Control of Uzbekistan (1969–84).

This kind of case was not so unique during the Khrushchev era, especially after the suicide of Aleksei Larionov (the first secretary of Ryazan *obkom* in Russia) in September 1960. Larionov organized massive padding of meat production in the province in order to deliver his promise that the province would enhance meat production in 1959 three times more than the previous year. Appealing to the Soviet peasants to catch up with (and even 'leave behind') the United States in meat and milk production within a short period of time, Khrushchev himself ardently supported this Ryazan's unreasonable initiative, the failure of which in turn called forth the all-out search for every deceptions by local officials in the fulfilment of production plans throughout the Soviet Union.[23] The dismissals of Tursunbai Uljabaev (Tajikistan) and Iskhak Razzakov (Kyrgyzstan) from the Republican Party first secretaries were related to this anti-cheating campaign, though the former was the actual organizer, while the latter just overlooked the cases in his republic.[24]

What can we learn from these incidents in terms of the comparative aspect? First, the Khrushchev regime paid great attention to the motion from below and ordered the republican Central Committees to take actual measures in local personnel affairs. Second, Moscow dispatched its representatives to the locality for inspection and control of incidents at the level of 'district'. Third, the vertical intervention in local affairs through the party line, nonetheless, still remained *ad hoc* and selective. Fourth, party-based control had its limit and there was a certain level of difficulty to engage in reshuffling of local personnel, if targeted cadres had strong connections with politically influential figures on the all-Union level, as was clearly shown in the case of Makhmudov.

Party Control During the Brejnev Era and the Intra-Elite Relations

As is well known, the Brejnev regime placed stress on 'collectivity' or 'collegiate style' of decision-making from the very beginning. It was necessary for republican elites to pursue consistent and stable policy management through consensus building, while easing hostility among the republican elites. In Kyrgyzstan, Tajikistan and Turkmenistan, three relatively small republics in Central Asia, it took a certain amount of time to consolidate cooperative and collegiate relations among them, which obliged the centre to take a role as a mediator of intra-elite conflicts in some occasions. On the contrary, the intra-elite relations were quite stable in Kazakhstan and Uzbekistan from the outset of the Brejnev era. The leaders of the Communist Party in the latter republics enjoyed noticeable authority in the centre, gaining candidate membership in the Politburo of the CPSU Central Committee,[25] which made it easier for the republican authorities to gain approval of their personnel policy line from Moscow and contributed to stabilize the political condition in the republics.

As Graeme Gill and Roderic Pitty argue, the Brejnev regime occasionally but continuously offered traditional criticism and encouraged self-criticism on fraudulence and deficiencies of local cadres with the purpose of 'the development of intra-party democracy' and 'the simultaneous improvement of intra-party discipline',[26] which, though, did not follow the campaign-styled control from above as during the Khrushchev period. On the contrary, as will be discussed below, the Brejnev regime more or less trusted the republican authorities from the beginning, entrusting internal investigations about personnel issues to the republics themselves. In this sense, the meaning of party control transformed itself.

The next section will focus on the analysis of the intra-elite relations in all five republics and how Moscow got involved in personnel matters in the republics during the Brejnev era. In addition, the 'generality' and 'particularity' of party control in Central Asia will be examined in further detail.

Kyrgyzstan

In Kyrgyzstan, there was a serious fallout in the relationship between the first secretary of the CC of the Communist Party of Kyrgyzstan (CPKyr), Turdakun Usubaliev, and the chairman of the Council of Ministers, Bolot Mambetov, after the fall of the Khrushchev regime in 1964. Usubaliev was born in 1919 and 12 years younger than Mambetov. The former got a higher education in the Pedagogical Institute in Frunze, the republican capital, but the latter graduated from the Moscow Institute for Water Transportation. Usubaliev built his career in the ideological and propaganda sector, while Mambetov was one of the first-generation native highly-educated technocrats (a hydraulic engineer) in Kyrgyzstan, who regarded Usubaliev as an amateur in management of agriculture and republican economy as a whole. Both assumed their post at the same time in 1961. Usubaliev was born in Naryn Province and from the Sarybagysh tribe, but

Mambetov was born in Issyk-Kul Province and likely from the Bugu tribe.[27] However, their confrontation seemed to be devoid of local or tribal background, but rather could be explained by the generational and career gap between the two figures.

The final break-up of their relationship occurred in September 1965 due to the adoption of the Resolution of the CPSU Central Committee, 'On the work of the party organizations in Kirghiz SSR in selection, placement and training of managerial personnel in construction', which severely criticized the republican party organization for the defective personnel policy and the weak party control in this sector.[28] The Central Committee Plenum of the republican Communist Party in January 1966 discussed this resolution, which resulted in the blame avoidance between Usubaliev and Mambetov. Usubaliev in his memoir selectively chose speeches of some Central Committee members at this plenum from the archival materials, including that of Mambetov. According to his memoir, Mambetov ironically mentioned at the plenum, 'In some sections of our [republic] exist servility, toadying, creation of unscrupulous situation, and an attempt to replace normal party relationship by deference to rank. I openly and frankly dare to say that an endeavor exists to substitute one-man decision for collective and collegial decision-making'.[29] Mambetov implicitly tried to make an insinuation about the working style of Usubaliev by referring to him as 'one-man decision'. The CPSU Central Committee had been receiving several written and verbal accusations from Kyrgyzstan about the working style of Usubaliev throughout 1966. Seemingly, Mambetov himself sent an accusatorial statement to Leonid Brejnev, too. According to the report by the Department of Organizational-Party Work of the CPSU Central Committee in January 1967, Usubaliev 'sometimes showed absolutely unjustified persistence with his own suggestions, against which in fact an overwhelming majority of the Central Committee Bureau members was offering opposition.'[30] The report also criticized his poor knowledge on agriculture and malevolent relationship with Mambetov. The officials of the department had a personal meeting with Usubaliev in December 1966 to have him reflect on his past conduct. He promised to 'absorb lessons from these for future practical assignments'.[31] It is worthwhile to note that Usubaliev himself in his memoir stated that he did not know anything about the statement of Mambetov and 'no one from the CPSU Central Committee talked about it with me'.[32]

Usubaliev attempted to return fire to Mambetov almost at the same time. According to Usubaliev's memoir, the CC of the CPKyr received letters and statements from the republican Council of Ministers and ministries in 1965–66 about the concrete facts of egregious breaches in expenditure of material and cash assets by the officials of the Council of Ministers and its head, Mambetov himself. Usubaliev recalled that Moscow also caught this signal and ordered the Bureau of the CC of the CPKyr to make a detailed examination of this scandal.[33] The investigation disclosed false receipt of a large amount of excessive medical allowances by Mambetov. Torobai Kulatov (the chairman of the Supreme Soviet) also violated the regulation about the acceptance of medical allowances. The Bureau of the Central Committee adopted a special resolution about these incidents in March 1967, which, solely ordered Mambetov and Kulatov to 'pay back' the excesses to the republican coffer. Mambetov tried to extinguish the fire by thrusting responsibility to and dismissing the account officers of the Council of Ministers, i.e. the executors of these fraudulent account procedures.[34]

However, this was not the end. Evgenii Kudriavtsev, the accountant general of the Central Committee of the CPKyr, sent a letter to Moscow in June 1967, which once again accused Mambetov of being responsible for this fraudulence, explicitly expressing his dissatisfaction with indecisive and equivocal measures to him. In fact, Kudriavtsev was the chief executor of the inspection. A 26-page final report of his investigation was attached to his letter, which gave a detailed elucidation about the various facts of infringement of financial discipline by officials of the Council of Ministers,[35] including not only indigenous Kyrgyz cadres, but some non-native elites, such as Nikolai Minich, the chairman of the Committee for People's Control, who improperly spent the fund of the Council of Ministers to repair his apartment.[36] He was a Ukrainian born in Ukraine, but started his job career in Kyrgyzstan from kolkhoz level.

This sort of abuse of their offices and privileges seemed to be quite popular among non-native elites as well as indigenous officials. It would have not been so difficult for the Republican Party leadership to camouflage the cases, but they dared to uncover them in detail at this timing. Kudriavtsev's action was not completely disfavored by the Republican Party leadership, evidence to the face that he served as the accountant general of the CC even after 1976.[37] At last, Mambetov was obliged to retire to pension in January 1968. Other than Mambetov, K. Danilin, the deputy chairman of the republican Council of Ministers, was the only other person ousted in June 1968, of whom Usubaliev undoubtedly had a low opinion, as was well shown in his memoir.[38] He did not touch upon other high-rank officials that were listed in Kudriavtsev's report. After this, Usubaliev established his authority and stable intra-elite relations in the republic.

Tajikistan

The intra-elite confrontation in Tajikistan assumed a different character. All the first secretaries of the CC of the Communist Party of Tajikistan (CPTaj) after the Second World War were people from Leninabad Province (today's Sogd Province) in Northern Tajikistan. According to Oliver Roy, Babajan Gafurov's 'secretaryship [from 1946] inaugurated the uninterrupted power of the Leninabad faction over a period which was to last right through to 1992'.[39] Uljabaev replaced Gafurov in 1956, and Jabbar Rasulov was called back from diplomatic work in Africa (Togo) to Tajikistan to replace Uljabaev in April 1961. The author has no material to substantiate whether the power of 'the Leninabad faction' was really 'uninterrupted' or not, but archival materials demonstrate that the centre at least was aware of the signals from within Tajikistan.

The centre received an anonymous letter from Tajikistan in fall 1966, informing of the increasing parochial tendencies and localism in the cadre policy in Tajikistan. According to this letter, the anti-party principle of localism started to appear on the political arena in Tajikistan soon after the Second World War, and became the general phenomena under the ruling of Uljabaev.[40] The republican leaders of that time, Rasulov and Ivan Koval (the second secretary of the CC, a Ukrainian) did not interrupt these malicious tendencies, but rather promoted the Tajiks from Leninbad Province, who were to take a role as promoters of localism.[41] Moreover, the writer of this letter complained that the former Tajik elites from Bukhara and Samarkand were driven out to give posts to those from Leninabad,[42] and, as the Leninabad faction grew, Tajiks from other regions also began to mobilize countrymen to form their regional factions of Pamir, Garm, Samarkand and so forth.[43] He further exposed the illicit acts by Muhammed Asimov, the former chairman of the Committee for Party-State Control of Tajik SSR and the president of the republican Academy of Sciences at that time, and wrongful dismissals of Tajik scholars born in Samarkand from the Institute of Economy under the initiative of the director, Rakhimov, a 'brother' of Ibodat Rakhimova (the secretary of the CC).[44] Both Asimov and Rakhimova came from Leninabad Province, too.

Rasulov reported to the CC of the CPSU that the republican CC also received the same letter, after the query from Moscow.[45] According to this report, Tajikistan actually conducted a number of personnel changes for the purpose of improving the quality of cadres, especially their educational background,[46] which was in accordance with Moscow's policy line and not unique for Tajikistan. However, he further admitted that some farms, enterprises and schools 'tolerated vicious parochial approach in cadre selection and placement, contradictory to Lenin's spirit, with which [Tajikistan] had to definitely fight in the future', but, at the same time, maintained that the removal and reshuffling of some Samarkand Tajiks were duly conducted on the grounds of their 'illness' or 'other practical reasons'.[47] Of course, he absolutely denied the accusation in the letter to the party elites of their engagement in and promotion of localism in the cadre policy.[48] He left no reference to the incidents concerning Asimov and Rakhimova. What was striking was that Moscow trusted and agreed to the conclusion made by the very accused Tajik elites themselves.

In December 1969, one more scandal involving the party elites from Leninabad occurred. As a result of the inquiry by the CC of the CPTaj, some middle-class officials were ousted from their post, but the accused Tajiks in the higher echelon remained unscathed.[49] It was not a coincidence when 'the need for a cleansing of the republican party from degenerates and fraudsters was stressed at a plenum in March 1970'. 'Localism' was also the target of criticism at this plenum.[50] However, this sort of 'self-criticism' eased in the republican capital after that.

Rasulov succeeded in stabilizing the intra-elite relations at least in Dushanbe, but, in turn, the target of criticism was directed toward the Pamir Region, or more specifically toward Gorno-Badakhshan *obkom* and its first secretary, Khushkadam Davliatkadamov. The CC of the CPTaj became aware of the unmerited 'cadre selection on the ground of homeland, kinship and personal loyalty', in the Gorno-Badakhshan Autonomous Province.[51] The republican CC repeatedly carried out investigations in 1973, 1975 and 1978. Interestingly, according to Davliatkadamov's explanation, the Committee for Party Control of the Central Committee of the CPSU also sent an inspector to Pamir and conducted a statistic research with an official from Dushanbe, the republican capital, about the composition of 'home districts' among *obkom* officials. This inquiry demonstrated that people from two districts (Shugnan and Rushan) had a majority in *obkom*.[52] The Rushan District was the homeland of Davliatkadamov.[53] In fact, the indigenous people in Badakhshan consisted of various ethnic groups, including the Shugnans, Rushans, Wakhans, Yazgulyams, Ishkashms, although all of them had been officially categorized as Tajiks since the 1939 census.[54] The bureau of the republican CC ordered him to employ more officials from different districts.[55] Second and third investigations were held in 1975 and 1978, which also confirmed a long-lasting tendency of localism and nepotism in cadre selection in the autonomous province.[56] Davliatkadamov could not put up with the pressure from Dushanbe, and wrote an explanatory letter directly to Moscow in 1968. According to him, the *obkom* quit promoting people from the Rushan District to executive posts in the autonomous province from

1975 and onward. However, he also admitted that two of his relatives were still working in the provincial consumers' association.[57] The Department for Organizational-Party Work of the CC of the CPSU spurned his petition and ordered the republican CC to 'take up a problem about consolidation of the *obkom* in near future'.[58] Davliatkadamov was finally ousted in the same year.

As long as the party leaders of Tajikistan did not allow direct intervention from the centre into 'their' personnel matters in Dushanbe, it was not so difficult for them to block on-site inspections in Gorno-Badakhshan by an official from Moscow. However, the reality was that they allowed the inspection. This implied a certain difficulty for Dushanbe to control the Pamir region by themselves. In addition, a confrontation likely occurred between the two regional groupings of 'Leninabad' and 'Pamir', and ethnic Rushans and Shugnans seemed to predominate in the Pamir faction.

Turkmenistan

It took a very long time to stabilize the political situation in Turkmenistan. Balysh Ovezov, the first secretary of the CC of the Communist Party of Turkmenistan (CPTur) from 1960–69, was accused of his deficiencies and fraudulence from the earliest days in office. Moscow almost immediately received anonymous written accusations against him after his inauguration as the first secretary. A wide variety of criticism was directed at Ovezov. Not only did the Turkmen SSR not achieve the cotton production plan in 1960, but also was exposed for a number of padding and whitewashes. Nonetheless, the republican leadership did not take any stern measure against them.[59] As mentioned above, such kinds of criticism was common all over the Soviet Union at that time. However, what was unusual in Turkmenistan, according to these letters, was that as soon as he became the republican Communist Party head, he started to promote his henchmen and relatives, especially people from his homeland Tashauz Province (today's Dashoguz Province) in Northern Turkmenistan. In addition, many of the newly appointed were previously fired from former managerial posts due to their misbehaviours and fraudulence.[60] One anonymous accusation even said that he also encouraged his 'close relative and friend', Jumamurad Kurbanov (the first secretary of Tashauz *obkom*), to camouflage the fulfillment of the plan for cotton production in his province.[61] The Department for Organizational-Party Work of the CC of the CPSU took these charges seriously against the Turkmen party head from within the republic and decided to conduct on-site investigations, which actually corroborated a majority of these cases. The officials of the CC of the CPSU held several meetings with Ovezov throughout 1961, but Moscow confined to reprehension on him without substantial punishment.[62]

This kind of written accusation intermittently came to Moscow. In 1963, the report of an instructor of the Department for Organizational-Party Work of the CPSU Central Committee once again enumerated fraudulent acts of Ovezov, including his overt protectionism of his countrymen in Tashauz Province. He also helped annul the party penalty of the above-mentioned Kurbanov, imposed in 1962 as a result of massive padding in his province.[63] In November 1964, Moscow received one more anonymous letter about his excessive drinking and bribe-taking.[64] Moscow again sent an official to Ashkhabad to conduct an on-site inspection, but did not find any firm evidence.[65]

The flow of written accusations against Ovezov did not cease after the fall of Khrushchev. In 1968, the department made a reference to an anonymous letter from Ashkhabad, which explicitly stated that Ovezov was 'stirring up the remnants of intertribal and interethnic strife of the past'.[66] According to the reference, the letter disclosed that all the leading officials in the republican apparatus were replaced by his tribesmen, though, without indicating any concrete name of a tribe.[67] It is worth noting here that Ovezov was from the Northern Yomut tribe.[68] In addition, the letter further exposed the following instances: allocation of crucial posts in law-enforcement organizations to his henchmen, bribe-taking from kolkhozes, dubious biography of his colleagues Oraz Orazmukhamedov (the chairman of the republican Council of Ministers) and Chary Ataev (the secretary of the CC) etc.[69] It seemed that the accumulation of the above-mentioned discreditable 'facts' drove the centre to reach a decision to oust him from the position of first secretary in December 1969. His downfall was coincided with the timing, when the newly appointed all-union KGB head, Yurii Andropov, started to stuck the knife into fraudulent and corruptive acts in several republics. Mukhamednazar Gapurov replaced him. Gapurov was from Charjou Province (today's Lebap Province) and from the Ersari tribe.

After the replacement of the first secretary, the blame was directed at the party-state elites, who were appointed during the rule of Ovezov. In June 1970, Moscow received an anonymous letter, which severely accused Vasilii Rykov, the second secretary of the CC, who was transferred from the CC of the CPSU in 1963. According to the letter, Rykov overlooked the misdeeds of republican elites, and allowed increasing criminality in the republic (such as bribery, the spread of narcotics etc.)[70] The letter further reproached that he surrounded himself with suspicious officials such as Orazmukhamedov, Ataev, A. Mukhamedov (Minister of Interior Affairs), Nikolai Sapozhnikov (the republican Superintending Prosecutor) and Viktor Pereudin (the head of the Organizational-Party Work of the CC). Orazmukhamedov and Ataev were once again condemned for their pretensions of their backgrounds and bribe-taking. Mukhamedov was depicted both as a bribe-taker from society and bribe-giver to Rykov. Concealment of the above-mentioned crimes by Sapozhnikov was also mentioned in the letter. Pereudin was described as a harsh executor of Rykov's policy line.[71] The Department for Organizational-Party Work in Moscow concluded without any in-depth investigation that the letter was just 'slanderous' and did not represent any truth.[72] The matters of personation by Orazmukhamedov and Ataev were also denied, since repeated investigations in the past did not find any firm evidence.[73] However, this conclusion evoked a scandal in Turkmenistan.

In March 1974, Moscow received one more anonymous letter from Turkmenistan about the family background of Orazmukhamedov and his protectionism to protégés.[74] Moscow ordered the CC of the CPTur to check his and his father's biography once again, which at last proved the personation of his father's past as a 'trader and *bai* (well-to-do peasant).' Furthermore, several his family members were 'clerics'. Orazmukhamedov had stated in his official biography that he was a son of a 'poor peasant' until that time.[75] Owing to the above-mentioned misjudgment before, Moscow and Ashkhabad seemingly could not remove him from office immediately. At last, he was dismissed in December 1975 by the resolution of the Bureau of the CC, which also confirmed the existence of protectionism to his protégés, relatives and countrymen.[76] As for Ataev, the editorial office of the all-Union party daily 'Pravda' received a signal from Turkmenistan in June 1965.[77] In accordance with the order from Moscow, Gapurov's authority once again investigated his biography, which exposed his suppression of the fact that he was once excluded from the Communist Party due to 'criminally negligent attitude toward storage of secret documents' during the Second World War.[78] He also falsified his year of birth.[79] The CC of the CCTur 'severely warned [him about] his conduct',[80] and told Moscow that it would 'make a suggestion about the move of Ataev to another post in the near future'.[81] He seemed to be dismissed shortly thereafter. Interestingly, the dismissals of both Orazmukhamedov and Ataev were conducted only after Rykov left Turkmenistan in April 1975 to a diplomatic post in Algeria as an ambassador. Pereudin assumed the position of second secretary, who had 26 years of job experience in Turkmenistan and well knew the specificity and complexity of the position and the republic. Gafurov eventually succeeded in stabilizing the political situation in the republic.

The purpose of this chapter is not to find or prove whether the accusations of the republican elites were right or not. Much less, it is impossible to make a 'true-or-false' judgment regarding the above-mentioned 'facts'. Rather, the noteworthy and remarkably interesting point that should be mentioned here is that these kinds of acrid accusations had been made quite frequently from within Turkmenistan, and many archival documents were left in Moscow about these incidents, which implies the intensity of the intra-elite conflicts in Turkmenistan and Moscow's consistent attention to them. However, the centre apparently entrusted in-house investigations to the authority in Ashkhabad after the dismissal of Ovezov. According to

Khlevniuk's typology, Ovezov can be categorized as a 'secretary-dictator', who had certain weaknesses in his inability to consolidate a wide variety of interests in the republic.[82] His 'dictator-styled' governance provoked repugnance.[83] Gafurov could obtain trust from Moscow by showing his effort to strengthen internal discipline and ease frustrations spread in the republic, by forcing out appointees during the reign of Ovezov.

Moreover, the point regarding *mestnichestvo* and tribalism in Turkmenistan should be brought to attention. Regardless of his overt partiality for people from Tashauz, Ovezov still cared about maintaining a certain balance of regional (or possibly tribal) composition of the republican elites. As seen above, Ovezov was from Tashauz Province. Orazmukhamedov was from Mary Province in Central-South Turkmenistan, Annamukhamed Klychev (the chairman of the Presidium of Supreme Soviet) from Cheleken District on the shore of the Caspian Sea, and Ataev from Ashkhabad Province close to the capital. Gafurov also appointed Bally Yazkuliev from Tashauz Province as the chairman of the Council of Ministers after the removal of Orazmukhamedov.

Kazakhstan

Dinmukhamed Kunaev enjoyed a very close and positive relationship with Leonid Brejnev, since Kunaev served as the chairman of the Council of Ministers of the republic during Brejnev's service as the First Secretary of the Communist Party of Kazakhstan (1955–56). In addition to this, he had two years working experience as the first secretary during the Khrushchev era (1960–62). He was a mining engineer with 'technical' higher education in Moscow. Moreover, he served as the president of the republican Academy of Sciences (1952–55). All these factors contributed to establish his undoubted authority in Kazakhstan.

No documents were found in the files of RGANI, indicating the intra-elite confrontation among the political elites in Kazakhstan. Some sporadic letters from within the republic accused some officials on the provincial, city and district level, but the CC or *obkoms* of the republican Communist party conducted all the investigations regarding these cases. Moscow seemed not to intervene in personnel affairs in Kazakhstan. The embezzlement of socialistic properties in Karaganda Province in 1974 was the biggest scandal, but Kunaev moved quickly, dismissing and severely punishing criminal officials, including those of the provincial law-enforcement agencies.[84] Anonymous letters accused two *obkom* first secretaries: Erkin Auelibekov in 1973 (construction of a deluxe personal residence) and Aleksandr Protozanov in 1978 (coercive style of leadership, excessive drinking and abuse of office), both of which were concluded as complete fabrications by the investigation of the CC of the republican Communist Party.[85]

The lack of documents in the archive implied that Moscow did not think that the in-depth control from above was necessary in Kazakhstan, but it did not necessarily mean the absence of intra-elite discords or grouping of elites in the republic. Possibly the cases did not rise up to the surface. In this respect, one suggestive document was found in the archive. In December 1970, one Kazakh writer and propagandist sent a letter to Moscow, which condemned the re-emergence of 'partiality for genealogy [*rodofil'stvo*]' among officials of ideological, cultural and pedagogical spheres in the republic. According to the letter, Sattar Imashev (the secretary for ideology of the CC) stood at the centre of *rodofil'stvo.*[86] He was born in Gurev Province (today's Atyrau Province) in North-Western Kazakhstan and genealogically originated from *Kishi juz.*[87] The writer of this letter mentioned, 'Imashev is clearly distorting the party line in selection, placement and training of cadres in favor of hidden and creeping ideology of *rodofil'stvo*. He created the iron wall of tribesmen, kinsmen and relatives from *Kishi juz* in all of ideological authorities and institutes.'[88] In fact, it was confirmed that some of those criticized were really born in Gurev, Uralisk and Kyzyl-Orda Provinces in Kazakhstan or Saratov and Astrakhan Provinces in Russia, where a majority of Kazakhs was of *Kishi juz.*[89] The author of the letter himself was a Kazakh from Karaganda Province, almost certainly, a Kazakh of *Orta juz*. However, Alma-Ata and Moscow both denied the facts of Imashev's *rodofil'stvo*.

It is insufficient to make a definite assertion about tribalism in Kazakhstan based solely on this document, but it is certain that as Ovezov and Gapurov did in Turkmenistan, Kunaev also gave consideration to the regional (or tribal) and ethnic composition of the republican elites.[90] Kunaev himself was a Kazakh of *Ulu juz*, born in Alma-Ata Province. It was the most politically stable time in Kazakhstan, when the triple heads, Kunaev, Baiken Ashimov (the chairman of the Council of Ministers, a Kazakh of *Orta juz*) and Imashev (the chairman of the Presidium of Supreme Soviet), governed the republic from December 1979 to February 1984. In addition, it should be noted that the power of some Slavic elites was also very strong. For example, Andrei Borodin (the first secretary of Kustanai *obkom* from 1959–81) and Vasilii Demidenko (the first secretary of Northern-Kazakhstan and Kustanai *obkoms* from 1965–88) were very influential figures in the Virgin Land Region in Northern Kazakhstan.

Uzbekistan

Sharaf Rashidov was one of the Central Asian elites, who rose to prominent success along with Kunaev. Rashidov took a candidate seat in the Politburo of the CC of the CPSU from 1961. However, his educational and career background was completely different from that of Kunaev. Like Usubaliev, Ovezov and Gapurov, he graduated from a 'pedagogical' institute and built his career as an ideological worker. As Robert Blackwell Jr. indicates, the status of cadres with some agricultural and industrial experiences increased during the Khrushchev era.[91] Some technocratic elites in Uzbekistan expressed their opinions, opposing to the candidacy of Rashidov to the Republican Party head. One of them was Mirza-Ali Mukhamedjanov, an eminent agronomist, who served as the deputy chairman of the Council of Ministers of Uzbekistan at the time of Rashidov's inauguration. According to his letter to Moscow in July 1968, he mentioned at the meeting of the Bureau of the CC in 1959, 'Rashidov in fact knows neither agriculture nor industry nor construction, since he never worked before in lower party, Soviet and economic organizations. His level of knowledge and experience was ill-fit to the post of the first secretary.'[92] At the time when he wrote the letter, he worked as an advisor of agriculture and irrigation in Afghanistan. Mukhamedjanov insisted that he must have been terminated from all governmental and academic posts under the initiative of Rashidov, but the latter quickly agreed to send the former to work in Afghanistan.[93] He further criticized Rashidov for the unfair dismissal of Khabib Abdullaev from the presidency of the republican Academy of Sciences in 1962,[94] and of his cadre selection on the basis of 'kinship, homeland and personal loyalty'.[95] As seen in this case, Rashidov seemed to succeed in establishing his unequivocal authority by forcing out real and potential enemies from elite posts until the end of the Khrushchev era.

After the fall of Khrushchev, archival materials tell us little about the political situation in Uzbekistan. Therefore, the case studies available are limited to the following two. After the earthquake disaster in Tashkent in April 1966, a number of party-state elites in Tashkent abused their status to obtain additional subsidies to repair their apartments and houses. These included high-rank officials such as G. Gabrieliants (the deputy chairman of the Council of Ministers), Malik Abdurazakov (the first secretary of Tashkent *obkom*), Mirzamakhmud Musakhanov (the deputy chairman of the Council of Ministers), among others. Moscow did not send a representative to Tashkent for an on-site investigation. The accused officials received the lightest penalty 'pointing out' their dishonest behaviour.[96]

In 1968, the Bureau of the CC of the CPUz adopted a resolution, which decided to dismiss all the secretaries of Andijan *obkom*. Andijan Province is located in Ferghana Valley in Eastern Uzbekistan. The self-investigation by the republican CC disclosed a big scandal that Slavic as well as Uzbek secretaries of the *obkom* protected and took bribes from the chairmen of several kolkhozes, who embezzled kolkhoz properties for their self-interest.[97] A number of scholars categorized those from Andijan Province as a part of the Tashkent-Ferghana regional faction, who were in confrontation with the Rashidov's Jizzak-Samarkand faction.[98] However, it may be an overstatement to say that this incident in Andijan was a lesson for the

Ferghana faction from Rashidov due to the lack of detailed biographical data of those dismissed.[99] Rather, what is notable from these cases are that Slavic officials actually engaged in corrupt acts in cooperation with natives.

The author found absolutely no documents dating all the way up to 1981 concerning party control from above over personnel affairs in Uzbekistan in the files of RGANI. As Ronald Carlisle states, the so-called 'Pakhtakor Incident' in April 1969 (the sole mass anti-Russian demonstration in Uzbekistan during the Brejnev era) 'shocked the Uzbek elite and eventually brought a direct intervention in Uzbek politics by Moscow', which at last dismissed Rakhmankul Kurbanov from the chairman of the Council of Ministers and Yalgar Nasriddinova from the chairwoman of Presidium of the Supreme Soviet. The former was relegated to the first deputy minister of Sovkhoz in February 1971, and the latter was transferred to Moscow as the chairwoman of the Soviet of Nationalities of the USSR Supreme Soviet in July 1970. According to Carlisle, Rashidov succeeded in dominating all the three key posts by appointing his close allies.[100] Demian Viseman added Rafik Nishanov, the secretary of the CC of the CPUz on ideology, to the group of Kurbanov and Nasriddinova, which orchestrated to shift responsibility only to Rashidov for the incident and oust him.[101] Nishanov was dismissed and sent to a diplomatic work in Sri Lanka as an ambassador in 1970. The author has not found any document about the event in the archive. However, it seemed that Rashidov had been powerful enough and well 'trusted' from above until that time, and, in all probability, even until the fall of Khrushchev.

'Trust in Cadres' in Central Asia: Generality and Particularity

The volume of archival documents over personnel matters in Central Asian republics decreased as time went on. Lack of documents in the files of the cadre department in Moscow does not mean lack of 'interest' by Moscow in personnel matters in Central Asia, but rather the lack of the 'practical action from above'. Most of the documents may have either been destroyed or kept in the files of the General

Department, responsible for correspondence. The archival authority of the Russian Federation has not declassified the documents of the General Department of the CC of the CPSU in the Brejnev period. Some important documents should be preserved in the files of the Politburo and Secretariat of the CC of the CPSU, if these documents directly relate to party resolutions.[102] Notwithstanding, it is at least certain that Moscow had increasingly entrusted personnel affairs to the republican heads, even if the republican elites were struggling with each other. The Brejnev regime obviously ceased *ad hoc* intervention in personnel matters in the republics in search for criminals or frauds among the republican officials. This sort of policy line was significantly different from that of the Khrushchev regime. Much less, Moscow never dispatched their officials to the district or city level over personnel matters.[103] These were the general tendencies of 'trust in cadres' in Central Asia.

In this respect, it is important to reconsider the meaning of the party-based control during the Brejnev era. The party officials in Moscow concentrated more upon 'information gathering' than 'real action.' Occasions of on-site control were limited to the moments of official events like the republican party congresses, plenums, conferences and so on, where officials in charge of each republic had to participate. In this sense, it is plausible to say that the party control from above was 'routinized' at least over personnel affairs in national republics. The moves made by the centre became more apparent and the republican leadership was able to foresee them. The republican leadership even made use of the party-based control from above in order to resolve internal personnel problems in their favour on some occasions, as seen in the case of Davliatkadamov's dismissal in Tajikistan.

Furthermore, it is also worthy to reconsider the role and position of the party second secretaries in Central Asia. As mentioned above, previous studies tended to describe them as 'watchdogs' of the centre, although their authority under any circumstances did not surpass that of the first secretaries.[104] However, as seen in the case of Vasilii Rykov in Turkmenistan, the surveillance by the second secretaries of native elites and internal politics had its limit. Moreover, as Pereudin in Turkmenistan, several second secretaries had gained enough job experiences (more than 20 years) inside their national republics until the accession to second secretary.[105] It is quite possible that they embroiled themselves in the republican inner circles and pursued narrow interests with native officials.

Now let us turn to 'particularities'. First, the degree and longevity of party control was different for each republic. Moscow continuously kept its interest in the intra-elite confrontation and illicit acts by the republican elites in Turkmenistan up to 1975, but paid much less attention to analogous phenomena in Kazakhstan and Uzbekistan from the beginning of the Brejnev era, which could be explained by the degree of 'trust' toward the leadership of these republics by Moscow.

Second, it is still too early to make any concrete conclusion about localism and tribalism in Central Asia solely on the analysis of archival materials for this study. Nevertheless, it is certainly possible to indicate the existence of *mestnichestvo* and some regional factions (Leninabad and Pamir at least) in Tajikistan and the strength of people from Tashauz Province in Turkmenistan under the leadership of Ovezov. On the contrary, the confrontation between Usubaliev and Mambetov can be explained by the generational and career gap between the two figures. Archival materials suggest localism in Uzbekistan and cliques by *juz* in Kazakhstan, but there are no clues about tribalism and localism in Kyrgyzstan.

Some points should be added about the tribal situation in Turkmenistan and Kazakhstan. In the case of Turkmenistan, the written accusations against Ovezov and his surroundings obviously jumbled tribal, local and kinship factors without mentioning concrete tribal belonging of the accused. In Kazakhstan, the largest tribal coalition and the smallest kinship factor were confused. On the one hand, these facts indicate the usability of this sort of calumny to opponents with terms related to 'tribalism', which must have been uprooted during the 1920–30s. On the other hand, it also shows the real social transformation among former nomads under the socialistic rule, by which 'tribal' belonging no longer was the sole factor for the creation of patron–client relations, and their genealogical and geographical identities often intermingled.[106] The genealogical and tribal ideas were transformed and modernized up to the Brejnev era. The tribal belonging of various lineage levels (up to *juz* in case of Kazakhstan) became one of the factors to define 'closeness' of human relationship, which in turn related to the accessibility to political and material resources.

At the same time, the republican leaders persistently paid attention to the balance of the regional composition of the republican elites (Tajikistan is questionable in this sense). Thus, 'too much' emphasis on localism and tribalism can be misleading and preclude to recognize a certain level of unity of the republican elites around the 'pseudo' nation-states in Central Asia, which gradually but steadily developed during the Brejnev era.[107]

Conclusion

Brejnev's 'trust in cadres' policy finally brought about the 'stability of cadres' in every Central Asian republic. In reality, the 'stability of cadres' had a threefold meaning for national republics: 'stability' of elites' incumbency, 'stability' of intra-elite relations and 'stability' of centre–republican relations. Concurrently, liberation from *ad hoc* intervention from above in local personnel matters steadily pushed forward the centrifugal process of republican politics. Political autonomy in national republics was enhanced. Indigenous officials of the younger generation were fostered and promoted to elite posts during the second half of the Brejnev era. As long as 'strong' leaders survived both in Moscow and in the capitals of national republics and were able to coordinate a wide variety of interests inside the Soviet Union and national republics, the incumbents in the peripheries were comfortable and felt no pressure to change the status quo.[108]

It was under these circumstances that Brejnev passed away in November 1982. As Blackwell Jr. predicts accurately, after the end of a stable gerontocracy, younger leaders preferred to 'define the issues in terms of correcting ills and stimulating development through major policy departures.'[109] However, what Moscow and national republics intended was quite different in terms of 'policy departure'. Moscow endeavoured to develop the state through the recentralization and subordination of republics to the centre, but the Central Asian republics did not want to change the rule of the game and strived to maintain a certain level of political autonomy, which they gained during the Brejnev era. The centre–republican relations became so strained, which was further escalated by the 'anti-corruption campaign' from above. This was the situation in 1983–88. However, lacking enough resources to (re)distribute, Moscow lost its legitimacy to maintain centralization. Mikhail Gorbachev abruptly altered the course to democratization and decentralization from the middle of 1988. Then, as Steven Burg accurately states, 'engendered disputes over just what the "common good" actually is, and these quickly turn into disputes over the method of determining it'.[110] The declarations of sovereignty of national republics in 1988–90 should be understood in this regard. 'Pseudo' nation-states now obtained real substance. 'Trust in cadres' and 'stability of cadres' policy was the starting point of these historical trends, which gave the Central Asian republics the preliminary stage of independence, although republican elites did not intend for this at all.

The Soviet Union during the Brejnev era remained as a multinational 'particularistic' empire. The Central Asian republics gained significant political autonomy in their personnel matters including their ability to form some regional (or tribal in some regards) groupings that their leadership could determine cadre positioning by themselves within the rules of the game (i.e. ethnic composition, regional balance etc.) but without *ad hoc* intervention from above.

Notes

1 Slezkine, Y., 'The USSR as a Communal Apartment, or How a Socialist State Promoted Ethnic Particularlism', *Slavic Review*, 1994, vol. 53/2, pp. 414–52.

2 Martin, T., *The Affirmative Action Empire: Nations and Nationalism in the Soviet Union, 1923–1939*, Ithaca: Cornell University Press, 2001, ch. 4.

3 Bialar, S., *Stalin's Successors: Leadership, stability, and change in the Soviet Union*, Cambridge: Cambridge University Press, 1980, p. 209.

4 One case study about the centre-republican (Kyrgyzstan) relationship during the Khrushchev era, see Chida, T., 'The Relationship Between the Kyrgyz SSR

and the Centre in the Middle Khrushchev Period (1957–61): Based on Materials from Four Archives in Moscow and Bishkek', *Central Eurasian Studies Review*, 2007, vol. 6/1–2, pp. 15–20.

5 Хлевнюк, О., 'Региональная власть в СССР в 1953-конце 1950-х годов: Устойчивость и конфликты', *Отечественная история*, 2007, n°3, p. 48.

6 Gill, G., Pitty, R., *Power in the Party: The Organization of Power and Central-Republican Relationship in the CPSU*, New York: St. Martin's Press, 1997, p. 45.

7 Gorlizki, Y., 'Too Much Trust: Regional Party Leaders and Local Political Networks Under Brejnev', *Slavic Review*, 2010, vol. 69/3, p. 697.

8 Hough, J.F., *The Soviet Prefects: The Local Party Organs in Industrial Decision-Making*, Cambridge: Harvard University Press, 1969; Blackwell Jr., R.E., 'Elite Recruitment and Functional Change: An Analysis of the Soviet Obkom Elite 1950–1968', *The Journal of Politics*, 1972, vol. 34/1, pp. 124–52; Blackwell Jr., R.E., 'Cadres Policy in the Brejnev Era', *Problems of Communism*, 1979, vol. 28/2, pp. 29–42; Clark, W.A., *Soviet Regional Elite Mobility after Khrushchev*, New York: Praeger, 1989. There are many other works with this approach.

9 Rakowska-Harmstone, T., *Russia and Nationalism in Central Asia. The Case of Tadzhikistan*, Baltimore: John Hopkins Press, 1970; Miller, J.H., 'Cadres Policy in Nationality Areas: Recruitment of CPSU First and Second Secretaries in Non-Russian Republics of the USSR', *Soviet Studies*, 1977, vol. 24/1, pp. 3–36; Rywkin, M., *Moscow's Muslim Challenge: Soviet Central Asia (second edition)*, Armonk: M. E. Sharpe, 1990, ch. 9.

10 Carlisle, D.S., 'The Uzbek Power Elite: Politburo and Secretariat (1938–83)', *Central Asian Survey*, 1986, vol. 5/3–4, pp. 91–132; Vaisman, D., 'Regionalism and Clan Loyalty in the Political Life of Uzbekistan', in Ro'i Y. (ed.), *Muslim Eurasia: Conflicting Legacies*, London: Frank Cass, 1995, pp. 105–22; Jones Luong, P., *Institutional Change and Political Continuity in Post-Soviet Central Asia: Power, Perceptions, and Pact*, Cambridge: Cambridge University Press, 2002, ch. 3; Collins, K., *Clan Politics and Regime Transition in Central Asia*, Cambridge: Cambridge University Press, 2006, Chapter 4; Dadabaev, T., 'Regionalism (Localism) and the State. The Soviet Cadre Policy and its Implications in Uzbekistan and Tajikistan', *International Politics and Economics (Kokusai Seiji-Keizaigaku Kenkyuu)*, 2008, n°21, pp. 13–37 (in Japanese).

11 In this regard, Adrienne Edgar mentions that 'like the "Turkmen people" as a whole, tribes such as the Tekes and the Yomuts (note of the author: i.e. the largest genealogical subgroups of Turkmens) were too large and impersonal to inspire unqualified loyalty' (see Edgar, A.L., *Tribal Nation: The Making of Soviet Turkmenistan*, Princeton: Princeton University Press, 2004, p. 21).

12 Chvyr, L., 'Central Asia's Tajiks: Self-Identification and Ethnic Identity', in Naumkin V. (ed.), *State, Religion and Society in Central Asia: A Post-Soviet Critique*, Reading: Ithaca Press, 1993, p. 250.

13 Исмагамбетов, Т., 'Трайбализм: историческое прошлое или реалии дня?' *Мысль*, 1997, n°2, p. 46; Гуллетт, Д, 'Трайбализм в Кыргызстане: точка зрения', *Центральная Азия и Кавказ*, 2002, n°2, p. 43.
14 Хлевнюк, О., *op. cit.*, pp. 31–49; Gorlizki, Y., *op. cit.*, pp. 676–700.
15 Российский государственный архив новейшей истории (РГАНИ). Ф. 5. Оп. 31. Д. 146. Л. 44–48.
16 'К новым рубежам семилетки', *Хлопководство*, 1960, n°2, p. 1.
17 РГАНИ. Ф. 5. Оп. 31. Д. 146. Л. 39–43.
18 РГАНИ. Ф. 5. Оп. 31. Д. 170. Л. 186–190.
19 РГАНИ. Ф. 5. Оп. 31. Д. 170. Л. 177об–178.
20 РГАНИ. Ф. 5. Оп. 31. Д. 170. Л. 176об.
21 РГАНИ. Ф. 5. Оп. 31. Д. 170. Л. 177об.
22 РГАНИ. Ф. 5. Оп. 31. Д. 170. Л. 185.
23 About the scandals in Ryazan Province, see Medvedev, R.A., Medvedev, Zh.A., *Khrushchev: The Years in Power*, Oxford: Oxford University Press, 1977, ch. 9.
24 About the dismissal of Uljabaev, see Rakowska-Harmstone, T., *op. cit.*, pp. 161–2. As to the removal of Razzakov, see Chida, T., *op. cit.*, pp. 18–19.
25 Rashidov had already become a candidate member of Politburo in 1961 during the Khrushchev era. Kunaev became a candidate member in 1966 and a full-fledged member in 1971.
26 Gill, G., Pitty, R., *op. cit.*, p. 117.
27 Ethnic 'Kyrgyz' consists of triadic coalition of tribes including *On kanat*, *Sol kanat* and *Ichkilik*, which inhabit geographically separate areas: *On kanat* in Eastern, Northern and central, *Sol kanat* in Western and *Ichikilik* in Southern Kyrgyzstan. Each coalition can be divided into separate tribes such as Sarybagysh, Bugu, Saiak, Saruu, Kypchak etc. and further lower groupings including lineage ones. Junushaliev and Ploskikh state that the intertribal struggles had been flared in the Communist Party during the 1920–30s, which remained as a constant factor in the political and economic decision-making in the republic throughout the Soviet time. Kathleen Collins cites the word of a Kyrgyz democratic activist that Usubaliev gave preferencial treatments to his kins in promotion. Nikolai Borisov emphasizes the political strength of Kyrgyzs from Northern Kyrgyzstan during Razzakov-Usubaliev era. Such discourses clearly show the tangled character of the concept of 'tribalism' among Kyrgyzs. Борисов, Н.А., *Между современностью и традицией. Политические альтер нативы постсоветской Центральной Азии*, Москва: Российский государственный гуманитарный университет, 2010, p. 70; Джунушалиев, Д., Плоских, В., 'Трайбализм и проблемы развития Кыргызстана', *Центральная Азия и Кавказ*, 2000, n° 3, p. 152; Collins, K., *op. cit.*, pp. 106–7.
28 For the full text of the resolution, refer to *Справочник партийного работника. Выпуск шестой*, Москва: Издательство политической литературы, 1966, pp. 386–92.
29 Усубалиев, Т.У., '*Не могу молчать. Ответы недругам*'. *Книга IV (вторая часть III книги)*, Бишкек: Шам, 1997, p. 460.
30 РГАНИ. Ф. 5. Оп. 59. Д. 3. Л. 2.

31 РГАНИ. Ф. 5. Оп. 59. Д. 3. Л. 2–3.
32 Усубалиев; Т.У., *op. cit.*, p. 422.
33 *Ibid.*, p. 423.
34 РГАНИ. Ф. 5. Оп. 59. Д. 3. Л. 45.; Центральный государственный архив политической документации Кыргызской Республики. Ф. 56. Оп. 159. Д. 14. Л. 32–34.
35 РГАНИ. Ф. 5. Оп. 59. Д. 3. Л. 49–75.
36 РГАНИ. Ф. 5. Оп. 59. Д. 3. Л. 58.
37 *Ibid.*; Kudriavtsev was elected as a deputy of the Supreme Soviet of Kyrgyz SSR of the ninth convocation in 1976. His biography can be found in: *Депутаты Верховного Совета Киргизской ССР девятого созыва*, Фрунзе: Кыргызстан, 1976, p. 164.
38 Усубалиев, Т.У., *op. cit.*, pp. 437–8.
39 Roy, O., *The New Central Asia: The Creation of Nations*, New York: New York University Press, 2000, p. 113.
40 РГАНИ. Ф. 5. Оп. 58. Д. 3. Л. 113.
41 РГАНИ. Ф. 5. Оп. 58. Д. 3. Л. 114.
42 РГАНИ. Ф. 5. Оп. 58. Д. 3. Л. 113.
43 РГАНИ. Ф. 5. Оп. 58. Д. 3. Л. 114.
44 РГАНИ. Ф. 5. Оп. 58. Д. 3. Л. 113–4.
45 РГАНИ. Ф. 5. Оп. 58. Д. 3. Л. 109.
46 РГАНИ. Ф. 5. Оп. 58. Д. 3. Л. 110.
47 РГАНИ. Ф. 5. Оп. 58. Д. 3. Л. 111–2.
48 РГАНИ. Ф. 5. Оп. 58. Д. 3. Л. 112.
49 The author cannot supply details about this incident, since the relevant archival documents of RGANI are labeled as 'limited usage (*ogranichennoe ispol'zovanie*)'.
50 Gill, G., Pitty, R., *op. cit.*, p. 51.
51 РГАНИ. Ф. 5. Оп. 75. Д. 158. Л. 29.
52 РГАНИ. Ф. 5. Оп. 75. Д. 158. Л. 25, 29.
53 РГАНИ. Ф. 5. Оп. 75. Д. 158. Л. 26.
54 About the ethnic issues in Badakhshan, refer to Бушков, В., Моногарова, Л., 'Этнические процессы в Горно-Бадахшанской автономной области Таджикистана', *Центральная Азия и Кавказ*, 2000, n°5, pp. 215–24.
55 РГАНИ. Ф. 5. Оп. 75. Д. 158. Л. 25.
56 РГАНИ. Ф. 5. Оп. 75. Д. 158. Л. 26, 28.
57 РГАНИ. Ф. 5. Оп. 75. Д. 158. Л. 26.
58 РГАНИ. Ф. 5. Оп. 75. Д. 158. Л. 30.
59 РГАНИ. Ф. 5. Оп. 31. Д. 170. Л. 115,
60 РГАНИ. Ф. 5. Оп. 31. Д. 170. Л. 116–117, 121–2.
61 РГАНИ. Ф. 5. Оп. 31. Д. 170. Л. 124.
62 РГАНИ. Ф. 5. Оп. 31. Д. 170. Л. 119.
63 РГАНИ. Ф. 5. Оп. 31. Д. 220. Л. 71–3.
64 РГАНИ. Ф. 5. Оп. 31. Д. 239. Л. 78–81.

65 РГАНИ. Ф. 5. Оп. 31. Д. 239. Л. 89–90.
66 РГАНИ. Ф. 5. Оп. 60. Д. 3. Л. 25.
67 *Ibid.*
68 Unlike Kazakhs and Kyrgyzs, the tribal structure of ethnic Turkmen is not triadic, which can be clearly divided into several tribes (Teke, Yomud, Saryk, Ersari etc.). Each tribe geographically concentrates in certain area. More importantly, according to Adrienne Edgar, 'in contrast to Kazakh society, which featured an aristocratic stratum claiming a hereditary right to rule, Turkmen leaders lacked coercive authority and chosen by group consensus.' Therefore, 'despite [the] belief in a common ancestry, one cannot speak in the singular of "Turkmen history" or the "Turkmen people" before 1917. Relations between tribes and lower lineage groups had been tense, which could not be settled under the sovietization during the 1920–30s' (see Edgar, A.L., *op. cit.*, pp. 20, 171 and 195). According to Paul Geiss, Turkmen tribalism had been basically 'acephalous' and tribsmen had been equal under *däp* or their traditional customs (see Geiss, P.G., 'Turkman Tribalism', *Central Asian Survey*, 1999, vol. 18/3, pp. 347–9). At the same time, Shokhrat Kadyrov, a Turkmen scholar in exile, referred to the 'westernized' (or sovietized) Turkmen elites as 'Euroturkmens,' who received their education in either Russia, especially in Moscow or Leningrad, or in Tashkent, and came under the influence of certain type of Western culture. According to him, the less westernized a Turkmen elite was, the closer his mentality was to the subethnic group of him, thus, members in turn undoubtfully knew who were in the republican authority from their tribes and could be their patron (see Кадыров, Ш., *'Нация' племен. Этнические истоки, трансформация, перспективы государственности в Туркменистане*, Москва, 2003, p. 109; Кадыров, Ш., 'Туркменистан: политические, этнокультурные и демографические факторы смены элит', *Азия и Африка сегодня*, 2003, n°11, p. 33).
69 РГАНИ. Ф. 5. Оп. 60. Д. 3. Л. 25–6.
70 РГАНИ. Ф. 5. Оп. 62. Д. 5. Л. 92–3.
71 РГАНИ. Ф. 5. Оп. 62. Д. 5. Л. 95–6.
72 In March 1974, Moscow received an analogous, but this time signed, letter, written by some Bagiev, a former officer of the republican Ministry of Interior Affairs. Beforehand, he had sent several written accusations against the high-rank officials of the republican party and government. At this time, too, Moscow determined that the accusations in the letter was ungrounded and rejected Bagiev's appeal to be rehabilitated as a member of the CPSU. What is interesting, this Bagiev wrote in the letter that 'after [I sent letters to Moscow], I was harassed and persecuted for the purpose of revenge and hiding the facts, mentioned [in the letters]'. This sort of manhunt and suppression on indicer seems to have been a typical reaction from the 'accused' local party-government organizations. РГАНИ. Ф. 5. Оп. 67. Д. 79. Л. 14–25, 39–40.
73 РГАНИ. Ф. 5. Оп. 62. Д. 5. Л. 105.
74 РГАНИ. Ф. 5. Оп. 67. Д. 79. Л. 43–4.

75 РГАНИ. Ф. 5. Оп. 67. Д. 79. Л. 46.
76 РГАНИ. Ф. 5. Оп. 67. Д. 79. Л. 53–4.
77 РГАНИ. Ф. 5. Оп. 68. Д. 267. Л. 109–10.
78 РГАНИ. Ф. 5. Оп. 68. Д. 267. Л. 112.
79 РГАНИ. Ф. 5. Оп. 68. Д. 267. Л. 113.
80 РГАНИ. Ф. 5. Оп. 68. Д. 267. Л. 112.
81 РГАНИ. Ф. 5. Оп. 68. Д. 267. Л. 114.
82 Хлевнюк, О., *op. cit.*, pp. 33–5.
83 Kadyrov described Ovezov as an 'outstanding figure'. According to him, Ovezov's 'unyieldingness in the struggle for power and the rise and fall of his careers called forth respects for him not only among his landsmen' (see Кадыров, Ш., *op. cit.*, p. 130).
84 РГАНИ. Ф. 5. Оп. 67. Д. 80. Л. 6–12.
85 РГАНИ. Ф. 5. Оп. 66. Д. 108. Л. 23–7об.
86 РГАНИ. Ф. 5. Оп. 63. Д. 68. Л. 26–7.
87 *Juz* is a general term that refers to the coalitions of Kazakh tribes, which can be divided into three groups: *Ulu*, *Orta* and *Kishi*, which respectively coincide with a geographical area. *Ulu juz* is concentrated over the South-Eastern region, *Orta juz* the North-Eastern and central regions, and *Kishi juz* the Western region respectively, where Kazakhs dwell. Like the Kyrgyzs and Turkmens, the tribal structure of Kazakhs is treelike, and lower genealogical groups (*ru* and *taipa*) also bear critical importance for their identity. As Edward Schatz argues, social transformation of Kazakhs during the Soviet time made tribal divisions to be 'no longer the paramount wellsprings of social, cultural, and political identity that had been in the nineteenth century' (see Schatz, E., *Modern Clan Politics: The Power of 'Blood' in Kazakhstan and Beyond*, Seattle: University of Washington Press, 2004, p. 19). According to Nurlan Amrekulov, 'in years of the Soviet rule, *juz* and tribal division receded into the background. However, the subordination system of *juz* structure once again was revived during the time of decay of the communist system and stagnation, when national party nomenclature gained preference over Russian elite' (see Амрекулов, Н., 'Жузы в социально-политической жизни Казахстана', *Центральная Азия и Кавказ*, 2000, n°3, p. 135). While this argument needs to be elaborated further with more detail, nonetheless, at least the Gorbachev regime thought so, since the Kazakh elites singled out for condemnation during 1985–87 did concentrate on those who originated from *Ulu juz* (i.e. *juz* of Kunaev's origin) or took elite posts in Southern provinces of Kazakhstan during the Brejnev era. This last point has been verified to some extent by the author (see Chida, T., 'The Central-Republican Relationship and Party Elites in the Soviet Union: Kazakhstan (1980–1991)', *Slavic Studies (Suravu Kenkyuu)*, 2004, n°51, pp. 44–5, 60 (in Japanese)).
88 РГАНИ. Ф. 5. Оп. 63. Д. 68. Л. 28.
89 Nurbulat Masanov pointed out that Kazakhs of *Kishi juz* continuously occupied the position of the ideological secretary of the CC during the 1970s

(see Масанов, Н., 'Казахская политическая и интеллектуальная элита: клановая принадлежность и внутриэтническое соперничество', *Вестник Евразии*, 1996, n°1, pp. 52–3).

90 Furthermore, Askar Tulegulov argues that the central authority of the USSR in itself rigidly kept the balance of *juz* and clans of Kazakhs in personnel allocations (see Тулегулов, А.К., 'Рекрутирование политической элиты Казахстана: вчера и сегодня', *Саясат-Policy*, 1997, vol. 11, p. 50).

91 Blackwell Jr., R.E., *op. cit.*, p. 140.

92 РГАНИ. Ф. 5. Оп. 60. Д. 3. Л. 95–6.

93 РГАНИ. Ф. 5. Оп. 60. Д. 3. Л. 94–5.

94 РГАНИ. Ф. 5. Оп. 60. Д. 3. Л. 100–1.

95 РГАНИ. Ф. 5. Оп. 60. Д. 3. Л. 103.

96 РГАНИ. Ф. 5. Оп. 59. Д. 3. Л. 8–9.

97 РГАНИ. Ф. 5. Оп. 60. Д. 3. Л. 10–11.

98 For example, see Vaisman, D., *op. cit.*; Jones Luong, P., *op. cit.*, p. 88; Collins, K., *op. cit.*, pp. 105–106; Dadabaev, T., *op. cit.*

99 Actually, Rafik Nishanov, the secretary of the CC of the CPUz at that time, provides an opposite view about the ouster of the provincial party leaders, recalling in his memoir that Nishanov himself exposed corruption scandal in Andijan Province, although Rashidov asked him not to go deeply into the incident. Nishanov was born in Tashkent Province. *Деревья зеленеет до метелей: Рафик Нишанов рассказывает Марине Заваде и Юрию Куликову*, Москва: Молодая гвардия, 2012, pp. 98–99.

100 Carlisle, D.S., *op. cit.*, pp. 116–7.

101 Vaiseman, *op. cit.*, pp. 115–116.

102 In this regard, the author admits that he should have conducted thorough analysis about archival documents of Fond 89 in RGANI, which included declassified materials of Politburo and Secretariat, and documents of the republican CCs in the Russian State Archive of Social-Political History.

103 The author found archival documents about four incidents over personnel matters on the district or city level in RGANI. The republican CCs or *obkoms* took measure to all of these cases (see РГАНИ. Ф. 5. Оп. 61. Д. 5. Л. 2–12.; Ф. 5. Оп. 67. Д. 79. Л. 64–5, 87–92.; Ф. 5. Оп. 75. Д. 158. Л. 8–22).

104 Miller, J.H., *op. cit.*, p. 10; Rywkin, M., 'Power and Ethnicity: Regional and District Party Staffing in Uzbekistan (1983/84)', *Central Asian Survey*, vol. 4/1, pp. 5–6.

105 Viktor Pereudin (Turkmenistan), Viacheslav Makarenko (Kyrgyzstan), Aleksandr Korkin (Kazakhstan) and Oleg Miroshkhin (Kazakhstan) can be categorized as this sort of second secretary. Makarenko was an 'indigenous' Ukrainian, who was born in Frunze, the capital of Kyrgyzstan.

106 According to Saulesh Esenova, 'tribal identification is not understood as an identity which is based on kinship: it is a matter of attachment to a certain place', especially in the urban areas with population mixture (see Esenova, S., '"Tribalism" and Identity in Contemporary Circumstances: The Case of

Kazakhstan', *Central Asian Survey*, 1998, vol. 17/3, p. 451). Jenish Junushaliev and Vladimir Ploslikh also imply this sort of transformation of tribalism to 'regionalism' among Kyrgyz people (see Джунушалиев, Д, Плоских, В., *op. cit.*, pp. 153–4).

107 The author thinks that many of previous studies about the phenomena of localism and tribalism do not go much beyond 'impression'. More detailed 'facts' are needed to clarify these phenomena. In this connection, one point should be added to the argument by Kathleen Collins. She wrote: 'in Kyrgyzia, the Ichkilik clan based in Osh, a Southern *oblast* of the republic, gained significant control over republican politics when its leader, Razzakov, consolidated a power base from 1950 to 1961.' It is true that Razzakov was an Ichkilik (Kypchak), but he was born in Liailiak District (in today's Batken Province), located far from the provincial centre, Osh, and grew up in Tajikistan and Uzbekistan as an orphan. When he started to work in Kyrgyzstan in 1945, he was transferred from Tashkent, where he served as the secretary of the CC of the Communist Party of Uzbekistan. Given these facts, it is quite suspicious of his clan-based control over the republican politics. Collins does not make any in-depth explanation with concrete facts how he established this sort of tribal-based network (see Collins K., *op. cit.*, p. 106).

108 About this sort of feeling in the late Brejnev era, see Blackwell Jr., R.E., *op. cit.*, pp. 39–41.

109 *Ibid.*, p. 42.

110 Burg, S.L., 'Central Asian Elite Mobility and Political Change in the Soviet Union', *Central Asian Survey*, 1986, vol. 5/3–4, p. 85.

This article is based on research funded by Japan-Russia Youth Exchange Centre (Tokyo). The author sincerely appreciates the financial support of the Centre.

CHAPTER 3

NATIONS AND POST-COLONIALISM IN CENTRAL ASIA: TWENTY YEARS LATER[1]

Sergei Abashin
European University in St. Petersburg

The collapse of the USSR and the appearance instead of some 15 new states, not counting several territories declaring themselves to be states, has raised the inevitable question of how this space might now be reconfigured for analytical purposes. Should it, as used to be the case, be considered as an indivisible whole (as post-Soviet countries for example, or as Eurasia[2])? Or would it be better divided into separate parts, each correlated with other, wider delineations (North/South, West/East, the Christian/Islamic worlds etc.)? Both solutions have their reasons and goals, and, naturally, their pros and cons. In the first case, there is the risk of ascribing certain unique and uniform features to this space, while ignoring on the one hand its internal complexity and on the other its interaction with the rest of the world. In the second case, the opposite danger arises: of ignoring shared historical experiences and essentializing the borders, first and foremost the cultural borders, between the various communities that inhabit the space in question. Evidently, then, any strategy for analysis must be developed around the possibility of combining and aligning these two perspectives.

This chapter is an attempt to blitz through an overview of contemporary processes in Central Asian countries, along with a critical look at the analytical categories used to describe these processes. Of course, Central Asia is itself a somewhat arbitrary frame for scrutiny: it could be narrowed by splintering the territory into smaller parts (for instance Ferghana, the Pamirs, the Caspian Area, and so on) or, on the contrary, it could be expanded and reconfigured, resulting in different outlines to be analysed (for example the Muslim regions of the USSR). This chapter, nonetheless, assumes Central Asia to be a place that, for the greater number of readers, is already defined and already endowed with a whole range of features, even if only in their imagination.[3] It is familiar in the guise of an administratively-outlined territory comprising the five former Asiatic republics of the USSR, which at one time formed a distinctive Soviet 'other', being simultaneously exotic and backward. This place, being different, was—and still is—frequently absent from any discussion of the Russian Empire, the USSR and the post-Soviet period; only a few rare voices carry from 'over there'. Central Asia remains a (post-)Soviet backwater, on which the attention of scholars and lay people rests only infrequently, and then not for long.[4] This absence is another peculiarity which makes it possible to talk of an imagined unity within the region, at least from the point of view of those who continue to experience their own Europeaness and centrality in relation to it.

This chapter will centre its attention on three categories commonly applied to the new Central Asian states: nation, post-coloniality and post-Sovietness. It will consider the following: the ways in which these three categories are used to help describe modern Central Asian society (or societies); which schemas, classifications, and models are applied to it (or them); and the similarities, dissimilarities, new questions and further lines of inquiry which may arise.

Nations and Their Fragments?

The collapse of the USSR and the entire subsequent period are often perceived as the long-awaited triumph of the idea of the nation; a triumph which all preceding history (or all of the twentieth century, at least) had been preparing for, which sustained and intensified the consolidation of strong national states, national ideologies and national identities. Indeed, in Central Asian countries, the following phenomena have been observed: the creation of national mythologies and rituals; the rewriting of textbooks and the recasting of museum exhibits in the spirit of national histories; the strengthening of (or, at any rate, attempts to strengthen) the role of national languages; acute anxiety regarding demographic and cultural threats posed by foreign ethnic minorities etc.[5] Conflicts and contradictions can likewise be seen within Central Asian countries and between them, which take place under the banner of national interests (or the interests of the titular nations), while in bitter clashes in the media and on the internet nationally-charged accusations and insults, along with promises of victory and revanche, are hurled in the name of the nation.

This chapter aims not so much to undermine this perception as to show various facets of the process in which nation-states are consolidated. This process should not be seen as developing at its own accord, nor as teleologically preordained, but as the sum of the effects from varied and, at times, chaotic events and actions. These effects interlink with, structure and intensify one another, they are relayed into other spheres, and they shape not only the way in which one set of events or another are remembered, but also the way in which they are explained.

Certain of these effects are linked to the Soviet policy, begun in the 1920s, of constructing and shaping national republics, national cultures and national elites.[6] The elites thus learned to speak Soviet in their national languages (not necessarily literally: Russian was also spoken nationally). Reference to nationality became an official means of gaining access to power, privileges, and bonuses, while sometimes it was a stigma, a tool for repression and discrimination. The events of 1988–91, when regional elites began bargaining with the centre over their rights, did not—in Central Asia and Kazakhstan, at any rate—constitute a struggle for national liberation and a drive for independence. In fact, it was a continuation of the perennial negotiations between the centre and the republics over the redistribution of resources. The republics' leaders displayed complete loyalty to Moscow; the latter's decision to detach itself from Central Asia came as a surprise to them.

After 1991, when the Central Asian republics had been detached from Russia, new effects began to appear; measures and decisions that were sometimes arbitrary and sometimes unavoidable led to a new round of constructing national institutions, practices, identities and sentiments. Reference to the nation, it transpired, was convenient as a language of international law, as a means of transfer and comparison, as a language for communicating with other countries, international organizations, tourists, Western experts and politicians, for whom the nation is an understandable form of explanation. Reference to the nation also made it possible to talk of the past, the historical legacy, a golden age, authentic culture and continuity. This instilled primordial feelings in the population of the new states and attempted to smooth over dangerous contradictions and rifts within society.[7] Reference to the nation was and remains a tool for mobilizing modernization, and for constructing and promoting plans for a bright future. In each of these fields the national narrative is constructed in its own way, and is presented from particular perspectives. It performs specific and, at times, particularly concrete functions, but all these fields combine when matters turn to the legitimization of authoritarian regimes (or regimes tending towards authoritarianism) in Central Asia, who consider and assert that they are acting on behalf of and for the good of the nation.

The understanding that nationalism is not a primordially assigned programme or groove to follow but, rather, is linked to concrete contexts, allows the diverse trajectories of nationalisms in the independent countries of Central Asia to be discerned. Despite all the similar and parallel features that have existed for centuries or that arose under the unifying policy of the Soviet centre, despite the existence of multiple lines of interaction and mutual influence, of copying and of competition, there are significant differences between the national ideologies and state-building practices in the region. Simplifying greatly, it can be stated that Uzbek nationalism is concerned with strengthening the state; Tajik nationalism reaches out to its diasporas and struggles desperately with the alternative offered by Islam; Kyrgyz nationalism tries hard to support unity among the elite; Kazakh nationalism seeks a means of co-existence with the Russian-speaking community, while Turkmen nationalism is directed toward isolating the country from the outside world.[8] All these themes are present in each country, of course (that same issue of Muslim identity is to the fore everywhere), but they vary in the acuity, scale and specifics of the problems they pose.

Again, without going into detail, the point is that the differences mentioned, and similar issues, have arisen and continue to deepen simply because the new Central Asian states have differing weight categories and living standards, which did not seem too significant within the USSR. It turns out some of them have bigger populations, others have greater reserves of oil and gas; certain countries have an influential Russian-speaking community, others share a border with China and Afghanistan, and so on. The presence of some or other resources and the ability of particular individuals and groups within the elite to exploit these resources govern how national interests are formulated, foreign policies are oriented, and the examples and templates proffered for emulation are selected. So it is no surprise that Central Asian nations and nationalisms are different; they differ in their internal organization and they differ in the way they see their past and their future.

Nationalism is not a framework into which all people are inserted willy-nilly, but rather a particular combination of pre-meditated or spontaneous actions and their effects. Such an approach allows the various actors involved or not involved in producing such effects to be discerned. It becomes clear that there is no single dominant nationalism; rather, there are differing versions positioned in relationships of constant mutual debate and competition. For example, the group currently in power in Uzbekistan pays no attention whatsoever to the needs and challenges facing Uzbek minorities abroad, whereas a section of the establishment in Tashkent does hear the voices of their fellow nationals and lets them know that it is not indifferent to what they are saying. In exactly the same way, while one part of the local elite in Tajikistan expects a response from Tajik diasporas living in neighbouring countries, another part appeals for the focus to be on state-building within the ascribed borders. It is easy to imagine that these elite groups will replace each other in power, and will re-arrange their political emphases anew.

Alongside (and within) the political and intellectual elite in Central Asian countries there exist many different social classes and communities, each with their own interests and strategies. Sometimes these interests fit into national projects and strengthen them, while sometimes they do not—in the latter case other effects arise, offering alternatives to nationalism. Among these can be counted, for example, the formation of influential regional elite groups, which exist in every country in the region.[9] In Tajikistan in the 1990s, competition between such groups led to actual civil war; the periodic revolutions in Kyrgyzstan also have at their root a conflict of regional identities. Another alternative to nationalism, which has been gathering strength, albeit unevenly, throughout the post-Soviet period is presented by various Islamic/Islamist projects.[10] Some of these entirely abjure any national distinctions, seeing them as contrary to Islam and dictated by Russia or the West. Yet another alternative might be mentioned: women's movements, which formulate a particular view of nationalism.[11] And, finally, separate mention must be made of large-scale migration from some Central Asian countries into other states, for temporary employment and for permanent settlement.[12] It is not only that, for considerable periods of time, migrants are not subjected to the influence of nationalist propaganda, but also that they form new social networks, identities, and customs in their destinations. Complex trans-national communities are formed, in which the role of culture, history and language is considered anew.

When taking an overview of all these alternative or additional effects, which for the past 20 years have gradually been strengthening, spreading and combining into new projects and tendencies, it could be concluded that nationalism as a dominant official rhetoric is not capable of reducing so many private and collective interests and strategies to a common denominator. Moreover, the increasing tendency of the nation to fragment further along various fault-lines comes into view: rich regions and poor, the city (suburbs) and the village, Islamists, women, migrants, minorities etc. This does not mean that the nation has failed as a community or identity. It does, however, indicate that the process of national construction continues: reacting to new conditions, changing trajectory, and continually finding itself in competition with other identities.

From 'Empire' to Empire?

If the theme of nation and nationalism has appeared in the rhetoric of every Central Asian politician, and, correspondingly, in academic and specialist analyses of contemporary Central Asia throughout the last 20 years, and if the attention paid to it has not dimmed but rather increased, then the theme of post-coloniality as characteristic of post-Soviet societies in the region has developed only gradually and ambiguously.[13]

The question of post-coloniality usually arises in conjunction with other questions: was the USSR a colonial empire and, correspondingly, had society in Central Asia and Kazakhstan at that time been colonized? Academic opinion on this point is divided. Some of them do label the USSR an empire; in fact, specifically a colonial empire, in which entire peoples and regions found themselves in a subordinate position with fewer rights and governed by typically colonial methods.[14] Others argue that the Soviet Union was an atypical empire or perhaps not an empire at all, but rather, for example, a mobilizing, modernizing state, which does not alter the issue of subordination and resistance, but does allow it to be examined in other ways than just on the basis of the cultural differences between the oppressors and the oppressed.[15] In this case, academic discussion is of somewhat less interest than the attitude of Central Asian politicians, elites and publics to the question. The way in which people see themselves in their recent past suggests there may be important traits in present-day memory, identity and policy which require individual examination.

Criticism of the USSR is an important and inescapable element of modern national narratives in the region. The idea that the nation has taken the place of the previous unjust system, liberating people from it and overcoming its inadequacies, lies at the heart of the political apparatus of the new states. Their current status—i.e. the explanation of the new countries' origins and the basis of their claims to independence—cannot be legitimized without a rejection of the Soviet past. However, criticism of the USSR takes different forms in different Central Asian countries, each with its own peculiarities, and differing in its intensity.

Probably the harshest stance in this regard has been adopted by those in power in Uzbekistan, which consequently is pursuing a policy of de-Sovietization. Almost immediately following the collapse of the USSR, the president of Uzbekistan, Islam Karimov, promulgated the notion of *mustakillik* (i.e. independence) as the main goal towards which throughout history Uzbek society had been ever striving, and which it had finally achieved in 1991. Under the banner of this ideology, places have been rebuilt and/or renamed en masse, sites redolent symbolically of the Soviet era have been destroyed, while Soviet films, Soviet literature, Soviet textbooks and Soviet music have all been squeezed from view. This Uzbek policy of remembrance regarding the Soviet era is based on people's consciousness of trauma; a clear example of this is the Museum in Memory of the Victims of Repression.[16] The ideology of independence combines memory of the suffering caused by the colonial policies of the tsarist era with memory of Stalinist repressions and other hardships of the Soviet epoch to form one general sense of trauma. Although the colonialism of the Russian imperial period and the totalitarianism of the USSR period are treated separately in public rhetoric, in actuality no distinction is drawn between them: Soviet repressions are seen as the logical progression of the repressions of the Russian imperial era. This lack of distinction allows two political aims to be met: on the one hand, it multiplies the effect of criticism of the USSR by conflating it with criticism of the Romanov empire; on the other, it imbues arguments against Soviet totalitarianism with an anticolonial character and, consequently, shifts the emphasis from issues around human rights to questions of cultural difference.

Why should Uzbekistan in particular be leading the de-Sovietization drive? There are two factors: one subjective and one structural. Taking the second one first, Uzbekistan was considered by Moscow to be the main republic in the region: its representatives occasionally held positions in the Central Committee Politburo, and regional branches of Soviet ministries were located in Tashkent. But this meant that here was the place where connections between the centre and the Soviet periphery, the points of contact between them, were most direct, and the pressure was strongest.[17] The subjective factor is a continuation of the structural one, namely the so-called Cotton Scandal which Andropov exploited in the 1980s in the attempt to disavow earlier agreements between the Kremlin and the republic and to place matters in the region under harsher control, by demonstrating to all of local society that the centre's former power had not waned. This campaign of widespread criminal investigation into corruption was a painful blow to the pride of the Uzbek elite. To a great extent, this affair shaped the elite's anti-Kremlin/anti-Soviet mood, which made itself felt when the USSR unexpectedly collapsed.

In the other Central Asian countries, efforts are likewise under way to dismantle the symbolic constructions of the Russian and Soviet legacies. Moreover, after 20 years, this process is not only slowing down but, on the contrary, appears to be gradually gathering steam. However, in pursuing this, their rulers and elites are not, in contrast to the Uzbeks, striving to make criticism of the USSR evoke trauma, to make the latter appear exclusively negative, nor to force out fondly-remembered Soviet books, films and music.

Attention should be turned to one important feature shared by all Central Asian countries: there is not a single one in which the authorities or a majority of the public are prepared to label the Soviet period colonial, or the former Soviet republics colonies. Not even in

Uzbekistan, although this is where the ideological narrative about gaining independence came closest of all to classical forms of decolonialization narratives. Uzbek authorities restrict themselves to dropping obvious hints about the Soviet period being a continuation of the colonial period of the Russian Empire, although they cannot bring themselves to draw the logical conclusion of this comparison by declaring the USSR to be a colonial empire and present-day Uzbekistan to be post-colonial.

This fact may be explained by returning to what was mentioned earlier: the fact that Central Asian society is not homogeneous, but divided into a multiplicity of classes, groups, strata and communities, each with their own interests. The intensifying fragmentation of Central Asian societies explains the absence of any consensus regarding the Soviet past, the wide array of opinions and assessments, and the continuation, at times indeed the escalation, of the discussion.

Differing assessments of the Soviet past in Central Asian countries are linked, for example, to the presence of a Russian-speaking section of the population. Kazakhstan and Kyrgyzstan have large Russian-speaking communities, including Russian-speaking ethnic Kazakhs and Kyrgyz, and so the powers-that-be have no interest in letting the issue of trauma caused by the process of de-Sovietization become a source of internal social tension.

One of the reasons behind this unwillingness to be remembered in the role of the colonized lies in the fact that a large proportion of the contemporary Central Asian elites have a Soviet biography of careers and successes. All the modern attributes of statehood—borders, institutions, imagery—likewise were formulated in the Soviet era and bear the stamp of Soviet construction. To publicly label these roots colonial would mean to call into question the legitimacy of their social and symbolic capital and, consequently, also their present-day political status, which the elites fear doing.

In addition, the elites have been compelled to take account of public opinion within their countries. A survey conducted in 2009 in former Soviet republics by the agency Evraziiskii Monitor (Eurasian Monitor) uncovered a wide range of opinions about Soviet history and, moreover, in so doing, revealed that, of the entire post-Soviet space, it was in these same Central Asian countries that the highest percentages of people expressing positive opinions about the main Soviet leadership (including such people as Stalin, Zhukov and Brejnev) and positive perceptions of the October Revolution in 1917 were found, while attitudes towards collectivization and repression were less negative than, say, in the Baltic States or Georgia.[18] It is possible to argue over the methodology of these surveys, or over the interpretation of their results, but it seems impossible to argue with the general conclusion that within, or alongside, official memory there exist many other memories which are not simply the products of state-sponsored policies on remembrance. For many sections of society, nostalgia for the Soviet era is a peculiar means of criticizing the present state of affairs. The decline in the economic and social spheres, instability, the increasing gap between rich and poor, the appearance and exacerbation of new ways in which power is wielded—all these are factors which, in the minds of many people, make the previous Soviet forms of hegemony appear less pressing, while the achievements of the past, which in 1991 seemed unimpressive and debatable, appear to be a now-unattainable ideal. It may have been in name only, but all the same, the support offered in a form of 'positive discrimination' in the Soviet Union for women, for people living in backward regions and for cultural minorities leaves many people with a feeling of gratitude, set against the increasing pressure on these sections of society today.

Finally, after the Soviet Union collapsed, the previous unequal relationships between the Soviet republics and the centre, in the shape of Russia (Moscow) were replaced by new relationships of dependence, both regional and global. So in Tajikistan and Kyrgyzstan, themes of anti-colonialism and anti-Sovietism generally are sidelined, in part because the elites of these countries now consider their main historical rival to be Uzbekistan, which in their opinion is now seeking to don the mantle of the new dominant centre. The elites of these countries therefore prefer to mobilize historical disputes in terms of a real or imagined 'Uzbek peril' rather than hark back to the Russian or Soviet eras. The active penetration of

Central Asia by world powers (the USA, China, European countries etc.) and by a variety of international organizations has been accompanied by the development of a new subordination, by intervention in the internal affairs of the region, and by the spread of unfamiliar cultural trends. Under these conditions, Central Asian countries are rapidly being transformed into global outsiders, which in the best-case scenario will supply the leading powers with raw material and labour, while acquiring in return yet greater dependency due to foreign credits, investments, and political benevolence, not to mention the threat of military invasion should the rules laid down by these same world powers be flouted.[19] This rapid marginalization sparks fears of a current or future subjugation to new geo-political leaders, which in turn strengthens the reluctance to wield the label (post)coloniality.

So Just When Will the Post-Soviet Period End?

The issue of the post-coloniality of current Central Asian societies is likewise linked to the extent to which the Soviet legacy and Soviet features have been preserved over 20 years of independence, and the extent to which these shape the specificity of the processes in Central Asian countries in comparison with, say, other countries of the Near and Middle East which are similar to them in terms of religion, culture and language.

The existence of such a legacy is suggested *a priori* by the term post-Soviet, which remains as popular and resilient as ever. It contains a diverse set of distinguishing features. Firstly, the term indicates certain very specific political, economic and social transformations that the region underwent in the 20th century, not so much under the influence of internal developmental processes as of the social engineering policies carried out by the USSR's centre. In every country, specific political, economic and social infrastructures were created, as were institutions and practices for wielding power; to a great extent these have been preserved and have shaped the modern structure of the state. For example, the current presidential machines, which concentrate within themselves the main levers of control and management, copy the machinery of the central committees of the Communist Party. Great weight is given to ideology, and to the symbols and rituals of statehood, while parliaments and the principle of the separation of powers are little more than ornamental. The security services play a major role in internal politics. An array of countries in the region have retained Soviet institutions such as academies of science, creative unions, state-controlled trade unions, and youth organizations. The economy is characterized by monopolies, and is based on the extensive exploitation of natural resources, while new economic projects are frequently, it transpires, the continuations of projects originally under development in the Soviet era. In the social sphere, as before, pensions and welfare payments survive (even if tiny in size), as do, formally at least, free education and healthcare: the rudiments of a socially-minded state, such as the USSR claimed itself to be. The authorities and the elite position themselves culturally as secular regimes.[20] Lastly, as many historians have commented, their very national identities were formed in the Soviet period, as a result of the national demarcation of the 1920s.[21] Similar traces of Sovietness can be found in literally every sphere of state life.

The second distinguishing feature is that the term post-Soviet suggests specific daily routines and identities that were instilled in the population in the Soviet period, regardless of their religious or national affiliation. Of most relevance here is the major role of the Russian language—practically all the Central Asian elite speak Russian to this day. Many daily habits of interaction have been preserved, especially in urban areas, as have ways of spending free time, preparing food, and marking public holidays such as International Women's Day on 8 March, New Year, and Victory Day. People retain memories of Soviet leaders, Soviet living conditions, Soviet films etc. Many social ties (mixed families and friendships) endure that were initially formed in that period.

Thirdly, the very prefix 'post' states that the Soviet period is over and Central Asia is in a condition of gradual drift along a trajectory that was set in the preceding era. As a rule, this drift is seen as a crisis, a process of degradation, and a continuing collapse without any clear new route towards progress.

Reference to post-Sovietness is a frequently encountered and very important explicatory model, but it does have its weaker moments. One such is the insistence on the unique nature of the Soviet experience. However, a comparison of this with the experience of many other countries shows that Soviet development can be understood as just one version of the general processes of development that European countries, and others too, underwent in the previous century. These processes include an accelerated, authoritarian model of modernization (implementing new technology in the economy, industrialization, the spread of mass education etc.); the socialization of the state (the appearance of state pensions, public-sector housing, a mass consumer culture etc); ultra-ideological political regimes; the collapse of empires and the creation of nation-states.[22] 1991, then, can be seen as a continuation of or, perhaps, as a new stage in these processes of integration into the global system of distribution of power and division of labour that were already under way, thanks to Soviet policies, throughout the 20th century.

Another drawback of the term 'post-Soviet' is the fact that it to a great extent ignores the changes and problems that have accumulated in Central Asian countries following the breakdown of the USSR. It is obvious that over that time each of these countries has managed to pursue its own particular path, and so quite distinct differences between Central Asian states can now be seen that, as was argued earlier, were much less obvious in Soviet times. Societies in the region have taken on new traits, for example mass labour migration, which had never previously existed in this form. The influence of such novelties as the internet, mobile telecommunications and much more, has started to be felt in the social realm, which also creates a completely new—un-Soviet—reality. A generation has grown up which neither remembers nor pines for Sovietness, and which does not know the Russian language well; a generation whose habits and identities—for example, Islamist—have nothing in common with the Soviet era. In the countries of the region today, a new transport infrastructure is being built which is directed towards Iran, Afghanistan, and especially towards China, and which is already partially complete. Resources, people, money, and ideas actively circulate along these routes. The currents of internal movement in Central Asia have changed in intensity—in some places increasing (for instance, the shift of the capital of Kazakhstan from Almaty to Astana, formerly Tselinograd) while in others decreasing (for example, at the borders between Uzbekistan and its neighbours). It is possible to spend as much time describing this kind of change as listing examples of the Soviet legacy.

And so, while reference to post-Sovietness may, just as before, be suited to one sort of analytical procedure, it is entirely unsuited for others. The reality to be observed has a fractured, hybrid nature; it cannot be folded up neatly into some ready-made model based on the example of other countries or regions, and it does not provide a basis for the creation of a separate model exclusively for Central Asia. Societies in transition, failed states, the new periphery (or the new South), authoritarian regimes (Islamic or post-Soviet, according to taste) etc.: each of these frameworks suggests its own view and its own line of argument, referring to particular traits in Central Asian societies which from another angle are either invisible or only partially seen, in distorted forms. Any explicatory model selected will itself impose restrictions, create interference in perception, and demand that reality, which spreads in different directions, be brought into line.

It is particularly important that the various frameworks exist not only in the vision of specialists, but also in the consciousness, the calculations and the identity of the region's inhabitants themselves—both elites and non-elites. As soon as discussion of Central Asia begins to use words like nation, empire, colonialism, and Sovietness, the question immediately arises of how to distinguish between categories of analysis and categories of practice, i.e. how to separate strictly defined academic usage from the many contexts in which these words are produced and used every hour, every day. This distinction is in itself problematical, in so far as any academic analysis can be understood both from the point of view of its ideological and political effects and from the point of view of the social and financial mechanisms which create expert knowledge. In particular, it should be noted that many models which are presented as neutral research transform into influential factors driving new divisions and distortions.[23] Categories of analysis are drawn from categories of practice and then, reprocessed, are returned to the realm of practice—this cycle continues endlessly, never ceasing. Whenever the next Marx declares that the task of a philosopher is to change the world, a new intermixing of categories takes place and the manipulation of their interchangeability begins.

Notes

1 The author is grateful to *La Maison des Sciences de l'Homme* for making it possible to work on the subject-matter of this article.

2 Grant, B., 'We are all Eurasian', *Ab Imperio*, 2011/4, pp. 21–34.

3 Abashin, S., 'Thoughts about "Central Asia Within the Russian Empire"', *Ab Imperio*, 2008/4, pp. 456–71.

4 Remember that in 1989 this region's territory and population accounted for roughly one-sixth of the USSR's overall territory and population.

5 Smith, G., Law, V., Wilson, A., Bohr, A., Allworth, E. (eds), *Nation-Building in the Post-Soviet Borderlands. The Politics of National Identities*, Cambridge: Cambridge University Press, 1998; Roy, O., *The New Central Asia: The Creation of Nations*, London: I.B.Tauris, 2000; Adams, L., *The Spectacular State: Culture and National Identity in Uzbekistan*, Durham: Duke University Press, 2010; Abashin, S., 'Nation-construction in post-Soviet Central Asia', in Bassin, M., Kelly, C. (eds), *Soviet and Post-Soviet Identities*, Cambridge: Cambridge University Press, 2011.

6 Slezkine, Y., 'The USSR as a Communal Apartment, or How a Socialist State Promoted Ethnic Particularism', *Slavic Review*, 1994, vol. 53/2. pp. 414–52; Martin, T., *The Affirmative Action Empire: Nation and Nationalism in the Soviet Union, 1923–1939*, Ithaca, New York: Cornell University Press, 2001.

7 Bregel, Y., 'Notes on the Study of Central Asia', *Papers on Inner Asia*, n°28, Bloomington: Indiana University, 1996; Laruelle; M., 'The Return of the Aryan Myth: Tajikistan in Search of a Secularized National Ideology', *Nationalities Papers*, 2007, vol. 35/1. pp. 51–70; Shnirelman, V., 'Aryans or Proto-Turks? Contested Ancestors in Contemporary Central Asia', *Nationalities Papers*, 2009, vol. 37/5, pp. 557–87.

8 Do not forget the Kara-Kalpak, Pamir, and likewise Uigur nationalisms, with their own particular interests and institutions that were established in the Soviet era; nor the existence of various diasporas–Russian, Caucasian, Korean etc.–who

are undergoing their own search for identity (see Kosmarskaia, N., *'Deti imperii' v postsovetskoi Tsentral'noi Azii: adaptivnye praktiki i mental'nye sdvigi (russkie v Kirgizii, 1992–2002)* [*'Children of the Empire' in Post-Soviet Central Asia: Adaptive Practices and Mental Shifts (Russians in Kyrgyzstan, 1992–2002)*], Moscow: Natalis, 2006.

9 Collins, K., *Clan Politics and Regime Transition in Central Asia*, Cambridge: Cambridge University Press, 2006; Schatz, E., *Modern Clan Politics: The Power of 'Blood' in Kazakhstan and Beyond*, Seattle: Washington University Press, 2004.

10 Babadzhanov, B., 'Islam v Uzbekistane: ot repressii k bor'be identichnostei' ['Islam in Uzbekistan: From Repression to a Struggle of Identities'], in Kokoshin, A. (ed.), *Rossiia–Sredniaia Azia: Politika i islam v XX–nachale XXI v.* [*Russia–Central Asia: Politics and Islam in the 20th and early 21st centuries*], Moscow: USSR, 2011, pp. 191–213; Babadzhanov, B., "Vakhkhabitskie reformatory": ot disputov k raskolam i politicheskoi aktivnosti' ["Wahhabist Reformers": From Disputes to Schisms and Political Activity'], in Kokoshin, A. (ed.), *Rossiia–Sredniaia Azia: Politika i islam v XX–nachale XXI v.* [*Russia–Central Asia: Politics and Islam in the 20th and early 21st centuries*], Moscow: USSR, 2011, pp. 214–56; Naumki, V., *Radical Islam in Central Asia: Between Pen and Rifle*, Bolder: Rowman and Littlefield, 2005; Khalid, A., *Islam after Communism: Religion and Politics in Central Asia*, Berkeley: University of California Press, 2007; Rasanayagam, J., *Islam in Post-Soviet Uzbekistan: The Morality of Experience*, Cambridge: Cambridge University Press, 2011; Louw, M., *Everyday Islam in Post-Soviet Central Asia*, London, New York: Routledge, 2007.

11 Kandiyoti, D., 'The Politics of Gender and the Soviet Paradox: Neither Colonized, Nor Modern?' *Central Asian Survey*, 2007, vol. 26/4, pp. 601–23.

12 Olimova, S., Bosc, I., *Trudovaia migratsiia iz Tadzhikistana* [*Labour Migration from Tajikistan*], International Organization for Migration–NITs Sharq: Dushanbe, 2003; Abdullaev, E.V. (ed.), *Trudovaia migratsiia v respublike Uzbekistan: sotsial'nye, pravovye i gendernie aspekty* [*Labour Migration in the Republic of Uzbekistan: Social, Legal and Gendered Aspects*], UNDP & gender program of the Swiss embassy: Tashkent, 2008; Laruelle, M. (ed.), *Dynamiques migratoires et changements societaux en Asie centrale* [*Migratory dynamics and social changes in Central Asia*], Paris: Editions Petra, 2010.

13 Adams, L., 'Can We Apply a Post-colonial Theory to Central Asia?' *Central Eurasia Studies Review*, 2008, vol. 7/1, pp. 2–8; Kandiyoti, D., 'Post-Colonialism Compared: Potentials and Limitations in the Middle East and Central Asia', *International Journal of Middle East Studies*, 2002, vol. 34/2, pp. 279–97; Remnev, A., 'Kolonial'nost', postkolonial'nost' i 'istoricheskaia politika' v sovremennom Kazakhstane' ['Coloniality, Post-coloniality and 'Historical Politics' in Contemporary Kazakhstan'], *Ab Imperio*, 2011/1, pp. 169–205.

14 Hirsch, F., *Empire of Nations: Ethnographic Knowledge and the Making of the Soviet Union*, Ithaca, London: Cornell University Press, 2005; Vaberovski, I., *Vrag est' vezde: Stalinizm na Kavkaze* [*The Enemy is Everywhere: Stalinism in the Caucasus*],

Moscow: Rosspen, 2010; Northrop, D., *Veiled Empire: Gender and Power in Stalinist Central Asia*, Ithaca, New York: Cornell University Press, 2004.

15 Khalid, A., 'The Soviet Union as an Imperial Formation: A View from Central Asia', in Stoler, A., McGranahan, C., Perdue, P. (eds), *Imperial Formations*, Santa Fe: School of Advanced Research Press, 2007. pp. 123–51.

16 Abashin, S., '*Mustakillik* and Remembrance of the Imperial Past: Passing Though the Halls of the Tashkent Museum in Memory of the Victims of Repression', *Russian Politics and Law*, 2010, vol. 48/5, pp. 78–92.

17 Critchlow, J., 'Prelude to "Independence": How the Uzbek Party Apparatus Broke Moscow's grip on Elite Recruitment', in W. Fierman (ed.), *Soviet Central Asia: The Failed Transformation*, Westview Press, 1991, pp. 131–56.

18 Research project 'Vospriiatie molodezh'iu novykh nezavisimykh gosudarstv istorii sovestkogo i postsovetskogo periodov', Aprel'-Mai 2009. Kratkii analiticheskii otchet [The Perception of Soviet and Post-Soviet History by Young People in Newly-Independent States, April-May 2009. A short analytical report], Mezhdunarodnoe issledovatel'skoe agentstvo 'Evraziiskii monitor' [International Research Agency 'Eurasian Monitor'] (http://www.eurasiamonitor.org/rus/research/event-162.html).

19 On the new configurations of dependency in the region, see e.g.: Petric, B.M., 'Post-Soviet Kyrgyzstan or the Birth of a Globalized Protectorate,' *Central Asian Survey*, 2005, vol. 24/3, pp. 319–32; Heathershaw, J., 'Tajikistan Amidst Globalization: State Failure or State Transformation?' *Central Asian Survey*, 2001, vol. 30/1, pp. 147–68.

20 Peyrouse, S., 'La gestion du fait religieux en Asie centrale in: maintien du cadre conceptuel soviétique et renouveau factice', *Cahiers d'Asie centrale*, 2004, vol. 13–14, pp. 77–120.

21 Arne Haugen, *The Establishment of National Republics in Soviet Central Asia*, New York: Palgrave Macmillan, 2003.

22 Kotkin, S., 'Modern Time: The Soviet Union and the Interwar Conjuncture', *Kritika*, 2001, vol. 2/1, pp. 111–64; Khalid, A., 'Backwardness and the Quest for Civilization: Early Soviet Central Asia in Comparative Perspective', *Slavic Review*, 2006, vol. 65/2, pp. 231–51; Edgar, A., 'Bolshevism, Patriarchy, and the Nation: The Soviet "Emancipation" of Muslim Women in Pan-Islamic Perspective', *Slavic Review*, 2006, vol. 65/2, pp. 252–72.

23 Megoran, N., 'Calming the Ferghana Valley Experts', *Central Asia Monitor*, 2000, vol. 5, pp. 20–25; Reeves, M., 'Locating Danger: *Konfliktologiia* and the Search for Fixity in the Ferghana Valley Borderlands', *Central Asian Survey*, 2005, vol. 24/1, pp. 67–81.

CHAPTER 4

FUNCTIONAL CLUSTERS AND DIVERGING PATHS IN POST-SOVIET SOUTH: THE GEORGIAN CASE

George Tarkhan-Mouravi
(Institute for Policy Studies, Georgia)

What is the Post-Soviet South?

As some authors have observed, on-going globalization is accompanied by the strengthening and restructuring of regionalization processes, competing integration and fragmentation trends, in particular following geopolitical changes such as the dissolution of the USSR. Indeed, it is now not uncommon to see mention of the 'post-Soviet South' or the 'former Soviet South' as a region facing similar problems, challenges, systems of governance and political culture.[1]

It is not surprising to find similarities between groups of post-Soviet states, due to the simple fact that they are post-Soviet *per se*. Some observers go as far as drawing parallels between any number of Southern states based on similarities in climate and the Southern temperament of its inhabitants.[2] However, the question arises as to the meaning of post-Soviet South? Is this term useful when analysing the Post-Soviet trajectories of the three countries of the South Caucasus and five of the former Soviet Central Asia?[3]

One of the reasons for considering Central Asia and the South Caucasus as a single region is the simple fact that, after the breakdown of the Soviet Union, a number of scholarly disciplines experienced a terminological crisis. The relevance of former Sovietologists was questioned as the focus of their discipline ceased to exist, the majority have since became either historians or specialized in post-Soviet Russia. Others moved to what is referred to as 'post-Soviet Studies', where the difficulty is the growing diversity within the post-Soviet space reflecting different models of political arrangements, not to mention cultural differences. Scholars specialized in the developing world, including so-called 'transitologists', also faced a new challenge–how to classify these countries so different from the more traditional third world states but also so different from one another.

A trend emerged to subdivide (or sometimes organize) the post-Soviet space into smaller groups of countries along cultural, geographic or coalitional lines, such as Slavic (Ukraine–Belorussia–Russia), Central Asia, South Caucasus, Eastern Partnership, CIS, EURAZES, etc. At the same time, a number of centres in the West, especially in the US, focused on 'Central Asia and the Caucasus' (Berkeley, SAIS, Harvard, among others, in particular after 9/11 when some centres previously covering just the Caucasus started to include Central Asia), which would be the equivalent to the 'post-Soviet South'. The question that arises is: are there political and cultural similarities and geographic considerations that justify such grouping of countries? Or is this just a bureaucratic convenience that prompted some centres to rename? The aim of this chapter is not to justify or criticize administrative decisions or scholarly classifications, but rather to use this opportunity to better understand certain processes ongoing within the region. While grouping together the countries of the Caucasus and Central Asia under the term 'South' may be prone to controversy and criticism, this chapter aims to understand the similarities and differences between the societies of the post-Soviet South, what are the current trends, and why?

The heritage of the Soviet past, in the form of underdeveloped democratic institutions and political culture, coupled with the long-term effects of civil tensions and ethno-territorial conflicts, still continues to haunt political processes, narrowing the space for political dialogue and threatening democratic transition. The legacy of decades of totalitarian rule is unlikely to diminish quickly. The complexity of Soviet reality, considerable geographical variety and temporal dynamism, extreme intricacy of practised Communist ideology and of societal and political arrangements have all contributed to the specificity and diversity of the Soviet state, the particular character of its Southern periphery, and the impact of Soviet legacy on today's political and social reality. Soviet statehood was not a standardized version of the static, geographically uniform and easily describable phenomenon, although the Soviet system as a whole is a good illustration of the anti-ideal of a totalitarian concept, especially during the Great Purges of the 1930s.

Since the dissolution of the USSR, the former Soviet South has become a new strategic crossroads for energy security, tensions and conflicts, labour migration and trafficking, transportation and trade links and other key policy areas, where the interests of Europe, Russia, China, the United States, among other significant players intersect and compete. While defining this region in purely geographic terms is not difficult, its diversity in terms of size, cultural traditions, political systems, economic wealth or geopolitical orientations, should not be overlooked. Having said this, the region of Eurasia is to a certain extent united from a European perspective, linked by issues such as political instability, geostrategic importance (e.g. land access to Afghanistan, Caspian oil riches, neighbouring Iran's nuclear ambitions), drugs and weapons trafficking, as well as access to huge energy resources. One way to understand the complex nature and the essential diversity of the region is to categorize or group the countries on the basis of various markers or criteria.

Differences

It is essential to consider the differences between the countries of the region that are not often examined as it is against a background of differences that similarities become more apparent.

The previously mentioned geographic location, but also the sheer size of the countries in question plays an important role in determining the political trajectories of these states as this defines the scale of resources controlled by central governments as well as the level of self-sufficiency and openness to the outside world. Some of the states are considerable in size. Kazakhstan is 9 times bigger than Italy, and even Turkmenistan, with its comparatively small population of 5 million, is significantly bigger than Italy or Germany. At the other end of the scale lie the tiny former Soviet republics–Azerbaijan, Georgia, and Armenia in the South Caucasus, and the relatively small Tajikistan and Kyrgyzstan in Central Asia (see Table 4.1).

It becomes apparent that the countries in question greatly differ not only in size (e.g. Kazakhstan is 90 times bigger than Armenia,

Table 4.1 Area and Population of the Countries in the Region and Some of Their Neighbours

State	Area (mln km^2)	Population (mln)	Density (pop/km^2)	Birth rate (per 1,000)
Kazakhstan	2.725	16.6	6	23
Uzbekistan	0.447	28.5	64	24
Kyrgyzstan	0.198	5.6	28	26
Tajikistan	0.143	7.5	53	28
Turkmenistan	0.488	5.1	10	22
Azerbaijan	0.087	9.2	106	17
Georgia	0.070	4.3	62	14
Armenia	0.030	3.1	105	14
Russia	17.045	142.8	8	13
Iran	1.648	77.9	47	19
Turkey	0.784	74.0	94	18
China	9.759	1,345.9	141	12

Source: Population Reference Bureau, *World Population Data Sheet*, Washington D.C., 2011 (http://www.prb.org/pdf11/2011population-data-sheet_sp.pdf)

and Central Asia, with 4.001 mln km,^{2} is more than 20 times bigger than the South Caucasus with a total area of 0.187 mln km^2), and population (the population of Uzbekistan is nine times that of Armenia, whilst the population of Central Asia, 63.3 mln, is almost four times that of the total population of the South Caucasus, 16.6 mln strong), but also in population density (105–6 persons per sq. km in Armenia and Azerbaijan as compared to six in Kazakhstan and ten in Turkmenistan), and even more importantly–birth rates (22 to 28 in the countries of Central Asia and 14 to 17 in the South Caucasian states). These demographic differences strongly influence the labour market and generational structure, and thus necessarily the economic and political prospects of the countries.

The economic power of the concerned states is closely linked to their size, with the exception of small but oil-rich Azerbaijan. Another criterion for grouping is the role played by energy resources within the economy. The littoral states of the Caspian Sea (Azerbaijan, Turkmenistan and Kazakhstan) and Uzbekistan are rich in oil and gas, alone controlling a noticeable portion of the world's energy resources, gas in particular. On the other hand, some states of the region are dependent on energy importations and, in some cases, on the transit of energy resources (Georgia, though rich in hydropower potential) while landlocked Kyrgyzstan, Tajikistan and Armenia do not possess a significant amount of natural resources, nor do they play a role as energy transit countries.

Size and economy are important characteristics, although there are several other factors to group countries, such as confessional and cultural tradition. Georgia is predominantly Eastern Orthodox, while Armenia is Gregorian Christian. Central Asian states are mainly Sunni Muslim (though formally secular states), with numerous Christians (mainly Slavs) in Kazakhstan, and Shiya (*Nizari Ismailites*) in Tajikistan's Badakhshan and Azerbaijan is predominately Shiya Islam: although about one-third of Azerbaijans' population is reportedly Sunni, the country has basically been a secular state since Soviet times.

Even during the post-Huntingtonian (and post-Fukuyama for that matter) era, certain correlations were made between civilization type and geopolitical orientation, although there is no linkage between confession and historical–cultural tradition. A certain geographical correlation can be noted,[4] as the states of the South Caucasus tend to reflect a pro-Western orientation and a supposedly higher degree of political pluralism, while those located in Central Asia in general tend towards authoritarianism and an interest in the East. To some extent this trend is also related to the 'oil curse' factor, when greater energy resources within a country correspond to a more centralized and concentrated power system.[5]

Another interesting dimension is the geopolitical orientation of the countries in the region. Georgia is keen to pursue Western integration. Armenia, landlocked and sandwiched between Azerbaijan and Turkey, is formally Russia's strategic partner, dependent on the latter for security and housing a Russian military base in Gyumri. In addition to providing security, Russia to a great extent controls Armenia's economy and, while a hostage to its own victory in the Karabagh conflict with Azerbaijan and therefore lacking the freedom of manoeuvre, Yerevan struggles to develop fully its relations not only with the EU and the US, but also with Turkey and NATO. Azerbaijan and Central Asian states all pursue a complex policy of balancing the influences of Russia, the West and, in the case of the latter, China. Their attitudes are unstable, permanently shifting in search of better deals.

Why is such categorization important? All of the above factors influence the political profiles of the states, in particular political stability, democracy as opposed to authoritarianism, and ethno-territorial conflicts in which they are involved. While open conflicts in the former Soviet space emerged in the late 1980s and early 1990s, it is worth mentioning that they were all located in the Caucasus and Central Asia, with the exception of Moldova, to a certain extent also a Southern state. These conflicts have had an impact on related state-building processes and the relationship between the two processes is rather complex.

It is interesting to observe that those states of the region rich in energy resources have authoritarian regimes and attempt to pass power on in a hereditary manner, for example Azerbaijan. In contrast, those states with limited natural resources claim to be moderately democratic when located closer to the West, or demonstrate hybrid regimes with softer semi-authoritarianism combined with non-consolidated democracy, such as Georgia, Kyrgyzstan, Armenia, or even Tajikistan. These latter countries have also experienced significant ethno-territorial conflicts.

Some further differences are worth noting. The states of the South Caucasus and Central Asia do not actually have that much in common from a confessional, linguistic and geographical viewpoint. Azerbaijan is an exception with the absolute majority Turkophone and Muslim population having more in common with the Central Asian states. From a political geography viewpoint, the South Caucasus may be considered as a European periphery with states being members of the Council of Europe, and at least formally entitled to request the EU membership. Central Asia is, in turn, unequivocally an essential part of Asia.

The confessional and linguistic characteristics of Central Asia have already been raised, noting the exception of Tajikistan, speaking Turkic languages and practising Sunni Islam. A specific difference is the geopolitical environment. For South Caucasus countries, the main neighbours are firstly Russia, then Turkey and Iran and, for Central Asia, China is an increasingly important neighbour. Afghanistan is another important and arguably dangerous neighbour, a potential source of Islamic radicalism and already a source of heroin and opium trafficking. Turkey, Iran and India, and to a lesser extent Pakistan, play an increasingly active role in the region.

Other characteristics such as energy and water resources (the latter of great importance in Central Asia), or the aforementioned level of authoritarianism, are sufficient to demonstrate that alongside the similarities characteristic of the post-Soviet South, there is also great diversity.

Similarities

An observant eye can easily see many similarities in the political and social realities of the post-Soviet South, reflecting both a common

Soviet past, and shared cultural influences with neighbouring civilizations such as Iran.[6]

As already noted, the current situation in the region is characterized by high volatility and unpredictability. The geopolitical environment in which the region finds itself is equally uncertain. In both the Caucasus and Central Asia, the heritage of the Soviet past, in the form of underdeveloped democratic institutions and political culture, along with the aftermath of an authoritarian suppression, civil wars and ethno-territorial conflicts, still continues to haunt political processes and civil society building, reducing the space for political and social dialogue. The situation further East, where authoritarianism has a stronger hold on societies, especially in Turkmenistan[7] and Uzbekistan,[8] is particularly difficult.

Understanding similarities between the eight countries of the post-Soviet South is a challenging task. It should be noted that some of these similarities are common to all, or almost all, post-Soviet states, whereas it would be interesting to highlight those characteristics common to the region but not easily observed from outside. On the other hand, different features are also noted in other countries of the Eurasian South, beyond the FSU (former Soviet Union). To a certain extent, the region in question can be located on the intersection of two broader regions – the post-Soviet space and the South/Greater Middle East[9] (although there are some telling similarities between these two bigger regions too).

One of the interesting political aspects of the region is the system of governance adopted by these countries. One may speak of 'post-Soviet governance contagion' (drawing a distant analogy with the Arab spring or the so-called 'Galton's problem'[10]), when elites borrow various models and approaches from one another, in particular methods for strengthening the power of the ruling party and weakening opposition, but also in terms of institutional arrangements. The presidential model is universal to all post-Soviet states, although some countries in the initial stages may have followed the parliamentary model too and there have been calls to revert to a parliamentary model in some countries (e.g. Georgia and Kyrgyzstan). Although Georgia has moved to a more mixed model with a relatively strong prime minister, the overall pattern remains unchanged.

Another characteristic is the absolute dominance of the executive, essentially the presidential power, over other branches and the particular weakness of the subservient judiciary system, which to a great extent serves and legitimizes decisions made by the executive. Parliaments too are mostly dominated by the executive and are little more than a symbolic agency rubber-stamping decisions from above. The police, and more broadly law enforcement, more so than the armed forces, seem to be the main pillar supporting incumbent governments, as the real threat to their hold on power comes from internal opposition, or so it is feared. The political arena is universally governed by the parties or coalitions controlled by respective presidents, ready to use administrative resources and populism to win elections, creating what is now fashionably called 'electoral authoritarianism'.[11] A weak and ineffective opposition as a rule fails as a viable alternative to incumbent elites, any real challenges come from the split of former allies in power. The same ruling elite attempts, and to varying degrees succeeds, to control mass media, in particular electronic media. Human rights abuses by law enforcement figures, readiness to use excessive force against the opposition and during mass protests are further characteristics of post-Soviet political reality in the region.

Other than Kyrgyzstan and Georgia, which tend to be politically more volatile, the same regimes rule for many years, with the same problems of succession. Although situations are comparable with the same clan retaining power, transition itself is resolved somewhat differently, for example in Azerbaijan from father to son, in Turkmenistan with the Health Minister turned acting President as opposed to the imprisoned Chairman of Assembly (thanks to the support of the top leadership), or in Armenia from President to Prime Minister. It is not yet clear how succession will occur in Uzbekistan, Kazakhstan and Tajikistan, with aging leaders still in place, although it is evident that the families and immediate circle here too play an important role.

In a paradoxical and maybe even ironic sense, Francis Fukuyama's concept of the 'end of history' can be seen in action in the post-Soviet South. While the arrival of a Western-style liberal democracy is still far off, governments have learned to imitate the formal aspects of democratic institutions, albeit in different ways, and leaders enjoy talking about democracy and the rule of law, both at national and international venues,[12] interpreting these concepts in their own ways.[13] Such imitational democracy is to some extent an extension of the old Soviet tradition of organizing fake elections with single candidates and no competition and thereafter no real power to elected officials, although this pattern can also be seen far beyond the post-Soviet space. As a result, imitations replace real democratic institutions, empty shells without democratic content.

Another imitation observed in these countries is that of the free market, as although legislation is quite liberal, property rights are not well protected, there is no independent judiciary to seek justice against the state (or persons close to the government), big businesses are owned by those with connections to the ruling elite, and little is done to support small and medium businesses. On the surface, all countries embrace economic freedom and private initiative to varying degrees; in reality, however, state bureaucracy has implemented informal mechanisms for controlling and reprimanding businesses. This is coupled with a total absence of labour protection, due to the lack of any effective trade unions, increasing gaps between the rich and poor and high-level corruption permeating all significant business transactions. As a result, and despite growing economies, the poor are still numerous, and the gap between the rich and the poor is rapidly increasing. In most cases this leads to massive labour migration, and for the poorest countries of the region, remittances from migrants make up a significant share of the GDP.

If the above are taken as characteristic for almost all post-Soviet states, North and South, some patterns can be argued to be more specific to Southern countries. These features concern 'southern' cultural tradition, based on a different set of values and patterns of interpersonal and intergroup relations. As already mentioned, some of these characteristics are related to strong kinship that helped with the resistance to totalitarian pressures in Soviet times, and today continue to play an equally important, albeit less beneficial, role. A significant role is also played by (sub-) ethnic and territorial clans, various patronage–clientele networks, and informal relationships. Group loyalties are often stronger than state patriotism, professional ethics or sense of responsibility. This in turn leads to anti-meritocratic personnel policies, ineffectiveness of governance and corruption. While the personality of a leader plays an important role throughout the post-Soviet space, one can argue that politics in the South are even more personality centred, and personality is more important than formal political ideology, agenda, declared values or institutions borrowed (sometimes only formally) from the Western models.

Clusters

It is not just similarities that allow the grouping of countries of the region, or differences that divide them. Another important way of considering regionalism and regionalization is the extent to which these countries could be seen as functional agglomerations, i.e. whether they create a geo-economic, geopolitical or regional security complexes, or alternatively should be considered as several overlapping clusters, united by functionalities such as membership to international alliances and organizations, being part of a transportation corridor, or interaction at other levels. Relations within this previously isolated region are very different today compared to before the dissolution of the USSR and the end of the Cold War, in part because of the openness to various developments and influences commonly attributed to globalization. It is also interesting to observe how regionalization and globalization dynamics interact and compete in this complex region, and how various integration and fragmentation processes contribute to the emergence of a system of regional clusters.

After the disappearance of the uniting Soviet power, the three states of South Caucasus and five of Central Asia drifted apart, more concerned with their own survival, with few common interests, although formally united within the Commonwealth of Independent States, a loose and basically symbolic association of former Soviet countries with coordinating powers in the areas of trade, finance and security (Georgia joined in 1993 and officially left in August 2009, applying for withdrawal in the immediate aftermath of the August 2008 war).

However, as years pass and regimes stabilize, both geo-economic and geopolitical factors have emerged that bring together at least some of these countries. While referring to full regional integration of the South Caucasus region is premature due to the existence of sometimes convergent but frequently irreconcilable interests and sporadic tensions, a regionalization process related to trade and transportation is taking form. Indeed, one of the first actions in this sphere was the linking of transportation routes, especially as regards countries with goods to export. Following a political and economic logic, those states keen to trade with the West sought ways of bypassing Russia and developing alternative routes to the new markets in Europe, but also in Asia.

However, economic relations sometimes give rise to economic divisions. One of the most notable dividing issues concern the exploitation of the mineral resources of the Caspian Sea and the delimitation of its borders. Unlike Iran and Russia, Azerbaijan, Kazakhstan and Turkmenistan are of the opinion that the sector outlines of each littoral country should be based on the median line (an outdated though essentially still formally valid legal arrangement of the Caspian Sea based on the agreements signed between Iran and the Soviet Union in 1921 and 1940), thus giving each state a share proportional to its Caspian coastline length. Disputes continue to flare up between Azerbaijan and Turkmenistan with regards to exploiting the shared oilfields. The most notable recent tension emerged between Tajikistan and Uzbekistan, as the former accused the latter of imposing an economic blockade around it in an attempt to trigger a humanitarian catastrophe and destabilize the country.[14] This is probably in connection with a dispute over the use of water resources and Tajik–Iranian joint plans to construct dams and hydropower stations thus reducing its dependence on energy imported from Uzbekistan. It is interesting to note that the problem of water shortages in Central Asia is in fact more to do with poor water management than a real water shortage.[15] Similar problems stemming from the misuse of natural resources can also be observed in the South Caucasus and non-effective agriculture as the main occupation of the population throughout the region is equally problematic.[16] Another important economic activity is the extraction, export and transit of raw materials.

It should be noted that both uniting and dividing issues and related tensions contribute to regional interdependence and regionalization. Indeed, regionalism depends on the existence of political, security or economic related issues that influence all countries within this region. However, the most explicit form of regionalization is belonging to, and being active in, regional institutions. In the case of the post-Soviet South, there are currently no institutions to which all states belong,[17] although there are some in which the majority of the countries participate. Save for membership in global agencies such as the UN and the Bretton-Woods institutions, and being signatories to a number of international conventions, the OSCE seems to be the only regional international organization (along with the Asian Development Bank) in which all of the countries of the region participate, although their effectiveness is frequently questioned.

Membership of these countries to various regional organizations once again reveals overlapping clusters that are formed to reflect varying interests and orientations. Thus, while all three South Caucasus countries are members of the Council of Europe, EU Eastern Partnership Programme, and EU Eastern Neighbourhood, only Armenia is a member of the Collective Security Treaty Organization (CSTO), along with the four Central Asian states (without Turkmenistan), Russia, and Belarus. Georgia and Azerbaijan are members of the GUAM Organization for Democracy and Economic Development along with Ukraine and Moldova, although it is currently semi-defunct. All Central Asian states and Azerbaijan are members of the Organization of Islamic Cooperation, and, along with Iran, Afghanistan, Turkey and Pakistan, of the

Economic Cooperation Organization. Kazakhstan, Kyrgyzstan, Tajikistan, and Uzbekistan, along with Russia and China are members of the Shanghai Cooperation Organization. Azerbaijan, Kazakhstan, Kyrgyzstan are members of the Turkic Council, along with Turkey, Uzbekistan and Turkmenistan are planning to join.

It is interesting to note that all eight countries of the post-Soviet South participate in the NATO Partnership for Peace programme. All three South Caucasian nations have contributed troops to the NATO-led security mission in Afghanistan, the International Security Assistance Force (ISAF). The Central Asian states have however assisted the mission in other ways, mainly by transporting military and non-military cargo, as the region is reinforced as a transit zone to Afghanistan through its growing role in the Northern Distribution Network.[18]

The states of the South Caucasus and Central Asia are institutionally and militarily weak, surrounded by larger regional powers and influenced by global players. However, it is not just different geopolitical environments that lead to the emergence of differing geostrategic orientations, although they do lead to the creation of two rather distinct regional security complexes,[19] or clusters.

Stability and security in the South Caucasian states are strongly connected for numerous reasons including conflicts and historical grievances (related to Karabakh in the first place), geography—i.e. being located between Russia, Turkey and Iran, westward transportation routes that almost all pass through Georgia and ethnic composition (important Azeri and Armenian communities in Georgia, ethnic Georgians in Azerbaijan, etc.) This also leads to close observation of the political and military developments of neighbouring states, and somewhat similar trajectories as regards international relations as well as participation in the same programmes avoiding exclusion at all costs (whether it is involvement in Afghanistan, or general relations with USA, NATO, EU or Russia). At the same time, external orientations are explicitly different. A strongly anti-Russian Georgia strives to enter NATO and the EU, Armenia is a member of CSTO, and a staunch

Russian ally, Azerbaijan, sits between the two. While Russian influence is strong, it fails to destabilize security processes in the South Caucasus or totally deform the security structure of the region. It manages to maintain a 'no war – no peace' balance between countries reflecting a frozen conflict (e.g. Armenia and Azerbaijan), while keeping Georgia under a permanent threat of destabilization, and, as a result, hinders the westernization of the region. Nevertheless, all three societies consider themselves to be part of Western civilization, although in Azerbaijan this is counter-balanced by a strong Turkic and Islamic identity.

Central Asia is faced with a totally different regional, geopolitical and security complex.[20] The strategic dynamic created by the cooperation of the great powers and the Central Asian states is multifaceted and constantly shifting. Central Asia is permanently exposed to significant extra-regional influences that affect the security structure of the region. This regional complexity is formed of different threats and influences, some shared with the South Caucasus, namely dominant Russia in the north and Iran in the South. The huge and growing influence of China (and increasingly India), and the USA, threats of an imminent drawdown of NATO forces in Afghanistan, internal disputes over water resources, rising ethnic nationalism and mutual hostility, authoritarian regimes acting aggressively in interstate relations, and the threat of radical Islamism all combine to create a complex situation. Besides intra-regional tensions, the biggest short and mid-term external threat concerns developments in Afghanistan. Mountainous Tajikistan, sharing a porous 1,352 km border with Afghanistan, is probably the most likely area through which Islamic militants would spread into Central Asia once NATO forces leave Afghanistan in 2014.

The only areas with common concerns between some Central Asian and Caucasian states (Azerbaijan in this case) concern the Caspian Sea and Iran, as Caspian littoral states create yet another important geopolitical cluster.

Diverging Paths

There are grounds for scepticism on considering the post-Soviet South as a single regional complex. Indeed, the above demonstrates that although there are significant similarities between the countries of the post-Soviet South, the structure of this region is complex, influenced by both integrating and disintegrating forces, and is naturally subdivided into a number of clusters with different roots and functionalities. The following question naturally arises, should one expect to see integrative forces triumph and lead to further convergence and regionalization of the area as a whole, or will the clusterization lead to further dissociation of the South Caucasus and Central Asia, thus going against the general trend towards globalized interdependence of the countries of world? Given the sheer number of geopolitical and geo-economic factors at play, it is virtually impossible to speak with any certainty of mid or long-term developments, although some trends seem more plausible than others.

Firstly, it would appear that integration and interdependence within South Caucasus and Central Asia will develop faster than interconnections between these two regions. The resolution of the legal status of the Caspian Sea would go a long way to boosting trade and transportation from Central Asia to Europe via the South Caucasus, including the Trans-Caspian gas pipeline. The development of new energy-related technologies, and in particular the commencement of extracting reserves of shale gas in China[21] and India,[22] may change the global energy market, and influence the prospects of pipeline geopolitics in the Caspian region, but at the same time diminish Russia's economic leverage and influence.

Russian evolution over the next couple of decades will greatly influence developments in the South, as concerns foreign policies and as the main destination for labour migrants, especially from Tajikistan, Kyrgyzstan and Uzbekistan,[23] but also proportionally from Armenia and Azerbaijan. A weaker Russian influence could be potentially replaced by the growing importance of China, and to a lesser extent India in Central Asia, although in the South Caucasus any new vacuum will be filled by the USA, the EU and Turkey.

The rise of China and India confronts Russia with many challenges, including rethinking Russia's traditional European drive and opening the country to Asia, refocusing on developing the Russian Far East and searching for a new balance in relations with China, re-energizing relations with India, and agreeing on a more multilateral approach with regards to Central Asia. These external influences could play a determining role in Central Asia due to the lack of a dominant power in the region to counter them and institutional weaknesses means increasing reliance on external support. In Central Asia, much will depend on leadership changes, currently due in both Uzbekistan and Kazakhstan, the two biggest countries of the region, with Uzbekistan particularly prone to destabilization. However, there is mid-term hope that democratization will take root in at least some of the Central Asian states, with relatively better prospects for Kyrgyzstan and Kazakhstan.

Democratization of the South Caucasus seems imminent as societies become increasingly frustrated by authoritarian tendencies and are keen to see change. Even modest progress in resolving the conflicts in Karabakh, Abkhazia and South Ossetia may lead to further democratization of governance in these areas, although the contrary is also possible. A system of integration by choice, whereby participating countries freely choose to co-operate at the highest level (e.g. the utopia of the Caucasian Federation), may one day become a reality, although this is not a short or even mid-term perspective. For the South Caucasus, lack of stability and persistence of conflicts make such prospects unlikely as external impacts and internal differences undermine the possibility of creating such a system.[24] The growing influence of the West, maturing of civil societies and political establishments, multiplication of Western-educated public servants and civil activists will surely encourage such changes.

Thus, further dissociation of the post-Soviet South into two loosely connected regions, with short and mid-term diverging paths, could become a reality. Whether this will lead to the erosion of the concept of the post-Soviet South itself remains to be seen. It is clear that its relevance will decrease as the common legacy of the Soviet past is gradually replaced by new geopolitical interests and civilization orientations.

Notes

1 Herzig, E., *Iran and the Former Soviet South*, RIIA, 1995; Allison, R. (ed.), *Challenges for the Former Soviet South*, Washington, DC: Brookings Institution Press, 1996; Baev, P.K., 'Conflict Management in the Former Soviet South: The Dead-End of Russian Interventions', *European Security*, 1997, vol. 6/4, pp. 111–29; Webber, M., *CIS Integration Trends: Russia and the Former Soviet South*, London: Royal Institute of International Affairs, Former Soviet South Key Paper, 1997; Aras, B., 'Turkey's Policy in the Former Soviet South', *Turkish Studies*, 2000, vol. 1/1, pp. 36–58; Kirmse, S.B., *Youth in the Former Soviet South: Everyday Lives between Experimentation and Regulation*, London: Routledge, 2011; Blum, D., *Cultural Globalization in the Post-Soviet 'South'*, paper at the conference: Two Decades of Post-Soviet Independence: What Have We Learned? December 7–8, 2011 The Elliott School of International Affairs; *Постсоветский юпошел против воли Запада.*(http://www.ng.ru/week/2007-07-09/8_sng.html); Игнатенко, А., 'СоединенныеШтатыусиливают свое проникновение в регион постсоветского Юга—на Кавказ и в Центральную Азию', *Независимая газета*, 10.03.1994. (http://i-r-p.ru/page/stream-library/index-20628.html).

2 Even after Montesquieu, this 'semi-mythical' concept of temperament from time to time emerges in cross-cultural studies. For example: Gartstein, M.A. *et al.*, 'A Cross-cultural Evaluation of Temperament: Japan, USA, Poland and Russia', *International Journal of Psychology and Psychological Therapy*, 2010, vol. 10/1, pp. 55–75; Tsai, J.L., Knutson, B., Fung, S., 'Cultural Variation in Affect Valuation', *Journal of Personality and Social Psychology*, 2006, vol. 90, pp. 288–307; Nisbett, R., *The Geography of Thought. How Asians and Westerners Think Differently, and Why?*, New York: The Free Press, 2003; Berry, J., Poortinga, Y., Segall, M., Dasen, P., *Cross-Cultural Psychology*, Cambridge, UK: Cambridge University Press, 2002 (2nd edn); Buss, A., Plomin, R., *Temperament: Early developing personality traits*, Hillsdale, NJ: Erlbaum, 1985.

3 Although in Soviet terminology Kazakhstan was considered separately, the region would be called 'Central Asia & Kazakhstan.'

4 A number of political geographers deal with this issue. For example: Dalby, S., Ó Tuathail, G. (eds), *Rethinking Geopolitics*, London: Routledge, 1998; Cox, K. R., Low, M., Robinson, J. (eds), *The Sage Handbook of Political Geography*, London: Sage, 2008; Anderson, K., Domosh, M., Pile, S., Thrift, N. (eds), *The Handbook of Cultural Geography*, Thousand Oaks: Sage, 2005; Slater, D., *Geopolitics and the Post-colonial: Rethinking North-South Relations*, Oxford: Blackwell, 2004. Kuus, M., *Critical Geopolitics*, Vancouver: University of British Columbia, 2008.

5 Humphreys, M., Sachs, J.D., Stiglitz, J.E. (eds), *Escaping the Resource Curse*, New York: Columbia University Press, 2007; Lynn Karl, T., *The Paradox of Plenty*, Berkeley: University of California Press, 1997; Gelb, A. *et al.*, *Oil Windfalls: Blessing or Curse?* New York, Oxford, London, Glasgow: Oxford University Press, 1988; Bayulgen O., *Foreign Investment and Political Regimes: The Oil Sector in Azerbaijan, Russia, and Norway*, 2010; Kalyuzhnova, Ye., *Economics of the Caspian Oil and Gas Wealth*, Basingstoke, UK: Palgrave-Macmillan, 2008; Shishkin, P., *Central Asia: Crisis of Governance*, Washington DC: Asia Society, 2012.

6 Memories of cultural interaction with Iran are particularly noticeable in Azerbaijan and Tajikistan, but are also strong throughout the South Caucasus, in Turkmenistan and Uzbekistan. See for example: 'The influence of Iran–although the core of its civilization lies in South-West Asia–was particularly strong, to the extent that it is sometimes difficult to establish a clear boundary between the civilization of the Iranian motherland and that of the outlying lands of Central Asia.' (Asimov, M.S., Bosworth, C.E. (eds), *History of Civilizations of Central Asia*. vol. 4/1, Paris: Unesco, 1999. p. 12). See also on current implications of cultural ties: Johnston, W.J. Jr, *From Revolution to Realpolitik: Iran's Foreign Policy in Central Asia and the South Caucasus since 1991*, Florida State University: 2007; Whitlock, E. (ed.), *Iran and Its Neighbors: Diverging Views on a Strategic Region*, Stiftung Wissenschaft und Politik (German Institute for International and Security Affairs): Berlin, 2003; Hooman, P.. *Regional Security and the Future of Central Asia: The Competition of Iran, Turkey, and Russia*, Westport, Connecticut: Praeger, 1998; Herzig, E., *Iran and the former Soviet South*, London: Royal Institute of International Affairs, 1995.

7 Here Gurbanguly the 'Protector' Berdymukhamedov, who seized power after 'Turkmenbashi' Saparmurat Niyazov's death back in 2006, on February 12, 2012, won presidential election with over 97 per cent of the vote. 'Turkmenistan: Cult of Berdymukhamedov Takes Only Logical Step', *EurasiaNet*, 15 February 2012 (http://www.eurasianet.org/node/65006). Human Rights Watch characterizes the situation in the country as follows: 'Five years after the death of dictator Saparmurad Niyazov, President Gurbanguly Berdymukhamedov's authoritarian rule remains entrenched, highlighting Turkmenistan's status as one of the world's most repressive countries. The country remains closed to independent scrutiny, media and religious freedoms are subject to draconian restrictions, human rights defenders face constant threat of government reprisal, and torture is widespread' (Human Rights Watch, *World Report 2012* (http://www.hrw.org/europecentral-asia/Uzbekistan)).

8 'Uzbekistan's human rights record remains appalling. Torture is endemic in the criminal justice system. Authorities target rights activists, opposition members, and journalists, and persecute religious believers who worship outside strict state controls. Freedom of expression remains severely limited. Government-sponsored forced child labor during the cotton harvest continues. Authorities deny justice for the 2005 Andijan massacre in which government forces shot and

killed hundreds of protestors, most of them unarmed. Reacting to the Arab Spring, authorities increased the presence of security forces across the country and widened control over the Internet. Despite this, the United States and European Union are pursuing closer relations with Tashkent, seeking cooperation in the war in Afghanistan' (*ibid.*)

9 Stephen Blank wrote 'undoubtedly the increasingly visible strategic linkage of these two adjoining regions–the former Soviet South comprising Central Asia and the Transcaucasus and the traditionally understood Middle East' (Blank, S., 'The Greater Middle East and Its Strategic Profile', *Alternatives: Turkish Journal of International Relations*, 2004, vol. 3/1 (http://www.alternativesjournal.net/volume3/number1/blank.pdf)). See also, e.g.: Oliker, O., Yefimova, N., *Carnegie-RAND Workshop on the Future of the Greater Middle East and the Prospects for U.S.-Russian Partnership*, vol. 118, 2004. (http://www.rand.org/content/dam/rand/pubs/occasional_papers/2005/RAND_OP118.pdf). However, in June 2006, while in Tel Aviv, Condoleeza Rice made an attempt to introduce the 'New Middle East' concept, roughly covering the same set of countries (Beale, J., 'Diary: Rice's Mid-East Mission', *BBC News*, 26 July 2006 (http://news.bbc.co.uk/2/hi/middle_east/5205164.stm); Nazemroaya, M.D., 'Plans for Redrawing the Middle East: The Project for a "New Middle East"', *Global Research*, 2006 (http://www.globalresearch.ca/index.php?context=viewArticle&code=NAZ20061116&articleId=3882)).

10 See e.g.: Neumayer, E., Plümper, T., 'Galton's Problem and Contagion in International Terrorism along Civilizational Lines', *Conflict Management and Peace Science*, 2010, vol. 27/4, pp. 308–25 (http://papers.ssrn.com/sol3/papers.cfm?abstract_id=1347949).

11 See e.g.: Schedler, A. (ed.), *Electoral Authoritarianism: The Dynamics of Unfree Competition*, Boulder: Lynne Rienner Publishers, 2006; Blaydes, L., *Who Votes in Authoritarian Elections and Why? Determinants of Voter Turnout in Contemporary Egypt*, 2006 (http://www.stanford.edu/~blaydes/Turnout.pdf); Abbott, J.P., 'Electoral Authoritarianism and the Print Media in Malaysia: Measuring Political Bias and Analyzing Its Cause', *Asian Affairs: An American Review*, 2011, vol. 38/1, pp. 1–38 (http://www.tandfonline.com/doi/pdf/10.1080/00927678.2010.520575).

12 Even in highly authoritarian Turkmenistan, authorities try to imitate political pluralism by creating additional pseudo-parties from above: 'Turkmenistan plans two political parties in democracy drive', *Reuters*, 27 March 2012 (http://af.reuters.com/article/energyOilNews/idAFL6E8ER8DS20120327), while Uzbekistan's Islam Kerimov, renowned for his brutality in suppressing opposition, put forward in November 2010 the 'Concept of intensifying democratic reforms and forming the civil society in the country' (http://mfa.uz/eng/press_and_media_service/dates/the_concept/executing_initiatives_of_concept.mgr).

13 A good and brief description of post-Soviet imitation style can be found in: Furman, D., 'Imitation Democracies: The Post-Soviet Penumbra', *New Left*

Review, 2008, vol. 54, pp. 29–47 (http://www.newleftreview.org/?page=article&view=2750). There was even a lecture course at the Cornell University titled 'Virtual Politics, Imitation Democracy: Society & Spectacle in Former USSR' by Prof. Michael Bobbick (http://cornell.chequerd.com/courses/6569).

14 See for example: Kilner, J., 'Tajikistan and Uzbekistan row over "economic blockade"', *Daily Telegraph*, 4 April 2012 (http://www.telegraph.co.uk/news/worldnews/asia/tajikistan/9186804/Tajikistan-and-Uzbekistan-row-over-economic-blockade.html).

15 'It is important to realize that, against the common perception, this region is not extremely water-scarce. The enormous environmental problems that have been created after 1960 are largely due to extremely uneconomic water use and due to policies that have not taken into consideration the sustainability of agricultural development, particularly in the basins of Syr Darya and Amu Darya Rivers. The per capita water use in the region is sky-high, being manifold in comparison to any other comparable part of the world. This waste of the valuable resource yields in very low economic gain, keeping the countries economically weak.' (Varis, O., Rahaman, M.M., 'The Aral Sea Keeps Drying out But Is Central Asia Short of Water?' in Rahaman, M.M, Varis, O. (eds), *Central Asian Waters: Social, Economic, Environmental and Governance Puzzle*, Helsinki University of Technology (Electronically published doctoral dissertation): Helsinki, 2008, p. 3.

16 In Georgia for instance, while more than half the population resides in rural areas and 55 per cent of the workforce is employed in agriculture, its portion of the GDP is no more than 8 to 9 per cent (http://www.geostat.ge/index.php?action=page&p_id=428&lang=eng).

17 Still, the five Central Asian states initially formed the Central Asian Commonwealth in 1991, changing membership and name several times, first to the Central Asian Economic Union (in 1994, with Tajikistan and Turkmenistan not participating); in 1998 it became the Central Asian Economic Cooperation (marked by the return of Tajikistan) and in 2002 it was renamed the Organization of Central Asian Cooperation (OCAC). However, Russia joined the OCAC in 2004, and a year later it was decided that OCAC plus Uzbekistan would merge with the Eurasian Economic Community. The organizations merged in January 2006 (http://www.eurasianhome.org/xml/t/databases.xml?lang=en&nic=databases&intorg=8&pid=15).

18 Laruelle, M., 'Involving Central Asia in Afghanistan's Future', *EUCAM*, 2011, vol. 20 (http://www.ceps.eu/ceps/download/5998).

19 Buzan, B., Wæver, O., *Regions and Powers: The Structure of International Security*, Cambridge, UK: Cambridge University Press, 2003.

20 See the latest discussion of Central Asia as a regional security complex in Tadjbakhsh, S., *Central Asia and Afghanistan: Insulation on the Silk Road, Between Eurasia and the Heart of Asia*, Oslo: Peace Research Institute, 2012 (http://www.prio.no/sptrans/-663265531/Tadjbakhsh,%20S%20(2012)%20Central%20Asia%20and%20Afghanistan%20(PRIO%20Paper).pdf).

21 Evans-Pritchard, A., 'China Claims World's Biggest Shale Gas Reserves', *Daily Telegraph*, 1 March 2012 (http://www.telegraph.co.uk/finance/comment/ambroseevans_pritchard/).

22 'India's ONGC to Sign Gas Exploration Pact With ConocoPhillips', *Reuters*, 30 March 2012 (http://www.reuters.com/article/2012/03/30/us-india-ongc-conocophillips-idUSBRE82T0JY20120330).

23 In the case of Tajikistan, remittances made up 31 per cent of the country's national income (2010 data), representing the highest proportion of any country in the world. In Kyrgyzstan, remittances made up 21 per cent of its total income (Kilner, J., 'Remittances account for a third of Tajikistan's national income', *Daily Telegraph*, 3 December 2011 (http://www.telegraph.co.uk/news/worldnews/asia/tajikistan/8940421/Remittances-account-for-a-third-of-Tajikistans-national-income.html).

24 Among many such utopias, the most detailed outline was proposed by a group of scholars at the Centre for European Policy Studies in Brussels back in 1999–2000 (see Celac, S., Emerson, M., Tocci, N., *A Stability Pact for the Caucasus*, Brussels: CEPS, 2000).

PART 2

DEVELOPMENT, INEQUALITIES AND POVERTY

CHAPTER 5

SYSTEMIC CHANGE IN TWO CENTRAL ASIAN RENTIER STATES: TURKMENISTAN AND KAZAKHSTAN

Hélène Rousselot
(EHESS—School of Advanced Studies in Social Sciences, Paris)

A comparison of oil and gas rent formation in the two landlocked former Soviet Central Asian republics of Kazakhstan and Turkmenistan is particularly topical following the tragic events in Zhanaozen and Shetpe on 16–18 December 2011 (at least 17 dead and over a hundred wounded according to official figures). Here in Western Kazakhstan, as Independence Day was being celebrated, fatal confrontations between the army and oil workers on strike since May 2011 put an end to an episode, unique in the history of independent Kazakhstan. The strikes began at the oil companies Karažanbasmunaj[1] and Ozenmunajgaz.[2] Until then increased oil revenues had enabled the government to ensure a certain industrial peace and unrest such as that at Ozenmunajgaz in 2008 had remained limited. To date, Turkmenistan has not experienced this sort of event.

In the early 1990s, many analysts considered that all the former Soviet bloc economies would follow similar paths towards a single model. However, as early as 1994, Michalopoulos and Tarr pointed out that their paths had diverged as they adopted various reforms, as had their economic performance and trading patterns.[3] This difference justifies the term 'systemic change' rather than 'transition', since the former Soviet bloc economies have not all followed 'the same itinerary towards a final destination, an "end of history" that marks the completion of their development'.[4]

This chapter first presents the two rentier state models of Kazakhstan and Turkmenistan, then their imperfect oil and gas markets (in the Walrasian sense), the subsequent appearance of rents and the two countries' macroeconomic choices. It is based on the work of Pauline Jones Luong and Erika Weinthal[5] among others, who assert that Turkmenistan's macroeconomic choices have caused it not to reform as quickly as Kazakhstan.

One of the main methodological problems is sources, particularly the two countries' macroeconomic data. Some figures are not available, especially for Turkmenistan (gas exports in 2003–04 and from 2007; GDP in local currency and dollars). In 2010, the Economist Intelligence Unit reported that the Turkmen authorities had still not provided any foreign trade data.[6] For Kazakhstan, uranium export revenues since 2002 are not available. This chapter does not address the question of transport costs, although this is a major issue for landlocked countries like Kazakhstan and Turkmenistan.[7]

Rents, Rentier States and Distributive States

The idea of economic rent as presented by Adam Smith arises from the fact that the exploitation, production and sale of the product are not the result of work (or only minimally so). For contemporary political science, the product that provides a rent is a 'gift of nature', and not the result of a major input of labour. Note that the term 'cotton rent' used in the English-language literature in connection with the Central Asian economies does not correspond to this definition. This apparently inappropriate use may be explained by the conditions in which cotton was farmed in the United States in the 19th century, using unpaid labour. In Central Asia, cotton farming is not highly mechanized and requires little capital but a large amount of labour. Manual cotton harvesting was indeed encouraged by the Turkmen government from 1992, because of mechanical problems with the machinery.[8] In 2007, the Economist Intelligence Unit reported that manual cotton harvesting was still frequent in Turkmenistan.[9]

The definition, theoretical underpinning and calculation of economic rent are all problematic. In her chapter on the concept of rent, Fatiha Talahite states that the concept 'has a plurality of meanings and it has not been possible to construct a unified theory of rent'.[10] In his critique of the theory of the rentier state, Yasuyuki Matsunaga[11] recalls that it was devised in the late 1960s by economists working on the oil-exporting countries of the Middle East and North Africa. They did not examine the case of the USSR, nor subsequently the post-Soviet republics. Under this theory the 'rentier state' draws its income essentially from external revenues, i.e. taxes paid by foreign companies exploiting oil and gas under contract to the state owning the subsurface minerals, and to a much lesser extent from local taxation.[12] This theory tends to neglect the income from the sale of national production, which is a major failing.

Esanov, Raiser and Buiter do not restrict the idea of rent to external revenue. They distinguish a number of rents from energy sources, shared between producers, transport infrastructure owners, governments and energy consumers. External rents (export rent plus total rent) are gained from exports. Internal rents (domestic consumer subsidies plus domestic producer rent) are gained from sales within the country. They are consequently a component of the redistribution of oil and gas revenues. According to the various beneficiaries, the authors present four definitions and ways of calculating the rents, ignoring internal transport costs:[13]

- Export rent = export volume × (export price − lifting cost − transport cost)
- Total rent = total production × (export price − lifting cost − transport cost)

- Domestic consumer subsidies = domestic consumption[14] × (import price − domestic price)
- Domestic producer rent = total rent − export rent − domestic consumer subsidies

These definitions do not include taxes paid by oil companies, or taxes paid locally. Consequently they do not include the fiscal aspect of rent.

Matsunaga uses the idea of a rentier state that draws a substantial proportion of its revenues from outside the country. He separates the concepts of 'rentier state' and 'distributive state', which are not mutually exclusive. A distributive state is one in which state budget expenditure is a considerable proportion of national revenue. But this approach is of limited relevance to this chapter, because it is not easy to know expenditure as a proportion of Turkmenistan's national revenue and the presence of off-budget funds, particularly in Turkmenistan, makes the state budget an unreliable indicator of the real state of public finance.

Auty, in the typology of rentier states he established with Gelb, introduces other criteria, such as the role of markets. He shows that domestic markets exercise a fairly weak constraint on the state, both in Kazakhstan and Turkmenistan, both of which maximize their capture of rent.[15] The difference between them is the larger number of players capturing the rent in Kazakhstan. From Matsunaga's and Auty and Gelb's models, a new one can be constructed as follows (Table 5.1).

Examination of oil and gas trade and macroeconomic choices, especially for foreign investment, shows why the two countries are so different (Kazakhstan more distributive and with less political autonomy from its population than Turkmenistan).

Oil and Gas Markets in Turkmenistan and Kazakhstan

In geographical and economic terms, the position of Turkmenistan and Kazakhstan's energy resources in the global oil and gas market is a strange one. The two countries are landlocked and were dependent on the Soviet pipeline network throughout the 1990s. Gazprom (and

Table 5.1 Pure Rentier and Distributive State

	Pure rentier state (Turkmenistan)	Distributive rentier state (Kazakhstan)
Rent capture	Maximized capture of substantial external rent	Maximized capture of external rent and rent capture by officials
Taxation	No fiscal extraction from domestic economy	Minimal fiscal extraction
Use of rent	No expenditure of rent inside the country	Limited distribution of rent
Type of economy	Predominantly central planning	Introduction of market economy mechanisms
Government and opposition	Social groups deprived of bargaining power Virtually autonomous predatory state	Opponents 'bought off,' population dependent on state for well-being Oligarchy based on factions
State/society relations	State immunity from democratic demands	Depoliticization and acceptance of regime by society
State political autonomy	Considerable fiscal and political autonomy	Relative political autonomy

its transport subsidiary) was Kazakhstan and Turkmenistan's obligatory partner for transport. Other Russian companies had similar roles in refining. At the start of the 1990s, neither Kazakhstan nor Turkmenistan could afford to build new oil and gas transport infrastructure. Yet both of them had to devise long-term export strategies for oil and gas. Not until some ten years later did they begin to free themselves from this dependency and modify their trade relations with Russia.

Gas Transport and Pricing in Turkmenistan

Throughout the 1990s Turkmenistan signed no long-term contracts for set quantities and prices adjusted each year with regular customers. Except for the contract with Iran to deliver 8 billion m^3 of

Table 5.2 Oil and Gas Production of Independent Kazakhstan and Turkmenistan (1991–2010)

	Oil (million tonnes) (*per cent of world total*)			Gas (billion m^3) (*per cent of world total*)		
Production	1991	2002	2010	1991	2002	2010
Kazakhstan	26.6	48.2 (*1.3%*)	81.6 (*2.1%*)	7.9	10.2 (*0.5%*)	33.6 (*1.1%*)
Turkmenistan	5.4	9.0 (*0.3%*)	10.7 (*0.3%*)	84.3	48.4 (*2.0%*)	42.4 (*1.3%*)

Source: British Petroleum, *BP Statistical Review of World Energy*, June 2011.

gas a year once the Korpeje–Kordkuy pipeline[16] came on stream in 1997. It was at the time the only pipeline not controlled by Russia and so most Turkmen gas was transported by the Central Asia-Centre pipeline system[17] until the end of 2009, when the Turkmenistan–China gas pipelines were completed.[18]

Assessing the value of Turkmen gas export revenues is a difficult matter, particularly for the years from 1995 to 1999, since not all payment was made in cash. Reportedly, barter of gas for other goods with no monetary compensation accounted for 60.2 per cent of the trade in 1995 and 55.9 per cent in 1996.[19] Until 1996, Gazprom's acquisition of Turkmen gas was on the basis of short-term intergovernmental agreements and Russia attempted unsuccessfully to obtain a long-term contract and the creation of a joint company for gas transport. In August 1996, Turkmenistan created a joint company. Turkmenrosgaz (Turkmenneftegaz: 51 per cent, Gazprom: 45 per cent and Itera International Energy Corporation: 4 per cent), with Russia/Gazprom, controlling most of the country's gas exports. Gazprom bought Turkmen gas for $40–42 per thousand m^3 at the Turkmenistan–Uzbekistan border[20] and sold it to Ukraine for $80. The guaranteed volume of gas exports was then 30 billion m^3. The advantage for Turkmenistan was that Gazprom guaranteed payment for the gas it bought.[21] Turkmenrosgaz was dissolved in 1997 and Itera[22] took over control of deliveries of Turkmen gas to Ukraine until 2002. The Turkmen government and Itera were in dispute and exports to Russia were stopped until 1999.

According to Milov, in the late 1990s and the early years of the millennium, the price Russia paid for Turkmen gas was roughly $42 per thousand m^3. This was well below what Russia charged Europe, especially after 2000, when selling prices in Europe were extremely high.[23] When Vladimir Putin came to power in 1999, he showed increasing interest in Turkmenistan. He told the new head of Gazprom, Aleksei Miller, to regain control of assets in the company from Itera and achieve what Boris Yeltsin had been unable to do, namely ensure Russia's long-term gas supplies.

After several years' negotiation, in April 2003 Turkmenneftegaz[24] signed a strategic 25-year agreement with Gazeksport (a wholly-owned subsidiary of Gazprom) including the delivery of 5 billion m^3 in 2004 up to 80 (or even 90) billion from 2009 at a renegotiable price. The price rose from $44 per thousand m^3 on 1 January 2007. But at the end of March 2009, the Turkmen president, Gurbanguly Berdymukhamedov, refused to sign a contract with Gazprom for the construction of the East–West gas pipeline intended to connect the South Yolotan field to the Caspian Sea. On 8 April, Gazprom demanded that Turkmengaz cut its deliveries by 80 per cent. The arrival of Turkmen gas at the Uzbekistan border was stopped and on 9 April there was an explosion on the Central Asia–Centre–4 pipeline. Moscow proposed to Ashgabat to review the terms of the delivery contracts. Under the agreement signed in January 2009, Gazprom had undertaken to buy from Turkmenistan 40 to 42 billion m^3 a year for $310–315 per thousand m^3. But the reduction in Gazprom's gas deliveries to Europe and the CIS forced the company to reduce its purchases when deliveries resumed in January 2010, at a price of $240–250 per thousand m^3.

Oil Transport and Pricing in Kazakhstan

Before 2002, Kazakh oil was mainly transported to the Baltic and European markets via CIS countries along the Atyrau–Samara pipeline.[25] Another route was examined by the Caspian Pipeline Consortium (CPC), created in 1992 by the Russian Federation (24 per cent), Kazakhstan (19 per cent), Chevron Caspian Pipeline Company (15 per cent), Lukarco BV (12.5 per cent) and Mobil Caspian Pipeline Company (7.5 per cent). The CPC pipeline[26] ran 1,510 km from the Tengiz oilfield[27] to the Russian port of Novorossiysk, also across Russian territory. The Atasu–Alashankou pipeline from the central oil fields of Kazakhstan to the Chinese border, opened on 15 December 2005, was the first outlet to the east for Kazakh oil.

Kazakhstan's total dependency on the Russian Federation resulted in oil prices to the detriment of Kazakhstan.[28] In 2000, the selling price to Russia for Karažanbas oil was 140 tenge (KZT)[29] a tonne,[30] or KZT 19.17 ($0.13) a barrel.[31] The 2000 price for Brent was $28.5, or KZT 4,050.7 a barrel (at roughly KZT 142.13 to $1). The difference between the selling price to Russia and Brent was thus enormous. Russia gained an export rent by buying this oil and gas, but the two Central Asian countries also gained a rent from their oil and gas.

Appearance of Rents in Kazakhstan and Turkmenistan

Overall, in 1992–2000, rents (except for domestic producer rents) were higher in Turkmenistan than Kazakhstan: the total rent in Kazakhstan was 20.9 per cent of GDP, while it was on average 45 per cent in Turkmenistan over that period. But from 2000, the situation altered and total rent as a percentage of GDP grew considerably in both countries. The export rent proportion doubled in Kazakhstan and rose significantly in Turkmenistan. The table below (Table 5.3) shows that the domestic producer rent was negative on average in Turkmenistan in 1992–2000. This means that it was lower than that distributed to consumers in the form of subsidies (otherwise the subsidies would be negative, which was not the case). This is consistent with the assertion that, at least in the first half of the 1990s, Turkmenistan needs revenues to finance social programmes (and consumer goods imports).[32] Although the share of domestic producer rent remained negative in Turkmenistan, in Kazakhstan it rose (the domestic producer rent in Kazakhstan was positive on average in 1992–2000). However, the proportion of consumer subsidies fell in Kazakhstan and rose in Turkmenistan to reach more than one-quarter of GDP in 2000. The high level of expenditure on subsidies within Turkmenistan, according to Sabonis-Helf, is characteristic of oil states.[33] However, these figures must be treated with caution, given the opacity of state accounts described above.

The appearance of these rents led to the creation of funds, along the Norwegian model, according to the authorities.

Creation of Funds

In Kazakhstan, the idea of saving for future generations dates from 1992,[34] when republic currency fund was set up under the direct authority of the ministerial cabinet. The idea therefore emerged long

Table 5.3 Types of Rent in Kazakhstan and Turkmenistan as Per Cent of GDP

	Export rent		Domestic producer rent		Total rent		Domestic consumer subsidies	
	1992–2000 mean	2000	1992–2000 mean	2000	1992–2000 mean	2000	1992–2000 mean	2000
Kazakhstan	10.1	20.2	5.7	9.8	20.9	33.6	5.1	3.6
Turkmenistan	25.7	43	−5.7	−5.2	44.4	65.3	24.4	27.5

Source: Esanov, A., Raiser, M., Buiter, W., *op. cit.*, p. 5.

before the total rent as a proportion of GDP began to soar. The initiative for an oil fund goes back to 1997[35] and Galymzhan Zhakiyanov. He was an advisor to the President and Director of the Strategic Resources Control Agency and proposed the creation of a development budget for Kazakhstan. The collapse of the oil price in 1998 (when it briefly fell below $10 a barrel) also moved the Kazakh authorities to consider creating a stabilization fund.

Finally, in September 2000, when oil was back at $28.2 a barrel and gas at $4.3 per Mtoe[36] (compared with $2.5 in 1998), the National Fund for Future Generations, also known as the National Fund of the Republic of Kazakhstan (NFRK), was created by presidential decree.[37] It is financed by fiscal duties, tax payments and other compulsory contributions, paid by enterprises in raw material sectors, in particular the nine biggest oil companies (Aktobmunajgaz Corporation, Kazahojl-Emba Corporation, TengizChevroil Joint Venture, Karačaganak Petroleum Operating B.V., Hurricane Kumkol Munaj Corporation, Turgaj Petroleum Limited Partnership, Mangistaumunajgaz Corporation, Uzenmunajgaz Corporation, OJSC Karažanbasmunaj) and three mining companies. These gas and oil companies, including KMG, make payments directly to the Fund without going through the state budget. It is impossible to know how much each company pays.[38] The total sum of these contributions was nearly $1.1 billion in 2001 (5.5 per cent of GDP at end 2001[39]), according to the budget report of the Finance Ministry, of which $576 million was allocated directly to the Fund and $500 million to local budgets. The Fund was estimated at $1.86 billion on 1 December 2002[40] and $30.89 billion at end 2009.[41]

In Turkmenistan, the history of this sort of fund is different but also starts in 1992, before the massive arrival of gas revenues in the years after the millennium. Officially there are two Turkmenistan Funds. There is the State Fund for the Development of the Oil and Gas Industries and Mineral Resources, created in 1996, and the Foreign Exchange Reserve Fund.[42] Revenues paid into the Foreign Exchange Reserve Fund are not included in state budget accounts, and the budget only receives 20 per cent of Turkmenistan's gas revenues. Some of the gas revenues from Ukraine avoided the budget because they were captured by a Cyprus-based company owned by Nyazov's son.[43] Consequently data concerning the state budget hardly reflect the full reality of Turkmenistan's public finances.

Oil Revenues and Conflicts

Until December 2011 Kazakhstan had managed to belie the observation that low per capita countries dependent on oil revenues are prone to conflict.[44] Its circumstances contradicted any deterministic correlation between the volume of oil revenues and the presence or absence of conflict. Turkmenistan, on the other hand, confirmed it. Neither Kazakhstan nor Turkmenistan had had violent movements or political renewal after free elections (continuation of a constant regime under the same head of state 1991–2011 in Kazakhstan, and non-violent coup by Gurbanguly Berdymukhamedov in 2007, continuing his predecessor Niyazov's regime).

Demonstrations in Kazakhstan were more frequent and widely reported, but had not endangered the regime of Nursultan Nazarbayev. The tragic events in Zhanaozen and Shetpe in December 2011 and subsequent political repression mark a turning point in the country's political history, revealing how much the long-serving Nazarbayev has lost touch with changes in Kazakh society and people's demands for the oil rent to be more fairly shared.

Demonstrations in Turkmenistan were recorded in early 1992, July 1995, 1996 (prison revolts), 1998 and 1999, end 2001–2002 and 2002, a year in which there were a number of protests by women against falling living standards and unemployment;[45] none of this has made the country unstable. One explanation of this 'Turkmen exception' is the macroeconomic choices made by President Niyazov based on the country's political and socio-economic past. Although the appearance of revenues paid to the state by foreign countries in a newly independent country contributes to the formation of an undemocratic government, the presence of a major 'agricultural rent' must also be considered in contributing to the authoritarian nature of the Turkmen regime.

The Two Countries' Macroeconomic Choices in the 1990s

Kazakhstan's GDP collapsed until 1995. From 1997, growth stabilized at around 2 per cent and then took off in 2000. Higher oil revenues brought 2001 to an end with a budget surplus. As the cost of oil rose in the early years of the millennium, Kazakhstan and Turkmenistan saw their growth rates soar (Table 5.4). Kazakhstan's external debt as a percentage of GDP continued to rise after independence and was over 73 per cent in 2002. As early as 1996, Kazakhstan was spending nearly 10 per cent of its budget on servicing this debt and made severe cuts to its welfare programmes.[46] Turkmenistan's external debt swelled from 1992, when it was virtually nil, to 1999. It is hard to evaluate as a percentage of GDP because that depends on the exchange rate chosen for the manat (TMT), official or parallel. In 2000, debt was apparently 55 per cent of GDP at the official rate, and 125 per cent at the parallel rate.[47] This debt is, however, counterbalanced by almost equivalent credit claims Turkmenistan holds on Ukraine, Georgia and Armenia for gas delivered but not paid for.

In 1992, Turkmenistan had a small population (3.5 million according to the 1989 census) and was not very industrialized. Growth in agriculture was then a high priority, since 42.5 per cent of the population depended on that sector in 1991 (compared with 26.1 per cent in Kazakhstan) and lived in conditions of extreme poverty.[48] This figure rose to 55 per cent in 2002[49] and then fell back to 48.2 per cent in 2010–11. The Turkmen government draws considerable revenues from agriculture.[50] Although in absolute terms cotton exports contribute less to the country's budget than gas exports, cotton provided an increasing quantity of revenue to the

Table 5.4 GDP Growth in Kazakhstan and Turkmenistan (in Per Cent)

	2001	2002	2010	2011
Kazakhstan	9.8	13.5	7.0	7.5
Turkmenistan	20.4	12.0	9.2	14.7

Source: EIU, *Country Report Profile Turkmenistan 2007*, The Economist Intelligence Unit Limited, p. 5; EBRD, *Strategy for Turkmenistan*, 2006, p. 49.

state after 1991, particularly in 1993 and 1996. These revenues fell from 1998 to 2001.

As the world's sixth largest gas producer in 1991,[51] the country was able to export a large proportion of its production.[52] But by 2002, it was only the 12th largest producer (48.4 billion m^3 according to BP) and by 2010 its share of global production had fallen even further.

Conversely, in Kazakhstan, the share of agriculture, which provided 29.5 per cent of GDP in 1991, fell to 4.5 per cent in 2010. Farmland fell during the same period from 34.9355 to 21.4387 million hectares.[53] Kazakhstan was a net farm produce exporter at the start of the 1990s; Its main farm exports from 1995 to 2002 were cereals and, to a much lesser extent, cotton and wool. Cereals and cotton were neither particularly subsidized nor taxed. This contrasts with the situation in the Turkmen cotton sector, from which the state took a large part of its rents.[54]

Foreign Direct Investment

From the earliest days of its independence, Kazakhstan considered diversifying its economy by attracting foreign direct investment (FDI). The Strategy on the Formation and Development of Kazakhstan as an Independent state, published in spring 1992, provided for greater FDI and continued reduction in the importance of commodities in the economy from 1996 to 2005.[55] Very little was achieved. And the Kazakh president's stated desire to diversify his country's economy had still not been implemented by the end of the 1990s, quite the contrary. Large amounts of FDI were attracted to Kazakhstan but mainly to the oil and gas sector. In contradiction with the 1992 Strategy, Kazakhstan in the early 1990s sought to stimulate FDI to increase its export potential and promote the creation of joint ventures to exploit natural resources. In 1996, FDI was $1,674 million in Kazakhstan, and $108 million in Turkmenistan.[56] Subsequently it grew much faster in Kazakhstan than in Turkmenistan (Figure 5.1). From 1996 to 2000, Kazakhstan attracted more than $1 billion in FDI flows per year and from 2001 annual FDI was at least $2 billion, of which more than 85 per cent was intended for the natural resource sectors.[57]

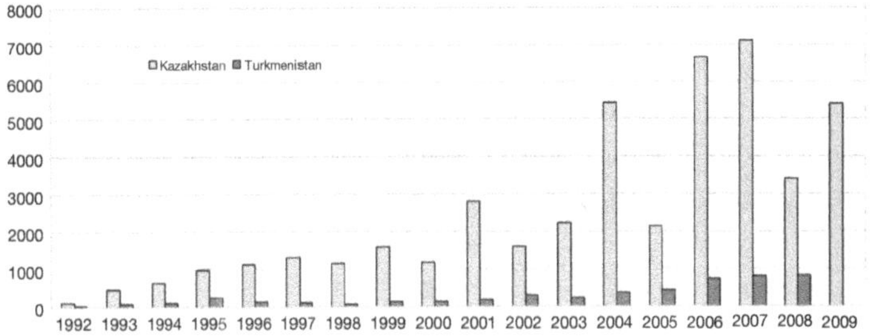

Figure 5.1 FDI Flows in Kazakhstan and Turkmenistan (1992–2009)
Source: *Le Courrier des pays de l'Est*, n°417, 428–29, 439, 1010, 1020, 1030, 1041, 1047, 1053, 1065; Peyrouse, S., *Turkménistan Un destin au carrefour des empires*, Paris: Belin, 2007; Pomfret, R., 'Resource Abundance and Long-Run Growth: When is Oil a Curse? The Effects of Oil Discovery on Kazakhstan's Economy', Canadian Network for Economic History Conference, 15–17 April 2005; EBRD, *Strategy for Kazakhstan*, 2010.

Turkmenistan did not attract foreign direct investment in anything like the same proportions as Kazakhstan, whatever the sector of the economy. However, until 1996 total FDI volume in dollars per capita was comparable in the two countries. Turkmenistan receives revenues from other exports than gas, namely cotton. These enabled Niyazov to postpone attracting FDI to the oil and gas sector, as Jones Luong and Weinthal have shown. This difference in FDI policy was due to transfers from agriculture to other sectors of the economy. The delay drastically reduced foreign presence in Turkmenistan and encouraged the establishment of a highly authoritarian regime, unlike Kazakhstan, where the indigenous elites in the oil sector, more numerous than in Turkmenistan,[58] took over the sector as soon they could.[59] The opportunity arose when Moscow called for foreign investors to exploit the Tengiz oilfield, but nothing similar occurred in Turkmenistan. These differing situations at independence also partly explain the differing developments in oil and gas sector institutions in the two countries and the slower appeal to foreign investment in the sector in Turkmenistan. A further explanation is the place of cotton in the Turkmen economy and exports.

Turkmen Exports: Gas and Cotton

Although Russia continued to buy Turkmen raw cotton, Turkmenistan turned after 1991 to other 'traditional' buyers of Soviet cotton. Moscow could not act as intermediary in this trade, a striking difference from its position in oil and gas. Furthermore, the country did not need to immediately invest considerable capital in cotton exports, as it would have done if it had wished to immediately increase its gas exports or diversify.[60] The exception is the construction of the Korpeje–Kordkuy gas pipeline for $190 million, financed 80 per cent by Iran and 20 per cent by Turkmenistan.

Nevertheless it had to borrow considerable sums from Western investors to finance the upgrading and development of its energy sector and its agriculture.[61] This strategy caused a rise in demand for oil and petrol and rapid growth in the production of wheat and cotton.

Transfers from Turkmen Agriculture to Other Sectors

The policy followed in Turkmenistan in the 1990s placed a heavy burden on cotton and wheat farmers, whose production was virtually

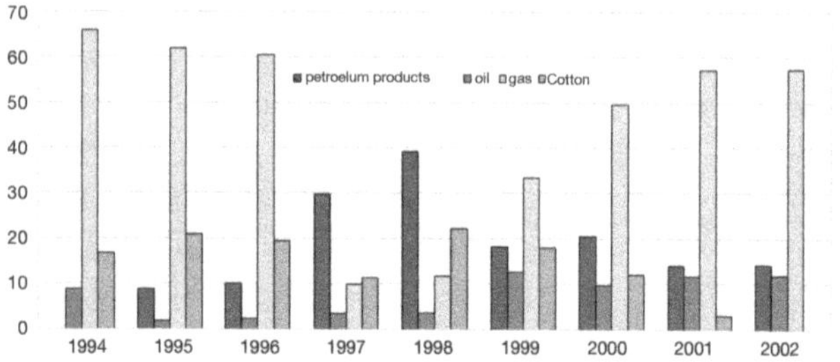

Figure 5.2 Exports of Petroleum Products, Oil, Gas and Cotton as a Percentage of Turkmenistan's Total Exports

Source: EIU, *Country Report Profile Turkmenistan 2007*, The Economist Intelligence Unit Limited, p. 26; International Monetary Fund, *op. cit.*; Statističeskij komitet Sodružestva nezavisimyh gosudarstv, *Vnešneèkonomičeskaâ deâtel'nost' gosudarstv Sodružestva*, Moskva: Finstatinform, 1993, p. 141; Asian Development Bank, *Economic data Turkmenistan*, 2008.

all bought up by the state. State purchase prices and exchange restrictions enabled large net transfers to be made from the agricultural sector to the rest of the economy. Pastor and Van Rooden[62] estimate that 15 per cent of GDP was transferred in this way in 1999. Other authors evaluate the figure at 11 per cent.[63] The state purchase prices for producers was set on average at 50–60 per cent of the world market prices for cotton and wheat at the official exchange rate. Some of the transfers in Turkmenistan (roughly 2 per cent of GDP according to Pastor and van Rooden, or 10 per cent according to the EIU[64]) were due to the difference between the state purchase price and the unsubsidized world price for cotton or wheat. The rest came from the difference between the product's value at the world market price at the usual official exchange rate and at a depreciated rate.[65] Conversely, Kazakhstan transferred roughly one-half of its GDP in 2000 to the agricultural sector (KZT 11.345 billion[66] out of a GDP of KZT 23.1 billion[67]).

This Turkmen policy of excessive transfers from the agricultural sector to the state budget had the effect of distorting the local market for cotton. With preferential prices for the domestic textile industry and subsidized inputs for cotton farmers (farm subsidies were $1 billion in 1998[68] while cotton exports earned $135.4 million that year), according to Pastor and van Rooden, this strategy of massive transfer was not sustainable because it endangered the state budget.[69] However, budget figures show no increase in the deficit, which was at worst 2.6 per cent of GDP in 1995, 2.8 per cent in 1998 and 2.7 per cent in 2002.[70] But although the official figures do not report a deficit, it should not be forgotten that policy decisions in 2003–04 drastically reduced retirement pensions, dismissed 12,000 to 13,000 teachers (shortening compulsory education) and abolished 15,000 health sector jobs, replacing them by military personnel. So there was indeed a budget problem. Pastor and van Rooden claim that transfers on this scale from agriculture to other sectors should have been made via direct fiscal measures rather than the exchange rates. But this could not be envisaged because citizens' incomes were not high enough to introduce such a tax system. This inability to make fiscal transfers reflects one aspect of the theory of the rentier state mentioned above, namely a high degree of fiscal (and perhaps political) autonomy and the argument comes full circle: because the state enjoys gas and cotton windfalls it can afford not to tax its citizens, and because there are high earnings from cotton exports, the state can transfer resources from agriculture to other economic sectors.

No similar policy was possible for Turkmenistan in the oil and gas sector. The use of foreign companies[71] to exploit its resources prevented that amount of distortion in this sector. The relations between the state as owner of its subsoil resources with foreign companies, restricted and uncooperative until 1996, are fundamentally different from those it has with its own farmers. The Turkmen state cannot treat these companies as it does its farmers, because it needs to negotiate agreements with them, denominated in dollars and not local currency. This is one reason why the Turkmen government initially chose not to attract FDI in its gas sector.

The social contract established in Soviet times and relations with the elites are key to understanding Turkmenistan's macroeconomic choices concerning FDI. Cotton production in Soviet Central Asia represented a crucial link between the elites at the top of the Soviet republic and those at lower levels. On this basis the republics' leaders had requested further transfers to Moscow.[72] They relied on regional leaders, who in turn relied on *rayon* leaders and kolkhoz managers to ensure that the cotton harvest plan was adhered to (at least on paper). Relations of this sort could not be formed in the oil sector, probably because of its capital-intensive nature.

Kazakhstan's Exports

In 1991, farm products accounted for only 8 to 10 per cent of Kazakhstan's export earnings, far behind oil and gas.[73] By 2000, the share of agriculture and the food industry in total exports had fallen to 6 per cent and 1 per cent respectively. Developments in the first decade of the millennium must be considered in both absolute and relative terms.

The table below (Table 5.5) shows that the main farm exports account for only a small share of Kazakhstan's total exports.

Table 5.5 Kazakhstan's Main Farm Exports 1995–2010 as Per Cent of Total Exports

	Cereals	Raw cotton	Wool
1995	5.6	0.07	0.95
2000	5.2	0.9	0.04
2005	0.788	0.587	0.095
2010	1.5	0.186	0.006

Source: Pomfret, R., *op. cit.*, p. 224; Kazakhstan's State Agency of Statistics, *Yearly bulletin 2010*, Astana, 2011, p. 413.

Furthermore, there was no clearly identified market for the cereals outside the former USSR, since most wheat had previously been intended for the rest of the Soviet Union. At independence, Kazakhstan had little access to sources of revenues other than oil and gas exports.

To increase its budget revenues, it could have made greater use of its major iron ore reserves in particular. But ore quality is poor and its long-term comparative advantage in world markets would have been limited. Kazakhstan also possesses 1.6 million tonnes of uranium reserves,[74] placing it second in the world in 2011. In 1997, it set up a national company, Kazatomprom, at the same time as the oil company Kazah Ojl (which became KMG in 2002). Kazatomprom controls the entire uranium exploration-production chain and nuclear product imports and exports. Kazakhstan's uranium export earnings were much lower than those from oil in 2001–02 (see Table 5.6 below) and the exploitation of uranium mines, like oil, gas and all extractive industries, requires

Table 5.6 Comparison of Kazakhstan's Uranium and Oil Export Earnings

Million dollars	Uranium	Oil
2001	125.38	4,254.7
2002	144.85	5,027.8

Source: *Otčët za 2002 g. ZAO Nacional'naâ atomnaâ kompaniâ Kazatomprom*, 2002, p. 26; International Monetary Fund, *Country report n°01/20*, 2001, p. 68.

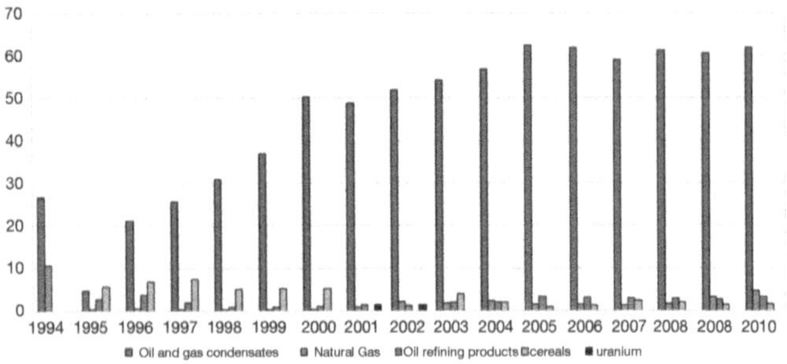

Figure 5.3 Export Share of Energy Products, Cereals and Uranium in Kazakhstan as Per Cent of Total Exports
Source: The World Bank, *Studies of Economies in Transformation. Statistical handbook 1994. States of The Former USSR*, Paper n°14, p. 277; Kazakhstan's State Agency of Statistics, *op. cit.*, pp. 234, 413–414; Statistical Committee of the CIS, *Vnešneèkonomičeskaâ deâtel'nost' gosudarstv Sodružestva*, Moskva: Finstatinform, 1993, pp. 32, 141; Tasmagambetov, I.N., *op. cit.*; International Monetary Fund, *Country Report n°01/20*, 2001, p. 68; International Monetary Fund, *Republic of Kazakhstan: Selected Issues and Statistical Appendix*, IMF Staff Country Report n°02/64, 2002; International Monetary Fund, Country Report n°04/363, 2004, p. 28; Pomfret, R., *The Economies in Central Asia*, Princeton N. J.: Princeton University Press, 1995.

huge investment because the business is also highly capital-intensive.

The lack of other sources of revenue comparable to Turkmenistan's cotton exports encouraged Kazakhstan in the early 1990s to invite foreign investors to develop its oil and gas reserves before Turkmenistan.[75]

N.B. The nominal price of a barrel rose from $15.82 in 1994 to $20.67 in 1996, fell to $19.09 in 1997 and $12.72 in 1999, and then rose sharply to $28.50 in 2000, and fell to $25.02 in 2002.

Comparison of Figures 5.2 and 5.3 shows that the share of gas in Turkmenistan's total exports was above 60 per cent until 1996, fell until 2000 and rose until 2002, whereas in Kazakhstan the share of oil exports only rose from 1995 to 2001, due mainly to differences of FDI in the two countries.

Kazakhstan, Highly Dependent on Oil, with High Oil Revenues in 2010

The 'resource curse' theory claims that in countries with low per capita oil revenues[76] high dependence on oil and gas exports[77] presents a risk of poor governance and lack of transparency. A country's governance, i.e., its traditions and institutions of government, is assessed by the World Bank according to dimensions including the perceived likelihood that the government will be destabilized or overthrown by unconstitutional or violent means, including politically motivated violence and terrorism.[78]

Turkmenistan and Kazakhstan were countries with low per capita hydrocarbon revenues in 2002: $283.7 for gas in Turkmenistan, $322 for oil in Kazakhstan. This indicator rose about above the $1,000 per capita threshold from 2004 to 2005 and was $2,255 in 2010. This considerable increase makes Kazakhstan currently a high per capita oil revenue country. In 2011, the country saw the biggest oil sector strike in its history and an unprecedented wave of terrorist acts.[79] In the case of Turkmenistan, this indicator cannot be calculated because the authorities have not published the value of gas exports since the middle of the last decade.

Kazakhstan and Turkmenistan's dependency on oil and gas varied over the 1993–2010 period (see Figures 5.2 and 5.3). It peaked for Turkmenistan in 1993 (gas was then 72.2 per cent of total exports, falling to 57.2 per cent in 2002; no figure is available for 2010). Kazakhstan's oil dependency was 51.9 per cent in 2002 and 61.8 per cent in 2010. So dependency has increased in Kazakhstan as a result of higher world oil prices and rapid increases in production.

Conclusions

The inadequacy of rentier state theory in the cases of Kazakhstan and Turkmenistan also reveals the difficulty of these two former Soviet republics' slide into the global South. Their development models defy classification. In 2011 the United Nations Development Programme ranked Kazakhstan 68th out of 187 countries (ahead, in particular, of Ukraine and Brazil) and Turkmenistan 102nd, just ahead of Thailand, on the Human Development Index.[80] The two countries' level of industrialization may be assessed by the urbanization rate and employment in the economy's main three sectors.[81] During the 1980s, the urbanization rate fell in the Turkmen SSR, against world trends at the time even in the countries of the 'global South' (from 48 per cent in 1980 to 45.1 per cent in 1991). This Turkmen exception disappeared in the years after independence and the current rate is 50 per cent.[82] This is still lower than Kazakhstan (58.8 per cent in 2010[83]), which continues to urbanize in line with the world trend.

Employment structure has seen an increase in the share of agriculture in Turkmenistan (42 per cent in 1990 and 48.2 per cent currently), whereas industrial employment has fallen from less than 30 per cent just before independence to 14 per cent now. The service sector employs 37 per cent of the working population. Kazakhstan, just before independence, fell somewhere between the four Central Asian republics and the Slav republics.[84] In 2010, employment was 25.9 per cent in agriculture, 11.9 per cent in industry and 62.2 per cent in services. In terms of employment structure, therefore, Turkmenistan may be classified among the unindustrialized countries and Kazakhstan among those with a highly developed service economy with industrial employment below agricultural employment, unlike the industrialized countries. These criteria present the two countries as atypical and different from each other.

Economic domination by a country of the 'North' might also be a criterion in assessing this Southward slide. But fear of domination, especially in Kazakhstan, is directed more by China, even though both Astana and Ashgabat are intensifying their oil and gas trade with that country. At the end of the 2000s, Moscow's desire to continue its policy of importing Turkmen gas caused Turkmenistan to open up its trade with China and not shut the door to the European Union. Kazakhstan, too, has opened up to the East and begun construction of the Kazakhstan–China oil pipeline.

Globalization, therefore, does mean something for these countries, which possess the two largest hydrocarbon reserves in Central Asia, attracting increasing attention from major gas and oil companies. They know how to play their cards and profit from this international attention by regaining the advantage over companies with which they had signed unfavourable contracts in the 1990s.

After noting the difficulty of assessing the two countries' slide towards the global South, one essential question for the future is whether they will continue growth without development or begin a policy of shaking off their dependency on hydrocarbons, and reducing poverty, since the economic fallout from the oil and gas industry does not trickle down to the entire social fabric. But that is not the avenue they have so far chosen.

Notes

1 Currently owned in equal parts by the Exploration & Production arm of the national company KazMunaiGaz (KMG) and the Chinese CITIC Group.

2 A subsidiary of KMG, based in Zhanaozen, with between 9,000 and 9,500 employees. The oilfield where Ozenmunajgaz operates is the fourth largest in Kazakhstan, after Tengiz.

3 Michalopoulos, C., Tarr, D.G., *Trade in the New Independent States, Studies of economies in transformation*, n°13, Washington D.C.: World Bank; New York: UNDP, 1994, p. 8.

4 Redor, D., *Les économies d'Europe de l'Est: Europe centrale, Europe orientale, Russie, depuis 1989*, Paris: Seuil, 1997, p. 22.

5 Jones Luong, P., Weinthal, E., 'Prelude to the Resource Curse: Oil and Gas Development Strategies in Central Asia and Beyond', *Comparative Political Studies*, 2001, vol. 34/4, pp. 367–99.

6 EIU, *Country Report Profile Turkmenistan 2010*, The Economist Intelligence Unit Limited, p. 22.

7 Raballand, G., *L'Asie centrale ou la fatalité de l'enclavement*, Paris: L'Harmattan; Tashkent: IFEAC, 2005.

8 World Bank, Turkmenistan, Washington: The World Bank, 1994, p. 129.

9 EIU, *Country Report Profile Turkmenistan 2007*, The Economist Intelligence Unit Limited, p. 31.

10 Talahite, F., 'Le concept de rente: le cas des économies du Moyen-orient et de l'Afrique du nord', *Problèmes économiques*, 2006, vol. 2,902, p. 9.

11 Matsunaga, Y., 'L'Etat rentier est-il réfractaire à la démocratie?', *Critique internationale*, 2000, vol. 8.

12 Shirdel, M.-A., 'Le changement dans les stratégies du développement économique en Iran, 1980–1988: le socialisme islamique', *Politique et Sociétés*, 2007, vol. 26/1, p. 97.
13 Esanov, A., Raiser, M., Buiter, W., *Nature's Blessing or Nature's Curse: The Political Economy of Transition in Resource-Based Economies*, Working paper, EBRD, London, n°65, November 2001, pp. 1, 5–6.
14 Where national consumption equals total production minus export volume.
15 Auty, R., 'Natural Resources and 'Gradual' Reform in Uzbekistan and Turkmenistan', *Natural Resources Forum*, 2003, vol. 27/4, p. 257.
16 Supplemented by a pipeline in Northern Iran via Artyk, Lutfabad and Dargaz in 2000.
17 The first section was completed in 1967 and 'from 5 October 1967 Turkmen gas was taken by the Central Asia-Centre gas pipeline 2,750 km to the industrial districts of Moscow'; in the late 1960s, gas from Turkmenistan supplied the industrial enterprises of the Urals. The second section was then being built. In 1969, after the construction of the Mayskoye–Ashgabat–Bezmein (Abadan) pipeline, gas was delivered to enterprises in the latter two areas. Then, in 1974, the third section of the Central Asia–Centre gas pipeline, CAC III (Kotur-Tepe–Uzen), was completed to supply the European parts of the USSR with gas from Turkmenistan. Two branches run from the Gazli field in Uzbekistan, a third from the Okarem field and the fourth from the Shatlyk field in the Turkmen SSR. The latter two ran through Aleksandrov-Gaj to join the existing pipelines between Ukraine (Shebelinka), the Caucasus (Krasnodar and Stavropol) and Moscow.
18 The initiative for this pipeline came from the first president of independent Turkmenistan, Saparmurat Niyazov, who concluded the agreement with Beijing shortly before his death in 2006.
19 International Monetary Fund, *Turkmenistan: Recent Economic Developments*, IMF Staff Country report n°99/140, Washington D.C.: IMF, 1999, p. 121.
20 Miyamoto, A., *Natural Gas in Central Asia: Industries, Markets and Export Options of Kazakhstan, Turkmenistan and Uzbekistan*, London: Royal Institute of International Affairs, 1997, p. 50.
21 Farnsworth, G., *Encyclopedia of Caspian Oil and Gas Sector*, vol. 2, Tarzana (Calif.): Russian Petroleum Investor, 1997, p. 43.
22 Itera was founded in February 1994 (or 1992) in the United States by Igor Viktorovich Makarov (born in Ashgabat). He clearly had ties to the Turkmen government, according to Global Witness, which quotes him as saying that the key to his initial success was the fact that 'boyhood friends' were moving into key government positions in Turkmenistan.
23 Milov, V., 'Ups and Downs of the Russia–Turkmen Relationship', in Dellecker, A., Gomart, T. (eds), *Russian Energy, Security and Foreign Policy*, London: Routledge, 2011, pp. 92–4.
24 A structure created in 1996 to succeed the oil and gas ministry, then abolished by Niyazov in 2006 in order to bring the entire energy sector under his control.

CHAPTER 6

HUMAN CAPITAL AND INEQUALITY IN TAJIKISTAN: INTERCOMMUNICATION AND INTERDEPENDENCE

Saodat Olimova and Muzzafar Olimov
(Sharq Research Center, Tajikistan)

The former brethren republics of the Soviet Union chose differing economic and political models 20 years ago; however, the human factor, a phrase popular in the perestroika era, is the most critical factor in determining the course of development. How did the former 'Soviet people' change? What are they building in every specific former republic of the USSR? And how do they see themselves and their future? We had these questions in mind while researching the development of human capital in Tajikistan in the years after having gained independence. This study was conducted with the support of the European Training Foundation (ETF) in 2009 and 2010. Some of the results have served as the foundation for the chapter.

Theodore Shultz, Gary Becker and George Mintzer developed their theory of human capital at the turn of the 1950s and 1960s.[1] This theory recognizes humans and their knowledge as the chief factor in economic growth, thus defining the course of economic development, and sees the income inequality of the economically active population as the outcome of inequality in the productivity of human capital, which has been accumulated through various educational practices. Various factors besides labour productivity, however, may cause income inequality. Among such factors are cultural, climatic and political, those stemming from sustained gender, national and other barriers in the labour and education markets, substantial social mobility restrictions, and case interference.

Human-capital theory disregards the denoted factors by virtue of the premature global trend to weaken them. Specific case studies, however, demonstrate the complex relations between income distribution and the breakdown of the population's level of education.

In particular, examining human capital development in Tajikistan allows the opportunity to scrutinize this connection at an intriguing point in the post-Soviet transformation. We believe that there is a strong interdependence between accumulated human capital (HC) and inequality. Tajikistan, just like other former Soviet republics, has seen social stratification after the fall of the USSR that has been accompanied by a drastic rise in income differentiation, which in effect has created significant social and economic inequality. Simultaneously, the quality and quantity of human capital dropped, with the young people being less educated than their parents and the quality of education having fallen. Access inequality to education for various groups of the population is on the rise, especially among women, the poor and rural residents. Together this strengthens the dismantling of modernization that has unfurled itself in Tajikistan after having obtained independence. Meanwhile, experience from a number of countries shows that social and economic inequalities stimulate the efficient accumulation, redistribution and use of human capital. The objective of this study is to research what the chief trends and progress of the development of HC within Tajikistan's transition are, and to determine what conditions help turn social and economic inequalities from a stimulus of public development into what serves as obstacles to it.

We use the following definition of human capital in our study: the knowledge, skills, capabilities and motivations, which humanity may use during the labour process and which make a difference in a country's social and economic development. We limit ourselves to researching issues in education, training, acquiring professional knowledge and skills, and using them in the labour market. We exclude health and nutrition, because these spheres require being researched separately.

In analysing the changes in human capital during the post-Soviet period, we study the current level and courses of development in the context of Tajikistan's general economic processes. These processes include the following: transitioning to a market economy and the structured reconstruction of the economy after having gained independence, labour migration, the shaping of economic inequality and poverty, and the change in the role of state and public institutions.

Official statistical data, material from the authors' research from over the past six years, materials from the 2007 Tajikistan Living Standards Survey (TLSS, 2007), and interviews with experts in education in Tajikistan, conducted in 2009 and 2010, serve as the empirical base for this chapter.

The development of human capital (HC) during the period of independence

Tajikistan, along with the other Soviet republics, was undergoing belated industrialization. Moreover, Tajikistan was able to achieve a high level of human capital, despite the industrial modernization's having been incomplete.[2] The ideologies of reform during the initial years of the transition see this factor as the chief condition for successful reforms in Tajikistan. It was assumed that both educated and patriotic people would make every effort to build an independent nation state with a democratic government and market economy. Simon Kuznets's theory serves as the foundation for these views. According to this theory, having sufficient HC at the beginning is the most important factor for economic growth in countries going through industrialization.[3] The transition from the Soviet period, however, was accompanied by significant difficulties, which, first and foremost, include the civil war of 1992–97 and the human and material losses, as well as the mass forced emigration that came along with it. Moreover, Tajikistan, with its limited resources and very small domestic market, was much more dependent on the USSR than the other Soviet republics, and thus suffered from the fall of the Soviet Union more than the others.[4] Along with the loss of subsidies from Moscow and the emigration of qualified Russian technical personnel, scholars and managers, Tajikistan was also dealing with the quick dissolution of its institutes and the weakening of the state during this transition.

The fall in economic activity, the growth in joblessness, the majority of the people being plunged into poverty, the unprecedented increase in poverty and the overall decline in the social and economic situation plagued the country during its transition to a market economy. This all served as the backdrop for political, social and cultural reforms. They determined the areas for developing HC in post-Soviet Tajikistan.

If we are to look at HC development in Tajikistan over the past 20 years, then we will see that it has been gradually declining.[5] If during the Soviet era all children were provided with an education, there is now a group of people who have never gone to school and are illiterate. The censuses from 1989 and 2000 do not have information on people who have no education at all, although the 1989 census showed that 0.3 per cent of people ranging in age from 9 to 49 were illiterate. The number of such people in the 2000 census was equal to 0.2 per cent.[6] In 2007, however, 0.7 per cent of the Tajik population 15 years of age or older said that they never went to school and are not literate.[7] Moreover, from 1989 to 2007, the share of people with higher or secondary professional education, shrank by 1.8 per cent and 2.1 per cent, respectively.[8]

The labour force's level of education is currently limited to general secondary education, which poorly encompasses all levels of professional education. Therefore, around half of the economically active population has only a secondary education, while a third of the working population have a professional or higher education. At the same time, the USSR census of 1989 showed that 87.7 per cent of the working population in Tajikistan had a professional or higher education.[9]

The level of education has noticeably fallen, and there is a discrepancy between the length of study (number of years) and its quality (the knowledge and skills learned while studying). When keeping a relatively long study period (the average is 11 years), students obtain a significantly smaller aggregate of knowledge and skills than before.[10] The decline in the quality of education leads to a growth in the inequality of access to education, which is especially noticeable among rural residents, the poor and girls. The low quality of education available for the poor rural population and women limits their chances to make the transition to higher levels of education and, as a whole, leads to the stagnation and stammering of the country's development.

The Decline in Human Capital: Reasons and Factors

What helped cause the decline in HC in Tajikistan? In studying the different factors impacting the development of HC, we have highlighted four chief ones: a) a decline in the education system as part of the removal of state services; b) the effect of the economy's structural rebuilding; c) the impact of large-scale labour migration; d) the development of social and economic inequalities, and inclusion.

A Glance at the Educational System in Tajikistan

To understand the state of HC in Tajikistan, it is necessary to give an overview of the educational system in Tajikistan. Tajikistan has an educational system, which is a legacy of comprehensive and free public education system of the Soviet Union. The current education system in Tajikistan consists of the following levels: (1) voluntary pre-school for ages 2–6, (2) compulsory secondary education for ages 7–15, (3) voluntary complete secondary or technical/professional education, and (4) voluntary higher/university education. While pre-school education in Tajikistan is voluntary, the 1993 law on education establishes that the 9-year secondary school education is compulsory for all citizens of Tajikistan. The 9-year secondary education consists of the following two stages: 4-year primary education for ages 7–10 (grades 1–4); 5-year basic or incomplete secondary education for ages 11–15 (grades 5–9).

After successful completion of the 5-year basic education, students are issued a state endorsed certificate of incomplete secondary education. Given this certificate, students can complete a voluntary two-year general secondary education (grades 10–11). Upon completion of the general secondary education, students are issued a state diploma of complete secondary education. Only the diploma of complete secondary education allows students to apply to colleges and university in Tajikistan.

An alternative route for students with incomplete secondary education is to continue education at professional/technical colleges and schools. There are two types of professional/technical education available in Tajikistan. The first type is professional/technical education provided by professional schools and colleges subordinate to the Ministry of Education. Depending on the duration of study (two to four years), students can get a variety of professional-technical qualifications. Upon completion of two years of instruction a student can obtain a certificate of basic professional-technical qualification without complete secondary education. Students can obtain basic professional-technical qualification together with complete secondary education after four years of instruction. After graduation with complete secondary education, students can have two years of instruction and obtain professional-technical qualification.

The second type of professional/technical education is provided by educational centres of professional education under supervision of the Ministry of Labour and Social Protection (MLSP). Unlike in the professional-technical schools of the first type, the duration of study at educational centres of MLSP usually does not exceed one year. In general the curriculum at these institutions is designed for the needs of adults with complete secondary or professional-technical qualification.

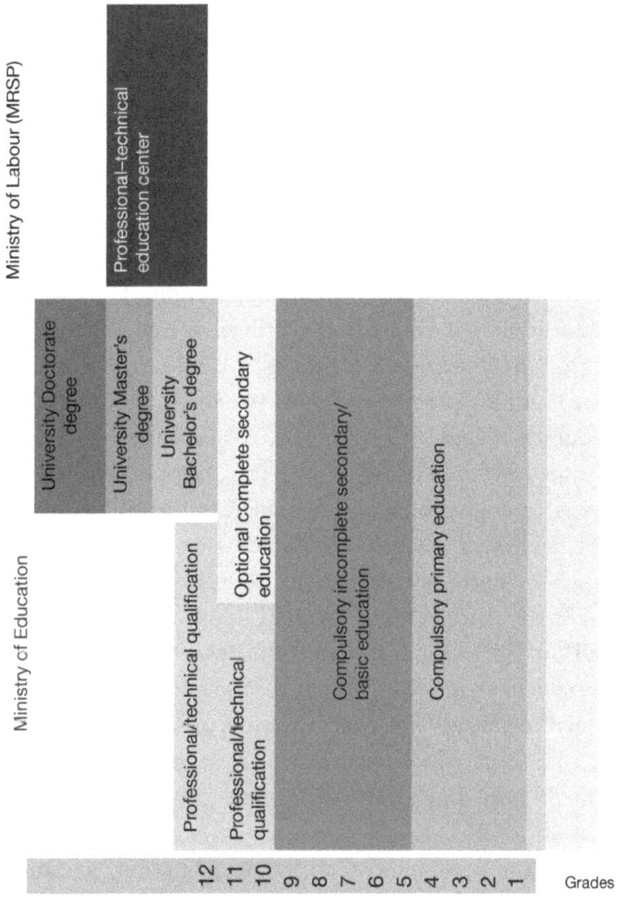

Figure 6.1 Structure of Education System in Tajikistan

Individuals with complete secondary education can apply to institutions of higher education. After four years of instruction at a university, students are awarded a bachelor's degree. Five-year university programmes offer specialist diplomas. Having obtained a bachelor's or a specialist degree, students can continue education in two-year long masters programmes and doctorate programmes. Tajik law stipulates that incomplete and complete secondary education at public schools is free and guaranteed for all citizens of Tajikistan. Admission into public professional-technical schools and universities is competitive and can require payment. The Figure 6.1 below depicts the structure of educational system in Tajikistan.

The Decline in Education During the Transitional Period

Despite preserving a developed system of education, this very system declined significantly during the transitional period. The problems with education in Tajikistan, as a rule, are linked to the aftermath of the civil war that took place from 1992–97, and to the emigration of the most educated people during the initial years after the fall of the Soviet Union. While recognizing the importance of these circumstances, it ought to be pointed out that the following factors aided in the decline of education in Tajikistan.

The drop in state investment in education and the overall contraction of the share of GDP invested in education, from 9.7 per cent of GDP in 1991 to 4.1 per cent of GDP in 2008.[11] The fall in state investments in education came at the same time as the sources of financing for the educational system were diversified, including the foundation of private educational institutions and the development of a system of providing households with informal payments for education at all levels.

Speaking of the development of private education, it should be noted that it is advancing very slowly and under the state's complete control. The first private educational institutions (secondary schools, lyceums and gymnasia) were opened in 1994 when a new law was passed that regulates educational institutions financed by private sources. There were eight educational institutions in 1999–2000 with a total of 1,012 students, while in 2003–04 the number of private schools grew to 50 and had 14,126 students overall. There are currently 53 privately financed general education institutions.[12] There are courses that teach foreign languages, how to use computers, and other similar skills.

The system of providing households with informal payments for education, including expenditures for basic education, plays a much more significant role in financing educating in the Republic of Tajikistan than does investment in private education. The constitution of the Republic of Tajikistan may guarantee the right to free secondary education, but the practice of collecting payments from parents for education is ubiquitous, as is making contributions for remodelling work, buying equipment, conducting school events, etc. Professional and technical education institutions and universities, along with official contributions, also unofficially collect payments from students.

Even when taking into account the diversification of the sources of financing and the growth in the share of GDP invested in education, the aggregate state and private investments made in education still did not match the level of 1991 (see Table 6.1).[13] The calculated data shows that the annual share of expenditures on education should be at least 6 per cent of GDP to satisfy the minimal requirements for preserving and developing the educational system.[14]

The decline in teacher qualifications

The key problems with the educational system in Tajikistan have to do not only with the unsatisfactory material and technical equipment provided in educational institutions and inefficient school

Table 6.1 Expenditures on Education in Tajikistan (2000–07)

Year	2000	2001	2002	2003	2004	2005	2006	2007
Share of GDP spent on education	2.3	2.4	2.6	2.4	2.7	3.5	3.4	3.4
Share of state budget spent on education	15.9	16.0	16.0	14.5	15.0	18.0	17.9	12.5

Source: State Statistics Committee of the Republic of Tajikistan, 2009, *op. cit.*, p. 7.

administration, but also with the low level of teacher and professor qualifications. This is especially typical for rural areas and has to do, first and foremost, with the lack of qualified teachers. In 2008, 10,809 teachers quit their job.[15] Low salaries and the hardships of village life, especially in distant mountain regions, were the chief reasons for these teachers leaving their jobs. In order to fill the deficit of professors, the Tajik Ministry of Education took the decision to send university graduate students to rural schools and to allow graduates to teach lower schools.

In 2008–09, 61 per cent of 96,127 teachers working in Tajikistan had completed their higher education, 59 per cent had an incomplete higher education, 59 per cent had a secondary professional or

Table 6.2 Main Demographic Indicators

		Per cent	Number
Location type	Urban	26.3%	1,857,700
	Rural	73.7%	5,206,100
Oblast (region)	Dushanbe	9.4%	660,900
	Sughd	29.7%	2,095,700
	Khatlon	35.7%	2,519,600
	DRD	22.2%	1,567,200
	GBAO	3.1%	220,400
Gender	Male	48.6%	3,436,289
	Female	51.4%	3,627,511
Age groups	0–9	22.8%	1,612,137
	10–19	25.1%	1,771,342
	20–29	17.9%	1,266,972
	30–39	11.3%	792,801
	40–49	10.2%	720,169
	50–59	6.5%	465,521
	60–69	3.2%	225,727
	70 +	3.0%	209,131
TOTAL		100.0%	7,063,800

Source: State Statistics Committee of the Republic of Tajikistan, *Tajikistan Living Standards Measurement Survey 2007*, Dushanbe, 2009.

technical education, and 6.3 per cent had a secondary education.[16] The unsatisfactory level of professional education in pedagogical universities has a negative impact on the level of teachers' qualifications in Tajikistan, as do out-of-date and inefficient advanced teacher training programmes.

The demographic squeeze

Ever since Tajikistan gained its independence, not only has the country's population grown significantly, from 5,108,600 people in 1989 to 7,565,000 in 2010,[17] but the share of school-aged children has also risen (see Table 6.2), which has created an ever-increasing burden on the country's educational system. The especially fast growth in the number of children and young people ages 5 to 19 took place from 1989 to 2000, when their population grew by almost a third, from 1,811,100 people to 2,404,600 people.[18] Even though the population of this group grew from 2000 to 2010 by 1,058,500 people,[19] its growth, nonetheless, slowed significantly, and the process for increasing the burden on Tajikistan's educational system weakened.

Consequently, despite all the cataclysms, over the past 20 years that Tajikistan has been independent, the number of students has grown steadily. Moreover, the number of schools and teachers has increased as well (Table 6.3). If the number of students in schools in Tajikistan during the 1991–92 academic year was 1,325,400 people,

Table 6.3 General Education Institutions, Number of Students and Teachers (1988–89, 2000–01 and 2008–09 Academic Years), per Thousand

Year	1988–89	2000–01	2008–09
Number of schools	2,954.0	3,604.0	3,817.0
Number of students	1,204.5	1,529.7	1,691.9
Number of teachers	88.6	100.2	96.1

Source: State Statistics Committee of the Tajik SSR, 1989, pp. 13–4; State Statistics Committee of the Republic of Tajikistan, 2004, pp. 13, 15, 29 State Statistics Committee of the Republic of Tajikistan, 2009, pp. 15, 26 and in 2001 it was 1,529,700 people, then during the 2008–09 academic year it was 1,691,900 people. While there has been a significant increase in the number of schools, the number of teachers has been rising at slower rates. Therefore, there has been some increase in the burden on teachers. If during the 2004–05 academic year there was an average of one teacher per 11 students, then during the 2008–09 academic year, the average was one teacher per 13 students. Although the burden on teachers cannot be considered excessive, it should be kept in mind that teachers in Tajikistan carry out a large and unaccountable volume of work related to public functions. They serve in the electoral process at all levels, push for government measures and act as direct organizers of all public events in communities.

Impoverishment of the People of Tajikistan

In 1990, the per capita income of the Tajik people was roughly $1,050. Two years later, it declined by 50 per cent (to $480 in 1992), and then 10 years after that it was $150. In other words, per capita income shrank by 85 per cent.[20] Despite the fast economic growth that has taken place during the reconstruction after the civil war, the level of per-capita income remains low. In 2008, per-capita income was $600.[21] Tajikistan continues to be the poorest country among the former Soviet republics and in the Eurasia region overall.

The Impact of the Economy's Structural Reconstruction

The structural transformation of Tajikistan's economy has had the biggest impact on HC. This very transformation was accompanied by de-industrialization, de-urbanization, social stratification and inequality. De-industrialization was a result of industrial production coming to a halt during the fall of Soviet agriculture. If, in 1991, 21 per cent of the Tajik population was in working industry, then in 2009 only 4.8 per cent of all workers were employed in industry.[22] The shutdown of industrial factories also led to an unemployment rate that, according to government documents, reached 30 per cent.[23] The number of jobless shrank from 16 per cent in 1999 to 11.4 per cent in 2002, and then fell yet again to 7.4 per cent after 2003[24] or, in other words, after a significant part of the economically active Tajik population began to emigrate and enter international labour markets.

Together with de-industrialization, the urban population also fell. In 1989, 1,668,100 people, or 33 per cent, of the country's 5,108,600 people, were living in cities. The latest census, conducted in 2010, showed that the population of Tajikistan was 7,564,500 people, including 2,005,000, or 26.5 per cent of the population, living in urban areas.[25] The increase in the rural population can be explained not only by the higher birth rate in rural areas, but also by the emigration of mostly Russians and other non-native peoples during the Tajik civil war.[26] The growth in the rural population led to an increase in employment in agriculture. Cultivating food cultures, including wheat, rice and potatoes, and raising live stock and poultry was a survival strategy for many households during the difficult years of the civil war and shock reforms.

The expansion of the subsistence economy and labour emigration has swallowed up more and more people who have stopped entering the domestic labour market. This is how Tajikistan's public economic activity, statistically low and continuing to fall, came about. This economic activity, moreover, has invisible, unofficial employment that made up for 52 per cent of the work force in Tajikistan in 2010.[27] The majority of them are women who make up two-thirds of the economically inactive population of Tajikistan.

Research on Tajikistan's shadow economy in 2007 showed that the majority of unofficially employed people in rural areas work on personal land plots and family farms producing food for consumption, trade and sale. Many economically inactive people in rural areas, in fact, work for their relatives at small family factories or are self-employed. This research shows that the household production of goods and services for personal consumption and sale make up 23.3 per cent (in other words, almost a fourth) of the overall income of households in Tajikistan. Producing goods and services at home was the only source of income for 16.2 per cent of households. The volume of goods production for personal consumption in 2007 was 14.7 per cent of GDP.[28]

The changes to the structure of Tajikistan's GDP, which took place between 1995 and 2007, caused the share of sectors with more qualified labour to shrink and the share of sectors with less qualified labour to increase. For example, industrial production that requires qualified labour decreased by more than 50 per cent, while the volume of trade, which has not been modernized in the country and requires relatively less qualified workers, has almost tripled. The construction and services sectors, which in Tajikistan use primarily traditional materials and technologies, have seen the fastest growth, and therefore they require less-qualified workers. All this together has resulted in changes in the quality of workers in the labour market and in a drop in the demand for human capital in terms of professional or technical qualifications.

The demand for professional and technical education dropped as a result of the changes taking place during the post-Soviet-era transition, while the demand for higher education grew. The number of students in technical schools shrank from 40,700 in 1992 to 34,000 in 2008. Moreover, the biggest decrease was seen in the first five years after the fall of the USSR: 1992–98. Even when taking into account the civil war, which caused the student population in all types of educational institutions to decrease, the recovery in student numbers in vocational schools and primary schools went much slower than in other educational institutions, and still have not reached the level attained in 1991.

Low-qualified workers continue to be in demand, while the demand for highly qualified labour has fallen, even though it has not been satisfied over the past seven years. Research of the shadow economy in Tajikistan has shown that 32 per cent of polled companies have experienced a deficit in qualified employees.[29] The World Bank reports that in 2009, 40 per cent of companies labelled the deficit of qualified labour as a problem ranging from moderate to significant.[30] This deficit had taken shape in education, industry, construction, housing, healthcare and communications.[31]

The Impact of Migration on Education

A number of studies have been conducted in various countries that examine the impact of migration on human capital. Most studies show that migration has a positive effect on HC by decreasing extreme poverty, increasing incomes through money transfers (which as a result escalates migrant family expenditures on education), and by obtaining additional knowledge and skills from the process of migration.[32] Contrary to these studies, McKenzie and Rapoport point out that migration has a negative effect on school attendance and the overall level of education. These authors believe that the negative influence migration has on education, stemming from the heighted demand for child labour, is more significant that the positive influence of migration coming from money transfers, which provide a higher income level.[33] This study, just like others, shows that the type of impact migration has on human capital is swayed not only by purely economic factors, but also by various social and cultural factors, such as dominate values and ideologies, gender and age roles and models, and social structures.

The materials from the latest studies show that labour migration has a significant impact on the development of HC in Tajikistan by having a full-circle influence, both positive and negative, on education.[34] Migrants with a higher education send home more money more often than migrants with a lower level of education; however, since they rarely work according to their profession abroad,[35] their knowledge and skills that they obtained before they left go to waste.[36] Migrants that return home make a definite contribution to the development of small business and agriculture by using new technology, tools, instruments, knowledge and skills; however, this contribution has little effect on the country's technological development.[37] The increase in migrant household incomes, and, consequently, the improvement in the diet and health of these families' children, is the most positive impact that labour migration has. The proliferation of child labour in migrant households, nonetheless, is a negative side effect from the increase in income from migration.[38] Overall, migration's negative impact on HC in Tajikistan is greater than its positive aspects.

Table 6.4 Education Level of People Aged 15 and Above

		Education level					
Description		None	Primary	Basic	Secondary general	Secondary special/technical	Higher
Location type	Urban	0.5%	7.4%	17.4%	43.6%	14.9%	16.2%
	Rural	0.8%	9.1%	23.7%	50.6%	9.6%	6.1%
Region	Dushanbe	0.3%	7.1%	17.4%	36.2%	14.9%	24.1%
	Sughd	0.5%	6.8%	19.8%	55.7%	8.9%	8.3%
	Khatlon	0.8%	9.5%	22.9%	49.5%	11.2%	6.2%
	SRR	1.1%	10.8%	27.0%	43.3%	11.1%	6.7%
	GBAO	0.3%	7.5%	14.8%	50.0%	15.7%	11.7%
Gender	Male	0.5%	7.1%	17.6%	45.9%	15.7%	13.2%
	Female	0.9%	10.1%	26.1%	51.4%	6.7%	4.8%

Source: State Statistics Committee of the Republic of Tajikistan, 2007, *op. cit.*

Social and Economic Inequality and the Development of Human Capital

Developing human capital requires significant investment not only from the state, but also from the people. After the fall of the socialist system and its guaranteed, state-funded education, the Tajik people came to a crossroads: either invest in their own children's education, or spend this money on their immediate needs. This alternative created a complex connection between the growing social and economic inequalities and the development of HC. This connection can be viewed through the prism of direct dependence–as the influence of income differentiation on access to education, and through the prism of reverse dependence–as the influence of accumulated HC on the income differentiation. We will first take a look at how social and economic inequality impact access education.

Gender Inequality in Access to Education

Social and economic inequality has a gender dimension to it and includes gender inequality in access to education. If the share of young boys ages 8–18 who are provided with an education is 95 per cent, then the same indicator for young girls is 87 per cent.[39] Gender inequality in access to education has increased notably after the fall of the USSR. If in the academic year of 1990–91 the number of women among university students was 36.6 per cent, then ten years later their share dropped to 23.7 per cent,[40] and then rose in 2010 to 29 per cent.[41]

Inequality is found in elementary school, with the gender coefficient being close to 1.00, which is indicative of the differences in terms of elementary school attendance between boys and girls. This indicator, however, dips to 0.83 in secondary school, or in other words ten boys for every eight girls (see Table 6.2).

Table 6.4 indicates that boys are more likely to receive a general secondary education than girls, who often quit school after the fourth grade. This type of situation is most prevalent in poor families in rural areas. Moreover, there is a notable difference in gender inequality between regions in Tajikistan, with the number of girls after the end of the fourth grade being the highest in Khatlon region and Subordinate Republic Regions (SRR), where only 70.5 per cent of girls continued on to study in the fifth grade, while the number of boys to continue on to study in the fifth grade stays at 91.5 per cent. The gender inequality after the fourth grade is less evident in Gorno Badakhshan and in Sughd region, just as it is among children in well-off families and in urban areas. The regional difference is to a large extent explained by social and cultural factors, the peculiarities of the regions' demographic development, and each type of regional economy.

Women residing in Gorno Badakhshan, a district with a small population in the Pamir Mountains where the share of the urban population is just 13.6 per cent, had the highest level of education in the Tajik SSR; this trend continues to this very day. Moreover, the Aga Khan Development Network (AKDN)[42] provides programmes to support women's education and gender equality in the Gorno Badakhshan. Women residing in Sughd region, which is in Northern Tajikistan and is part of the Ferghana Valley, also have more opportunities than in other regions of Tajikistan, finish secondary school and obtain a professional education. This is a densely populated district with the highest rate of urbanization in Tajikistan (25 per cent[43]), with a significant share of industry in the economy and a relatively high rate of participation by women in administration. Dushanbe, the capital, the surrounding regions of the republic and Khatlon region (Southern Tajikistan), which are all located in central Tajikistan, have the highest level of gender inequality. Central and Southern Tajikistan's rural population is employed in traditional agriculture and has preserved its traditional cultural and economic way of life, which is based on male authority.

Mothers' education level has a notable impact on their children's level of education. Households with a mother who has an elementary education see only 45.1 per cent of girls and 79.4 per cent of boys continue to attend school after the fourth grade. Among the children of mothers with a higher education, 93.3 per cent of girls and 96.3 per cent of boys attend secondary school (see Table 6.5).

Table 6.5 Gender Inequality in Elementary and Secondary School in Tajikistan (2005) NAC = Net Attendance Coefficient, EGRI = Equal Gender Rights Index

	Elementary School			Secondary School		
	NAC for girls	NAC boys	EGRI	NAC for girls	NAC for boys	EGRI
Place of residence						
City	90.6	87.9	1.03	77.9	90.7	0.86
Village	87.3	89.5	0.98	73.1	88.7	0.82
Mother education						
No education	52.0	81.7	0.64	52.2	74.3	0.70
Elementary	81.6	79.2	1.03	45.1	79.4	0.57
Unfinished secondary	85.9	88.4	0.97	65.5	87.2	0.75
Secondary	88.7	88.9	1.00	75.8	89.1	0.85
Secondary special	88.6	91.2	0.97	74.3	92.5	0.80
Higher	96.5	95.6	1.01	93.3	96.3	0.97
Quintile welfare index						
Poorest	85.8	90.2	0.95	69.7	84.6	0.82
Second	87.3	89.1	0.98	66.9	90.2	0.74
Average	87.8	87.3	1.01	74.8	90.1	0.83
Fourth	87.3	87.8	0.99	77.4	87.7	0.88
Richest	93.3	91.0	1.03	84.8	94.1	0.90
Total	88.2	89.1	0.99	74.4	89.3	0.83

Source: State Statistics Committee of the Republic of Tajikistan, *Tajikistan: Multi-Cluster Survey, 2005*, Dushanbe, 2005.

The high rate of girls engaged in housekeeping is, first and foremost, one of the reasons for gender inequality in schools. Girls take care of household chores and look after their younger brothers and sisters. Research on child labour in Tajikistan shows that girls spend much more time on housekeeping than boys. Girls ranging from 13 to 15 years of age spend the most time on household chores.[44] They are strong enough, skilled enough and able enough to perform difficult chores, such as cooking, cleaning, looking after the children, gardening, sewing and repairing clothing. This is explained by the fairly high level of the group of girls after finishing elementary school. Girls from poor families are the most burdened with household chores and work in household agriculture. Therefore, they are the most restricted in obtaining access to education.

Higher education is one of the areas where gender inequality is most evident. Women made up only 29 per cent of university students in the 2009–10 academic year, while the coefficient between women and men receiving education is 0.36 per cent, which is the lowest among countries in the Central Asian region.[45] This can be explained to a large extent by the dominating gender ideologies in Tajikistan, which limit women in education. Poverty exasperates the situation, since low-income families prefer to invest their money in boys' education, but not girls'. Families believe that education can help boys find work in the future in Tajikistan or abroad, so that they can then support the elderly members of the family in the future. Parents do not see the use of their daughters receiving an education, because daughters traditionally get married at a young age, run the husband's household and do not enter the labour market. Therefore, parents prefer not to invest in the education of their daughters, but rather marry them off as soon as possible. This practice is ubiquitous in rural regions.

The low level of education of young girls and women causes an overall low level of education among the teenage generation, since poorly educated mothers do not encourage their children to study and receive a professional education. Research shows that a child's success in school depends much more on the mother than the father. Migrant families where women have much greater responsibility for the household than usual are in the toughest position. Overall, children from migrant households where mothers have a higher level of education and a profession, despite a father not being around, study much better and longer, and thus achieve a higher level of education than the children of mothers who lack an education and a profession.[46] In migrant households, however, young girls are the most limited in their access to education because of being engaged in child labour.[47]

Social and Economic Inequality as a Barrier for Development

Just like in other Central Asian countries, Tajikistan saw a significant rise in the public income differentiation during the first decade after the fall of the Soviet Union (see Table 6.6).

If in 1988 the Gini index was 0.27 in terms of per capita expenditures, then in 1999 it was equal to 0.33. This number grew in 2003 to 0.36.[48] In 2007, the Gini index was 0.39.[49]

The growing social and economic inequality has led to inequality in education when young people from high-income families have much more incentive and many more opportunities to receive a professional and higher education than people from poor parts of the

Table 6.6 Household Income Ranking in 1989 and 2006 (Number of Respondents)

	1–3 (Low Income)		4–7 (Medium Income)		8–10 (High Income)		I don't know		Total respondents
	2006	1989	2006	1989	2006	1989	2006	1989	
Kazakhstan	299	175	645	526	51	158	5	141	1,000
Kyrgyzstan	168	88	742	524	58	267	32	121	1,000
Tajikistan	225	59	709	450	44	245	22	246	1,000
Uzbekistan	225	82	756	596	16	217	3	105	1,000
Total	917	404	2,852	2,096	169	887	62	613	4,000

Source: EBRD, *Life in transition*, 2006 (http://www.ebrd.com/pages/research).

population. Therefore, according to the results of a poll taken by the authors in 2010 as part of the European Training Foundation research for the development of HC in Tajikistan, a third of primary school students taking part in the poll (33.8) do not plan to continue their education, because going to university or a secondary professional educational institution is too expensive for them. The poll also shows that 66.7 per cent of respondents believe that poor people in Tajikistan have limited educational opportunities and cannot afford to study in universities.[50]

Income differentiation has a negative impact on education accessibility right at the school level. Table 6.7 shows that children from families that belong to the richest quintile have a much higher attendance coefficient–89.2 per cent–than children from families belonging to the poorest quintile–79.6 per cent. Moreover, girls from rich households attend school at a rate of 83.6 per cent, which is much higher than that of girls from poor households, which is just 70.2 per cent. It should be kept in mind that come high school there

Table 6.7 Net Attendance Coefficient for Secondary Educational Institutions (2005)

		Total	Women	Men
Place of residence	City	84.8	77.9	90.7
	Village	81.4	73.1	88.7
Age	12	95.6	92.1	98.4
	13	93.4	89.3	97.0
	14	91.6	87.0	96.3
	15	84.1	72.8	93.3
	16	70.1	53.9	84.0
	17	61.6	45.4	76.7
Quintile consumption	Poorest	79.6	70.2	87.6
	Second	78.8	67.8	88.9
	Average	81.5	73.7	88.2
	Fourth	83.4	78.2	88.1
	Richest	89.2	83.6	94.1

Source: State Statistics Committee of the Republic of Tajikistan, 2005, *op. cit.*

are virtually no girls left. Almost all 17-year-old girls who continue their education come from families, which are part of the three most prosperous quintiles.

The high cost of education at all educational institutions in Tajikistan, including backdoor payments at schools, is a significant hurdle to receiving an education. Research from the World Bank tracks a clear link between money being collected in schools and the number of children who do not attend class for financial reasons.[51]

Tuition for secondary specialized, and especially higher, education is much higher than school expenses, and poor families have virtually no means to cover it. World Bank research shows that approximately 50 per cent of Tajik household expenses are spent on secondary education, while the majority of their expenses are spent on higher education.[52] For instance, the official annual tuition alone for paid groups in the Tajikistan Technical University is 1,200 dollars.

Moreover, students from rich families study for free much more often–or even receive state scholarships–than students from poor families. Almost half of university students study in groups paid for by the state. In other words, they do not pay for their education out of their own pocket. Since being accepted to university is non-transparent and involves graft, poor students are unable to make these unofficial payments when applying for state scholarships. Therefore, they are unable to get access to state financing. The cost of these unofficial payments when applying to university varies widely, from 1,500 dollars at the Tajikistan Technical University to 8,000 dollars at the Law School of Tajikistan National University, while at the Medical School they reach 15 to 20,000 dollars.[53]

The inequality, which set in during the years of the transitional period, in access to education at all stages between rich and poor groups of the population in Tajikistan continue to grow. The difference in the coefficients of inclusion of elementary education in the higher and lower quintiles of consumption increased from 1.05 (1999) to 1.07 (2007). The difference in the coefficients of inclusion, in terms of secondary education, between the richest and poorest quintiles rose from 1.09 (1999) to 1.24 (2007). Inequality among university students is even higher, with 72 per cent of students in

2007 having been from families belonging to the first two richest quintiles, while the share of students from the poorest quintile was only 5 per cent.[54]

In this respect, the most vulnerable are poor young people from rural areas. A poll conducted as part of HC research showed that school children from rural areas quit school twice as often because of school tuition costs and three times more often because of the need to make money.

Rural residents are also limited in their access to education because of a low level of education. Graduates of rural schools have few actual opportunities to continue their education at the university level. This claim is supported by the public opinion of the quality of school education: rural residents in Tajikistan are much less satisfied by the level of school education than urban residents. Only 43.1 per cent of urban respondents and 26.2 per cent of rural respondents gave high marks to the quality of secondary education, while 4.6 per cent of urban respondents and 30.8 per cent of rural respondents believe that the quality of secondary education in Tajikistan is very low.[55]

The Impact of Accumulated Human Capital on Income Differentiation

Now we will look at the reverse impact of human capital on income differentiation. If accumulated HC had a positive impact on income differentiation in a number of post-Soviet countries, such as Russia, in Tajikistan this dependence was much weaker.[56]

How much the accumulated HC factor impacts income differentiation can be judged according to how effective education is. If the years spent on education lead to higher income, then a person can take the decision to obtain a supplemental education and not search for work. Therefore, the expected benefit from education plays a critical role in analysing various stimuli for acquiring human capital.

Analysing the effect from education, as a rule, is done by comparing worker salaries with various levels of education. Since the information was not available, the coefficient between household incomes in Tajikistan and the education level of the heads of these households was studied. Of course, some distortions may be caused by a various number of workers in a household; nonetheless, this type of study can give us an idea of the main trends.[57]

Figure 6.2 shows that the incomes of households, the heads of which have an incomplete or complete secondary education, are virtually identical. Simultaneously, the line denoting the incomes of families, the heads of which have a professional education, is shifted to the right and reaches $88–145. The monthly incomes of households, the heads of which have a complete professional education, hit their peak at $145 and quickly fall to the level of households where the heads have a higher education and have a more uniform distribution of the level of income.

The denoted trends give the grounds to make several conclusions. First, a professional education is capable of significantly increasing monthly income, but does not raise a household's income to the highest level. A household head's university education helps increase the family's income from extremely low to average, while it can also raise the family's income to the extremely high level. Figure 6.2 shows that the positive effect of higher education on income is more

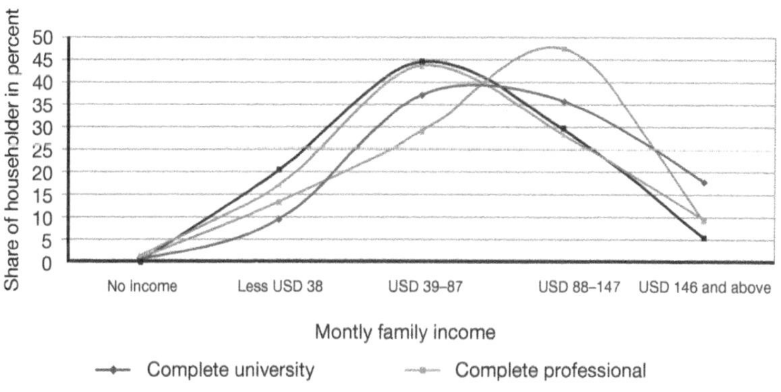

Figure 6.2 Distribution of Monthly Income by the Educational Status of Head of Household

Source: Author calculations based on materials from Household Research materials 2006.

stable than that of professional education. Therefore, professional education can be viewed as the chief tool in decreasing the scale of extreme poverty, but is not the best way to expand family income.

Figure 6.3 shows the dependence of a household's well-being on the head's educational status. This graph is similar to graph 2 in terms of the distribution of the level of dependence of a household's well being on the education level of family heads, namely basic, secondary, professional, technical and higher education. The curve, however, of the dependence of households on the level of their head's education shows a slight inclination toward less educated household heads. The curve levels of well-being for households, the heads of which have a secondary, professional or higher education, mainly coincide, while household heads with a higher education end up somewhat more often in the group of average and higher levels of well-being.

Models show that education and increasing human capital can lift households out of extreme poverty, but do not have a significant impact on achieving a higher level of well-being. The presumption can be made that the weak dependence of the level of income on the level of education in Tajikistan is explained by the condition of the institutional environment (weakness of formal institution, high level

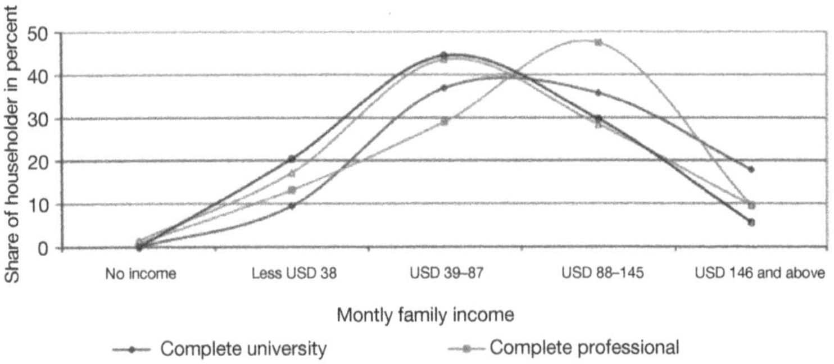

Figure 6.3 Distribution of Family Wealth Status by Educational Status of the Head of Household
Source: Author calculations based on materials from Household Research materials 2006.

of corruption, etc.), the unofficial, though steadfast, barriers in the labour market, which manifest themselves through the complex link in human and social capital (access to networks, communications, background, etc.). Empirical research was conducted on this topic in Russia.[58] The correlation of human and social capital during the transitional period, however, has barely been studied on the basis of materials of Central Asian countries.

Conclusions

In examining the development of human capital in Tajikistan during the post-Soviet era, features can be found that are characteristic of all post-Soviet countries: the decline in HC during the first decade after the collapse of the USSR stemming from armed conflict, the exasperation of massive social and economic difficulties, the fall in economic activity, the dismantling of the state, the degeneration of the structural transformation of the economy, which led to a change in the employment structure, and the waning of demand on the labour market. Tajikistan continues to see high economic growth rates that started at the beginning of the 21st century, which as a result has led to growth in the accumulation of HC, although the trend of its decline in terms of professional skills is continuing. Despite the specific quantitative increase in HC over the past years, Tajikistan has still not reached its level from back in 1991. When comparing the development of HC in Tajikistan with other countries, then we should denote that it is lagging behind Indonesia, China and Vietnam, which had the worst starting points at the beginning of the transitional period.[59] At the same time, Tajikistan continues to have a significantly higher level of human capital than countries with a similar level of GDP, such as sub-Saharan region countries.[60]

Overall, Tajikistan in many respects (income, level of corruption, institutional development, etc.) can be viewed as a part of the South; however, at the same time, this new South has a strong idiosyncracy to it that is the result of the previous years of Soviet modernization, with the development of HC being one of the most notable and original features of it.

In contemplating what determined the trajectory of the development of HC in post-Soviet Tajikistan, we highlighted the impact of social and economic inequalities as one of the most important factors. In examining the link between social and economic inequalities and the development of HC in terms of the impact of accumulated HC on income differentiation, we discovered that education and increasing HC in Tajikistan can serve as a tool for escaping extreme poverty, but they do not have a remarkable effect on achieving a higher level of well-being. Therefore, we can presuppose that a significant component of income differentiation can be explained not by the inequality in HC, but by other factors, such as political relations, the institutional environment and social capital. The last of these factors has a direct impact on HC, because part of HC is created by the development of social networks; however, in order to speak more specifically on these factors, research needs to be conducted on the unofficial and official social institutes and political networks, unofficial employment structures, and the network interactions of companies and markets.

When we were examining the impact of social and economic inequalities on the development of HC in Tajikistan, we discovered that they create large barriers to accumulating HC. Gender inequality in access to education has an especially negative effect on HC. The gender imbalance during the transitional period led to a decline in HC not only in the short term, but in the long term as well.

Income inequality has become a significant hurdle for developing HC. Even with a relatively low Genie index, income inequality is still a barrier to access professional, and especially higher, education that cannot be overcome. Therefore, the conclusion can be made that the growing social and economic inequalities in Tajikistan do not stimulate, but rather hinder, the accumulation, redistribution and effective use of HC.

Speaking of areas for further research in HC, it should be acknowledged that the political, social and cultural factors of the structural transformation of the economy and changes in the labour market that are linked to both the Soviet past and to the traditional culture in Central Asian countries, including Tajikistan, are important aspects, but they cannot be studied. Therefore, studying the chief social and economic factors impacting the development of HC is a relevant issue in researching the continuing transformative processes in countries of the so-called 'new South', Related social capital, social networks, and social and cultural factors also need to be researched; these factors are linked to employment and social transfers. The distribution of new information and communication technology and their impact on HC is an important area in future research.

Notes

1 Shultz, T., 'Human Capital', in *The International Encyclopaedia of the Social Sciences*, New York, vol. 6, 1968; Becker, G., *Human Capital*, New York: Columbia University Press, 1964; Mintzer, G., *The Production of Human Capital and The Life cycle of Earnings: Variations on a Theme*, Working Paper of the NBER, n°4838, 1994.

2 Vishnevsky, A.G., *The Sickle and Rouble: Conservative Modernisation in the USSR*, M.: OGI, 1998, pp. 290–6.

3 Kusnets, S., *Modern Economic Growth: Rate, Structure, and Spread*, Yale University Press: New Heaven, London, 1966, pp. 81–2 183–5, 286–93.

4 Dowling, Wignaraja, *Central Asia After Fifteen Years of Transition*, ADB, July 2006.

5 World Bank, *Republic of Tajikistan. Evaluating Poverty Statistics*, March 2009, p. 84.

6 State Statistics Committee of the Republic of Tajikistan, *Population of the Republic of Tajikistan 2000*, Dushanbe, 2002, p. 39.

7 State Statistics Committee of the Republic of Tajikistan, *Tajikistan Living Standards Measurement Survey 2007*, Dushanbe, 2009.

8 Unfortunately, the data from the Tajikistan census conducted in 2010 on the level of education of the public was not available at the time this chapter was being written. Two volumes are no longer in print: vol. 1 'The number and location of the population of the Republic of Tajikistan', and vol. 2 'Population of the Republic of Tajikistan in terms of sex, age and marriage'.

9 State Statistics Committee of the Republic of Tajikistan, *Results of the All-Union Census of 1989 for the Tajik SSR*, vol. II, Dushanbe, 1991.

10 IMF, *Republic of Tajikistan: Poverty Reduction Strategy Paper Progress Report*, IMF Country Report n°04/280, August 2004.
11 State Statistics Committee of the Republic of Tajikistan, *Education in the Republic of Tajikistan*, Dushanbe, 2009, p. 7.
12 *Ibid.*
13 To evaluate the scale and changes of investment in education in Tajikistan after gaining independence, let's compare it with the share of GDP invested in education in North African countries during the period of decolonization and 30 years later. If, at the beginning of the 1960s the aggregate private and state expenditures for education, healthcare and science in these countries did not exceed 4–5 per cent of GDP, then from 1994 to 1996 they grew on average up to 10–11 per cent of GDP (Global Competitiveness Report (http://data.worldbank.org/indicator/)).
14 World Bank, 2008.
15 State Statistics Committee of the Republic of Tajikistan, 2009, *op. cit.*, p. 9.
16 *Ibid.*, p. 27.
17 State Statistics Committee of the Republic of Tajikistan, 2010, *op. cit.*, p. 4.
18 State Statistics Committee of the Republic of Tajikistan, 2002, *op. cit.*, p. 65.
19 State Statistics Committee of the Republic of Tajikistan, *Preliminary Results of the 2010 Census and Housing Statistics*, Dushanbe, 2011, pp. 12–3.
20 World Bank, *IDA/WB Country Strategy Memorandum*, World Bank, 2003.
21 World Development Indicators database.
22 State Statistics Committee of the Republic of Tajikistan, 2010, *op. cit.*, p. 90.
23 PRSP, 2002, p. 23.
24 Kuddusov, J., *Labour Policy in Tajikistan*, IPC Soc-service: Dushanbe, 2010, p. 36 (http://www.labour.tj/Draft%203%20report%20Labour%20policy.pdf).
25 State Statistics Committee of the Republic of Tajikistan, *Amount and Location of the Population of the Republic of Tajikistan (vol. 1)*, State Statistical Committee publishing house: Dushanbe, 2012, p. 31.
26 UNDP, *Tajikistan Human Development Report*, Zhibek zholy publishing house: Dushanbe, 1997, p. 35.
27 State Statistics Committee of the Republic of Tajikistan, 2010, *op. cit.*
28 Olimov, J., *UNDP Human Development Report, The Informal Economy in Tajikistan,* Dushanbe, 2007, p. 11.
29 *Ibid.*, p. 98.
30 World Bank, *Republic of Tajikistan. Country Economic Memorandum*, 2011, p. 70.
31 Olimov, J., *op. cit.*, pp. 48–9.
32 Cox, E., Ureta, M., 'International Migration, Remittances and Schooling: Evidence from El Salvador', *Journal of Development Economics*, 2003, vol. 72/3, pp. 429–61; de Haan, A. 'Migration in the Development Studies Literature: Has it come out of marginality?' Paper For the UNU-WIDER Jubilee Conference Future of Development Economics, United Nations University, 2005.

33 McKenzie, D.J., Rapoport, H., *Can Migration reduce educational attainment? Evidence from Mexico*, World Bank Policy Research Working Paper n°3952, Washington, 2006.

34 Olimova, S., 'The Impact of Labour Migration on Human Capital: The Case of Tajikistan', *Revue Europeenne des Migrations Internationales*, 2010, vol. 26/3.

35 Only 28 per cent of labour migrants from Tajikistan are working in Russia according to their profession (Kuddusov, J., *op. cit.*)

36 Olimova, S., *op. cit.*

37 ILO, *Migration and Development in Tajikistan. Emigration, Return and Diaspora*, Moscow: ILO, 2010 (http://www.ilo.org/public/english/).

38 Unicef, *Impact of Labour Migration on 'Children Left Behind' in Tajikistan*, Dushanbe, 2011.

39 State Statistics Committee of the Republic of Tajikistan, 2007, *op. cit.*

40 State Statistics Committee of the Republic of Tajikistan, *Men and Women of the Republic of Tajikistan,* State Statistical Committee publishing house: Dushanbe, 2002b, p. 52.

41 State Statistics Committee of the Republic of Tajikistan, 2010, *op. cit.*, p. 62.

42 The Aga Khan Development Organisation (AKDO) includes agencies conducting programmes in economic development, supporting rural areas, education, culture, healthcare and financial services. Prince Karim Aga Khan, the spiritual leader of Nizarit-Ismaili, founded the AKDO. Ismaili Muslims make up the majority of the population of Gorno Badakhshan.

43 State Statistics Committee of the Republic of Tajikistan, 2012, *op. cit.*, p. 31.

44 Olimova, S., 'A Quick Analysis of Child Labour in the Cities of Tajikistan', Dushanbe, 2005; Unicef, *op. cit.*

45 State Statistics Committee of the Republic of Tajikistan, 2010, *op. cit.*, p. 62.

46 State Statistics Committee of the Republic of Tajikistan, 2005, *op. cit.*, pp. 75–6.

47 Unicef, *op. cit.*

48 World Income Inequality Database (WIID), May 2007; World Bank, 2005, *op. cit.*, p. 56.

49 Brown, R., Olimova, S., Boboev, M., 'Country Report on Remittances of International Migrants in Tajikistan', in Asian Development Bank, *Study on International Migrants' Remittances in Central Asia and South Caucasus*, 2008 (http://www.adb.org/Documents/Reports/Consultant/40038-REG/40038-04-REG-TACR.pdf).

50 Olimova, S., Olimov, M., *Relationship between Human Capital Development and Equity in the Republic of Tajikistan*, Torino, European Training Foundation, 2011. (http://www.etf.europa.eu/webatt.nsf/0/10EDEAE3D0D37987C125789D0036C28D/$file/Final%20report_Tajikistan_for%20copying.pdf).

51 World Bank, 2011, *op. cit.*, p. 72.

52 World Bank, 2009, *op. cit.*

53 Infomation collected through interviews.

54 State Statistics Committee of the Republic of Tajikistan, 2007, *op. cit.*

55 Olimova, S., Olimov, M., 2010, *op. cit.*

56 Mitra, P., Yemtsov, R., *Increasing Inequality in Transition Economies: Is There More to Come?* World Bank. Policy Research Working Paper n°4007, Washington, 2006; Sabirianova, K.Z., 'The Great Human Capital Reallocation: A Study of Occupational Mobility in Transitional Russia', *Journal of Comparative Economics*, 2002, vol. 30/1.

57 The link between household incomes and the education level of their heads was studied based on material from the data base, which was received as a result of Standard of Living Study that was conducted by the authors in 2006. The selection was representative of the entire country and included 1,000 households across Tajikistan. *Household Research materials, 2006*. Dushanbe: Sharq, 2006 (manuscript).

58 Dobrinin, A.I., Dyatlov, S.A., Tsyrenova, E.D., *Human Capital in the Transit Economy. Creation, Evaluation and Efficient Use*, St Petersburg: Science, 1999, pp. 7–29, 69–95; Cox, D. *et al.*, 'Economic Support of Families by Private Individuals during the Transition to a Market Economy' in Klugman, D. (ed.), *Poverty in Russia. State Policy and the Public's Reaction*, Washington: The Economic Development Institute of the World Bank, 1998, pp. 251–92.

59 The comparison with the second and third countries is especially interesting, because they also were making a transition, although they were following their own course (World Development Indicators database).

60 World Bank, 2009, *op. cit.*

CHAPTER 7

MEASURES OF POVERTY IN THE CAUCASUS AND CENTRAL ASIA: INTERNATIONAL APPROACHES AND SPECIFICITIES OF SOUTHERN COUNTRIES OF THE FORMER SOVIET UNION[1]

Cécile Lefèvre and Sophie Hohmann
(Ceped, University Paris Descartes, Sorbonne Paris Cité and Ined);
(Cercec, EHESS and Ined)

The Caucasus and Central Asia are rarely covered in studies regarding development. The principal international indicators for comparison (such as the HDI (Human Development Index), or absolute poverty measures of $1.25 or $2 per day) classify them as medium developed countries and their characteristics are difficult to interpret. Use of composite indicators (including HDI) 'raises' the country level due to high literacy and school attendance rates. The reality is that poverty concerns the majority of the population in these countries, still affected by the significant economic crises that followed the collapse of the USSR and struggling to find an appropriate development model. Inequalities have deepened, social spending remains low, access to social services, that was promoted under Soviet rule, is now being debated.

This chapter will consider the different means and concepts for measuring poverty (relative/absolute, monetary/living conditions, spending or resource based) and study how countries use these concepts, in particular with regard to international comparisons, recommendations of international organizations and the Millennium Development Goals (MDG). It contributes to works on the sociology of measure and quantification.[2] Focus will thus be on the measure of poverty and its uses and not on how populations perceive poverty and vulnerability.

Generally speaking, the Southern Caucasus and Central Asia implement an absolute monetary threshold above which a person can purchase a basket of basic goods based on calorie requirements. This is in fact the 'subsistence minimum'. However, several measures of poverty are calculated depending on the country, using methods which are not altogether explained, the relevance of which are more or less questioned. It appears that the method adopted reflects the political strategy of a given country. Georgia, for example, tends to minimize poverty figures in an attempt to align itself with the West whereas countries such as Tajikistan use poverty figures to justify their request for international aid.

Is the Question of the Measure of Poverty Asked in the Same Way When Considering the Caucasus and Central Asia and Other Developing Countries?

Few attempts have been made to examine the methods of analysis used to study developing countries in the context of research carried out on current developments in Central Asia and the Caucasus. Somewhat surprising given that these newly independent countries were also classified as 'developing' by international institutions and non-governmental organizations following the significant economic, social and political crises of the 1990s. International aid to Central Asia, and to a lesser extent to the Caucasus, thus tended towards development aid as opposed to transitional aid during the 1990s.

With this in mind, the entry of Central Asia and the Caucasus on to the global stage in the post Soviet period could be characterised as a form of 'third worldization'. It could be argued that the delimitation between 'developing' and 'developed' countries shifted from the frontier of the USSR to the Southern border of Russia.[3]

Opposing former metropolises and former colonies, the 'developing country' concept is a post-colonial phenomenon which begs the question of the imperial nature of the USSR and the use of theoretical concepts (dependency theory, post-colonial studies, etc.) that gave rise to the idea of the 'developing country'. The direction currently taken by Central Asia and the Caucasus also raises the issue of how development fits in with the idea of globalization. An analysis is necessary of the ideal of transition, and its application, as developed by international organizations in the 1990s to replace the socialist model with a democratic political system, an economy based on liberal capitalist principles and Euro–Atlantic geopolitical positioning.[4] A review of transition policies will throw light on the diverse paths taken by the eight countries that make up Central Asia (ex-republics of the USSR) and the Southern Caucasus and help to understand why only some of these countries moved into the South division after their independence.

The post-Soviet era corresponds to a period of differentiation and individualism for the societies, economies and territories of the new independent states. Proximity to Russia, however, remains a key element. Natural resources, in particular oil and gas, and the importance of migrations or international relations (the potential or not for migrant workers or diaspora to transfer money), among other factors, contribute to the varied socio-economic transformation of these countries, and could even be argued to have contributed towards creating the outlines of segmentation. As for the ex-USSR, all these countries experienced economic crises marked by de-industrialization and deep recession at the beginning of the 1990s.[5] In addition, Armenia suffered an earthquake in 1988 that adversely affected the socio-economic situation. Some countries were also affected by political conflicts, some armed; between Georgia and Russia, between Azerbaijan and Armenia (Nagorno-Karabakh conflict), civil war in Tajikistan, terrorist attacks in Uzbekistan, criminal massacres in Kyrgyzstan,[6] all of which hindered economic growth and social development.

The 1990s was a dark period for these countries. The disindustrialization process, the partial financial withdrawal of Russia, the breakdown of the labour market structure and privileged trading status that once existed at the heart of the ex-USSR, the increasingly important role of money in the economy and inflation all gave rise to a general impoverishment of the population (see Figure 7.1) (officially the percentage of the population touched by poverty was 50–60 per cent, at a time when the notion of poverty was only just coming into being) and increasing inequality as privatization commenced.[7] All of the above raised the question of a 'third world ex-USSR' as mentioned by Jacques Nagels in his work *La tiers-mondisation de l'ex-URSS?*[8]

Further study into the poverty measures in these countries and their influence on the 'measure of development' appeared necessary, for various reasons.

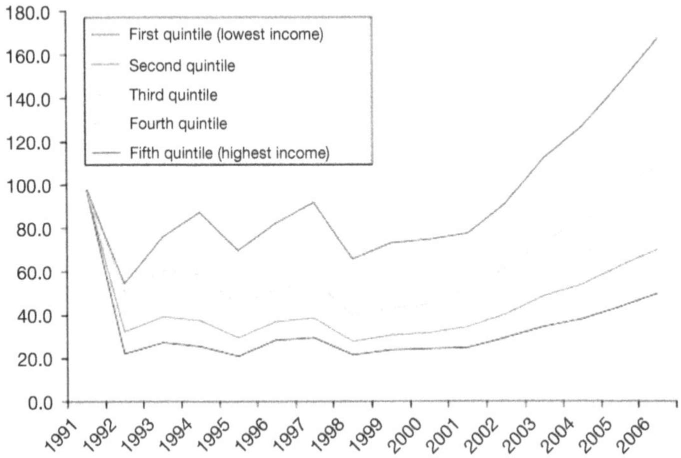

Figure 7.1 Progression of Real Income in Russia, per Quintile (base 100)
Source: Rosstat, Federal Service of Statistics (http://www.gks.ru/).

(1) **To reveal societal transformations**: This notion was not officially recognized until the 1990s, although measure thereof was crucial from the outset with a population becoming rapidly, noticeably and extensively impoverished. This raises the question of which indicators were used at the time? Were different approaches to poverty being discussed? What role did Soviet and national traditions play and what were the recommendations of international organizations?

(2) **To reveal the irrelevance of certain indicators**: At a time when the population was clearly becoming impoverished, standard international indicators were unable to provide a realistic picture of the situation in the Caucasus and Central Asia. These regions were perceived as having a high or medium HDI, it was difficult to estimate daily monetary incomes due to the weak monetization of the economy and services were still officially free or subsidized. We are thus looking at a region where poverty became evident albeit immeasurable when using classic international measures.

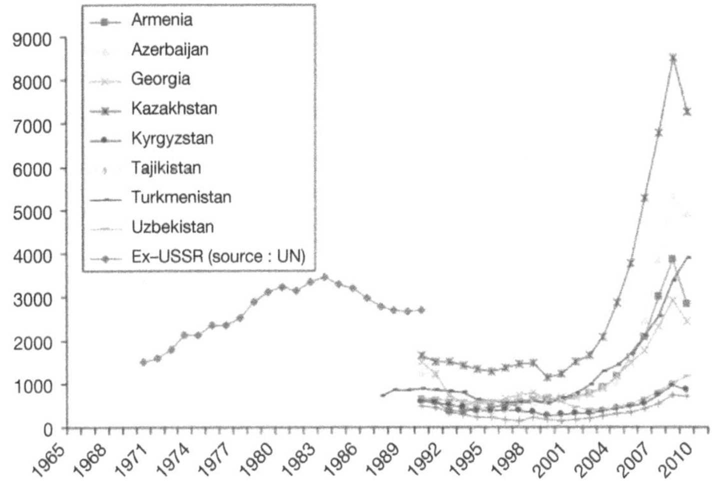

Figure 7.2 GDP Evolution Per Inhabitant in US Dollars in the Caucasus and Central Asia
Source: WHO (http://data.euro.who.int/hfadb/).

(3) **To reveal the different paths of development**: Oil rich countries (Kazakhstan, Azerbaijan, Turkmenistan) experienced rapid GDP growth in the 2000s, particularly during the second half. Georgia and Armenia experienced moderate growth, an improvement all the same, whereas countries with little resources such as Kyrgyzstan and Tajikistan remained poverty stricken (Figure 7.2). The various paths of development were thus mapped out. Tools for measuring poverty, and use thereof, have become more complex, given the different national and international contexts and issues for each country.

Different Ways of Measuring Poverty: Theoretical Concepts

Most publications link poverty rates (the percentage of the population living below a given threshold) to an unequivocal notion with no consideration of measurability or comparison. In reality, the rate is based on a number of choices and hypotheses and there are numerous official ways of measuring poverty.[9]

Relative Measure/Absolute Measure

One idea distinguishes relative and absolute measures of poverty. This concept differentiates European Union member states from developing countries but also from the United States and the former USSR.

The idea of measuring poverty absolutely is simple: a threshold for poverty is set and anyone living with financial resources below this threshold is considered to be poor. Two methods are used to set the threshold. Comparative studies and international organizations usually set the threshold at $1, or now more often $2, a day. A second method is to constitute a basket of basic needs goods and services and attribute monetary value to it. A threshold of $1 or $2 a day would seemingly have the advantage of being simple to use and facilitate international comparison. However, such simplicity fails to take into account the true value of the dollar in different countries. Although we consider dollars as 'purchasing power', the value and relevance of a given consumable item varies depending on the country.

The monetary value of a basket of goods takes into account local needs (for example, the cost of heating in colder countries) or specific needs (the basket of food items based on calorie requirements can be adjusted for men, women, infants and the elderly). Although the content of the basket is fixed, its monetary value can vary depending on market rates, an advantage in the event of significant price fluctuations. This method is thus more adaptable to real situations but less user friendly for comparisons at international level.

European countries have officially adopted a different method for measuring poverty, in relative terms. Strictly speaking, it is more a measure of inequalities than a measure of poverty. The poverty threshold is fixed based on the median income of the population (thus dividing the population in two, 50 per cent low income and 50 per cent high income). A person is considered poor when he/she brings in an income below or equal to 60 per cent of the median income.

Monetary or Living Conditions Measures

These measures apply to an economy where income and consumption are monetized, which is not always the case, particularly in countries where self-sufficiency and bartering are commonplace. The measures are also short term, the absolute measure of poverty in particular takes into account basic needs and consumption necessary for survival from a physiological viewpoint, but fails to consider the acquisition of equipment, for example.

These limits lead to the development of measures of poverty that focus more on an objective assessment of individual living conditions. So instead of setting a monetary threshold, we identify a number of criteria, possession of or access to, fixes the level of poverty. This could include running water and electricity in the household, eating meat at least twice a week, providing three meals a day, owning a motorized vehicle, a refrigerator, a mobile phone, etc. This measure can be used in statistical surveys on household budgets, living conditions, etc. and the basket is of course adjustable and flexible. This method has given rise to numerous works, in part methodological. For European countries, Jérôme Accardo and Thibaut de Saint Pol have shown that, based on population consensus, we can make a list of unacceptable deprivations or 'poverty in terms of living conditions'.[10] This list has its limits, however, as it refers only to vital needs. The 'list of deprivations' varies throughout Europe according to public opinion, making it difficult to use poverty in terms of living conditions in international comparisons. For sub-Saharan African countries and Uzbekistan, and based on standardized surveys (Demographic and Health Survey), S. Hohmann and M. Garenne[11] propose an index of material well-being (allowing for comparisons between developing countries) as opposed to an index based on deprivations. This index uses the same method: a list of criteria (in particular accommodation conditions and possession of goods) based on material living conditions that can be considered objectively.

Objective or Subjective Measure

The measures below (Figure 7.3) seek to identify and quantify the poor based on criteria used in studies or reviews. They do not, however, take into account the way an individual or household perceives their situation.

Do they see themselves as poor? Do they suffer from lack of money in certain situations? It is clearly not easy to incorporate these questions into statistical measures but some household surveys now seek to discern perceived poverty (questions such as 'Do you have difficulties to make the ends meet?', 'Do you see yourself as poor?').

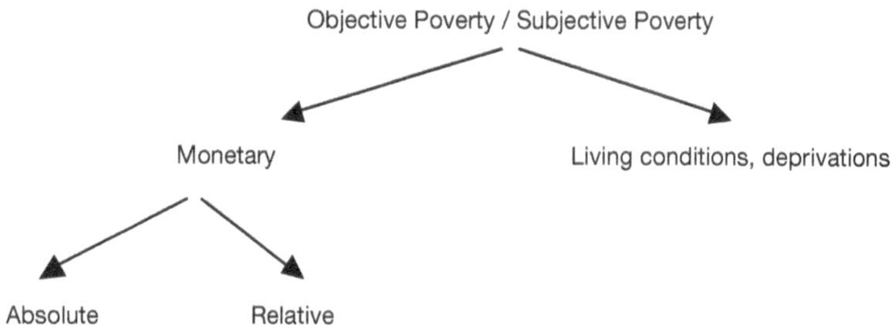

Figure 7.3 Connection Between the Different Concepts of Poverty Measures

When all Statistic Measures are Used and Compared

Numerous socio-economic works now combine these different concepts and data sources to highlight the complex and contextual nature of measuring poverty. Whether in Madagascar,[12] Romania[13] or Russia,[14] we note a certain overlapping of populations considered to be poor depending on the concept applied, thus confirming the multidimensional nature of poverty. Each indicator focuses on a population type or poverty factor. Subjective poverty is linked to socially related variables and transformations. Objective criteria identify different socio-demographic groups, for example living conditions and deprivation measures provide a finer analysis of the poverty of families with children and absolute monetary poverty highlights the poverty of the aged population in Russia. 'These results prove that poverty reduction strategies cannot be based on a sole instrument, or focus on one area, rather they need to refer to a variety of measures covering different dimensions.'[15]

The Measure of Poverty in Southern Countries of the ex-USSR: Soviet Tradition of 'Minimum Subsistence Level'

The notion of poverty has always had strong ideological connotations in the USSR. The change in terminology is telling. The word poverty (*bednost* in Russian) was first used in administrative texts and scientific, sociological and economic works with the arrival of perestroika in the mid-1980s.

Since 1986–87, the poverty measure has been based on one indicator, the poverty line or minimum subsistence level (*prožitočnyj minimum* in Russian). It plays a central role in the estimation and publication of the number of poor but also serves as criteria for operational thresholds in the social assistance system. The idea of minimum subsistence refers to poverty in absolute as opposed to relative and subjective terms. Although it was adopted at the end of the 1980s, the idea of defining poverty based on a minimum list of consumables had already been used during the first years of the Soviet regime.

According to Tatiana Jarygina,[16] first attempts to calculate a minimum subsistence level as a poverty indicator date from the October Revolution. It was initially conceived to ensure the creation of a minimum wage, as stated in the 1918 Employment Code. No single methodology was established and the minimum subsistence was calculated for different categories of workers and seen as a physiological minimum taking into consideration a list of essential food items and some other expenditures (non-food items and services). The list of consumables was determined in two different ways: a standard method based on an estimation of physiological needs or a more empirical method based on studies of actual consumption budgets. It is worth noting that considerable work had already been carried out at this time to provide statistics on family budgets, initiated by the local administration body in tsarist Russia, the *zemstva*.

The work carried on by the *zemstva*,[17] in both social and statistical domains, was two-fold. The 1864 Statute distinguished mandatory (state-delegated) and optional work for the *zemstva*. Mandatory work included the management and administration of a subsistence service, set up in 1834 to assist the population in case of food shortages, and the management and upkeep of provincial hospitals, hospices, orphanages and asylums. According to article 6 of the Statute, optional work meant the *zemstva* should 'contribute to the improvement of public health and education'. In order to do this, it was first necessary to determine the scale of work and better understand the population in question. The *zemstva* thus carried out important work to develop statistical studies,[18] in particular social studies on livelihoods and peasant poverty.

The *zemstva* approach in social statistics continued until the 1920s, the 1922 conference of Russian statisticians examining the statistics of family budgets. During the NEP era (1921–28), a minimum subsistence calculation was used to indicate the cost of living, but not as criteria for fixing the minimum wage. As for unemployment,[19] the 1930s brought with it the declaration of the eradication of the causes of poverty and thus the calculation of minimum(s) of subsistence was done away with. This occurred at a time when the Soviet state was failing to guarantee the living and security conditions promised to workers by the October Revolution and an increased social security debt, in the context of large-scale economic industrialization (with the launch of the first five year plan in 1928), hindered access to these rights and provided proof of a deep-rooted incoherence within the system.

From the 1960s to 1980s, new studies on family budgets were carried out but remained largely unpublished; neither were they used to fix a poverty threshold, as such was an unmentionable notion. Certain data on income distribution remained secret. According to the then acceptable concept of '*maloobespečennost*' (literally modest income, little social protection), families were considered to dispose of a low income if the average income per head was less than half of the average income of the population, which is finally a notion of relative poverty very similar to that used in Europe today.

A 1987 decree of the USSR Council of Ministers authorized the calculation of a minimum consumption budget as a tool for the reform of pension and salary calculations. The minimum wage was thus fixed at 150 per cent of this basket of minimum consumables. The budget corresponded to a list of 1,000 referenced products, comprising food items (half) and non-food items (including long-term goods). The value of the basket was established on the basis of prices fixed by the state. Prior to the reforms of 1989, between 16 and 25 per cent of the population were considered poor on the basis of this threshold (differences in evaluation were linked to the prices used to fix the value of the basket).[20] Inflation led to a marked increase in the rate in 1991–92 (up to 70 per cent). Consequently, a new minimum subsistence calculation was elaborated by the Ministry of Labour in 1992, restricting the products on the list.[21]

In light of the above, it appears that the notion and the calculation of a minimum subsistence level as a poverty threshold did not appear with the liberalization of the economy from 1991 onwards but rather with perestroika (1985–89), which reconsidered ideas that themselves first appeared in the period 1918–28, on the creation of the economy and of Soviet society. The concepts of absolute poverty and minimum subsistence continue to influence debates on poverty and the eligibility criteria of social assistance in Russia today.[22] Those with an average household income per head lower than the minimum subsistence level were considered to be poor. When revised in 1992, it was considered to be a short-term or 'transition' indicator, to cover a limited period of economic crisis. This explains the absence of expenditure on long-term goods and an insufficient representation of expenditure on clothes. The concept has, however, endured and even revised today still corresponds to a minimum list comprised largely of food items (representing 70 per cent) and a notion of absolute poverty.

All ex-USSR countries initially applied this analysis and poverty measure as set out by the USSR and later adopted by Russia. In the 1990s, Central Asia and the Caucasus adopted the concept of absolute poverty, based on the money value required to satisfy physiological needs, as was by then also applied in Russia. Thereafter, the concept was adapted and supplemented by each country, but the basis remained unchanged. The methodology of household surveys was reviewed, in particular after World Bank missions and recommendations. Influences diversified and the implications of a poverty measure became more complex.

Behind the Supposed Single Definition of Absolute Poverty, Various Methods and Indicators

Throughout the 1990s and early 2000s, the Caucasus and Central Asia followed the methodological stance employed by Russia, an absolute poverty approach, particularly as this corresponded to the views of international organizations and the World Bank. Most countries thus initially calculated a poverty threshold that corresponded to the notion of minimum subsistence (minimum value of a basket of basic goods, sometimes including services). They also measured the poverty rate using as a base an exogenously fixed limit of $1 or $2 per day. Some countries applied these measures simultaneously, to comply with the statistical requirements of international organizations, while others slowly prioritized the second method in favour of the first due to financial constraints or through a desire to simplify.

Table 7.1 Population Below the 'National Poverty Line', in Per Cent

Country	1995	1996	1997	1998	1999	2000	2001	2002	2003	2004	2005	2006	2007	2008
South-Eastern Europe														
Albania	–	–	–	–	–	–	–	25.4	–	–	18.5	–	–	12.4
Bosnia and Herzegovina	–	–	–	–	–	–	19.5	–	–	18.3	–	–	18.2	–
Croatia	–	–	–	–	–	–	17.2	18.2	16.9	16.7	17.5	17.0	18.0	–
Serbia	–	–	–	–	–	–	–	10.6	10.5	–	6.5	–	–	–
The former Yugoslav Republic of Macedonia	–	–	19.0	20.7	21.0	22.3	22.7	30.2	30.2	29.6	30.5	29.8	29.4	28.7
Turkey	–	–	–	–	–	–	–	27.0	28.1	25.6	20.5	17.8	17.8	17.1
Eastern Europe, Caucasus and Central Asia														
Armenia	–	–	–	–	–	–	50.9	49.7	42.9	34.6	29.8	26.5	25.0	23.5
Azerbaijan	68.1	–	–	–	–	–	49.6	46.7	44.7	40.2	29.3	20.8	15.8	13.2
Belarus	38.4	38.6	32.1	33.0	46.7	41.9	28.9	30.5	27.1	17.8	12.7	11.1	7.7	6.1
Georgia	–	–	46.2	50.2	51.8	51.8	51.1	52.1	54.5	27*	–	–	31.0	–
Kazakhstan	–	34.6	38.3	39.0	34.5	31.8	28.4	24.2	19.8	16.1	31.6*	18.2	12.7	12.1
Kyrgyzstan	–	43.5	43.0	54.9	55.3	62.6	56.4	54.8	49.9	45.9	43.1	39.9	35.0	31.7
Republic of Moldova	–	–	–	52.0	73.0	67.8	54.6	40.4	29.0	26.5	29.0	–	–	–
Russian Federation	–	–	–	–	–	29.0	–	19.6	20.3	17.6	17.7	15.2	13.3	13.5
Tajikistan	–	–	–	–	87.0	–	–	–	64.0	57.0	–	–	–	–
Ukraine	–	–	–	–	–	–	26.4	27.2	27.2	26.6	27.3	27.1	28.1	–
Uzbekistan	–	–	–	–	–	–	27.5	26.5	27.2	26.1	25.8	–	–	–

Source: UN, *The MDGs in Europe and Central Asia: Achievements, Challenges and the Way Forward*, Statistical Annex n°3, Table 1A, 2010, p. 109 (http://www.unece.org/fileadmin/DAM/commission/MDGs/2010_MDG_Optimized.pdf).

Reader's notes: The national poverty rate is the percentage of the total population living below the national poverty line. National poverty lines are set by individual countries, reflecting their population's basic needs for subsistence. The following are definitions applied in the reported countries.

Albania: Absolute poverty headcount (below Lek 4891 – Living Standards Measurement Survey), Source: Albania: Trends in Poverty 2002–2005–2008.

Bosnia and Herzegovina: National relative poverty line, set at 60% of median per capita consumption, Source: MDG update report, 2009.

Croatia: At risk of poverty, 60% of median equivalised income, Source: National Statistical Office – Household Budget Surveys for years 2001–2005, Eurostat for years 2006–2007.

Serbia: Population with money income below subsistence minimum level, Source: MDG report 2006.

The former Yugoslav Republic of Macedonia: Relative poverty (70% of median equivalised expenditure), Source: MDG report 2009, State Statistical Office.

Turkey: Income below subsistence minimum, complete poverty line (food and non-food), Source: MDG report 2005 for years 2002–2003, Poverty study 2008 for years 2004–2008.

Armenia: Consumption below the adult equivalent poverty line, Source: Integrated Living Conditions Survey (ILCS) 2004, 2008.

Azerbaijan: Absolute poverty line, Source: UNSD MDG database for years 1995–2001, State Statistical Committee (MDG indicators) for years 2002–2008.

Belarus: Below minimum subsistence budget, Source: National MDG report 2005 for years 1995–2004, National Statistical Office (Households Sample Surveys) for years 2005–2008.

Georgia: Official subsistence minimum, Source: National MDG report 2004–2005 for years 1997–2003, Human Development Report 2008 for years 2004 and 2007.

Kazakhstan: Population with income below official minimum subsistence, Source: National MDG report 2002, 2005, 2007 for years 1996–2006; National Statistical Office for year 2008.

Kyrgyzstan: Source: UNSD MDG database.

Republic of Moldova: Population with less than $2.15 per day PPP values, Source: National Human Development Report 2006.

Russian Federation: Population with money incomes below minimum subsistence level, Source: UNSD MDG database for year 2002, National Statistical Office – Russia in figures 2009 for years 2000, 2003–2008.

Tajikistan: Population living on less than US$2.15 per day. Source: Poverty Reduction Strategy of the republic of Tajikistan for 2007–2009.

Ukraine: Population below relative poverty line (75% of median individual total expenditure), Source: MDG report 2000 + 7.

Uzbekistan: Based on the 2,100 calories poverty line. Source: Welfare Improvement Strategy for Uzbekistan, 2007.

* Break in series due to change in methodology.

In light of the above, one must remain cautious. Although a poverty formula or official threshold may correspond to an absolute notion, it can also be based on varying indicators and definitions of poverty. Several poverty rates may be cited for the same country within one report. The latest 'country' report published by the UNDP states for example that 52 per cent of the Georgian population is poor according to the 2004 official subsistence minimum[23] and 27 per cent for the same year if we apply the income threshold of $2 per day per person. A United Nations report on the millennium development goals[24] cited several values for Tajikistan: 57 per cent of the population was considered to be poor in 2004 with the application of a threshold on $2.50 per day and 17 per cent if we apply the income threshold per person of $1 per day in 2008.

A table can apply one rate per country, but based on different definitions depending on the country. Definitions and readers' notes should be studied in detail (see Table 7.1). The information presented is not incorrect, each element has meaning and use, but caution should be exercised when using them to interpret and compare.

Use of Composite Scores (Human Development Indicator, Multidimensional Poverty Indicators, etc.): Insights and Limits for the Caucasus and Central Asia

As an alternative to the threshold of $1 to $2 per day, and particularly favoured by the World Bank, the UNDP developed the Human Development Indicator (HDI) in 1990, based on the works of Amartya Sen and Mahbub ul Haq. It rapidly became a reference in international comparisons of social development as it seemed less simplistic than the sole criteria of GDP per capita or dollars per day.

This indicator covers three aspects:

1. Health, measured by life expectancy at birth,
2. Education, measured in the 1990s by adult literacy rate and gross school attendance,
3. Standard of living in terms of GDP per inhabitant.

To what extent can this more complex indicator, going beyond a basic monetary approach, be applied to the developing countries of the ex-USSR? In reality, it does not reveal new data as these countries are shown to have an average life expectancy (compared internationally) and high literacy and school attendance rates. Hence, when international organizations applied the HDI to these countries, they were ranked high or medium (Map 7.1).

A characteristic, and by all means an accomplishment, of the former USSR is the high literacy rates attained several decades ago (Table 7.2). Literacy rates were officially in excess of 99 per cent in all countries according to data published by Unesco in 2009. The gross school attendance rate was between 95 per cent and 98 per cent. The sub-indicators of the 'education' dimension of the HDI thus rank the Caucasus and Central Asia at the top.

It is interesting to consider life expectancy at birth over an extended period of time. Alongside efforts on education, the Soviet state set up a branch-based health system that led to an initial epidemiological transition (fight against infectious diseases, generalised vaccinations and public health).[25] Thus, from the end of the 1960s to the end of the 1980s, life expectancy at birth in the Caucasus and Central Asia varied from 65 to 75 years. This

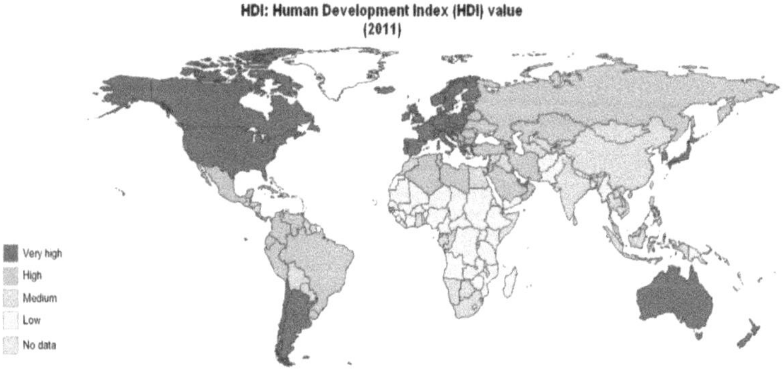

Map 7.1 Value of the Human Development Indicator in the World in 2007
Source: http://hdr.undp.org/en/data/map/.

Table 7.2 School Attendance and Literacy Indicators in the Caucasus and Central Asia (2009)

	Armenia	Georgia	Azerbaijan	Uzbekistan	Tajikistan	Kyrgyzstan
Primary school attendance rate						
Net	89%	89%	85%	89%	89%	89%
Gross	98%	98%	95%	98%	98%	98%
Adult literacy rate	99.5%	99.7%	99.5%	99.3%	99.7%	99.2%

Source: UNESCO Institute for Statistics (www.stats.uis.unesco.org).

intermediate situation, as compared to Mali and France on Figure 7.4, also contributed to a high HDI ranking for these countries.

However, and contrary to France, life expectancy in these countries did not improve during this period which is proof of a certain stagnation and a missed turning point in the 1960–70 era. The health system was unable to reform and it did not make the necessary move towards the treatment and prevention of non-infectious or chronic diseases (diabetes, cancer, cardiovascular illness, etc.). During the 1990s, this indicator highlighted political difficulties (conflicts in the Caucasus, civil war in Tajikistan), economic and environmental issues (epidemiological consequences of uranium and celsium pollution and contamination, in particular in abandoned sites in Kyrgyzstan and Tajikistan), as well as natural catastrophes (the Armenian earthquake in 1988, repeated earthquakes in Tajikistan, floods, landslides, etc.).

Since the end of the 1990s, life expectancy at birth has once again stabilized and in some countries has marginally improved (subject to data reliability), returning to 1980s levels. However, when compared to less developed health systems, in particular in sub-Saharan Africa where life expectancy in some areas is as low as 50 years, this indicator ranks the Caucasus and Central Asia at medium level with

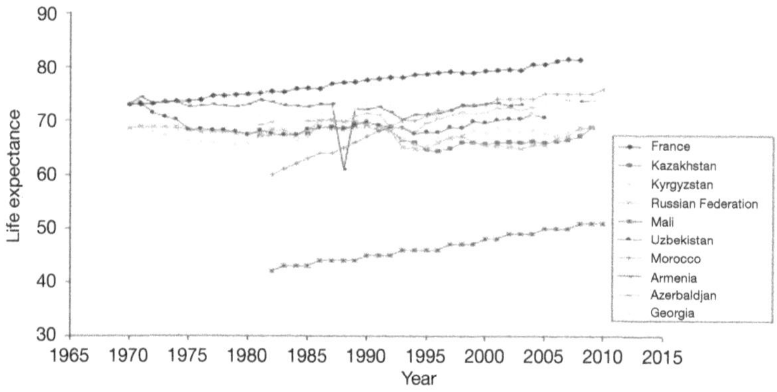

Figure 7.4 Trends in Life Expectancy at Birth in South Caucasus and Central Asia Compared with France and Mali (1970–2010)
Source: http://data.euro.who.int/hfadb/.

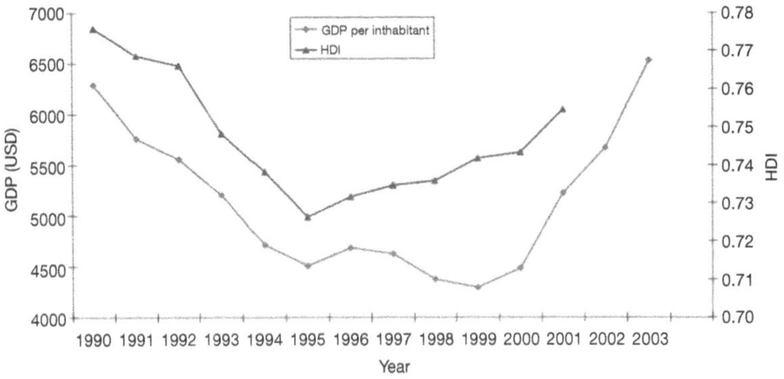

Figure 7.5 Gross Domestic Product (GDP) Per Capita and Human Development Index (HDI) in Kazakhstan
Source: Kazakhstan Statistics Office (www.stat.kz).

regards to the HDI. In reality, the HDI for these countries indicates the progress of the third element, GDP per capita, thus focusing on the economic and monetary dimension. Figure 7.11 highlights this phenomenon for Kazakhstan. The multi-faceted nature of the HDI becomes less relevant in this case Figure 7.5.

At the end of the 2000s, the UNDP decided to adopt a new composite indicator, the MPI (Multidimensional Poverty Indicator). The MPI follows the HDI three-dimensional approach of health, education and living standards Figure 7.6 but brings into play ten distinct sub-indicators:

1. Health: child mortality, nutrition,
2. Education: years of school, school leavers under 8 years,
3. Living standards: access to electricity, drinking water, toilet facilities, floor type, furnishings, heating.

This indicator is more accurate and allows for a finer assessment of the various aspects of socio-economic development. It relies on data collected by standardized international surveys DHS (Demographic Health Surveys) and MICS (Multiple Indicator Cluster Surveys). The

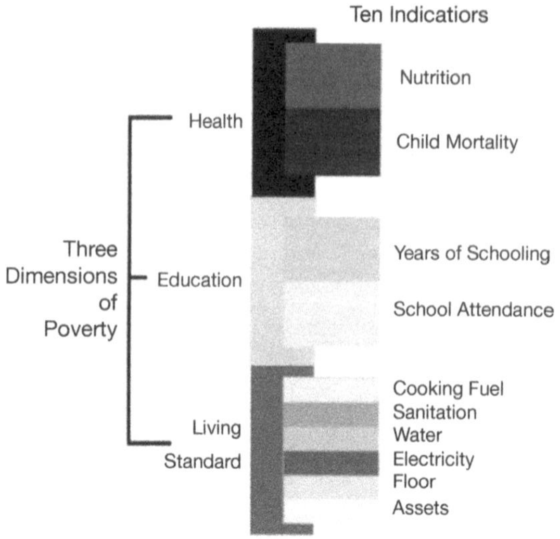

Figure 7.6 The Three Dimensions of the MPI (Multidimensional Poverty Index)
Source: http://ophi.qeh.ox.ac.uk.

MPI calculation thus corresponds to the year in which the survey was carried out. The MPI develops an absolute poverty approach with regard to living conditions, which are widely covered by the variables of the surveys.

The MPI raises the same questions with regards to the Caucasus and Central Asia as the HDI. Some indicators (nutrition, education) once again rank these countries at the top end. It does, however, throw up certain essential points that the HDI fails to unveil: the issue of infant mortality, with a rate which remains high in some countries, access to drinking water and heating (outdated networks and increase in the price of these services).

It is worth comparing the MPI to other one dimensional poverty indicators (thresholds of $1.25 and $2 a day, national poverty lines) to reveal a provisional typology of countries within the region.

Firstly, we take the national poverty rate as data reflecting the choice of each country in the way it measures poverty and the role this measure plays. This rate clearly refers to different definitions depending on the country. The following figures are from the Oxford Poverty and Human Development Initiative (OPHI)[26] 2010 and 2011 reports, the rates compared often refer to different years which should be taken into careful consideration.

We can highlight a first example of international dollar per day criteria indicating a low poverty rate (0 to 2 per cent) and national criteria revealing a considerably higher rate (15 per cent). This is true of Kazakhstan and Azerbaijan and can be compared to the situation in European countries (and Russia where the notions of poverty are respectively 1 per cent, 1 per cent, 2 per cent and 20 per cent as regards the Figures 7.7 and 7.8). This suggests that both Kazakhstan and Azerbaijan have low poverty rates when applying these indicators and inequality indicators should thus be considered further.

Both countries have experienced similar rapid economic growth due to oil extraction and refining. The GDP increases and the issues of redistribution among the population and rural development take priority over that of absolute physiological poverty.

The diagram depicts almost inexistent monetary poverty and Azerbaijan is the only country in South Caucasus with such a high MPI (5 per cent as compared to Georgia, 1 per cent, and Armenia, 2 per cent). The high MPI rate is due to child mortality and water access indicators that are linked to the question of rural development

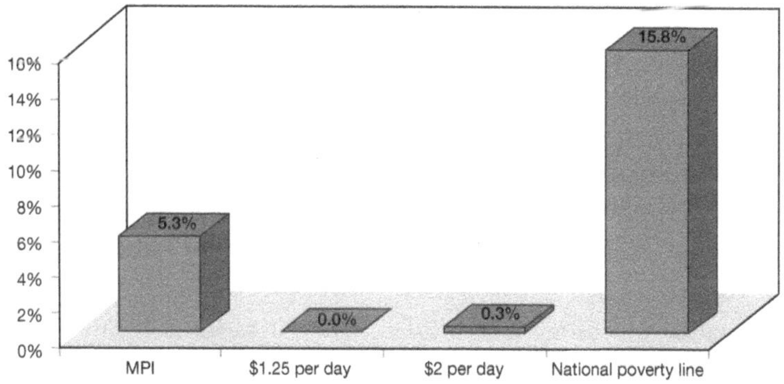

Figure 7.7 National and International Measures of Poverty in Azerbaijan
Source: http://ophi.qeh.ox.ac.uk (Country Briefing, Azerbaijan and Kazakhstan 2011)

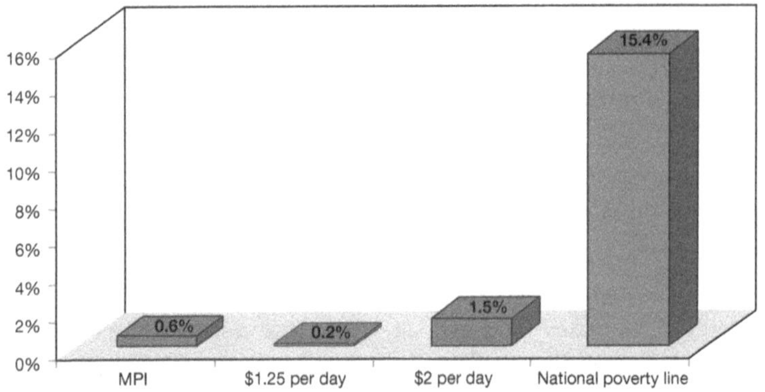

Figure 7.8 National and International Measures of Poverty in Kazakhstan
Source: http://ophi.qeh.ox.ac.uk (Country briefing: Azerbaijan and Kazakhstan, 2011).

and development policies that focus mainly on the capital city, which those in power have chosen to present as a country-wide success story.

A second case is that of Armenia Figure 7.9 and Georgia Figure 7.10. Absolute monetary poverty, measured using the international indicator of $1.25 or $2 per day, is more closely aligned to the national poverty rate. Georgia is interesting: in its thought process on the measure of poverty, it believed that monetary income alone could not provide a reliable assessment of poverty. It thus adopted the principle of *proxy means testing* with a complex indicator that takes into account the various aspects of living conditions (income but also housing, household composition, self-sufficiency, which is very common in Georgia, etc.) and also considers expenditure as well as consumption needs, including subjective ones. Two poverty measures appear: extreme poverty (15 per cent of the population) and poverty (37 per cent of the population). On the diagram below, the national line could correspond to the sum of the two poverty thresholds, but this is not specified by the OPHI.

How do we account for the fact that 30 to 40 per cent of the population do not have access to 2 dollars a day? The high rate of self-sufficiency in the countryside, low commoditization and monetization of certain goods could go some way to explaining this.

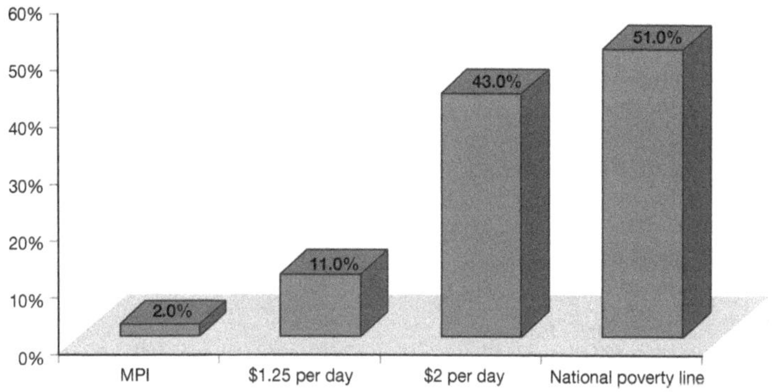

Figure 7.9 National and International Measures of Poverty in Armenia
Source: http://ophi.qeh.ox.ac.uk (Country Briefing, Armenia 2010).

A third configuration groups the lower Central Asian countries of Tajikistan, Kyrgyzstan and Uzbekistan, all with specific characteristics. For Tajikistan and Kyrgyzstan, the international monetary poverty rate, measured in dollars per day, is close to the national rate, even a bit higher. This is explained by the fact that in Tajikistan Figure 7.11 the national poverty threshold is based on an absolute monetary poverty threshold of $2.15 per day. Kyrgyzstan on the other hand bases its poverty rate on the calculation of the monetary value of a basket of food items that corresponds to 2,100 calories per day. The MPI is also high in Tajikistan compared to other countries

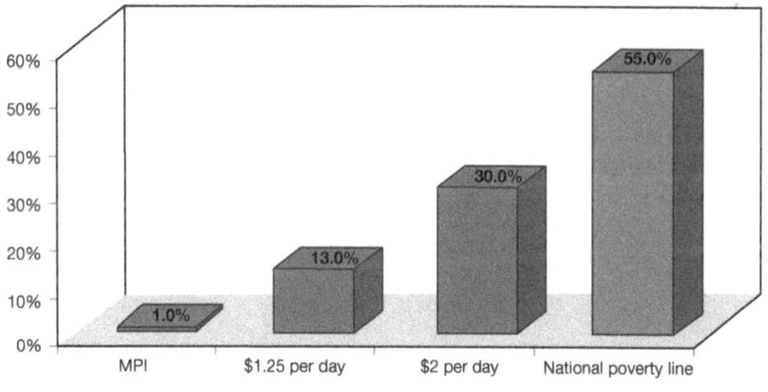

Figure 7.10 National and International Measures of Poverty in Georgia
Source: http://ophi.qeh.ox.ac.uk (Country briefing: Georgia 2010).

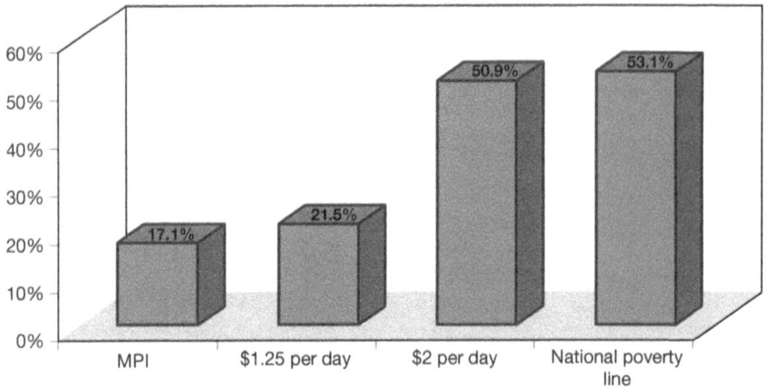

Figure 7.11 National and International Measures of Poverty in Tajikistan
Source: http://ophi.qeh.ox.ac.uk (Country Briefing, Tajikistan, 2011).

in the region. It almost corresponds to the extreme monetary poverty rate of $1.25 per day. The MPI rate is close to the high poverty rates of countries such as Mongolia, Bolivia or Peru. Although indicators may reveal different rates, they show significant poverty for the population of Tajikistan and Kyrgyzstan.

Uzbekistan Figure 7.12 is a specific case and the related data should be scrutinized. The notion and measure of poverty do not

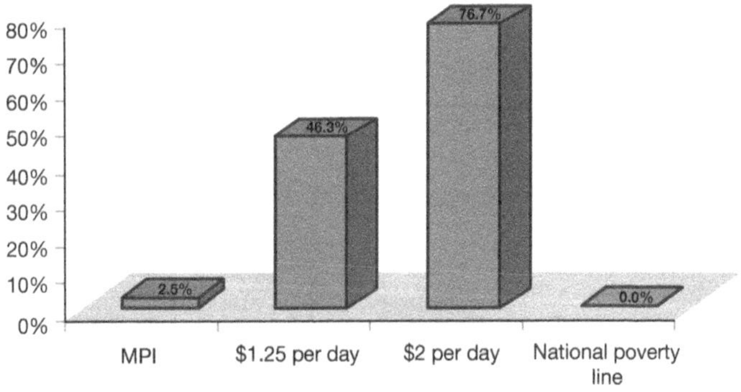

Figure 7.12 National and International Measures of Poverty in Uzbekistan
Source: http://ophi.qeh.ox.ac.uk (Country briefing: Uzbekistan 2011).

correspond to the vocabulary used by the authorities which prefer different approaches. This explains the absence of official data in respect of some years. The high poverty in terms of absolute monetary rate ($2) can similarly be explained by the rural nature of the country, the lack of monetization of certain agricultural products and bartering.

Conclusion

The aim of this comparative paper on indicators and countries of the Caucasus and Central Asia is not to determine 'the' best or the 'real' indicator, nor is it to discredit them due to their sheer number and disparities. There is no one measure of poverty, rather several and, moreover, a number of issues and uses of these measures.

It is interesting to compare the indicators for two reasons, to reveal their relevance but also their limits.[27] On a country basis, they paint a multi-faceted picture of the living conditions and income of the population.

One should remain cautious in the face of international comparative data (see table and notices in the annex) entitled 'poverty rate' without further explanation. There is often a difference between the rate calculated for (and sometimes by) international organizations and the rate provided by countries at national level. The official national poverty level may play a significant political role (in election campaigns or as indication of the success or failure of an economic policy). It is often used as operational criteria or as eligibility criteria for social assistance (assistance granted if income is below a 'subsistence minimum', for example).

Certain countries have adopted a more complex approach by developing two poverty thresholds at national level. Georgia, for example: one (as mentioned above with the country comparisons) that could be referred to as contextualized and multi-dimensional and used for social assistance policy, based on an in-depth analysis of social reality in Georgia, and the other, more unequivocal, of an income below the 'subsistence minimum' calculated to cater for long-term data and be used in political and media discourses.

Azerbaijan has used two poverty lines since 2001: the first is the absolute poverty line based on a basket of goods (subsistence minimum) corresponding to a food list of approximately 2,200 calories per person per day. Food represents 70 per cent of the list. The second poverty line is based on a relative approach to poverty that corresponds to 60 per cent of the average consumption level per person.

Tajikistan has adopted an absolute monetary poverty measure ($2.15 per day), facilitating comparisons with the World Bank indicator of $2 per day.

All of these choices are motivated by geopolitical issues and ways of entering on to the international stage. Depending on the situation, it is interesting (and sometimes necessary) to apply a simple rate, in terms of dollars per day, and one which is aligned with international standards, in order to respond more easily to international organizations (for example, in the case of PRSDs, (Poverty Reduction Strategic Directives) approved by the IMF and the World Bank, or MDGs, (Millennium Development Goals)[28]) and to apply for loans and credit facilities. In other cases, publishing relative rates facilitates a comparison with Europe and a study of inequality developments. It is this multitude of issues that needs to be considered with poverty measures.

Notes

1 A previous version of this chapter was communicated during the international GEMDEV conference on 'The measure of development', Unesco, Paris (held on 1–3 February 2012).

2 Desrosières, A., *La politique des grands nombres: histoire de la raison statistique*, Paris: La Découverte, 2000 (2nd edn); Desrosières, A., *Gouverner par les nombres*, Paris: Presses de l'Ecole des Mines (2 volumes), 2008.

3 Baumann, E., 'Se rapprocher de l'Ouest pour se démarquer du Sud sans perdre le nord? Questions à l'adresse de la Géorgie (Sud-Caucase)', *Revue Autrepart, 'On dirait le Sud...*, 2007, vol. 41, pp. 195–210.

4 Lefèvre, C., 'Organismes internationaux et protection sociale en Russie: analyse de trois types de discours des années 1990', *Le Courrier des pays de l'Est*, 2003, vol. 1040, pp. 16–25.

5 Numerous works have been published on social inequalities and impoverishment in post-Soviet Russia: Lefèvre, C., 'Inégalités, nouveaux modes de vie et politiques sociales', in Rousselet, K., Favarel-Garrigues, G. (eds), *La Russie contemporaine*, Paris: Fayard, 2010, pp. 296–307; Mespoulet, M., 'Des différences sociales accrues', in Rey, M.-P. (ed.), *Les Russes de Gorbatchev à Poutine*, Paris: Armand Colin, 2005, pp. 169–93; Kortchagina, I. *et al.*, 'Conditions de vie et pauvreté en Russie', *Economie et Statistique*, 2005, vol. 38, pp. 219–44; Guilluy-Sulikashvili, N., 'L'émergence d'une nouvelle classe moyenne en Russie ou les caractéristiques d'une nouvelle consommation', in Dupont-Dobrzynski, M., Galstyan, G. (eds), *Les influences du modèles de gouvernance de l'Union européenne sur les PECO et la CEI*, Lyon: ENS Lyon, 2011 (http://institut-est-ouest.ens-lyon.fr/spip.php?article351). Yet few have touched on the Caucasus and Central Asia: Baumann, E., 'Géorgie: la difficile équation entre économie néo-libérale et valeurs démocratiques', in Dupont-Dobrzynski, M., Galstyan, G. (eds), *Les influences du modèles de gouvernance de l'Union européenne sur les PECO et la CEI*, Lyon: ENS Lyon, 2011 (http://institut-est-ouest.ens-lyon.fr/spip.php?article290); Falkingham, J., 'The End of the Rollercoaster? Growth, Inequality and Poverty in Central Asia and the Caucasus', *Social Policy & Administration*, 2005, vol. 39/4, pp. 340–60, except for reports published by international organizations.

6 Djalili, M.-R., Kellner, T., *Géopolitique de la nouvelle Asie Centrale: de la fin de l'URSS à l'après 11 septembre*, Paris: PUF, 2003, p. 585; Merlin, A., Serrano, S. (eds), *Ordre et désordres au Caucase*, Brussels: Editions de l'Université de Bruxelles, 2010 and Radavanyi, J., Beroutchavili, N., *Atlas géopolitique du Caucase: Russie, Géorgie, Arménie, Azerbaïdjan: un avenir commun possible ?*, Paris: Autrement, 2010.

7 Lefèvre, C., 'Le système de protection sociale russe: héritages et transformations', *Revue d'études comparatives Est-Ouest*, 1995, vol. 4, pp. 25–54.

8 Nagels, J., *La tiers-mondisation de l'ex-URSS?*, Bruxelles: Editions de l'Université de Bruxelles, 1993, p. 228.

9 Verger, D., 'Bas revenus, consommation restreinte ou faible bien être: les approches statistiques de la pauvreté à l'épreuve des comparaisons internationales', *Economie et Statistique*, 2005, vol. 383–384–385.

10 Accardo, J., de Saint Pol, T., 'Qu'est-ce qu'être pauvre aujourd'hui en Europe? L'analyse du consensus sur les privations', *Economie et Statistique*, 2009, vol. 425, pp. 3–27.

11 Hohmann, S., Garenne, M., 'Health and Wealth in Uzbekistan and Sub-Saharan Africa in Comparative Perspective', *Economics and Human Biology*, 2010, vol. 8/3, pp. 346–60 and Hohmann, S., Garenne, M., 'Absolute Versus Relative Measures of Poverty: Application to DHS African Surveys', *Journal of US-China Public Administration*, 2011, vol. 8/7, pp. 748–62.

12 Razafindrakoto, M., Roubaud, F., 'Les multiples facettes de la pauvreté dans un pays en développement. Le cas de la capitale malgache', *Economie et Statistique*, 2005, vol. 383–384–385.

13 Duma, V., Molnar, M., Panduru, F., Verger, D., 'Roumanie: une agriculture de survie, après l'industrialisation forcée', *Economie et Statistique*, 2005, vol. 383–384–385.

14 Ovtcharova, L., Prokofieva, L., 'Pauvreté et solidarité familiale en Russie à l'heure de la transformation', *Revue d'études comparatives Est-Ouest*, 1998, vol. 31/4, pp. 151–82.

15 Razafindrakoto M., Roubaud F., *op. cit.*

16 Jarygina, T., 'Poverty in Rich Russia', *Problems of Economic Transition, a Journal of translations from Russia*, 1994, vol. 37/8.

17 The *zemstva (singular zemstvo)* are territorial assemblies created in 1864 under the administrative reform led by Alexander II with the aim of stimulating and organising administrative initiative and management at local level. The *zemstva* were created at two levels, provincial (*gubernija)* and district (*uezd*). An assembly and executive power were set up at each level. The term *zemstva* comes from the Russian word *zemlâ*, land. *Zemstvas* were set up in 34 of the 50 provinces of European Russia. Many local issues were dealt with by the *zemstvo*: land tax collection, public education and health, roads, stocks in case of food shortages, fire protection, management of institutions and charitable funds. *Zemstvas* ceased to exist in 1917 but their work formed the basis on which the USSR created its public health system.

18 For *zemstva* related statistics see Mespoulet, M., *Statistique et Révolution en Russie. Un compromis impossible (1880–1930)*, Rennes: Presses Universitaires de Rennes, 2001; Johnson, R.E., 'Liberal Professionals and Professional Liberals: The Zemstvo Statisticians and Their Work', in Emmons, T., Vucinich, W.S., *The Zemstvo in Russia. An Experiment in Local Self-Government*, Cambridge: Cambridge University Press, 1982, pp. 343–63; Stanziani, A., 'Statisticiens, zemstva et Etat dans la Russie des années 1880', *Cahiers du monde russe et soviétique*, 1991, vol. 22/4, pp. 445–68. In 1899, Lenine detailed the use and interpretation of zemstva statistics, in particular the 'zemstva statistics in peasant budgets', in *Le développement du capitalisme en Russie*, ch.2, Paris: Ed. Sociales.

19 Lefèvre, C., 'Note sur les notions de chômage et d'emploi dans les années 1920 et 1930 en URSS', *Cahiers du Monde russe*, 1997, vol. 38/4, pp. 617–27.

20 Ovtcharova, L., Prokofieva, L., *op. cit.*

21 Decree of the President of the Russian Federation dated March 2 1992 n°210 'System of minimum consumption budgets'.

22 For further information on these questions: Ovtcharova, L., 'Définition, niveau et facteurs de pauvreté dans la Russie actuelle', *Revue d'études comparatives Est-Ouest*, 2006, vol. 37/2, pp. 33–58 and Lefèvre, C., *Système de protection sociale et entreprises en Russie, Héritages et transformations, 1987–2001*, Ph.D thesis, Paris: EHESS, 2003.

23 Georgia Human Development Report 2008 (http://hdr.undp.org/en/reports/national/europethecis/georgia/NHDR-Georgia-2008.pdf).

24 Millennium Development Goals, Tajikistan Progress Report 2010, (http://www.undp.tj/files/WEB-MDG-Tajikistan-2010-Eng.pdf).

25 Hohmann, S., *La mortalité chez les jeunes enfants en Ouzbékistan. Des particularismes soviétiques aux réalités contemporaines*, Sarrebruck: EUE, September 2010, p. 67 and Hohmann, S., 'Santé publique en Ouzbékistan contemporain: continuités soviétiques et limites des processus engagés', *Les Cahiers d'Asie Centrale*, 2004, vol. 13–14, pp. 121–61.

26 http://www.ophi.org.uk/policy/multidimensional-poverty-index/.

27 This discussion could also cover the difference between individual and household poverty, as regards the equivalent levels between members of the household and the differences between the estimate of the household situation based on income or consumption.

28 A MDG (Target 1.A) is to halve the proportion of people living on less than $1 a day from 1990 to 2015.

PART 3

THE GROWTH OF LABOUR MIGRATIONS: TOWARD A NEW NORTH–SOUTH RELATION?

CHAPTER 8

THE POST-SOVIET SPACE BETWEEN NORTH AND SOUTH: DISCONTINUITIES, DISPARITIES AND MIGRATIONS

Julien Thorez
(CNRS, Paris)

Organization of the post-Soviet space has been fundamentally and permanently transformed since the collapse of the USSR.[1] A 'territorial transition' was sketched in the context of a diversification of actors in the political, economic and social fields, be it at state level, entrepreneurial or informal, national or international.[2] Marked by dynamics of fragmentation, disintegration, but also integration and unification, this process has been redrawing the map of Europe and Asia.[3] Depending on the regions and scales, these spatial dynamics give rise to a heterogeneous territory where both countries integrated into the European Union and countries linked to Western and Southern Asia co-exist now around Russia.

In this context, the restructuring of the means of production in times of economic crisis, the liberalization of exchange based on offer and demand and redefining the geopolitical balance modified the position of countries of Central Asia and the Caucasus within the global arena. In the bipolar world, as a Soviet region, Central Asia was generally perceived to be in the 'developed world' in scientific works[4] and expert reports,[5] although some works questioned its inclusion in the 'third-world'.[6] For many, the unity of the Soviet space, based on the centre–periphery model, outweighed regional inequalities although Central Asia was sometimes considered to be a 'dominated periphery'.[7] Twenty years on from the commencement of the 'transition' and in the context of a global world, Central Asian and Caucasian countries are associated with the idea of the 'South', irrespective of the different paths taken.[8] This 'third-worldization', an original evolution by all accounts, results from the magnitude of the economic and social crisis that followed the disintegration of the USSR.[9] But this idea is also based on a classic post-colonial analysis of the post-Soviet space, the frontier between 'North' and 'South' corresponding in almost all publications to the Southern border of the former metropole, Russia.[10]

Table 8.1 GDP Growth (1991–96) (in Per Cent)

	1991	1992	1993	1994	1995	1996
Estonia	−8.0	−21.2	−5.7	−1.6	+5.0	+5.0
Latvia	−12.6	−32.1	−5.0	+2.2	−0.9	+3.8
Lithuania	−5.7	−21.3	−16.2	−9.8	+3.3	+5.2
Belarus	−1.2	−9.6	−7.6	−11.7	−10.4	+2.8
Moldova	−16.0	−29.1	−1.2	−30.9	−1.4	−5.2
Ukraine	−8.4	−9.7	−14.2	−22.9	−12.2	−10.0
Russia	−5.0	−14.5	−8.7	−12.6	−4.1	−3.6
Armenia	−11.7	−41.8	−8.8	+5.4	+6.9	+5.9
Azerbaijan	−0.7	−22.6	−23.1	−19.7	−11.8	+1.3
Georgia	−21.1	−44.9	−29.3	−10.4	+2.6	+11.2
Kazakhstan	−11.0	−5.3	−9.2	−12.6	−8.2	+0.5
Kyrgyzstan	−7.9	−13.9	−15.5	−20.1	−5.4	+7.1
Uzbekistan	−0.5	−11.2	−2.3	−5.2	−0.9	+1.7
Tajikistan	−7.1	−29.0	−16.4	−21.3	−12.4	−16.7
Turkmenistan	−4.7	−5.30	−10.0	−17.3	−7.2	−6.7

Source: World Bank (www.data.worldbank.org).

This analysis is also based on the identification of characteristics of post-colonial situations: the expansion of landlockedness as a result of the internationalization of former inter-republican Soviet borders;[11] the increase in migrations of imperial populations to their homeland;[12] and the boom in labour migration towards the former metropole.[13] A new geography of development thus takes form in a post-Soviet world where, between 'North' and 'South', societies and territories are changing, in the context of increasing socio-political inequalities and transformation of practices of mobility.

Crisis and Inequalities: From East to South

Crisis and Impoverishment: The Third-Worldization of the Ex-USSR?

The division of the USSR into 15 independent and sovereign countries did not just signify the fracturing of a political territory. This 'spatial event' led to a long-term change in territorial organization by creating an area fundamentally different to its previous state,[14] and coincided with the questioning of regional geo-economic gradients as the post-Soviet transformation commenced with an exceptional economic and social crisis (Table 8.1).

At the turn of the 1990s, the disintegration of the Soviet production and exchange system, the adoption of principles of the market economy, as well as international opening, all had a far-reaching and long-term affect on national economies. From 1991 to 1994, the GDP of all post-Soviet countries decreased annually. This propagation of the crisis reveals the importance of interdependent relations created by Soviet planning. During this period of 'chaos',[15] the GDP of Uzbekistan, for whom the economy was officially less destabilized than others, fell by 20 per cent, whereas Estonia and Russia witnessed a 30 per cent reduction and Georgia, where the crisis was even more exacerbated, almost 80 per cent (Table 8.1). The geography of the independent states was initially coined a 'geography of crisis',[16] combining industrial decline, an explosion in unemployment rates and an impoverishment of the majority of the population.[17]

Most Baltic and Caucasian countries recorded positive growth from 1994–95, whereas the crisis continued to the end of the 1990s in Russia, Moldova and Ukraine. In addition, the recovering economic growth did not equate to post-Soviet countries returning quickly to pre-crisis levels. The GDP calculated in current dollars did not surpass 1990 levels before 2002 in Armenia, 2003 in Kazakhstan, 2004 in Russia and 2008 in Tajikistan. During the first years of independence, countries of the former USSR thus suffered from an unprecedented decrease of their position in regional and global hierarchy, since world growth increased on average by 3 per cent per annum from 1990 to 1999, according to the IMF. In this regards, the post-Soviet situation is not comparable to that of 'post-colonial Western Europe' as the period of independence corresponded to rapid economic growth in Africa and Western Europe.[18] This said, the collapse of the post-Soviet economies in a context where international institutions such as the IMF and the World Bank were increasingly present,[19] justified the status change regarding CIS countries in the globalized world and their integration into the category of 'emerging and developing countries'.

In Central Asia and the Caucasus, this trend could be reinforced by the landlockedness that accompanied the end of imperial territorial construction. This geographical situation has caused a political dependence on neighbouring transit countries and given rise to an economic growth deficit in contrast to littoral countries, since exchanges were limited by the inflated continental transit costs.[20] However, this element had little effect on the economic development of post-Soviet countries, because of the importance of the macroeconomic difficulties. Interestingly, littoral countries, such as Georgia and Ukraine, suffered from the crisis more than neighbouring landlocked countries such as Azerbaijan, Armenia or Belarus. The heterogeneity of trajectories in the countries of the former Soviet Union, resulting notably from the political, economic and geo-political decisions of the sovereign authorities, has now a spatial dimension. The post-Soviet world is unequal, segmented as much by new political borders as by economic discontinuities.

Inherited Inequalities? Central Asia as a Soviet Third World?

From a territorial organizational standpoint, the socialist political project of the Soviet authorities aimed to reduce regional differences by changing the location of the production and, more generally, to eradicate spatial inequalities by homogenizing national territory and doing away with social classes.[21] The territorial planning policy also aimed to unite the Soviet space by creating a uniform territorial grid and developing inter-regional relations that would be stimulated by the territorial division of work.[22] In this context, the unified transport system, whose organizing principles encouraged the movement of goods and people by minimizing transportation costs, should have played an important role by promoting the logics of regional specialization and national homogenization.[23]

Despite these principles, the territorial planning policy of the USSR, often oscillating between sectorial and territorial approaches, succeeded in creating a unified space, but it failed to eradicate

Table 8.2 GDP per Capita (in Dollars) and Country Differences (index number: 100 = the most developed country) from 1990 to 2010

	1990		1995		2000		2005		2010	
Estonia	3,193	*91*	3,030	*100*	4,144	*100*	10,329	*100*	14,341	*100*
Latvia	2,796	*80*	2,107	*69*	3,301	*79*	6,973	*67*	10,723	*74*
Lithuania	2,841	*81*	2,178	*71*	3,297	*79*	7,604	*73*	11,045	*77*
Belarus	1,705	*48*	1,371	*45*	1,273	*30*	3,090	*29*	5,765	*40*
Moldova	9,72	*27*	477	*15*	354	*8*	831	*8*	1,631	*11*
Ukraine	1,570	*45*	936	*30*	636	*15*	1,829	*17*	3,007	*21*
Russia	3,485	*100*	2,670	*88*	1,775	*42*	5,337	*51*	10,440	*72*
Armenia	637	*18*	546	*18*	621	*14*	1,598	*15*	3,031	*21*
Azerbaijan	1,237	*35*	397	*13*	655	*15*	1,578	*15*	5,718	*39*
Georgia	1,611	*46*	569	*18*	692	*16*	1,470	*14*	2,621	*18*
Kazakhstan	1,647	*47*	1,288	*42*	1,229	*29*	3,771	*36*	9,132	*63*
Kyrgyzstan	609	*17*	364	*12*	280	*6*	476	*4*	847	*6*
Uzbekistan	651	*18*	586	*19*	558	*13*	547	*5*	1,381	*9*
Tajikistan	496	*14*	213	*7*	139	*3*	358	*3*	820	*5*
Turkmenistan	881	*25*	558	*19*	645	*15*	1,707	*16*	3,967	*27*

Source: World Bank (www.data.worldbank.org).

regional inequalities.[24] On the contrary, while sector administrations privileged already developed regions, the gap in development grew slowly towards the end of the Soviet era to the detriment of the Southern republics of Central Asia, according to official indicators.[25] As a consequence, the GDP per capita in 1990 varied considerably between Soviet Socialist Republics, from 496 dollars in Tajikistan to 3,485 dollars in Russia (Table 8.2). The Soviet planned system's organization involved a territorial concentration of power, despite a real autonomization of the Soviet Socialist Republics, particularly in the Brejnev era. And the Soviet territory was structured in terms of a centre–periphery gradient, which reflected the imbalance of political and economic relationships.[26]

At the level of the Soviet Union, the political centre included the wealthiest regions whereas the republics furthest removed from the heart of the Soviet territory were also the poorest. Inequalities were in part a result of the varied development of the production system. In the planned production and exchange organization, Central Asia contributed to the supply of raw materials (minerals, hydrocarbons, cotton, wool, etc.) for the Western regions of the USSR (Volga, Urals, Central Russia, the Baltics, Belarus, etc.) but remained relatively non-industrialized, save for the expansion of some industrial poles like Tashkent, Alma-Ata and Karaganda.[27] Yet the transfer of funds by the authorities to the peripheries, representing 20 per cent of national income in Tajikistan and Kyrgyzstan, only partially compensated for these regional disparities.[28] To a certain extent, Central Asian societies could also be compared to those of developing countries in the neighbouring Iranian world. Despite the relative early literacy of Central Asian women, the demographic transition temporality in Central Asia coincided with that of Iran, with reduced birth rates only really starting in the 1970s.[29]

The inequalities of the Soviet space were in part a reproduction of spatial disparities under the Tsarist Empire.[30] Although Central Asia caught up significantly during the 20th century, it still reflects the deficiencies in the Soviet planning policy which failed to localize activities efficiently in order to ensure a homogenous and coherent regional development.[31] However, the centre–periphery model is not relevant to analyse Soviet Central Asian and Caucasian societies, because these societies were not faced with the poverty that would have been specific to the dominated peripheries.[32] Indeed sociological and economic publications of the end of the Soviet period portrayed Central Asian populations benefiting from a quality of life comparable to or better than the populations of European regions of the USSR, particularly in rural areas.[33] Despite small plots – 0.2 hectares in Tajikistan and 0.5 hectares in Kyrgyzstan – private agriculture ensured substantial revenues for collective farm workers and at the same time contributed to containing underemployment and limiting the cost of living both in the countryside and urban areas. On the eve of the collapse of the USSR, Central Asia, for the most part rural, was faced with a complex and ambivalent situation that highlighted the paradoxes of the path of development and the territory of the Soviet Union.

Increased Spatial Inequalities: When the 'South' Separates from the 'North'?

In addition to changes to the political map, the 'territorial transition' is marked by an increase in socio-spatial differences. In the first years of the post-Soviet crisis, territorial inequalities were reinforced between the newly independent countries, but also between regions, between cities and the countryside, between cities and between neighbourhoods. According to World Bank data, the wealth differences between Soviet republics, on the basis of GDP per capita per annum, ranged from 1 to 7 in 1990. By 2000, a difference of 1 to 29 separated Tajikistan and Estonia, with respective GDP per capita per annum of 139 and 4,144 dollars (Table 8.2). In the 2000s, this difference became slightly less significant due to the rapid economic growth of Central Asian and Caucasian countries which was in particular based on the expansion of raw material production (oil, gas, minerals, etc.). In 2010, GDP per capita per annum reached 820 dollars in Tajikistan, but it exceeded 14,000 dollars in Estonia, bringing the difference to 1 to 17. Over the past 20 years, disparities between post-Soviet countries have thus significantly increased from a social and economic viewpoint, in addition to their diverse geopolitical orientations. The Baltic States, members of the EU since

2004, have thus integrated into the European space and the 'triad' despite being poorer than the average EU country, while at the opposite end of the spectrum, Tajikistan and Kyrgyzstan show economic indicators comparable to those of sub-Saharan African countries. Consequently, the significant increase in spatial inequalities resulted in a radical geo-economic division of the post-Soviet space between countries of the 'North' and the 'South.'

Despite the downgrading of Central Asian and Caucasian countries in the 1990s, likened to a 'third-worldization', the differences in wealth do not correspond to the classic situation between a 'former metropole' and 'former colonies' as seen in Western European post-colonial configurations. Firstly, Russia has not the highest GDP per capita per annum, despite clearly being the strongest economy in the region with a GDP of 1,479 billion dollars in 2010 (Table 8.3). Furthermore, the main economic discontinuities are not located on the Southern borders of Russia but on the Southern borders of Kazakhstan (Map 8.1). Despite the continuation of a centre–periphery logic – though imperfect – this observation confirms the specific situation of Kazakhstan within the post-Soviet space. Kazakhstan is not only the sole Central Asian state member of the Common Economic Space (CES), founded with Russia and Belarus in 2012. It is now the second regional economic power. This further highlights the difficulty in locating the North–South border, which is still commonly defined by international

Table 8.3 GDP of Post-Soviet Countries in 2010 (in Billions of US dollars)

Estonia	19.2	Armenia	9.3
Latvia	24.0	Azerbaijan	54.7
Lithuania	36.3	Georgia	11.6
Belarus	54.7	Kazakhstan	149.0
Moldova	5.8	Kyrgyzstan	4.6
Ukraine	137.9	Uzbekistan	38.9
Russia	1,479.8	Tajikistan	5.6
		Turkmenistan	20.0

Source: World Bank (www.data.worldbank.org).

Map 8.1 GDP per Capita in 2010 (in Dollars)

organizations and researchers as the limit between Russia and Central Asia and the Caucasus.[34]

But despite this significant divide between the wealthiest and poorest countries, locating the North–South border seems to be a difficult quest, because spatial inequalities have increased at every scale. In all countries, the organization of space was locally transformed with the appearance of numerous 'crisis funnels' and some 'oases of prosperity'.[35]

At the national level, this increase in territorial disparities has deepened regional inequalities. For example within Kazakhstan, GDP per capita per annum currently varies from 1 to 10 depending on the region:[36] the *oblasts* of Zhambyl and Southern Kazakhstan contrast with the wealthy oil regions of Atyrau and Mangystau, and with the cities of Astana and Almaty, respectively the political and economic capitals of the country.[37] This indicator highlights a lack of cohesion in Kazakhstan's economic space. This is also assessed by the average salary, which varies considerably between the *oblasts* in question, from 1 to 4, even if these two indicators provide imperfect information on the real quality of life of the population.[38]

In each country, the increasing gap between the countryside and cities, from an economic and social standpoint, is also reflecting the fragmentation of the national space, and constitutes an incentive for migration towards principal agglomerations. Whereas numerous rural areas suffer from peripherization, cities, with Moscow at the fore, benefit from metropolization. Contrary to small and medium-sized towns, often sorely affected by the post-Soviet crisis, cities concentrate political functions, polarize investments, lure wealth and witness the development of their role in the territorial system.[39] The spaces within these cities also become differentiated due to a combination of socio-spatial aggregation and segregation processes resulting from the liberalization of the real estate and land market.[40] Gated communities made up of large individual houses reserved for the political and economic elite have been erected on the peripheries of the main agglomerations and a gentrification of the city centres can also be noted. Inversely, several cities, such as Bishkek and Almaty, have witnessed the spontaneous and illegal erection of residential neighbourhoods close to the *microrayon*, the vast residential areas built during the Soviet period.

While the Soviet plan sought to eradicate spatial inequality, the political, economic and social transition, which varied from one country to the next, accentuated territorial differences, commensurate with the growth in social inequalities.[41] This new geographical distribution of wealth, which reflects the political paradigm of capitalist orientation adopted by post-Soviet governments, represents one of the main forms of spatial injustice.[42] Yet the territorial planning policies carried out by post-Soviet states rarely sought to reduce territorial inequalities, despite some redistribution mechanisms of the profits from raw materials, which filter down through national territories, in particular via subsidized energy prices.[43] Besides the statehood crisis of the 1990s and their liberal economic orientations, the authorities privileged the 'territorial construction of independence', that is adapting territorial organization to the new status of independent and sovereign state by redefining border functions, adapting networks to the new borders or nationalizing the capitals or the places of power.[44] In addition no regional institution is now in a position to lead territorial policies at the level of the post-Soviet region. Thus, 20 years after the end of the USSR, political borders, economic discontinuities and social barriers reflect in the territorial organization the implementation by national elites of strategies of social and political differentiation and domination. At all levels, these discontinuities split up a region now situated between North and South along the principal divide of today's world, and following an exceptional economic crisis in the 1990s.

The Emergence of a Post-Colonial Space?

The territorial organization that emerged from the post-Soviet transition presents a significant contrast with Western European post-colonial situations, be it inherited from the Soviet period or resulting from the diverse paths taken by the newly independent countries (*supra*). Though it can be argued that the creation of an international migration field between Central Asia and Russia, sparked by the sheer number of labour migrants from South to North, is similar to relations between Africa, Asia and Western Europe since decolonization.

An Accessible 'Metropole:' The Boom in Labour Migrations to Russia

Two decades after the disintegration of the USSR, several million Central Asian nationals work on a seasonal, temporary or sometimes permanent basis in Russia where they make up almost half of the immigrant workforce.[45] In 2008, between 6 and 7 million labour migrants were employed in Russia, including 2.425 million with work permits.[46] Among these migrants, approximately 2 million originated from Uzbekistan, 1 million from Tajikistan and 0.5 million from Kyrgyzstan.[47] Labour migration is a major social and economic reality in contemporary Central Asia, Turkmenistan aside. But it developed only in the mid-1990s in Tajikistan, at the end of the decade in Kyrgyzstan and at the beginning of 2000s in Uzbekistan.[48] This labour migration, including a flow towards Kazakhstan, is proof of a radical change in the territoriality of Central

Asians as, prior to the 1990s, their migratory mobility was the lowest one in the Soviet population, despite encouragement from Soviet authorities at the time.[49]

The emergence of new migratory practices reflects the economic and social situation of Central Asian countries and the 'third-worldization' after the collapse of the USSR, although the elements which frame the demand for mobility are extremely complex.[50] The emigration of the workforce and the extraversion of the accumulation of capital materialize individual and family strategies to overcome economic difficulties in a situation where the average monthly wage is no more than 100 dollars in Tajikistan and 200 dollars in Kyrgyzstan (Table 8.4).

A classic case scenario, the poorest cannot mobilize resources needed to migrate although this part of the population suffer full exposure to employment market tensions provoked by a lengthy economic depression coupled with strong demographic growth.[51] In Tajikistan, the population reached 7.565 million according to the 2010 census, compared to 5.092 million in 1989. In Uzbekistan, the workforce went from 10.2 million in 1990 to 14.8 million in 2006 due to the arrival on the market of the generation born during the birth rate peak of the 1980s.[52] Although living below what they would deem a satisfactory level, the majority of the population has sufficient economic and social capital to start a migratory path towards Russia. Despite the xenophobic and racist environment, Russia remains an attractive option for migrants because of its strong economic growth after the 1998 crisis, its demographic subdued growth and its cultural proximity.

Table 8.4 Average Monthly Salary in CIS Countries in 2012 (in dollars)

Russia	795	Georgia	327
Kazakhstan	625	Armenia	286
Azerbaijan	469	Moldova	268
Belarus	360	Kyrgyzstan	208
Ukraine	339	Tajikistan	110

Source: Committee of Statistics of the CIS.

Like economic dissatisfaction, the unequal geographical distribution of wealth stimulates demand for migration from national to international level, although the relative closing of the post-Soviet borders at the same time appears to hinder regional circulation.[53] The increase in the difference in salaries during the transition (Table 8.4) encourages migrations, even though migrants from Uzbekistan, Kyrgyzstan and Tajikistan do not claim the same salary as their Russian counterpart for the same job.[54] Central Asian migrants are paid between one-third and one-half of a Russian worker's salary but try to make up for it by working more. On average, the migrant working week is 20 hours longer than Russian workers and in a third of cases exceeds 70 hours.[55] As such, migrant worker salaries can equal those of the Russians and exceed by far the average salary paid in their country of origin.

Entry to Russia for Central Asian nationals is (in theory) relatively easy from a legal perspective. The agreement signed by CIS countries in Bishkek in 1992 officially grants their citizens free movement within the post-Soviet space. In practice, Russian legislation provides that nationals from Kyrgyzstan, Uzbekistan and Tajikistan can enter the national territory without a visa and, after registering, can stay for 90 days with a temporary residency authorization (*vremennoe pribyvanie*) (Figure 8.1). However, it is much harder to obtain a work permit, due to annual quota fixed by the authorities, or get three- or five-year residence permits. Consequently, the majority of Central Asian migrants work illegally in Russia.[56] Russia nevertheless appears accessible from Central Asia, with multilateral agreements introducing real fluidity within a politically fragmented post-Soviet space. In this sense, the status of the new borders between Central Asia and its former metropole differs considerably from the Southern borders of the European Union, which are in some cases materialized by a wall and play a significant role in migration policy, aiming at controlling and limiting access of migrants from the South to the territory of Europe.[57] However in practice, crossing borders and transiting via a foreign country often means difficulties and dangers for migrants.[58]

The accessibility to Russia is largely due to the numerous air, rail and road connections between Central Asia and Russia, operated by companies of both sides (*infra*). This transport supply constitutes a dense and diversified network that facilitates access to Russia for Central Asian migrant workers. Transport costs remain relatively low, particularly in light of the income migrant workers hope to make in Russia, and despite an increase related to post-Soviet restructuring and reduced mobility subsidies for transport companies. In September 2008, a second class train ticket from Tashkent to Saratov cost 140,000 *sums* (the equivalent of 70 Euros or 105 dollars), from Tashkent to Moscow 260,000 *sums* (130 Euros or 195 dollars). At the same time, a flight from Tashkent to Ufa, Rostov, Chelyabinsk or Novosibirsk cost 200 Euros (or 280 dollars).[59] Migrants can in addition reduce travel costs to Russia by taking a coach, an uncomfortable and long journey. From Bishkek to large towns in Western Siberia (Novosibirsk, Omsk), the journey takes

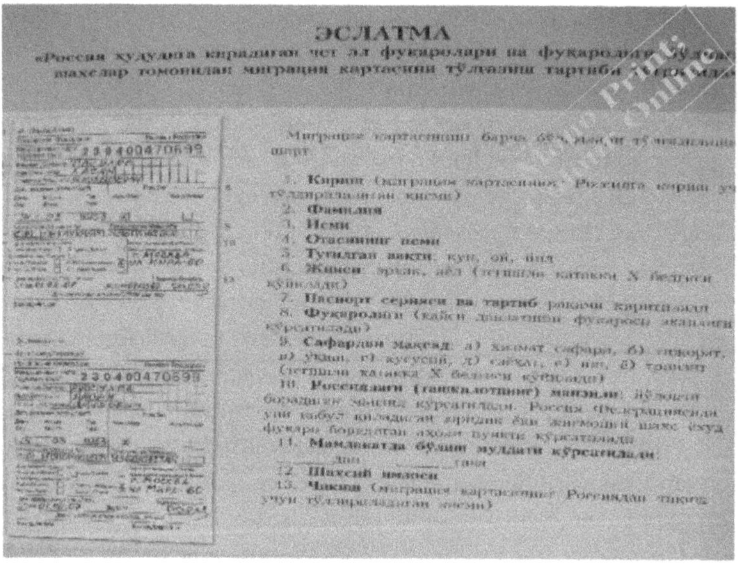

Figure 8.1 *Uzbekistan Airways* In-Flight Magazine (J. Thorez)
Uzbekistan Airways in-flight magazine distributed by Uzbekistan Airways has a page to assist migrants with the administrative steps involved with arrival in Russia, highlighting the role of national companies in the transportation of workers from Uzbekistan.

approximately 48 hours. In spring 2012, a ticket from Bishkek to Novosibirsk cost 3,250 *soms* (55 Euros or 70 dollars), from Bishkek to Krasnoyarsk 4,450 *soms* (75 Euros or 95 dollars), and from Bishkek to Moscow 6,000 *soms* (100 Euros or 130 dollars). The lack of a financial barrier encourages Central Asian population mobility and a concentration of migration towards Russia. The possibility to travel from Central Asia to Russia legally and cheaply also goes a long way to explaining the seasonal nature of migrant movement, regardless of dependency on weather conditions for certain types of work in Russia (construction, agriculture, etc.).

From Disintegration to Reactivation: A New Regional Space

Whereas the initial years of territorial transition were marked by the fragmentation and disintegration of the Soviet space,[60] labour migrations shattered this dynamic and contributed to the creation of a new regional space. In the 1990s, the end of the unified Soviet transport system led to regional connections being replaced by national and international links. This process was in line with the geopolitical imperatives of newly independent states waiting to integrate into the globalized world and affirm their sovereignty by reinforcing their unity.[61] Numerous air and rail liaisons ceased to be run by transport operators, who were created after the dismemberment of Soviet companies. On the eve of the collapse of the USSR, 148 trains circulated weekly in both directions between Southern Central Asia and other Soviet regions. Ten years after independence, only 14 weekly trains continued to connect Uzbekistan, Tajikistan and Kyrgyzstan to Russia. It should be noted that Moscow was no longer accessible from Turkmenistan.[62] Rail-related difficulties (reorganization of transit traffic, lack of agreement on tariffs, erection of customs barriers) did not give rise to a modal shift towards air transportation. Quite the opposite, the latter experienced a similar crisis. Regional traffic through Nukus (Uzbekistan) plummeted from 140,000 to 14,000 passengers between 1990 and 1993.[63] The *Aeroflot* network between Southern Central Asia and other Soviet regions comprised 140 regular connections in 1984 but only 43 were operated in 1996 by Russian and Central Asian companies (Maps 8.2–8.5 at the end of the chapter).

The development of charter flights to a certain extent compensated for the cessation of regular connections, for example Dushanbe–Moscow, but did not have a significant effect on general development. The reduced frequency of flights was accompanied by the shrinking of the geographical coverage of airlines network. This decrease in air and rail links affected relations between Central Asia and Russia as well as between Central Asia, the Caucasus and Eastern Europe. In 1989, *Aeroflot* operated 27 weekly flights between Kiev and Uzbekistan and 10 between Kiev and Tajikistan. By 1994, no company was flying these routes.[64] This clearly shows that the reduced transport network largely contributed to the simplification of territorial organization and the disintegration of the Soviet space.

Since the end of the 1990s, the process of the deconstruction of Soviet territorial links has decreased and been replaced by a regional reintegration dynamic stimulated by labour migrations. In the context of the normalization and stabilization of transport companies, the transport supply between Central Asia and Russia has increased and diversified to meet the demand for mobility of Central Asian migrant workers. Road links made by coaches, *mikroavtobus* or even taxis have appeared. In Soviet times, this mode of transport was reserved for short distances.[65] But now dozens of coaches cross the Kazakh Steppes on their way to Siberia, the Urals or

Table 8.5 Air Links between Uzbekistan and Russia (1984–2008)

	1984	1996	2002	2008
Uzbek cities connected to Russia	8	9	8	11
Russian cities reachable from Uzbekistan	30	15	15	17
Lines operated between Uzbekistan and Russia	53	19	22	36
Lines between Uzbekistan and Moscow	8	5	5	11
Lines between Uzbekistan and St Petersburg	3	1	1	6
Lines between Uzbekistan and Minvody	8	1	3	1

Source: airlines (*Aeroflot, Uzbekistan Airways, Tajik Air, Somon Air, Air Bishkek*, etc.), airports.

Central Russia, in particular from Northern Kyrgyzstan and Western Uzbekistan.[66] Air and rail networks have also developed with new liaisons and increased frequencies.

In 1996, one regular airline existed between Tajikistan and Russia, 11 in 2002 and 29 in 2008 (Maps 8.5, 8.7 at the end of the chapter). Between Uzbekistan and Russia, airlines of the two countries operated 36 regular flights in 2008, as opposed to 19 in 1996 and 22 in 2002 (Table 8.5, Maps 8.4 and 8.6 at the end of the chapter).

The geographical expansion of the transport network considerably improved access to Russia and Central Asia. All major cities in Uzbekistan, Tajikistan and Kyrgyzstan are now connected with Russia. Linked only by charters until 2006, Osh airport has now regular flights to eight airports in Russia (Moscow, Novosibirsk, St Petersburg, Kazan, Yekaterinburg, Samara, Krasnoyarsk and Irkutsk). Consequently its international traffic, including passengers to the Chinese town of Urumchi, rose from 25,000 to 271,000 passengers between 2005 and 2010. Despite a slower development rate, rail transport experienced similar changes, in particular from Uzbekistan. Thus, after a short decade of detachment, Central Asia seems to be restoring a coherent spatial entity with Russia, structured by the circulation of persons, goods and capital, and this despite significant territorial inequalities.

Run by Central Asian and Russian companies,[67] the creation of new air and rail links does not correspond to a reproduction of the Soviet transport network. Firstly, the flow remains less intense than in the 1980s. At that time, two to three daily trains connected Tashkent to Moscow, whereas today this connection is made four times a week. Further, the geography of regional connections has changed. On the one hand, the traffic increase initially focused on the Central Asia–Russia axis, whereas transversal connections to the Caucasus and Eastern Europe are rudimentary. In particular, there are no longer regular flights from Tajikistan and Kyrgyzstan to the Caucasus or Eastern Europe. There are few remaining flights from Tashkent to these destinations. But the quasi-disappearance of transverse air connections contributes to accentuate the polarization around the former Russian metropole of the whole regional transport network. This greatly contrasts with the diversity of regional relations formerly ensured by the Soviet transport system.

On the other hand, air, rail and road services to Russia are reorganized to the detriment of tourist regions and the benefit of industrial areas. Minvody, located at the heart of the large hot springs area in the Northern foothills of the Caucasus, was linked to eight airports in Uzbekistan on the eve of independence. One weekly flight now connects it to Tashkent (Table 8.5, Map 8.6 at the end of the chapter). Inversely, the airports of Surgut and Nizhnevartovsk, serving the important oil and gas producing region of Western Siberia, are now connected to several towns in Uzbekistan and Tajikistan. Polarized by Moscow, which is the best connected city from Central Asia, the regional transport network has thus fundamentally changed due to the generalization of labour migrations and the decrease in leisure-related mobility. The structural evolution of the transport system is significant of post-Soviet spatial changes: it contributes to ensure the sustainability of a coherent regional space built around Russia, but also to the 'move' of Kyrgyzstan, Uzbekistan and Tajikistan towards the South. To this extent, the re-organization of the transport system contributes to reformulating relations between Russia and Central Asia.

Conclusion

At the end of the post-socialist territorial transition, the development of socio-spatial differences in the context of an economic crisis projected the border between the North and the South to the heart of the post-Soviet space. Although this boundary does not correspond to the borders of the former Russian metropole,[68] this socio-economic discontinuity shapes societies and regional territories based on a centre–periphery model that confirms the third-worldization of Caucasian and Central Asian countries. In this context, the emergence of an international migratory field between Central Asia and Russia corresponds to a classic post-colonial situation, structured on the basis of unbalanced relations between the North and the South. Twenty years after independence, new forms of domination traverse the regional geopolitical field, while migrant mobility is accompanied by a large capital circulation. According to the Central Bank of Russia, in 2011, remittances from Russia to Uzbekistan represented 4,909 million dollars, 2,752 million dollars to Tajikistan and 1,407 million dollars to Kyrgyzstan. The accumulated capital officially transferred by migrants, representing almost half of the GDP for Tajikistan,[69] appears today fundamental for the families and societies of Central Asia.

This dependence places migration at the forefront of inter-state relations (Figure 8.2). It takes the form of geopolitics from below, exploited by Russia, recognized and accepted by Kyrgyzstan and Tajikistan but hidden and rejected by Uzbekistan. The authorities of the country are keen to free themselves from post-colonial domination and are often perceived to have, in this context, a policy to limit labour migration, especially to their former metropole.[70] But despite geo-economic and geopolitical constraints linked to labour

Figure 8.2 Western Union Advertisement (Samarkand, Uzbekistan, 2006) (J. Thorez)

Both the subject and the graphics of this advertisement for a money transfer company reflect this asymmetric relations between Russia and Uzbekistan.

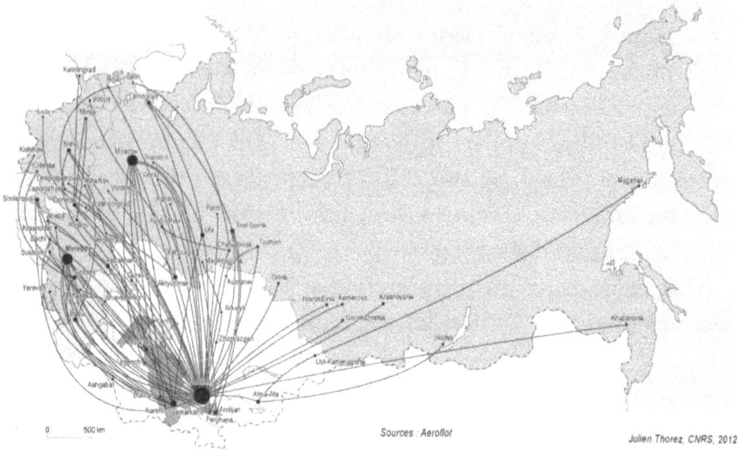

Map 8.2 Regular Air Links Between Uzbekistan and USSR in 1984 (Except Central Asia)

migration on the international position of the country, the state indirectly encourages labour migration via the development strategies of national transport companies, which have sought to

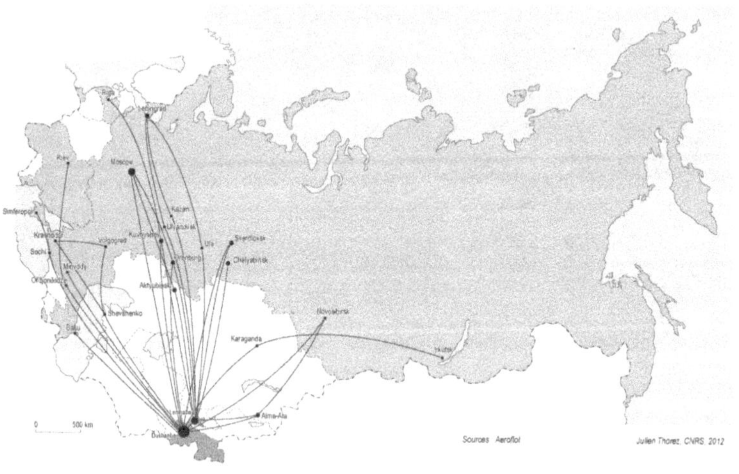

Map 8.3 Regular Air Links Between Tajikistan and USSR in 1984 (Except Central Asia)

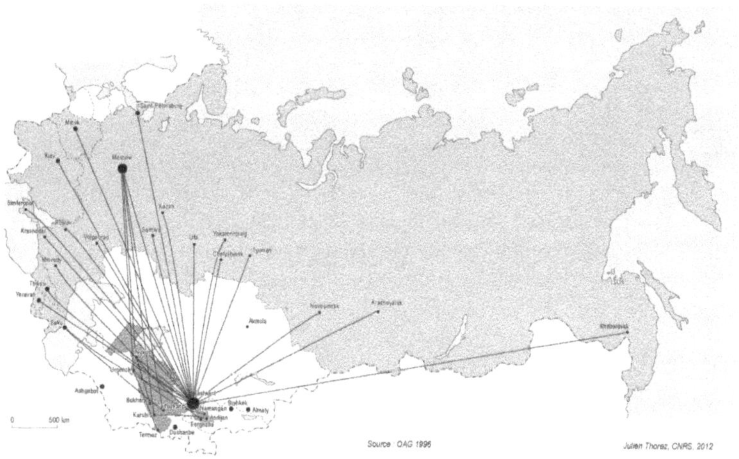

Map 8.4 Regular Air Links Between Uzbekistan and Former Soviet Union in 1996 (Except Central Asia)

reinforce the route between Uzbekistan and Russia since the 2000s (Figure 8.1).[71] At a time when states analyse the situation by confronting the pros and cons of this new migration flows within the

Map 8.5 Regular Air Links Between Tajikistan and Former Soviet Union in 1996 (Except Central Asia)

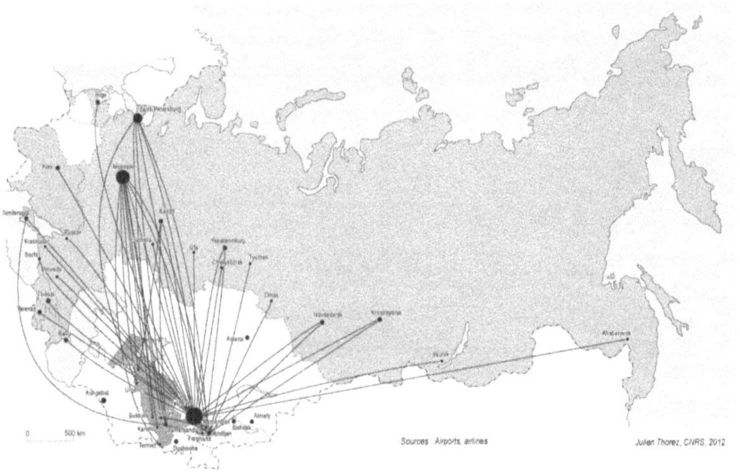

Map 8.6 Regular Air Links Between Uzbekistan and Former Soviet Union in 2008–09 (Except Central Asia)

economic, social and political arenas, this ambivalent attitude of Uzbekistan underlines the complexity of today's relations between Central Asia and Russia. Recent publications have not only described

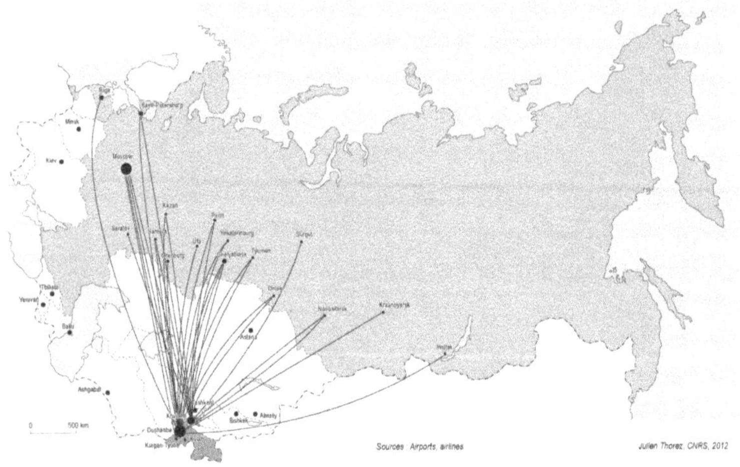

Map 8.7 Regular Air Links Between Tajikistan and Former Soviet Union in 2008–09 (Except Central Asia)

the new dependence of Central Asian societies but also raised the necessity for Russia to ensure a regular workforce flow. Thus one should be wary of univoqual approaches to geopolitical and geo-economic mutations stemming from labour migrations and strictly opposing North and South, post-imperial Russia against post-colonial Central Asian countries, and eager Russian businessmen against Central Asian workers, exploited and victims of racism. Firstly, the geographical diversification of labour migration, particularly through the migration flows from Uzbekistan and Kyrgyzstan to Kazakhstan, helps preserve Central Asia's exclusive relationship with Russia. Secondly, the generalization of socio-spatial differentiation mechanisms, socio-economic hierarchy and geopolitical domination go beyond post-colonialism and affect all countries and societies, in the globalized post-Soviet region.

Notes

1 Bradshaw, M.J. (ed.), *Geography and Transition in the Post-Soviet Republics*, Chichester: J. Wiley, 1997, p. 233.

2 Elissalde, B., 'Géographie, temps et changement spatial', *L'espace géographique*, 2000, vol. 3, pp. 224–36.

3 Thorez, J., *Flux et dynamiques spatiales en Asie centrale. Géographie de la transformation post-soviétique*, Thèse de doctorat, Université Paris 10 – Nanterre, 2005, p. 570.

4 Lacoste, Y., *Géographie du sous-développement*, Paris: PUF, 1965, p. 284; Chapuis, R., Brossard, T., *Les quatre mondes du Tiers-Monde*, Paris: Armand Colin, 1997, p. 247.

5 Brandt, W. (ed.), *Nord-Sud: un programme de survie*, Paris: Gallimard, 1980, p. 535.

6 Beaucourt, C., Chambre, H., Miklasz, C., *Tiers monde soviétique? Le Kazakhstan*, Paris: Cahier de l'Institut de Science économique appliquée, 1963, p. 329 ; Maurel, M.-C., *Territoire et stratégie soviétique*, Paris: Economica, 1982, p. 196 ; Blum, A., 'L'Asie centrale ex-soviétique, espace culturel et espace démographique', *Cahiers d'études sur la Méditerranée orientale et le monde turco-iranien*, 1993, vol. 16, pp. 335–49.

7 Maurel, M.-C., 'Les logiques territoriales du pouvoir soviétique', *Bulletin de la société languedocienne de géographie*, 1987, vol. 110, pp. 7–20.

8 Atlani-Duault, L., Lautier, B., 'Quand le second monde bascule au sud,' *Revue Tiers Monde*, 2008, vol. 193, pp. 5–11.

9 Nagels, J., *La tiers-mondisation de l'ex-URSS?*, Bruxelles: Éditions de l'université de Bruxelles, 1993, p. 226.

10 Nagels covers the whole of the post-Soviet world in his works written during the economic crisis at the beginning of the 1990s (*ibid.*)

11 Doumenge, F., *Enclavement et développement*, Paris: Agence de coopération culturelle et technique, 1986, p. 92.

12 Laitin, D., *Identity in Formation, the Russian-speaking Population in the Near Abroad*, Ithaca-London: Cornell University Press, 1998, p. 417.

13 Zajončkovskaâ, Ž.A., Vitkovskaâ, G.S. (eds), *Postsovetskie transformacii: otraženie v migraciâh* [*Post-Soviet transformations: in the Face of Migrations*], Moscow: Adamant, 2009, p. 412; Laruelle, M. (ed.), *Dynamiques migratoires et changements sociétaux en Asie centrale*, Paris: Pétra, 2010, p. 320.

14 EPEES (Laboratoire Espaces post-euclidiens et événements spatiaux), 'Événement spatial', *L'espace géographique*, 2000, vol. 3, pp. 193–9.

15 Sapir, J., *Le Chaos russe*, Paris: La Découverte, 1996, p. 329.

16 Trejviš, A.I., 'Geografiâ rossijskih krizisov' ['A geography of Russian crises'], *Izvestiâ RAN – seriâ geografičeskaâ*, 1999, vol. 2, pp. 7–16.

17 Bertin, A., Clément, M., 'Pauvreté, pénurie et transition en Russie: de l'économie soviétique à l'économie de marché', *Revue d'études comparatives Est-Ouest*, 2008, vol. 39/1, pp. 179–202.

18 From 1950 to 1973, annual economic growth averaged 4.5 per cent for Africa, 3 per cent for the United Kingdom and 5 per cent for France (Maddison, A., *The World Economy: A Millennial Perspective*, Paris: OECD, 2001, p. 384).

19 Lefèvre, C., 'Organismes internationaux et protection sociale en Russie', *Le Courrier des pays de l'Est*, 2003, vol. 1040, pp. 16–25.

20 Raballand, G., 'Determinants of the Negative Impact of Being Landlocked on Trade: An Empirical Investigation through the Central Asian Case', *Comparative economic studies*, 2003, vol. 45/4, pp. 520–36.

21 Richard, Y., *La Biélorussie, une géographie historique*, Paris: L'Harmattan, 2002, 310 p.

22 Maurel, M.-C., 1982, *op. cit.*; Wild, G., 'De la politique d'aménagement du territoire à la logique de fragmentation', in de Tinguy, A. (ed.), *L'effondrement de l'Empire soviétique*, Bruxelles: Bruylant, 1998, pp. 277–96.

23 Nikol'skij, V.V., *Geografiâ transporta SSSR* [*Geography of transport in the USSR*], Moscow: Izdatel'stvo Moskovskogo Universiteta, 1978, p. 286.

24 Radvanyi, J., *Le géant aux paradoxes – Fondements géographiques de la puissance soviétique*, Paris: Messidor – Éditions sociales, 1982, p. 423.

25 Wild, G., *op. cit.*

26 Maurel, M.-C., 1982, *op. cit.*

27 Minc, A.A. (ed.), *Srednââ Aziâ. Èkonomiko-geografičeskaâ harakteristika i problemy razvitiâ hozâjstva* [*Central Asia: Economic and geographical characteristics and problems of the development of the economy*], Moscow: Mysl', 1969, p. 504.

28 Wild, G., *op. cit.*

29 Blum, A., *op. cit.* On the other hand, the relatively rapid decrease in mortality rates corresponded to a contemporary evolution of other Soviet regions.

30 However, at the onset of the First World War, Western regions of the Tsarist Empire (Baltic Area, Poland, etc.) were more developed than the two-headed heart of European Russia. Among European empires, this situation was unique to Russia. Kappeler, A., *La Russie, empire multiethnique*, Paris: Institut d'études slaves, 1996, p. 415.

31 Wild, G., *op. cit.*

32 Maurel, M.-C., 1987, *op. cit.*

33 Tašbaeva, T.H., Savurov, M.D, *Novoe i tradicionnoe v bytu sels'koj sem'i Uzbekov* [*Novelty and tradition of rural Uzbek family lifestyles*], Tashkent: Fan, 1989, 162 p.; Zûzin, D.I, 'Pričini nizkoj mobilnosti korennogo naseleniâ respublik Srednej Azii' ['Causes of low level mobility of Central Asian populations'], *Sociologičeskie issledovaniâ*, 1983, vol. 1, pp. 109–18.

34 Carroué, L., *Géographie de la mondialisation*, Paris: A. Colin, 2004, p. 252; Capdepuy, V., 'La limite Nord/Sud', *M@ppemonde*, 2007, vol. 88 (http://mappemonde.mgm.fr/actualites/lim_ns.html); Atlani-Duault, L., Lautier, B., *op. cit.*

35 Trejviš, A.I., 1999, *op. cit.*

36 Ibraeva, A.N., Kazbek, B.E., *Puti i perspektivy mežregional'nogo vzaimodejstviâ v respublike Kazahstan* [*Regional cooperation paths and perspectives in Kazakhstan*], Astana, 2010, p. 234.

37 In comparison, in France, GDP per capita per annum varies from 1 to 2 depending on the region, due to the dominance of Paris. Outside the Paris region *(Ile-de-France)*, differences with the national average do not exceed 25 per cent.

38 *Ibid.*

39 Kolossov, V., O'Loughlin, J., 'How Moscow is becoming a Capitalist Mega-City', *International Social Sciences Journal,* 2004, vol. 56/181, pp. 413–27.

40 Vendina, O., 'Social Polarization and Ethnic Segregation in Moscow', *Eurasian Geography and Economics*, 2002, vol. 43/3, pp. 216–43.

41 Škaratan, O.I. (ed.), *Social'no-èkonomičeskoe neravenstvo i ego vozproizvodstvo v sovremennoj Rossii* [*Socio-economic inequalities and their reproduction in contemporary Russia*], Moscow: Olma Media Group, 2009, p. 556.

42 Bret, B., Gervais-Lambony, P., Hancock, C., Landy, F. (eds), *Justice et injustices spatiales*, Paris: Presses Universitaire de Paris Ouest, 2010, p. 315.

43 Bradshaw, M.J., 'Observations on the Geographical Dimension of Russia's Resource Abundance', *Eurasian Geography and Economics*, 2006, vol. 47/6, pp. 724–46.

44 Thorez, J., 'La construction territoriale de l'indépendance: réseaux et souveraineté en Asie Centrale post-soviétique', *Flux*, 2007, vol. 70, pp. 33–48.

45 Zajončkovskaâ, Ž.A., Tûrûkanova, E.V., Florinskaâ, Û.F., *Trudovaâ migraciâ v Rossiû: kak dvigat'sâ dal'še?* [*Labour migrations to Russia: where to go from now?*], Moscow: Maks Press, 2011, p. 52 (http://www.neweurasia.ru/media/1Labour_migration_to_Russia_r.pdf).

46 According to the Federal Migration Service, the number of officially registered migrant workers represents 3 per cent of the active population (*ibid.*). Including illegal workers, the figure increases to almost 10 per cent, comparable to figures for Germany or Belgium.

47 Zajončkovskaâ, Ž.A., Mkrtčân, N.V., Tûrûkanova, E.V., 'Rossiâ pered vyzovami immigracii' ['Russia and the call of immigration'] in Zajončkovskaâ, Ž.A., Vitkovskaâ, G.S. (eds), *Postsovetskie transformacii: otraženie v migraciâh*, Moscow: Adamant, 2009, pp. 9–62.

48 Brusina, O., 'Migranty iz Srednej Azii v Rossii: ètapy i pričiny priezda, social'nye tipy, organizacii diaspor' ['Migrants from Central Asian to Russia: migration stages and causes, social profiles and diaspora organisation'], *Vestnik Evrazii*, 2008, vol. 2/40, pp. 66–95.

49 Zûzin, D.I., *op. cit.*; Tarasova, N.V., 'Problema povyšeniâ migracionnoj aktivnosti naseleniâ' ['Problem of increased migration of the working population'], in *Sovremennye problemy migracii* [*Contemporary migration problems*], Moscow: Mysl', 1985, pp. 47–63; Patnaik, A., 'Agriculture and Rural Out-migration in Central Asia (1960–1991)', *Europe-Asia Studies*, 1995, vol. 47/1, pp. 147–69.

50 Migration is not only an economic strategy. The works of M. Reeves reveal how the migratory experience has become an important element in masculine identity, to some extent replacing military service for the Red Army (Reeves, M., 'Migrations, masculinité et transformation de l'espace social dans la vallée de Sokh', in Laruelle, M. (ed.), *Dynamiques migratoires et changements sociétaux en Asie centrale*, Paris: Pétra, 2010, pp. 217–45). Further, these migration flows are nation-specific: Tajikistan's legislation *de facto* encourages young men to migrate to avoid military service; in Uzbekistan, national migration restrictions linked to the administrative residents authorization system (*propiska*), or business activities through the control and taxation of imported goods, encouraged migrations in the early 2000s with some business owners developing their international mobility experience (Sadovskaâ, E.Û., 'Kazahstan v central'noaziatskoj migracionnoj subsisteme' ['Kazakhstan in the Central Asian migration sub-system'], in Zajončkovskaâ, Ž.A., Vitkovskaâ, G.S. (eds), *op. cit.*, pp. 279–322).

51 Olimova, S.K., 'Tadžikistan: ot vynuždennoj k trudovoj migracii' ['Tajikistan: from forced migrations to labour migrations'], in Zajončkovskaâ, Ž.A., Vitkovskaâ, G.S. (eds), *op. cit.*, pp. 350–76; Maksakova, L.P., 'Uzbekistan v sisteme meždunarodnyh migracii' ['Uzbekistan in the international migration system'], in Zajončkovskaâ, Ž.A., Vitkovskaâ, G.S. (eds), *op. cit.*, pp. 323–49.

52 Thorez, J., 'La mobilité des migrants d'Ouzbékistan: transport, frontières et circulation migratoire', *Revue Européenne des Migrations Internationales*, 2010, vol. 26/3, pp. 31–57.

53 *Ibid.*; Thorez J., 'Les nouvelles frontières de l'Asie Centrale: Etats, nations et régions en recomposition', *Cybergeo*, 2011, p. 28 (http://cybergeo.revues.org/23707).

54 Zajončkovskaâ, Ž.A., Mkrtčân, N.V., Tûrûkanova, E.V., *op. cit.*

55 *Ibid.*

56 *Ibid.*; Braux, A., 'Politique migratoire et gestion de la diversité culturelle en Russie: l'exemple de Moscou', *Les études du CERI*, 2009, vol. 158, p. 37.

57 Clochard, O. (ed.), *Atlas des migrants en Europe – Géographie critique des politiques migratoires*, Paris: A. Colin, 2009, p. 144.

58 Thorez, J., 2010, *op. cit.*; Thorez, J., 2011, *op. cit.*

59 Thorez, J., 2010, *op. cit.*

60 Tarhov, S.A., 'Transportnaâ integraciâ i dezintegraciâ postsovetskogo prostranstva: izmenenie passažirskih svâzej posle raspada SSSR' ['Integration and disintegration of the transport system in the post-Soviet space: changes to passenger lines after the break-up of the USSR'], *Izvestiâ RAN – seriâ geografičeskaâ*, 1997, vol. 3, pp. 73–82; Kolossov, V.A. (ed.), *Geopolitičeskoe položenie Rossii: predstavleniâ i realnost* [*The geopolitical situation of Russia: representations and reality*], Moscow: Art-kur'er – IGRAN, 2000, p. 352; Thorez, J., 2005, *op. cit.*

61 Thorez, J., 2007, *op. cit.*

62 Thorez, J., 2005, *op. cit.*

63 *Ibid.*

64 Tarhov, S.A., 1997, *op. cit.*

65 Nikol'kij, V.V., 1978, *op. cit.*

66 Thorez, J., 2010, *op. cit.*

67 From 2000 to 2005, the traffic of Russian airlines to Tajikistan increased from 6,000 to 274,000 passengers.

68 In some ways, the socioeconomic characteristics of the Russian North Caucasus are similar to South Caucasus countries'. In Central Asia the main economic discontinuities are located, at international level, on the Southern borders of Kazakhstan.

69 In Tajikistan, the share of remittances in GDP is the highest in the world, according to the World Bank.

70 Labour migrations can also be seen to reflect the incoherencies of the development model adopted since independence. Laruelle, M., 2010, *op. cit.*

71 Thorez, J., 2010, *op. cit.*

CHAPTER 9

FEMALE MIGRATION INTO RUSSIA FROM CENTRAL ASIAN COUNTRIES: MIGRANTS RESEARCHING MIGRANTS[1]

Natalia Zotova and Victor Agadjanian
(Institute of Ethnology and Anthropology, Russian Academy of Sciences, Moscow); (Arizona State University, USA)

This chapter considers some observations made during a project entitled 'Sexual Vulnerability and Sexual Risks of Central Asian Female Migrants in Moscow', which was conducted in the autumn of 2010. It examines the experience of research into migrants being conducted by other migrants, who were hired by the project to act as interviewers: their successes, the difficulties they encountered, and the reflections and conclusions that the interviewers made for themselves. It provides extracts from the interviewers' own accounts, in conjunction with comments and scholarly analysis from the authors. The chapter approaches the study of migration from the standpoint of cultural anthropology, which allows details to be highlighted, migratory processes to be viewed through the eyes of direct participants, and the research focus to be deepened.

Introduction

In Central Asia, the collapse of the Soviet Union brought in its wake large upheavals in the social and economic realms (and in others). This set in motion processes which had previously not been observed in the Central Asian region: in particular, large-scale migration abroad.

The overwhelming majority of migrants from Central Asia head for Russia, where the major point of attraction is the Central Federal District, with Moscow and the Moscow region in first place. According to figures from Russia's Federal Migration Service concerning the distribution of Central Asian workers among Russian federal districts in the first half of 2007, 38.2 per cent of migrants from Kyrgyzstan were working in the Central Federal District (including 35.3 per cent in Moscow and Moscow *oblast*). For migrants from Uzbekistan, these figures were 34.8 per cent and 23.4 per cent, respectively.[2] It should be noted that these figures refer to the number of migrants who had received work permits. If undocumented migrants (i.e. those working illegally) are taken into account, then higher rates are possible. Thus, according to Saodat Olimova,[3] the most attractive area for Tajik migrants in Russia is the Moscow conurbation (49 per cent of all migrants from Tajikistan working in Russia).[4]

This snowballing growth in the number of migrants has led to important structural shifts in the way society is organized. A huge wave of male labour migration has brought in its wake an exodus of women seeking work in a foreign country. Female migration is a new phenomenon in Central Asian society, although in general it typifies the broad pattern of evolution in migratory processes throughout the world at the end of the last century and the beginning of this. Experts have noted that the feminisation of migratory flows since the 1990s has become a characteristic feature of the most recent developments in international labour migration.[5] According to various assessments, women account for up to 40–50 per cent of the overall total of migrants throughout the world.[6]

It is vital to note that, until very recently, no special studies or monographs devoted to female migration from Central Asian countries into Russia have been published. It is possible to highlight several works that concern gendered aspects of post-Soviet migration, but in these, female migration from Central Asian countries is not considered separately. These works are, namely, a book by Elena Tiuriukanova and Marina Malysheva,[7] research by Dmitry Poletaev,[8] and a number of articles published in an issue of the journal *Diaspora*.[9] The first major research into female migrants and, undoubtedly, a significant step forward in the study of female migration came with work conducted under the aegis of UNIFEM by groups of experts in Tajikistan, Uzbekistan, Kyrgyzstan, Kazakhstan and Russia in 2008–09.[10] In the report published on the results of this research, a wide range of issues were illuminated: the factors which encourage women to travel away in search of work; models and projections of female labour migration; the opportunities and resources which they can utilize; the problems encountered in the receiving country; the effect of migration on their families etc. Nonetheless, the number of women surveyed in each country was not that high, and the resultant data do not reflect the regional, social and other variations that exist as a whole in the countries of the region, and in particular between the women of these countries.

Large-scale migration from the countries in the region is a relatively new occurrence; in this context, Tajik migration is the oldest and best established. An analysis of labour migration from Tajikistan can be found in the body of work by Saodat Olimova and Muzaffar Olimov.[11] There has yet to be any similar complex research conducted into migration from Kyrgyzstan and, until recently, there was none such regarding Uzbekistan. Moreover, due to the evident secrecy of Uzbekistan, and the unwillingness of that country's leadership to admit to the existence of significant migratory flows out across the country's borders, it was difficult to imagine that any such research would occur in the near future. For this reason it is important to mention an anthology of articles published under the aegis of the United Nations development programme in 2008.[12] This anthology contains articles and research on internal and external labour migration in Uzbekistan, including the results of two sociological research projects into the social and gendered aspects of migration. In the section on external migration, the data on women's attitudes to migration are of particular interest. Thus, 14.2 per cent of the women surveyed expressed a firm desire to leave Uzbekistan in search of work. 5.9 per cent had yet to make a firm decision, while not discounting the possibility of leaving.[13]

In sum, then, studies of large-scale migration from Central Asian countries into Russia over the last 10–15 years – a phenomenon which is relatively new, viewed from a historical perspective – have resulted in the publication of a significant quantity of generalizing works on issues concerning labour migration: the demographic and economic aspects; financial remittances and governmental attempts to regulate migratory processes; and international migration.[14] However, in both Russia and in Central Asia, a significant proportion of these publications have been written in a similar way: they contain figures and reflections on migration as a whole. Sociological research projects into migratory processes are being conducted in the countries of Central Asia, which are the main sources of labour migration into Russia. Several publications offer results from qualitative sociological research, extracts from in-depth interviews with participants in migratory processes, focus group analyses, and reflections on the transformation of gender relations as a consequence of mass migrations.[15] However, generalizing works cannot satisfy the interest of many researchers in the details. Nor do they have the necessary tools to identify and describe the causes, processes and consequences of migration from the point of view of the actual participants in these migratory processes, or to recount their personal life histories and their fates.

As the Lebanese researcher into migration Ghassan Hage wrote,

> 'After spending so many years examining all kinds of work in the areas of migration and diasporic studies, I have consistently found it to be the case that of all the disciplines deployed in studying globalization, migration and mobility, none are better equipped to capture the complexities of such social realities

> than an ethnographic analysis. This is because, more than ever, such realities still require the double gaze capable of capturing both descriptively the lived cultures with all their subtleties and analytically the global which structures them.'[16]

For a long time now, this has been the approach often taken by Western research into migration.[17]

Against this background of generalizing research which presents the reader with migration as statistics, very little work in the Russian research tradition has emerged which has been written from the stance of cultural anthropology, in which the story of the migrants and their families, their strategies and decisions, their intentions, and perceptions of success or failure in working abroad are presented with the help of the view 'from inside'. Few studies of Central Asian migration have so far been published that are written from this standpoint, which is characterized by a combination of macro-analysis of structural processes and such micro-analysis. Here, one might pick out research by Madeleine Reeves, who studied issues of migration from rural areas in Southern Kyrgyzstan. She was interested in how the decision to migrate was discussed and made, in the effect these decisions had on the local economy, in how departing to work abroad changed life for the settlement and for individuals, and so on. In addition, an array of interesting observations by the authors of a French publication on issues of migration from Central Asia[18] might be mentioned at this point, as might also several articles by Natalia Zotova which consider various aspects of female migration from Tajikistan and which present a view of migratory processes in the country as seen through the eyes of women.[19]

Implementation of the Project and the Experience of the Interviewers

Research into migration, and its place in the evolution of anthropology as a whole, has been the subject of a significant amount of Western scholarship.[20] As Steven Vertovic remarks: 'Migration and migration-related topics currently have a prominent place in the discipline of anthropology. Among an assortment of topics, anthropologists are involved in the study of areas such as migration and identities, citizenship, law and legal status, religion, family and kinship, children and the second-generation, language, education, health, media consumption, internet use, the construction of home, sexuality, remittances, hometown associations, development, local politics, workplaces and labour markets."[21] Anthropologists' attention is drawn to details, and to a combination of micro-analytical methods and tools with reflections on how the observed phenomena are located within the context of global migratory processes. A specific research focus in anthropology is described by Caroline Brettell, who discusses how the attention of these scholars is drawn to such questions as:

> 'the articulation between the place whence a migrant originates and the place or places to which he or she goes. This includes exploration of how people in local places respond to global processes. Equally, anthropology's focus on cultures, which includes the study of the interaction between beliefs and behaviour, of corporate groups, and of social relationships, has resulted in an emphasis in migration studies on matters of adaptation and culture change, on forms of social organization that are characteristic of both the migration process and the immigrant community, and on questions of identity and ethnicity.'[22]

The present chapter continues this tradition of cultural anthropology in the study of migration: it attempts to present a view of the issues surrounding female migration from Central Asian countries as seen through the eyes of those directly involved in these migratory processes. It draws on the findings of research conducted in Moscow in October–December 2010 into female migrants from the Central Asian countries of Kyrgyzstan, Tajikistan and Uzbekistan. 224 women between the ages of 18 and 40 were surveyed; they belonged to the three main ethnic groups: Kyrgyz, Uzbek and Tajik. Three sectors of the urban economy in which the representation of female migrants is relatively high were selected, namely: markets (sellers), catering establishments (mainly waitresses and cleaners), and small food shops (sellers, cashiers, merchandisers and cleaners). Kyrgyz, Uzbek and Tajik women were selected since they represent a significant proportion of the migrants in Moscow. While these three ethnic groups share many common features, especially when compared with the local population, there are ethnocultural differences between them; the attempt was made to capture these using a range of research tools.

The search for respondents took place via probability sampling in workplaces. Markets were selected by random sample, and then had a single one of the ethnic groups allotted to them. This was done in order to avoid the interviewers intruding on one another. To find respondents on the markets, we used a random walk algorithm. For work to be carried out in catering establishments (cafes and restaurants) and shops, lines on the Moscow Metro were selected. Two of the longest radial lines were chosen, on the basis of their colour on the network map coinciding to some degree with the colours on the national flags of the migrant women's countries of origin. Stations were selected at random along the chosen lines. All the cafes, restaurants and shops within a 500-metre radius (300 metres for central stations) were identified by traversing the location on foot, recording their names and marking them on a map. As a result, two separate lists were obtained: one for catering establishments and the other for shops. The places on the list were re-arranged randomly; in order to complete questionnaires with the required number of women, the interviewers visited each place in the order they now appeared on the list. A questionnaire consisting of several modules was designed for conducting the research. The modules were entitled: 'Individual characteristics'; 'Marriage and husband/partner's characteristics'; 'Health and reproductive behaviour'; 'Migration and life in Moscow'; 'Social ties'; 'Family and gender attitudes'; and 'Migration plans.' When the questionnaires had been completed, in-depth interviews were conducted with 21 of the women who had responded (seven from each ethnic group) to add precision and additional information to the responses received.[23]

The life of migrants in an urban setting differs significantly from life in their home country. As Anatolii Vishnevskii notes, the history of migration on a global scale can be characterized as the movement of the world village to the world city.[24] Even if migrants have moved from the capitals of their countries, for example Bishkek or Tashkent, life in Moscow presents them with different problems and compels them to find solutions. Moreover, migrants in Moscow are living in a different ethnic and cultural setting. Conducting research into migrants in the receiving country presents some difficulties: they are unwilling to make contact, they fear potential complications, and they are scared of officials from law-enforcement agencies etc. It is undoubtedly possible to make arrangements for meetings and interviews through migrants who are acquaintances or through those NGOs defending human rights, which migrants approach for help and advice. However, when migrants talk to local researchers, there still emerges a twin barrier effect: there is the language barrier, since not every migrant has a sufficiently high ability to speak Russian, and also their image of the researcher as 'other'. As a result of these obstacles, a significant amount of information may be missed or misapprehended by the researcher. Sherna Gluck remarks:

> The outsider can sometimes delve into certain kinds of experiences that insiders cannot. There might be specific topics that are more easily discussed with outsiders. Also, because outsiders are less conversant with the culture or subculture, they may take less for granted and ask for more clarification than insiders. On the whole, though, my experience has been that cultural likeness can greatly promote trust and openness, whereas dissimilarity reinforces cultural and social distance.[25]

To ease making contact with female migrants, and to resolve the problems of the language barrier and of alienation, interviewers from the countries being studied were selected; their ethnic self-identification matched that of the women migrants being surveyed by the project. The migration stories of the five young women acting as interviewers to a great extent matched the stories of their respondents: they had come to Russia to study or work. Two interviewers had come from Kyrgyzstan, from the cities of Bishkek and Osh. They were ethnic Kyrgyz. Two interviewers were from the Pamir mountains in Tajikistan (they were Shughni). The ethnic affiliation of the last interviewer was difficult to pin down, as always happens when dealing with people from Samarkand. She had grown up in a Russian-speaking family, and to the question 'What nationality do you consider yourself to be?' she replied archly 'Well, it says in our passports we're Uzbeks.' Four of the interviewers had degrees (graduating from universities in Bishkek, Khorog and Samarkand, and from the medical institute in Dushanbe). The youngest woman was a student at the Mendeleev Chemical Technology Institute in Moscow. The interviewers' ages ranged between 20 and 35. The student had lived in Russia longest of all: for six years. All the other women had spent between two and seven months in Moscow at the time the research was conducted.

The interviewers' task was to complete questionnaires and conduct in-depth interviews with Kyrgyz, Uzbek and Tajik migrant women. The two women from the Pamir mountains spoke fluent Tajik, and were responsible for the Tajik element of the project. The young woman from Bishkek worked with the Kyrgyz, and the two from Samarkand and Osh worked with the Uzbeks. The overwhelming majority of interviews were conducted in the native language of the respondents: Kyrgyz, Uzbek, Tajik, and several languages spoken in the Pamirs.

The somewhat unusual format of the research–'Migrants interviewing migrants'–allows the discussion of a distinctive focus that arises in such situations: a bifocal lens effect. Four of the five interviewers had arrived in Moscow very recently: the two from Tajikistan planned to further their education, the Kyrgyz woman from Bishkek had been compelled by difficult circumstances to travel to Russia to seek work, while the young woman from Samarkand had only just got married, and had arrived in Moscow with her husband, who had been living, studying and working in the city for some considerable time previously. No matter how different their circumstances were, they nonetheless each sought to find some source of employment or supplementary income in Moscow. And so each of them had lived her personal story of migration, had sought to realize her plans, and somehow to arrange her life in the unfamiliar and complex conditions of a huge megapolis. At the same time the women were working as interviewers: they were not only living their own story, but also observing and recording stories that were in effect very similar to their personal experience. As Ann Oakley remarks:

> When the social position of both [the interviewer and the interviewee] are the same, and their life experience is similar, the social distance reduces to a minimum. When the interviewer and interviewee belong to one and the same social minority, a notion of equality might be particularly clearly expressed in the mind of the interviewer.[26]

Note that the suggested methodology may have some potential drawbacks: due to this significant cultural closeness the interviewer may stray from the theme of the discussion or may become absorbed in details personally significant to her and the interviewee, and so on. When analysing the material obtained during the in-depth interviews, attempts were made to assess it in isolation from the respondent's own views and reflections. At the same time, the fact that the in-depth interview had been structured along previously determined lines helped to lower these possible risks.

As regards their personal circumstances, some of the interviewers found matters easier than others. Since they had come to join relatives, they were not faced with the threat of being left homeless if they could not earn enough to buy food and pay the rent. But some found things significantly harder. Things were worst for N. from Bishkek: in the spring of 2010, she and her husband had arrived in St Petersburg, where acquaintances helped them find work in a fish-processing business. However, their wages were regularly delayed, and consequently only a fraction of their earnings were actually paid out. Similar things happened with many of the other jobs that N. was forced to try. The young woman had enjoyed high social status in her home country: she had trained to be a lawyer, and had spent a long time working in that capacity for Kyrgyzstan's Ministry of Internal Affairs. In Russia, she had to live through a psychological crisis linked to the sharp decline in her status. N.'s fate was as grim as that of many migrants: she was forced to encounter deceits, insults, threats, unpleasant attitudes, difficult housing conditions etc. Since the memory of the offences she had suffered personally was so sharp, she approached all the respondents' life stories with great interest and sympathy. It could be said that she channelled absolutely everything through herself. She remembered each respondent and their situation, and could recount their details and particulars. She reflected on their fates, made subtle observations, analysed each case and drew conclusions. As a function of her temperament and straightforward personality, very many things upset her: discrimination, unfair treatment of migrants etc. At the bottom of the questionnaire was a field for any comments by the interviewer. N.'s comments were consistently interesting, reflecting both analysis and observation of the respondent along with the personality of the researcher herself. Some examples follow:

> Munara is a girl who smiles a lot, but I think she has a strong personality. She worked hard, but without enthusiasm. She defers to her managers and other [Russian] colleagues at work, scared of saying a word out of turn. To my question why she acted like that with them, she replied that she *had no rights* [underlined by N.] and would get nowhere if anything happened. Also, that they would always be right, even if the truth was on her side. She explained her refusal to leave her contact details [to allow a follow-up] by saying she did not want extra problems with her husband, on top of the ones she already had. And so every day she is stressed by contact with *representatives of the titular nationality* [underlined by N.]

> Zarina is a free-thinking girl, sociable and straightforward. She responded to the questions with ease, without embarrassment. Her free-thinking is either a consequence of her long sojourn in Moscow [four years] or of her *life in a city* [underlined by the

author: she was born and raised in Bishkek] because the mentality of eastern women does not allow them to be so open.

> I don't understand what such highly educated and well-brought-up people are doing in markets [author's note: the respondent worked on a market-stall]. I simply have nothing more to say, this kind of situation with migrants is an outrage and an insult.

At the same time it would be a mistake to assume that N. was identifying with the migrant women when taking their stories so close to her heart. On the contrary, the role of interviewer placed her in a certain sense above them.

> How did you feel during the research? How did you picture yourself when talking with the women, as their equal?

> No, to be honest, I felt I was a little above them, as though I was studying them.[27]

N.'s perception of her role offers an example of the bifocal lens effect mentioned earlier: on the one hand, she sympathized with migrant women living through a similar story. On the other hand, the role of observer distanced her from the Kyrgyz respondents and in some sense served to buttress N.'s social status in her own eyes and encouraged an increase in her sense of self-worth.

Interviewer A. encountered problems of a different kind. A Kyrgyz woman from the city of Osh (in Southern Kyrgyzstan), she had come to Moscow while still a schoolgirl, whereas at this point she was a student at one of the best higher education establishments in Moscow, and held Russian citizenship. She was a beautiful, petite young woman with a typically Kyrgyz appearance. While the research was being conducted, for a variety of reasons A. worked with Uzbek respondents; she spoke fluent Uzbek.[28] She encountered no problems gaining access to her respondents, but certain incongruities between her appearance and her chosen working language gave rise to doubts in some of the women being interviewed.

> Everyone used to ask why I would only interview Uzbek women. After we had the war [authors' note: the reference is to events in the city of Osh in the summer of 2010], everyone was on their guard–something here doesn't seem quite right. And also everyone was scared for their jobs–that they'd be sacked if they told anyone about their work. While some were even scared to talk at all. I was surprised that they were scared of me, after all, I don't look completely awful. They were scared for themselves, many of them thought they might do themselves no favours. Still more, after the war, after those things that took place back home.[29]

Some Uzbek refugees from Osh participated in the research. They had come to Moscow with all their relatives following the events in question. Other participants were women who had already been living and working in Moscow, but following the summer of 2010 were joined by relatives. Due to this sense of suspicion from the Uzbeks, A. had to introduce herself in a variety of ways:

> In some cases I would say I was Kyrgyz. Because they would ask straight away 'Here, you're a Kyrgyz, so why are you interviewing Uzbek women?' They were like 'something's not right here'. To some I would say I was an Uzbek girl from Ferghana. To others I said I was Uzbek on my father's side, which was why I looked like a Kyrgyz girl.

An excerpt follows from A.'s recollections of a conversation with ethnic Uzbeks who had become refugees after the events in Osh:

> I had this interview once – their entire family had come here from Kyrgyzstan. They had had their home burnt down, everything burnt down, there was nothing left. And they had such hatred of the Kyrgyz, it was just unreal ... They talked

> with such hatred, and at the same time they were crying because they had been treated so cruelly. But what they were telling me about – it really surprised me that Kyrgyz people could do such things.

This echo of the tragic events in Osh forced the young woman to dwell on problems that were new to her:

> (N.Z.): Had you ever thought about this before? In Moscow, everyone lives together, in Osh they used to live together. Did you ever think that Uzbeks and Kyrgyz were . . . different? Or had this never even crossed your mind before?
>
> Before? No. Because before, if, for example, some Russian lad on the street had started to harass me, then an Uzbek or even a Tajik man would immediately stand up for me. . . . And then, you can't believe it, that happens [authors' note: meaning the events in Osh]. I had never even thought that we might somehow be different from the Uzbeks. But after we had the war . . . now, when I walk past Komsomol'skaya [authors' note: Komsomol'skaya Metro station, alongside which are three railway stations] and the Uzbeks stare such daggers at you . . . there was none of that before. Before, Uzbeks, Kyrgyz, they were all friendly.

When considering A.'s situation as a researcher, it is, perhaps, necessary to talk, not of bifocal but of tri-focal lenses. Being a long-term resident in Moscow, the young woman was linked in to two social structures simultaneously. Since she had lived for a long time in Russia, she was fully integrated into Russian society. Her relationships, friendships and social ties were based upon it, and her relatives held Russian citizenship. Her elder sister had married an ethnic Russian Muscovite. The young woman herself was in higher education, and had many female friends among her coursemates. Simultaneously, she perceived herself to be part of a Kyrgyz social structure, with friends and relatives living in

Kyrgyzstan. A. tried to help her female friends who came to Moscow from Osh with the aim of finding employment. She was waiting for her boyfriend to complete his military service and was planning to marry him. Sometimes, she would discuss matters in terms of here and there.

> (N.Z.) You say of some respondents that they have turned Russian. Have I understood correctly that you mean those who have begun to act differently?
>
> Yes, I mean those who act, well, as though it was the twenty-first century, let's put it that way. Because there are some who, well, I don't understand them. They come here, and here they wear a long dress, they go about here in a headscarf [...] Of course, if you're married, and your husband won't allow any different, you can walk around in a headscarf and a long dress. But some of them begun to judge the others – they're like why do they behave like that? They put on jeans, they don't wear headscarves, not like us. But, well, is that how it is for us, here? We're in Russia, after all, we're in a different country. Here, you have to live like everyone else. For example, if I was there, in Kyrgyzstan, I would probably wear a long dress there, and a headscarf, and walk around like that. Because that's the custom, there. But here, it's not the custom.

At this point A. went on to discuss the accepted standards of behaviour in Moscow, commenting with a certain irony on some of her friends who went straight to the other extreme almost immediately after arriving in Moscow:

> They immediately put on mini-skirts, everything on view. Immediately, mind you, and they have only just arrived in long dresses [authors' note: i.e. from Kyrgyzstan] ... They let their hair down, put on a mini-dress and nylon tights. I saw a friend yesterday, she was in nylon tights, a really short skirt. She is big-breasted, but she had on a really thin blouse, that she could

> hardly button up. My god, what did she look like? And it's snowing at the moment ... Anyway, she only got here a month ago.

In this way, the interviewer's personal ideas about what is and is not acceptable, and the dichotomy between turning Russian and clinging to tradition shaped her analysis of her respondents' life histories. Reflections on Uzbek women from an ethnic Kyrgyz woman who had been resident for a long time in Moscow offer a deeper focus, by adding a third component to it. On the one hand, A.'s affiliation to a different ethnic group allowed her to maintain that minimum distance which is vital to an interviewer if she is to hear out and record the very varied life stories of her respondents. While undoubtedly empathising with the people she spoke to, the interviewer nonetheless was able to avoid becoming completely engaged emotionally in those women's experiences, which allowed her to keep to the general structure of the interview. On the other hand, her respondents construed their contact with A. as a woman-to-woman chat. They shared with her their difficulties around their husbands and partners. Some even offered guidance and homilies to the young woman, telling her about the potential dangers of sexual liaisons, about a variety of feminine health problems, about sexually transmitted diseases and also the methods they believed to be effective in preventing these. Several respondents sought to develop a friendship with A., ringing her after the project was over to suggest meeting up.

Recent arrivals from Central Asian countries, like the interviewers in this project, master the urban space. Within it, they form personal ties, and develop conceptions about a reality that had previously been alien to them. They construct their own mental map of the place where they now live. As Olga Brednikova and Olga Tkach remark:

> When changing their place of residence, migrants do not simply move from one population centre to another, they also reshape the space encompassed by their lives and significantly expand the boundaries of their day-to-day reality. ... They live

> simultaneously in several places and are integrated into more than one community or society.[30]

These authors discuss the way in which migrants gradually make a city their own:

> Easily swapping jobs and carrying their home in a box with them, women move around the city, gradually assimilating it and appropriating it. The association between home and work migrates and reproduces throughout the whole urban territory, filling a previously empty space with points that have meaning for the women. At the same time, their city is structured exclusively around the Metro map ... Metro stations become little centres which accumulate space around themselves.[31]

Likewise, during the design of this project, the map of the Moscow Metropolitan was used. Each of the ethnic groups being studied was allocated points along the two longest Metro lines, and then the stations along these lines were re-ordered at random. As a result, the interviewers had to do a great deal of travelling around the city, assimilating the space and exploring regions far from the city centre that were new to them. Here, the experience of Az., the interviewer from Samarkand (Uzbekistan), is worthy of note. Immediately prior to being introduced and beginning work on the project, Az. had spent no more than a month in Moscow, arriving in the city shortly after her wedding. Her husband had been working and living in Moscow for several years, but to the young woman the city was entirely new and unfamiliar; she only knew the small area around her home. This was in a distant suburb of Moscow, from which the easiest way to get to the centre or to the nearest Metro station was to take a suburban train. As work on the project progressed, she assimilated the city, spending time around Metro stations in regions all over Moscow. This experience was recounted with pride by Az. to her relatives, who found her new knowledge surprising. They commented that there was a whole set of regions in the city where they had never been, although they had been living in Moscow for some considerable time.

The authors of this chapter, as researchers, were not only interested to note the experiences of the interviewers as they worked on this project, but also to find out what happened to them subsequently. At the time of writing, of the five interviewers, only Az. has returned to her home country, for family reasons. She became pregnant, and spent most of her pregnancy in Moscow with her husband, but he and other relatives insisted she return home to Samarkand to give birth. Nonetheless, she enjoyed working as an interviewer very much. Her husband contacted Natalia Zotova to pass on his wife's comments that she would very much like to return to Moscow and be involved in any potential continuation of the project. The other four interviewers also remarked that they had gained valuable experience and qualifications. On Natalia Zotova's recommendation, all the interviewers were invited to take part in two other sociological research projects on migration, a testimonial to their professional abilities.

Conclusion

This chapter has attempted to highlight several points of interest which have emerged from this field-work, and to offer reflections on the way in which personal life stories and experiences of migration influence the way interviewers perceive their respondents. The unusual format of the research – 'Migrants interviewing migrants' – was of great interest to both the project leaders and to the young women who took part in the project as interviewers. When analysing the material gained during the in-depth interviews, a number of potential problems might have arisen – an interviewer deviating from the topic, a narrative being contaminated by the interviewer's interpretation, and so on. During the analysis, the respondents' personal views and judgements must be accounted for and isolated. Nonetheless, the fact that the in-depth interview had been structured along previously determined lines helped to lower these possible risks. Interviewer N. commented: 'It's simultaneously difficult and interesting. You're listening to the respondents' views, you're following the twists in the conversation, but at the same time you're keeping in mind the whole set of sample questions that you need to touch on in the discussion. You're trying not to miss anything out.' It could be claimed that the cultural closeness between the respondents and the interviewers, in conjunction with the latter's diligence and qualifications for the task, allowed for some high-quality, meaningful material to be collected as research progressed. The assessments and comments of the interviewers helped verify the material gathered, and also to perform a higher level of analysis.

By conducting research via interviewers who themselves are from the Central Asian countries being studied, much new information can be learned about the migration, feelings and self-identification of the new inhabitants of the great Moscow megapolis; about their problems and difficulties, their successes and joys; about their personal life stories and their plans for the future. In the arena of Russian research at the time of writing the vast majority of projects devoted to studying migrants in Russia were being carried out by Russian scholars with the addition of local interviewers and other collaborators. Notwithstanding all the interesting results obtained by these researchers, such work continues the tradition of a somewhat one-dimensional view on migratory processes: a view focused solely on the receiving country. Bringing on board interviewers who are themselves from the countries being studied offers more than the immediately obvious advantage of obtaining information on sensitive subjects that might be simply inaccessible for Russian researchers. It has allowed the following: the performance of a more complex analysis; the presentation of the interaction of migrants with both the society receiving them and with the ties binding them to the country they originate from; and the recognition of migration from Central Asian countries through the prism of trans-nationalism studies as a mobile, dynamic system in which migrants are actors integrated into several societies simultaneously. The interaction of migrants with the society receiving them and their conception of themselves in a new cultural setting depends on many factors, both internal and external. Internal factors include personal life and migration history, education, cultural and professional baggage, the age of the individual, the time spent living and working in the receiving country, and future plans and migration strategies. External factors include the state's migration policies, the receiving society's attitude to migrants, and interactions between different ethnic groups of migrants.

Taking the paradigm of cultural anthropology as the basis of any approach to researching migration may be of benefit to further analysis of, inter alia, the following: migrant identity in a Russian social setting; migrant adaptation to a new cultural environment; aligning systems of mutual aid with the legal system; using the resources of social support and social networks; the persistence or transformation of gender roles; and changes in attitudes to family and marriage.

Notes

1 This project was made possible thanks to a grant from the School of Social and Family Dynamics, Arizona State University, USA.

2 Abdullaev, E.V., *Trudovaia migratsiia v Respublike Uzbekistan: sotsial'nye, pravovye i gendernie aspekty* [*Labour Migration in the Republic of Uzbekistan: social, legal and gendered aspects*], Tashkent, 2008, p. 34.

3 This assessment is based on data from surveys conducted for the Sharq fund in Tajikistan.

4 Golunov, S.V., *Regional'noe izmerenie transgranichnoi migratsii v Rossiiu* [*Regional measurement of cross-border migration into Russia*], Moscow: Aspekt-press, 2008, p. 83.

5 Castles, S., Miller, J., *The Age of Migration. International Population Movements in the Modern World*. London: Macmillan, 1998.

6 International Organization for Migration. *World Migration Report 2008: Managing Labour Mobility in the Evolving Global Economy*, Geneva: IOM, 2008, pp. 10–11.

7 Tiuriukanova, E.V., Malysheva, M.M., *Zhenshchiny. Migratsiia. Gosudarstvo* [*Women. Migration. The State*]. Moscow: Academia, 2001.

8 Poletaev, D., 'Zhenshchiny-migranty iz zarubezhniykh stran v Rossii' ['Female migrants from foreign countries in Russia'], *Vestnik Evrazii*, 2005, vol. 1.

9 The issue in question is n°1 from 2005. See in particular the foreword 'Ot sostavitelia' ['From the Editor'], written by Natalia Kosmarskaia, and Elena Tiuriukanova's article 'Gendernye aspekty trudovoi migratsii iz stran SNG v

Rossiyu' ['Gendered aspects of labour migration from CIS countries into Russia'].

10 *Otsenka nuzhd i potrebnostei zhenshchin trudiashchikhsia-migrantov. Tsentral'naia Aziia i Rossiya* [*Assessing the needs and requirements of women labour migrants. Central Asia and Russia*], Ex Libris: Almaty, 2009.

11 The results of this complex research are set out in the following publication: Olimova, S., Bosc, I., *Trudovaia migratsiia iz Tadzhikistana* [*Labour Migration from Tajikistan*], Dushanbe: IOM-NITs Sharq, 2003. S. Olimova and M Olimov are likewise the authors of chapters on migration from Tajikistan published in an array of later publications: see e.g. Golunov, S.V., *Regional'noe izmerenie transgranichnoi migratsii v Rossiiu* [*Regional measurement of cross-border migration into Russia*], Moscow: Aspekt-press, 2008.

12 *Trudovaia migratsiia v Respublike Uzbekistan: sotsial'nye, pravovye i gendernie aspekty* [*Labour Migration in the Republic of Uzbekistan: social, legal and gendered aspects*], Tashkent, 2008.

13 *Ibid*., p. 158.

14 For a detailed overview of the existing publications, see: Zotova, N., 'Uzbekskie obshchiny v Rossii: novye "diaspory" (na primere Sankt-Peterburga, Astrakhani, Krasnoiarska)' ['Uzbek communities in Russia: new "diasporas" (on the examples of St. Petersburg, Astrakhan, Krasnoyarsk)'], *Issledovaniia po prikladnoi i neotlozhnoi etnologii* [*Studies in Applied and Urgent Ethnology*], 2010, vol. 222.

15 Of recent publications, see e.g.: Kasymova, S., *Transformatsiia gendernogo poriadka v tadzhikskom obshchestve* [*Transformations of gender structures in Tajik society*], Dushanbe: Irfon, 2007; Olimova S., Olimov M., 'Labor Migration from Mountainous Areas in the Central Asian Region: Good or Evil?', *Mountain Research and Development*, 2007, vol. 27/2, pp. 104–8; International Labour Organization & Sharq, *Families of Migrants in Tajikistan*, Dushanbe: Irfon, 2007.

16 Hage, G., 'A Not So Multi-Sited Ethnography of a Not So Imagined Community', *Anthropological Theory*, 2005, vol. 5/4, p. 474.

17 For an analysis of the existing literature and methods, see e.g.: Vertovec, S., 'Introduction: New Directions in the Anthropology of Migration and Multiculturalism', *Ethnic and Racial Studies*, 2007, vol. 30/6, pp. 961–78.

18 See the articles by Madeleine Reeves, Nafisa Khusenova and Stéphanie Bélouin in the anthology of Laruelle, Marlène, *Dynamiques migratoires et changements sociétaux en Asie central*, Paris: Editions Petra, 2010.

19 Zotova, N.A., 'Zhenskaia trudovaia migratsiia i vera v sobstvennye sily' ['Female labour migration and faith in one's own powers'], http://ferghana.ru/article.php?id=4715; Zotova, N.A. 'Zhenshchiny–trudovye migranty iz Tadzhikistana (starshaiya vozrastnaia gruppa)' ['Female labour migrants from Tajikistan (the older age cohort)'], *Vestnik Evrazii*, 2007, vol. 2/36, pp. 72–88; Zotova, N.A., 'Vospriiatie migratsii v strane iskhoda: Tadzhikistan' ['Perceptions of Migration in the Country of Origin: Tajikistan'], *Vestnik Evrazii*, 2008, vol. 2, pp. 29–43.

20 See e.g.: Gmelch, G., 'Return Migration', *Annual Review of Anthropology*, 1980, vol. 9, pp. 135–59; Kearney, M., 'From the Invisible Hand to Visible Feet:

Anthropological Studies of Migration and Development', *Annual Review of Anthropology*, 1986, vol. 15, pp. 331–61; Eades, J., 'Anthropologists and Migrants: Changing Models and Realities' in J. Eades (ed.), *Migrants, Workers and the Social Order*, London: Tavistock, 1987, pp. 1–16; Malkki, L., 'Refugees and Exile: From 'Refugee Studies' to the National Order of Things', *Annual Review of Anthropology*, 1995, vol. 24, pp. 495–523; Brettell, C.B, 'Theorizing Migration in Anthropology: The Social Construction of Networks, Identities, Communities and Globalscapes', in Brettell, C.B., Hollifield, J.F. (eds), *Migration Theory*, NY: Routledge, 2000, pp. 97–135; Foner, N., 'Anthropology and the Study of Immigration' in Foner, N. *et al.* (eds), *Immigration Research for a New Century*, NY: Russell Sage Foundation, 2000, pp. 49–53; Sanjek, R., 'Rethinking Migration, Ancient to Future', *Global Networks*, 2003, vol. 3/3, pp. 315–36.

21 Vertovec, S., *op. cit.*, p. 961.

22 Brettell, C.B., *op. cit.*, p. 98.

23 For a detailed description of the methodology used in this research project, see: Agadjanian, V., Zotova, N., 'Sampling and Surveying Hard-to-Reach Populations for Demographic Research: A Study of Female Labor Migrants in Moscow, Russia', *Demographic Research*, 2012, vol. 26, pp. 131–50.

24 Vishnevskii, A.G., *Rossiia pered demograficheskim vyborom. Vystupleniia i interv'iu* [*The Demographic Choice Facing Russia. Speeches and Interviews*], Moscow: GU-VShE, 2007, p. 190, p. 222.

25 Gluck, S., 'V chem osobennosti zhenshchin? Zhenskayi ustnaia istoriia' ['What's so Special about Women? Women's Oral History'], in Peto, Andrea (ed.), *Zhenskaia ustnaia istoriia 1* [*Women's Oral History 1*], Bishkek: Women's Network Programme of the Open Society Institute, 2004, p. 203.

26 Oakley, Ann, 'Sotsiologicheskie oprosi zhenshchin: protivorechiia mezhdu teoriei i praktikoi' ['Interviewing women: a contradiction in terms'], in Peto, Andrea (ed.), *Zhenskaia ustnaia istoriia 1* [*Women's Oral History 1*], Bishkek: Women's Network Programme of the Open Society Institute, 2004, pp. 168–9.

27 Excerpt from an interview with N. conducted by Natalia Zotova after the end of the research project.

28 The population of the city of Osh, which is situated in Kyrgyzstan, consists largely of two ethnic groups–Kyrgyz and Uzbeks. As a result, many residents of the city speak both languages.

29 Excerpt from an interview with A. conducted by Natalia Zotova after the end of the research project.

30 Brednikova, O., Tkach, O., 'Dom dlia nomady' ['A home for a Nomad'], *Laboratorium*, 2010, vol. 3, pp. 72–3.

31 *Ibid.*, p. 86.

CHAPTER 10

LABOUR MIGRATIONS IN THE OMSK REGION: ADMINISTRATIVE AND ECONOMIC WORKFORCE MANAGEMENT PRACTICES AND CONSTRUCTION OF NEW SOCIAL RELATIONS[1]

Anne Le Huérou
(CERCEC, Paris)

Whether by force or voluntarily, as a consequence of conflicts or in response to the economic necessities resulting from social and economic changes post-1991, migration to Russia has played a key role in public policies and has been continually raised in public debate since the second half of the 2000s.

This chapter proposes an off-centre study, more specifically to the region of Omsk, located in Southern Siberia on the border with Kazakhstan. An *oblast* characterized by the length of time in office of its rulers,[2] political stability often referred to as immobile and apathetic.[3] During the 1990s, the region experienced a flux of immigration of citizens from Kazakhstan, comprising Russians, Germans and ethnic Kazakhs, the latter joining a minority already present in the region.[4] Russian-speaking populations from other Central Asian republics also emigrated to the region in the early 1990s, leaving behind them the political and social instability of the newly independent states of Central Asia. The situation became more complex in the 2000s as the region of Omsk itself was subject to a wave of departures, including a return to an economically stronger and more dynamic Kazakhstan.[5] However, the city of Omsk witnessed important economic expansion in the second half of the 2000s, based on high consumption levels, significant commercial and service activities and a construction boom. These sectors rely on local workforce and are therefore the most likely to resort to migrants in a context of demographic decline.

Based on field research carried out mainly in the Omsk region in 2009 and 2010,[6] this contribution is a reflection on contemporary labour migrations in Russia, considering migration policy as well as the strategies and experience of the stakeholders in the migration field: administration, employers, migrants and diasporas.[7] Consideration will also be given to understanding how the question of migrant workers is addressed and debated at regional level and how or, indeed, whether it is integrated into 'national' or 'ethno-cultural' debates.[8]

Although this chapter does not result from a lengthy ethnographic study, it reviews the migration experience in a global context taking various factors into consideration, from the legality dimension up to daily work experience and to the mediating role of a variety of intermediaries.[9] It takes into account the migratory experience, or *micro*-level, and the regional policies applied to migrant workers as well as the role played by other actors in the migration field: employers, intermediary firms and diasporas – the *meso*-level. The *macro*-level of global processes, in particular economic dynamics linked to globalization, a concept newer to Russia than other regions in the world and the extent of which remains to be seen, should also be taken into account.[10] This is particularly true when considering how migration between Russia and its periphery affects the post-Soviet era within an increasingly globalized international context. Whether at micro, meso or macro level, two main points can be raised from the analysis: firstly, labour migrations appear as an 'adjustment variable' for which many diverse and sometimes contradictory economic and administrative regulations are implemented; secondly, observations of this process help to understand how a new post-Soviet and post-imperial social rapport is created, marked by an ethnicization of social processes.

Regional Migration Policies: Responding to Bureaucratic Necessity and Helping the Rational Management of Labour Flux

A compromise between various administrative, political and economic actors' agendas, the migration policy of the Omsk region can be described, in what may seem contradictory terms, as strong administrative control destined to accompany a liberal stance of migrating workforce management, with migrants as an adjustment variable. A complicated and game between municipal and regional administrations, the Regional Direction of the Federal Migration Service,[11] and employers takes place on the basis of annual quotas and foreign workforce registration. The necessity to concord with the federal economic ministries policies and with the FMS injunctions from Moscow brings additional layers to the procedure.

In the general context of a marked recentralization of power in Russia in the 2000s, the policy adopted by the Omsk region for the most part followed the development of federal legislation and its application. It is worth noting that a turning point came in autumn 2006, when Russian public decision-makers, in line with an all too common pattern, took advantage of the highly emotional issue of Kondopoga riots[12] to push through reforms. As regards migration policies, debates that had been ongoing for several years between supporters of a liberalization to accompany Russian economic growth and those who fought for a restrictive policy highlighting the dangers and magnitude of illegal immigration,[13] coincided with this event that radicalized and ethnicized political views on the question of migration, often confused with the situation of 'non'-Russian citizens of the Russian Federation.[14] The xenophobic feelings sparked by Kondopoga were used by certain politicians who spoke of an exceeded 'tolerance level' and called for 'selective immigration' to attract compatriots *(sootechestvenniki)*, Russians living abroad, particularly in former Soviet republics, with a new welcome programme.[15]

This conjunction gave rise to two new series of measures at the end of 2006 and the end of 2007, revealing a double-sided movement of liberalization and limitation:[16] On the one side, a law limiting market access to foreign workers, claiming priority for national producers, testifies the politicization of the question of migration;[17] on the other side, the facilitation of entry, residency and employment conditions for foreigners, raises mixed feelings among observers and actors of migration policies, and are often seen as the result of contradictory trends of politicians.[18] After some years of existence, these measures can be seen to have simplified access to residency and employment, tending towards a more flexible workforce.[19] In 2010, new legislation on individual work licence (*patent*) was introduced to simplify the professional activity of migrants on an individual basis, in particular in the care services and catering sectors.[20] New initiatives were then launched in 2012 and 2013, such as the introduction of a compulsory Russian language test for migrants applying for a work permit in the Russian Federation.[21]

With the above in mind, consideration shall now be given to how these new provisions were accepted, interpreted and applied in the region. Interviewed administrative staff confirmed that 2007 was a real breakthrough. The simplification of entry procedures in the Russian Federation, in particular as concerns nationals of countries that do not require a visa for visits of less than three months, immediately legalized numerous seasonal migrations. As Omsk lies on the border with Kazakhstan, it is relatively easy for migrant workers to cross back and thereby avoid illegal status.

Replacing obligatory residency registration (*registraciïa po mestu prebyvaniïa*) with a simple declaration to register a temporary resident (*uchët po mestu prebyvaniïa*) is a major innovation of the law aimed at prevention and legalizing immigrants for a limited period of three months, occasionally six. This provision reflects a desire to relax the rule and facilitate the employment of foreign workers.

Another development of the 2007 provisions and further proof of a relative liberalization, obtaining a work permit no longer depends solely on the employer, whereas before the migrant worker was totally dependent on an employment contract entered into with the employer.[22] Considerable efforts were made by the UFMS in Omsk to explain the new legislative and statutory provisions to potential employers of foreign workers. A brochure published in 2008 detailed the steps to be taken by the employer and migrant worker, on a case-by-case basis, to ensure that all parties respect the new laws.[23]

Another procedure, considered by the interviewees in Omsk to be equally as important, completes and regulates this liberalization by installing a quota system fixing the number of work permits to be delivered by a given region on an annual basis.[24] For foreigners from the 'far abroad' (beyond the ex-Soviet external borders), a quota is established at federal level based on information on workforce needs in each region. Thereafter, a back and forth negotiation process ensues between federal and regional bodies.[25] For the largest group of migrant workers, coming from neighbouring areas and thus benefitting from entry on to Russian territory without a visa, a multi-party commission piloted by the regional Labour ministry sets the maximum number of work permits for the coming year, based on employer requests.[26] Labour Ministry officials admit that the provisions of the 2007 law make the process more difficult for employers but at the same time 'clarify' things allowing access across the board, 'an employer is guaranteed to have his application taken into consideration, it is no longer a case of first come first served'.[27]

The year 2008 saw a maximum number of authorizations being issued to close and remote foreigners, in total 12,500, of which 2,500 were for remote foreigners.[28] According to administrative documentation,[29] a specific procedure is followed: an employers' request for 15 unskilled workers can either be fully granted by the commission, refused or partially authorized based on the company activity for the previous year, its forecast, compliance with rules on migrant workers (accommodation, health, wages). A request by a company for 60 Chinese workers was pending on the basis that the company wages are too low compared to the average wage in the sector.

From autumn 2008, the economic crisis affecting Russia, particularly sectors requiring foreign labour, such as in construction, gave rise to a progressive revision of policies. Initial forecasts for 2009 showed a slight decrease in employer requests. Administrations also tightened control over real needs and introduced a new provision whereby employers are obliged to prove that they are unable to find an equivalent worker locally. As the crisis continued, 2010 quotas were halved,[30] in line with the significant decrease of employers applications.

Like other regions, Omsk introduced the new compulsory Russian language test in 2012, although to date it does not appear to be fully implemented. Fewer than 20 people have come to the Omsk pedagogical university to pass the test,[31] and it is considered as 'yet another law that doesn't work in practice'.[32]

From the municipal administration viewpoint, the quota system is only partially effective as it is in practice difficult to ensure that a reduced number of work permits truly lead to a decrease in the number of foreign workers employed. Observers were quick to note that after the onset of the crisis, the decrease in the number of work permits meant that a considerable number of workers, for whom the new regulations meant a newfound legal status, reverted to an illegal situation. Further, despite reports referring to Tajik workers leaving en masse on trains from Kazan station in Moscow, this did not correspond to a large number returning to their country of origin.

Although public debate over illegal migration is prominent in Russia, with unverifiable figures and estimations mainly motivated by political necessities,[33] Omsk region appears to be less concerned by the issue for several reasons. Proximity to the Kazakh border makes it easy for migrant workers to leave and re-enter Russian territory every three months with temporary resident permits; the presence of a large number of individual houses[34] known as the 'private sector', progressively abandoned by owners and developing into an important pool of informal rentals for migrants; and up until 2009, the possibility for Kazakh, Uzbek and Kyrgyz nationals to rapidly acquire Russian citizenship.

In the Omsk region, the most publicized and visible cases concern Chinese workers often employed in markets or restaurants. This category of migrants is largely dealt with by the police and immigration services reporting to their superiors using various procedures of control, arrest, detention and expulsion. Observation of the large 'Chinese market' on the left bank of the city reveals the forms of control carried out and the noticeable tension that exists in the face of plain clothed patrols. Although the Chinese are present in the shops, and indeed often own them, they do not actually sell, prohibited by provisions that came into force in 2006, and leave this to Russians or former Central Asia nationals having acquired Russian citizenship. The administration seems more determined to control the commercial activity of this category of migrants coming from nearby countries than the 'close foreigner', meaning from ex-Soviet states.

A special brigade of an Interior Ministry regiment assists the UFMS in the crackdown on illegal immigrants by carrying out raids and arrests in the markets. The illegal migrants are then transferred to the FMS and can be sent to an administrative detention centre prior to expulsion. Such raids were conducted in 2013 on the circles of owners of *Marshrutki*.[35] A report of the UFMS advisory council refers to the existence of an administrative detention centre operating under good conditions in Omsk, contrary to neighbouring regions such as Novosibirsk. However, the brigade leader in charge of these operations is clear on the effectiveness of his work: 'I'm like any official, I meet my set objectives and after that it's out of my hands but I think that the illegal workers are useful to a lot of people, we all know they work for almost nothing.' He notes that the authorities, who referred to 300 expulsions in 2007 and 2008[36] are in no hurry to carry out mass expulsions due to the costs involved.[37]

The ambiguity, characteristic of Russian migration policy, is also apparent with regards to illegal practices and corruption. In addition to authorities overlooking the numerous illegal outlets selling work permits or medical certificates to migrants, the migration department itself was caught up in a case of corruption concerning foreign workers.[38] A scandal unveiled in 2010 led to the suspension and arrest of the head of the regional department of the FMS, V. Allès, accused of using his wife to organize the mass supply of work permits to Chinese employers importing workers without going through official channels. This case seriously damaged the reputation of the UFMS, undermining the policy of procedural rigour, severity in the face of non-compliant employers and respect of migrant rights applied since 2008. A review of the documents produced by the service confirms this policy, for example the minutes of internal meetings and the views of the regional deputy director who wants to see the rights of migrant workers respected and prevent ethicizing and stigmatizing opinions.[39]

Generally speaking, interviews with UFMS officials and various municipal or regional departments highlighted contradictory attitudes. On the one hand, a desire to substantiate the adopted policy around economic necessities and administrative procedures (i.e. registration, medical certificates, etc.) to ensure the legality of migrant workers present on the territory and protect their rights. Work inspectors confirmed that they frequently visit companies employing large numbers of migrants to verify working and living conditions, particularly when workers live on the premises. Employers that do not respect minimum wages and health and safety requirements can be sanctioned and refused future foreign worker applications. Since the law of January 2007, illegal work is in theory punishable by heavy fines, which, according to the deputy director of the FMS, should be sufficient to dissuade employers.[40] On the other hand, their discourse and the way they explain their practices reveal underlying dimensions of the historical construction of the nationalities question and its legacy in the post-Soviet period

Administrative Practices and Labour Management: Caught Between the Legacy of the Nationalities Policy and Promotion of Economic Interests?

Former republics with proclaimed equal rights, Soviet peripheries were nevertheless part of the Soviet nationalities policy and thus subject to a set of rights and duties, promotion and repression policies, embedded in complex processes of modernization and domination. Focus can be on the colonial nature of the Soviet statehood with its proactive construction of a national élite,[41] or the emancipator dimension of the 'affirmative action Empire'[42] or simply a 'family resemblance'[43] between the Soviet Empire and other imperial experiences. New independent states of the Caucasus and Central Asia have inherited a specific place in their relationship with the new Russian state. In part due to tsarist Russia and Soviet legacy, this place has been renegotiated since 1991 with multiple factors involved.

A continuation of this situation can still be seen in administrative practices and working relations in Omsk at the end of the 2000s. Migrant workers, and in particular those from neighbouring former Soviet Union republics, are caught up in a tangle of perceptions concerning their origins inherited from previous periods and combined with current political discourse and social representations. These perceptions contribute to the implementation of policies that aim to restrict and control them, either individually or as a 'community'.

An illustration can be provided with public health policies towards migrants founded on a hygienist and prophylactic vision inherited from the Soviet era and reinforced by fears of contagious diseases imported from abroad. According to an official at the regional Health Ministry, 'it is important that we do not let in migrants carrying socially dangerous diseases'.[44] Despite many surveys which testimonies that diseases, especially STD's are often 'brought back' from Russia by migrants. The 'one way' direction of these diseases is an undisputable fact for the authorities. Meanwhile, the officials seemed well aware of and without illusions about the widespread corruption of medical certificates.[45]

The Advisory Council of the UFMS: 'Communities' Without Migrants

The advisory council working with the FMS, convening actors of local civil society on a quarterly basis, is another example of a clear desire to supervise communities.[46] Administrative officials present their policies, get advice from experts, entrepreneurs, universities, religious representatives and representatives of various diasporas to ensure that they have fully understood and respect the legislation, to anticipate tensions between communities, and in turn to show good will in the face of the xenophobic tendencies of political parties as presented by the media. In line with this attitude, the president of the consultative council to the FMS at federal level, V. Volokh, tried to present a non-xenophobic view of migrants in a 2008 broadcast by showing that criminal statistics contradicted the widespread view that migrants made up the majority of criminals and delinquents,[47] but proceeded to show poor knowledge of migration figures.[48]

In the Omsk region, meetings of the consultative council to the UFMS are in sum a report on the quantitative and qualitative activity of the FMS for a given period, focusing on salient facts or incidents. The existence of this council alongside the UFMS raises the question of whether there is another dimension to the migration policy: what local vision of the migrants is the policy based on and how can it be argued to stem from the more classic nationalities policy as regards 'non-Russians' present in the region, be they Russian citizens belonging to national minorities or migrant workers? The composition of the council is interesting in this regard: the religious representative of the Muslim community is the Tatar Mufti, not a religious leader coming from one of the countries of origin of the migrants, but a representative of the Siberian Tatars, a long-established minority of the local population. Specialists of Islam in the region confirm that mosques' attendance follows a strict division of nationalities: the Tatars do not go to the Kazakh mosque and vice versa, and the Tajiks and Uzbeks do not go to either it would seem.[49] The Kazakhs, mostly citizens of the Russian Federation, and so not so affected by the main labour migration problems, also have their own council representative. The presence on the council of an Armenian representative is further testimony of the way this consultative body is built: a set of people who are identified representatives of 'non-Russian' populations but often Russian citizens, much more concerned with addressing classical issues of cultural and symbolic rights of local minorities, rather than challenging administrative issues or promoting the social or economic rights of the labour migrants.[50]

Despite the fact that most of the actors ensuring the 'civic control' required by the law on migratory policy are not migrants but representatives of local minorities, some more direct work with the diasporas representing the countries of origin of the migrant workers has also been carried out. Convened by the FMS to explain the new legislation, representatives of the diasporas then disseminate information to the members of their respective communities to ensure that the migrant workers have fully understood and are respecting the new rules and regulations.[51] Here again, we can see a partial repetition of nationalities and minorities policies applied during the Soviet era. The requested loyalty gives rise to a certain control over the communities via their official representatives. In return, these representatives can expect authorities to be severe in the face of employer abuse. For example, the annual report prepared for the advisory council which referred to a complaint lodged by Kyrgyz workers for the non-payment of salaries led to the condemnation of the company following an inquiry.

Should we conclude from this that 'local minorities' are embedded as a symbolic intermediary between labour migrants and the administration? To an extent this is true and can be explained by the fact that local administration efforts to be efficient and pragmatic are constrained by traditional Soviet schemes giving particular weight to the construction of groups based on nationalities and their representatives who are supposedly organized and controlled by diasporas. A more pragmatic explanation refers to local specificity: the implementation of an official federal policy on the ground reveals a significant measure of flexibility on the part of local authorities who naturally turn to people and modalities that they are familiar with.

On a more pragmatic level, this clientelistic and asymmetric relationship between authorities and minority representatives assimilated to migrants takes on varying forms and intensity depending on the way in which 'inter-ethnic relations' are built in a given region.[52] Local observers present Omsk as a region where ethnicity plays a minor role and raise the question whether this is due to the lack of public debate on issues like 'tolerance levels' or migrant related criminality, or does it reflect a more genuine stance in favour of the idea of a multinational Russia? This provincial characteristic was observed in Kazan where the multinational character of the city is again not essentially linked to labour migrations.[53]

The Kazakhs: A Local Diaspora on the Border

The above observation should be studied in more detail and begs the question of the role of the geographical situation of the Siberian Region, land of immigration on the one hand, and a border with Kazakhstan on the other. Co-existence with 'non-Russian' nationalities such as Tatars and Kazakhs is an integral part of the regional identity make-up and supported by the authorities. The stability of this composition lies in the history of settlement and frontiers as much as the economic and political ties of the current governor with Kazakhstan.[54] Questions referring to 'Kazakh migrants' generally surprise FMS and administrative officials in so far as the Kazakhs are clearly considered as part of the local population. The common response is 'oni zhe mestnye' ['but they are from here']. They are perceived as locals or neighbours, not as migrants, even by the authorities: 'there are no real migrants from Kazakhstan, those wishing to stay obtain Russian citizenship after three months'.[55] It is worth noting that prior to the 2008 crisis, Kazakhstan was the principal investor in the region.[56] Also, during the long lasting conflict between the former mayor Valery Roshchupkin and the governor, the Kazakh diaspora clearly sided with the governor L. Polezhaev.

Indeed, the history and geography of this area comprising Kazakhstan and Southern Siberia together contribute to a new territorial and politico-economic make-up. Long-lasting economic and territorial links, the effects of the significant arrival of Russian migrants[57] in Kazakhstan at the beginning of the 1990s, and the strong economic growth of Kazakhstan in the 2000s, all contribute to draw continuity between the two territories. Contrary to other conflict-ridden former Soviet entities, this continuity stems from a desire to seek mutual interests on an equal basis[58] and is epitomized in the numerous normative acts related to the border zones and economic and commercial cooperation.[59] The difference is that they concern on the one side a sovereign state and on the other a region, ever loyal to federal organs. The Customs Union between the Russian Federation, Belarus and Kazakhstan, ratified on 1 July 2010, ended all administrative procedures for both workers and employers. Commentators noted at the time that this ratification would have little effect on the migration flux from Kazakhstan, save for certain border regions. In order to reassure public opinion, supposedly reticent to the liberalization of migration procedures, it was argued that Russians or Ukrainians were more likely to be affected, and that Kazakhstan, which had become a country of immigration,[60] should expect to see an influx of workers.[61]

Relations between state officials are historically anchored, based on geographical and economical factors, and are reflected in both daily practice and social representations between Russians and Kazakhs in the region. The case of Kazakhstan highlights the differential treatment of migrant communities from other Russian peripheries. A hierarchy of nationalities is applied between *svoi* (our) and *chuzhie* (the others, the foreigners). These nationalities are controlled and integrated on an economic and demographic needs basis. This global approach is a direct reminder of how the Russian empire and thereafter the Soviet Union dealt with the question of nationalities, including having recourse to experts or prominent figures as they appear on the advisory council of the UFMS.[62] The studies, opinion polls and monitoring carried out by various academic or independent research centres on the inter-ethnic climate and/or tensions in the region that group together labour migrants with Russian citizens considered as 'ethnic minorities are worth investigating further'.[63]

Though quite secluded, the Kazakh community in Omsk appears to be integrated from an administrative viewpoint and in the eyes of the local population. Successful in business, they are indeed perceived in the region as an integral part of the multinational population including Germans and Siberian Tatars, and to a lesser extent Chechens, Armenians, Tajiks and Uzbeks. This observation supports the argument that the Soviet-style hierarchy of nations and peoples is being reshaped by the contemporary administrative and economic context.

In this respect, it could be interesting to consider in more detail how the Soviet nationalities policy and the scientific construction of nationalities[64] continue to influence administrative practices. Some French scholars suggest that the Algerian war contributed to the creation by the French police of the notion of 'inner enemy' within French society.[65] Sylvain Laurens analyses the post-decolonization role played by French administrative staff in defining migration policies by looking at the administrative careers of federal and local officials of migration and national policies.[66] A study could be made of Russian civil servants who have spent part of their career in the peripheries of the Soviet Union, in particular army personnel and police, to reveal the connection between orders from above and personal experience. Such attitudes can be seen with employers in Omsk, in the way they build labour and, more generally, social relations with migrants.

Working Relations and Use of Intermediaries: A New Social Rapport Between Flexibility and Control

Employers and Migrants

Observations of hiring practices and working relations during field work shed new light on the situation, indicating their ambiguous rationale: employers' opportunistic use of cheap labour contributes to creating social relationships with a strong post-colonial dimension.

Employers of labour migrants play an important role in the dissemination of perceptions at local level. Interviews revealed opinions close to those of administrative representatives' in terms of stereotypes about minorities and/or migrants, on the other hand, views linked to new business positions highlighting a more pragmatic attitude based on the idea that for practical needs, labour migration is more a solution than a problem.

Employers often try to take advantage of migration laws, for example by bargaining for official quotas, or even flouting the law by making deals with middlemen (*brigadiry*) from migrant communities who provide them with labour. Reliable, hard working and cheap, migrants have the upper hand provided they remain discreet and do not create trouble in public to avoid attracting the attention of law enforcement agencies.

Despite a certain proximity due to small sized enterprises, and the fact that migrants and their employers were part of the same Soviet society in the not-so-distant past, the latter show little knowledge of migrant life or culture, often confusing their country of origin and language, speaking of them as a collective using the plural, or making quite unexpected comparisons. For example, a former criminal police officer,[67] law abiding and sympathetic towards regularly employed Kyrgyz workers, berates employers' abuse of migrants but goes on to compare the situation with that of Russians subject to 'massive labour slavery' at the hands of people from the North Caucasus, as witnessed during his years working as a policeman.

Xenophobic attitudes and acts have become widespread in Russia in the last decade and are increasingly marked by the confusion of labour migrants with Russian citizens of 'non-ethnic Russian' or 'Slavic' appearance, as demonstrated by the events of Manezh Square on 11 December 2010. Public discourse, media coverage and misinterpreted statistics,[68] are proof of an anti-migrant attitude that has become more widespread since the 2008 crisis. Existing xenophobia can thus be linked to former Russian nationalist discourses and to contemporary ways of presenting migrant issues in the political arena. This can also be observed in Western states with liberal and globalized economies. While the fact that Russia has 'joined' the club does not make it automatically an ordinary Western state conducting post-colonial policy, there is no doubt a link between Western and Russian policies.

The most frequent ethnic and racial stereotypes propounded by both employers and local authorities are the result of two concepts inherited from the colonial component of the Soviet empire, affirmative action and elite promotion.[69] Coupled with scientific knowledge,[70] this forms the basis of a classification and hierarchy of nationalities.

This reveals a strong state capacity to construct and implement stringent norms that do not go against a certain 'liberalization'. In the case of migration policies, the state thus establishes close ties with concerned neighbouring states to ensure they will conduct appropriate law enforcement and security measures that satisfy their Russian colleagues. As such, a new form of management by diasporas has appeared, a tool ensuring social control of migrants and political security between states. The increased popularity for the enforcement of visas for migrants from Central Asia is in line with this tendency and indicates a move away from liberal economic circles towards a policy of control.[71] This policy is successfully implemented by relying on intermediaries that combine a community organization role in Russia and have close ties with the country of origin in order to control migration flux at source.

The Reshaping of Traditional Diasporas into Useful Intermediaries

At least two organizations, emblematic of this tension between state and employer practices, were observed. Representatives of the local migrant communities, sometimes self-proclaimed, can act as intermediaries between migrants and authorities and migrants and employers at different levels and with different strategies.

Run by a resident of Omsk since the 1960s, overtly nostalgic of the Soviet Union, the official Omsk Kyrgyz diaspora appears to be a part of the Soviet scheme of nationalities, albeit a more modern version. It has adapted to new conditions by hiring youngsters to work as recruitment intermediaries alongside the migration or law enforcement services on cases of abuse concerning Kyrgyz workers.

The diaspora is encouraged by the promises of a local politician close to United Russia to request their contribution with regards to the creation of new municipal legislature as a part of civil society.

Full integration for Kyrgyz citizens working as middlemen and active members of the official Kyrgyz diaspora organization would be obtaining Russian citizenship. In practice, however, they are already integrated and self-assured to the point that they blend in and go unnoticed by the police, who 'think they are Kazakhs'.[72]

The Centre for Migrant Recruitment (*Centr po trudoustrojstvu migrantov*) and Society for Uzbekistan's Friendship (*obshchestvo sodruzhestva Uzbekistana*) is an example of matching offer and demand. The organization, created in 2007 and registered in 2009, works on the majority of migrant related issues.[73] Founded and run by an ex-member of the prosecution office (*prokuratura*) and veteran from the Soviet war in Afghanistan (*Afganets*), born in Tajikistan, an 'ethnic' Kyrgyz arriving from Uzbekistan in the late 1980s,[74] the organization is mainly geared towards Uzbekistan and Uzbek citizens of all ethnic origins, including Russians. It represents a new model of hybrid institution, carrying out several activities including business supervision and protection. The organization strives to be an indispensable element for employers and authorities in the selection and recruitment of migrants directly from Uzbekistan. It aims to clean the place of unofficial intermediaries and prevent the arrival by train of 'unexpected workers' by establishing ties with official Uzbek migration agencies in several regions. The director was also hoping to extend activities to other *oblasts* of the Siberian Federal District, relying on his *Afgantsy* networks in regional administrations and legislatures.

The more cultural 'diaspora' activities are carried out from the same building and officially recognized by both sides. Community control is, however, an important part of their activity as the organization is regularly required by law enforcement authorities to control potential unrest inside the community or between communities, such as in June 2010 when violent clashes took place in the Region of Osh (Southern Kyrgyzstan). This kind of organization can be said to satisfy the interests of both countries of origin and receiving countries, Russia in this case.

The above suggests a post-Soviet model of co-operation and co-production applied to migration policies. It has the advantage of suiting some actors as it satisfies the desire of the Russian state and the migrant countries of origin to control and regulate the workforce through the creation of more institutionalized bodies. Close relations between the state apparatus of the country of origin and Russia, and the fact that people engaged in these activities often have Soviet careers (especially as concerns security services) making them true children of the 'affirmative action empire',[75] are undoubtedly enabling elements for this type of social and administrative construction.

However, it is unclear to what extent this type of organization suits migrants themselves, despite claims of acting as a kind of trade union, for example by negotiating decent wages with employers, although still lower than Russian workers rates. It is less likely to see this kind of organization working in contemporary Western countries, although leaders may not be altogether against the idea. This double inheritance of the policy of nationalities on the one side and Soviet social control on the other promotes the creation of such mechanisms in the post-Soviet context.

The extent to which these organizations are instrumental in influencing migration flows and procedures requires further study. Traditional channels of immigration continue to represent by far the most significant number of migrants. Observations of and interviews with migrants reveal a gap between self-legitimating strategies based on economic interest and/or political ambitions, their legitimization from above by state authorities, and the few regular contacts these organizations have with ordinary migrants, living in isolation, and often arriving via local middlemen or indeed family ties.

Conclusion

The study of various actors of the labour migration field in a regional context reveals diverse perceptions stemming from Soviet-style national policies and national minority representations which distance labour migrants from their former identity.

Both old and new concepts are deployed to shape the form of a new relationship between Russia and its former Southern republics. Colonial-type labour force management is combined with economic pragmatism serving market oriented objectives while the ever present desire for social and political control over the workforce makes it difficult to speak of a 'liberal' model. The (post-)colonial scheme is at the same time weakened and strengthened by the strong legacy of Soviet mechanisms.

In the light of field observations and both old and new concepts of migrants and minorities, one could conclude that the word 'post' should be removed and replaced by two main ideas:

- A strongly anchored Soviet-style labour management, with migrants representing successful workforce management and a level of global social control hitherto never attained in the Soviet economy. The profile of many of the employers interviewed (former army personnel or policemen with part of their career spanning the Soviet era) has certainly influenced this conclusion.
- Colonial-style perceptions, attitudes and practices fostered by state discourse and public opinion. These (post-)colonial attitudes could be compared to the experience of certain Western European countries, admittedly on a different time scale. As J.F. Bayart and R. Bertrand suggest, the post-colonial legacy, beyond historical dimension, has direct implications on the way contemporary policies are undertaken and implemented.[76]

Together, the above ideas, more so than a strict importation of the post-colonial theory, can lead to an in-depth study of the way state formation and contemporary contexts meet to give rise to complex forms of political and social domination.[77]

Notes

1 Research for this chapter, field trips in particular, was carried out in the framework of the project ANR 'Caucase et Asie Centrale post soviétique: un autre Sud (SUDSOV)', lead by the CERCEC (UMR 8083 CNRS/EHESS).

2 The governor Leonid Konstantinovitch Polezhaev has been at the head of the region in various positions from 1987 up to 2012.

3 A long-term and difficult conflict between the mayor of the city of Omsk and the governor of the region was resolved in the 2000s with the election of mayors loyal to the governor.

4 The Kazakhs have long been present in this vast expanse of the steppes, particularly in the South. Omsk was founded as the outpost of the Russian advance in Siberia in 1716 and in the 19th century became the seat of the governorate-general of the Steppes Territory which covered most of today's northern Kazakhstan. As with most federal subjects, Omsk today has National Cultural Autonomies (NCAs) (Erofeev, Yu.I., *Nacional'no-kulturnye avtonomii: statistiki i kommentarii* [*National-Cultural Autonomies: statistics and comments*], Moscow, 2010, p. 146), structures recognised by the authorities pursuant to a federal law of 1996, since amended, representing 'national minorities' within different regions and to a certain extent organizing the 'diasporas'. For Omsk, the two most significant diasporas are the Germans (the Azov German National Municipal district was created in 1992) and the Kazakhs due to their numbers and their status as an indigenous population. NCAs are also discussed by experts on national policies in post-Soviet Russia, in particular researchers, sociologists and anthropologists (see for instance Ossipov 2004). Recent migrant workers do not have NCAs but can establish 'ethnic' associations *(etničeskie social'nye ob"edineniâ)* (see *infra* on the role of the diasporas).

5 Hopes of a boost to the Omsk region were undermined with the reorganization of the oil sector in the mid-1990s, in particular when a merger of the then locally based company Sibneft with Yukos was announced and then cancelled. A second attempt failed in 2003 just before the clash between President Putin and then Yukos' head Khodorkovsky.

6 This chapter is based on field research conducted by the author in 2009 and 2010 in the Omsk region. The author is deeply thankful to the members of the Independent research centre *Guepitsentr* for their help during the research, in particular for their participation in the interview process with migrant workers. Interviews with migrants, NGOs, and experts were also conducted in Moscow by the author from 2008 to 2011. Material used for this chapter comprises qualitative interviews with State authorities in charge of migration policies in the region and in the municipality of Omsk (including local office of the Federal migration service, economic, labor and health regional and local administrations), with responsible from companies employing migrant workers, with intermediary firms, with representatives from *diaspora*, with migrant workers from various countries,

experts and journalists, as well as official documents (normative acts, official statistics) and press articles (printed or internet).

7 Regional Branch of the Federal Migration Service (UFMS), persons in charge of the economy, health, etc.

8 The use of inverted comas corresponds to the way in which these concepts are publicly referred to in Russia.

9 Reeves, M., 'Black work, green money: remittances, ritual and domestic economies in Southern Kyrgyzstan', *Slavic Review*, 2010, vol. 71/1, pp. 108–34.

10 Willen, S., 'Perspectives on Labour Migration in Israel', *Revue européenne des migrations internationales*, 2003, vol. 19/3, p. 8 (http://remi.revues.org/index2xw691.html).

11 UFMS is used for regional direction whereas FMS is for Federal direction.

12 In September 2006, a murder in a restaurant owned by Caucasians sparked several days of riots against, in particular, Chechens living in the town. This crisis, as social and political (angry rioters often also targeting local administrations) as it was inter-ethnic, highlighted the organizational capacity of ultra nationalist groups such as DPNI (Movement Against Illegal Immigration). See Kozhevnikova, G., 'Autumn 2006: Under the Kondopoga Banner', *Sova Center Analytical Report*, 2007 (http://www.sova-center.ru/en/xenophobia/reports-analyses/2007/01/d9912/?_ftn12); Shlapentokh, D., 'Kondopoga – Ethnic/Social Tension in Putin's Russia', *European Review*, 2010, vol. 18, pp. 177–206.

13 Yudina, T., 'Labour Migration into Russia: The Response of State and Society', *Current Sociology*, 2005, vol. 53, pp. 583–606; Tiuriukanova, E., 'Trudovaja migracija v Rossii' ['work migrations in Russia'], *Otechestvennye zapiski*, 2004, vol. 4 (http://www.strana-oz.ru/?numid=19&article=901); de Tinguy, A., Zaiontchkovskaja, Zh., 'Regards franco-russes sur l'immigration', *Migrations et société*, 2005, vol. 101; Mukomel, V., 'Immigration and Russian Migration Policy: Debating the Future', *Russian Analytical Digest*, 2006 (http://www.css.ethz.ch/publications/pdfs/RAD-7-2-5.pdf); Mukomel, V., *Migracionnaja politika Rossii: postsovetskie konteksty* [*Migration policies: post-Soviet contexts*], Moscow: Vladimir Dipol-T, 2005; Mukomel, V.I., Païn, E.A. (eds), *Nuzhny li imigranty rossiiskomu obshestvu?* [*Does Russian society need migrants?*], Moscow: Liberal Mission Fondation, 2006; Mukomel V, *Integration of Migrants: Russian Federation*, CARIM-East Research Report 2013/02 (http://www.carim-east.eu/media/CARIM-East-RR-2013-02.pdf); Ryazantsev S., Horie N., Kumo K., 'Migrant Workers from Central Asia into the Russian Federation', *Center for Economic Institutions Working Paper Series*, October 2010 (http://cei.ier.hit-u.ac.jp/English/database/documents/wp2010-1revised.pdf).

14 In the 'ethnic' sense used when referring to *russkij*, that is the nationality as formerly stated in passports. Regarding these debates, the impact and political–media coverage in Russia of the French suburban riots of autumn 2005 should also be noted.

15 See http://www.fms.gov.ru/programs/fmsuds/.

16 Federal Law n°271 of 30 December 2006 on 'Retail markets and amendments to the employment code'. Federal Law n°2 of 6 January 2007 (adopted by the Duma on 22 December 2006 and approved by the Federation Council on 27 December) on 'The amendments of the federal Law on Foreign Citizens'.

17 Shnirelman, V., 'Lukavye tsifry i obmanchivye teorii: o nekotoryh podhodah k izucheniu migrantov' ['Biased figures and misleading theories: on the approaches of migrant studies'], *Vestnik Evrazii*, 2008, vol. 2/40, pp. 125–50.

18 FIDH / Assistance Civique–Comité Assistance civique, *Migrations en Russie. Des populations fragilisées, premières victimes des crises politiques internes et externes*, Paris, 2007 (http://www.fidh.org/IMG/pdf/Migranrussie472fr2007.pdf/); Regamey, A., Le Huérou, A., 'Nécessaires et indésirables? Les migrants en Russie', *La Revue Nouvelle*, 2007, vol. 8, pp. 44–9.

19 Schenk, C., 'Open Borders, Closed Minds Russia's Changing Migration Policies: Liberalization or Xenophobia?' *Demokratizatsiya: The Journal of Post-Soviet Democratization*, 2010, vol. 18/2, pp. 101–21; Vitovskaja, G., Platonova, A., Shkolnikova, V., *Novoe migracionnoe zakonadel'stvo Rossijskioj Federacii: pravoprimenitel'naja praktika* [*New migration legislation in the Russian Federation: Application*], Moscow: OIM-FMS-OSCE, 2009; Zajontchkovskaja, Zh.A., Tiuriukanova, E.V., *Migracija i demograficheskij krizis v Rossii* [*Migrations and the demographic crisis in Russia*], Moscow: Maks Press, 2010, p. 112.

20 Ryazantsev S. *et al.* Praktika ispol'zovanija patentov na osushchestvlenie trudovoj dejatel'nosti inostrannymi grazhdanami v Rossijskoj Federacii (rezul'taty issledovanija) ['The practice of using *patents* by migrant workers for working activity in Russia (research results)'], IOM report, 2012, (http://moscow.iom.int/russian/publications/Practica_patent.pdf)].

21 http://ria.ru/society/20120824/729814591.html.

22 According to the new provisions, the migrant worker gives the UFMS a migration card received at the border, corresponding to a work permit request mentioning the sector of activity and passport details. Within ten days, he should receive a work permit that he can then present to any employer in the sector.

23 The brochure was drafted with the administrative law department of the Academy of the Interior Ministry, located in the region. It includes diagrams and graphs to ease employers' comprehension of the procedures. The 'foreign citizen' awaiting employment is represented on a picture as a business man in a suit and does not correspond to a migrant worker arriving from Central Asia looking for work on a construction site.

24 Interviews with several officials of municipal and regional administrations, Omsk February 2009, administrative documents consulted. The Russian term is *Kommissia po ispolzovaniju inostrannoj rabochej sily* [Commission for the use of foreign work force].

25 Interview with the Labour vice-minister of Omsk region, 27 February 2009.

26 In addition to the Labour ministry, the commission includes officials from the Interior ministry, migration services, the Health and Education Ministries, unions, the employment agency and employers.
27 Interview with the Labour vice-minister for Omsk region, 27 February 2009.
28 Of the documents consulted, figures vary slightly depending on adjustments made during the year.
29 Consulted during field work.
30 'Sokrashchena kvota na inostrannuju rabochuju silu' ['The quota for foreign workers has been decreased'] (http://www.rabotaomsk.ru/firmnews/news_body.php?id=43900).
31 http://omsk.rfn.ru/rnews.html?id=11318441.
32 http://www.omskarbitr.ru/review/Zakon_ob_ekzamene_po_russkomu_dlya_migrantov_poka_ne_rabotaet.
33 Shnirelman, V., 'Lukavye tsifry i obmanchivye teorii . . .':*op. cit.*
34 The existence of old houses in the town centre characteristic of several towns in Siberia, including Omsk, largely untouched by the construction boom of the 2000s and whose population is decreasing.
35 Private minibuses, a popular alternative to public transport.
36 *Argumeny i fakty v Omske*, n°8, 20 February 2008, consultation of an internal UFMS document dated 2009.
37 Interview with the brigade commander, 25 February 2009.
38 See in particular *Bisness Kurs*, 30 March 2010.
39 Interview dated 27 February 2009. During the interview, she was interested in the French situation and referred to the role played by social problems and discrimination in the 2005 troubles (much commented on in Russia).
40 *Ibid.*
41 Hirsch, F., *Empire of Nations: Ethnographic knowledge and the Making of the Soviet Union*, Ithaca: Cornell University Press, 2005.
42 Martin, T., *The Affirmative Action Empire: Nations and Nationalism in the Soviet Union, 1923–1939*, Ithaca: Cornell University Press, 2001.
43 Beissinger, M.R, 'Soviet Empire as "Family Resemblance"', *Slavic Review*, 2006, vol. 65/2, pp. 294–303.
44 Interview with an official of the Health Ministry responsible for this issue, Omsk 26 February 2009.
45 The ministry set up a system of secure forms distributed only to the senior doctors of the four services authorised to deliver certificates in the region. The spokesman interviewed added 'the holograms are also made by a human being'.
46 The general administrative reform ongoing in Russia since 2005 is accompanied by a law on social control (*obshchestvennyj kontrol*) that armed many administrations with councils made up of representatives of civil society. Depending on the current and regional political issues, these councils can either be a simple formality or a real force of independent organizations with experience and expertise on a given question. In 2009 and 2010, these councils

were active at federal level and within the Interior Ministry in Moscow as regards the preparation of police reforms.

47 Radio programme from the *Moscow Echo* station dated 4 December 2008 with V. Volokh (http://www.echo.msk.ru/programs/poehali/557038-echo/#element-text).

48 The official of the advisory council fails to explain the difference between the 7 million persons declared to the FMS for one year, that is to say the total number that passed through the Moscow migration services at some point, and the number of working migrants estimated by Moscow.

49 Interview with V.B. Yashin, expert on national questions and a history lecturer at the University of Omsk, 7 July 2010.

50 Armenians are often cited as employers or intermediaries for migrants from Central Asia. Interviews with several Kyrgyz migrants in February 2009 and with a small construction business owner of Armenian origin, July 2010. For the Kazakh diaspora, see above.

51 The diasporas assisted the UFMS by posting the new provisions in native languages in the migration service offices. Interview, 27 February 2009, documents of the advisory council for 2007, interview with representatives of the Kyrgyz community 28 February 2009.

52 This is the term used officially, as found in studies and surveys on the question regularly requested by regional administrations.

53 Khodjaeva, E., 'Etnicheskie men'shinstva i sotrudniki milicii: sluchaj Kazani' ['Ethnic minorities and the police: the case of Kazan'], in Voronkov, V., Gladarev, B., Sagitova, L., *Milicia i etnicheskie migranty* [*Police and migrants*], St Petersburg: Aletey, 2011.

54 Interview with V. B Yashin, expert on national questions and history lecturer at the University of Omsk, 7 July 2010.

55 Interview with an official of the UFMS, 27 February 2009.

56 34 Per cent of foreign investment. Regional statistics for 2006 and 2007.

57 Numerous Germans from Kazakhstan also emigrated to the Omsk region following the break-up of the USSR.

58 Larina, E., Naoumova, E., 'Migracija kazakhov v zapadnoj chasti rossijsko-kazakhstanskogo pogranichia' ['The migrations of Kazakhs to the Western part of the Russian-Kazak border zone'], *Vestnik Evrazii,* 2006, vol. 4/34, pp. 32–47.

59 Numerous agreements, decisions of the governor and regulations were introduced between 1998 and 2010.

60 Laruelle, M., 'Le Kazakhstan, nouveau carrefour migratoire d'Asie centrale', in Laruelle, M., *Dynamique migratoires et changements sociétaux en Asie Centrale* [*Migratory dynamics and social change in Central Asia*], Paris, Petra, 2010.

61 http://www.customsunion.ru/info/4439.html http://rus.azattyq.org/content/migration_guest_workers_/24257872.html http://wfin.kz/node/.

62 Hirsh, F., *op. cit.* Cadiot, J., *Le Laboratoire impérial, Russie-URSS 1860–1940*, Paris: CNRS Éditions, 2007, p.267; Kappeler, A., *La Russie, un Etat multi-*

ethnique, Paris: Institut d'Etudes Slave, 1994; Martin, T., 'Affirmative action Empire', *op. cit*.

63 Savin, I., 'Labor Migration From Central Asia to Russia: Mutual Social Perception in the Orenburg *oblast*', *China and Eurasia Forum Quarterly*, 2010, vol. 8/3, pp. 173–84.

64 Hirsh, F., *op. cit*;

65 Rigouste, M., *L'ennemi intérieur. Des guerres coloniales au nouvel ordre sécuritaire*, Paris: La Découverte, 2009.

66 Laurens, S., *Une politisation feutrée. Les hauts fonctionnaires et l'immigration en France*, Paris: Belin, coll. « Socio Histoire », 2009.

67 Interview, July 2010.

68 Schnirelman, V., *op. cit.*; Malakhov, V., *Ponaehali tut... Ocherki o nacionalizme, rasizme i kul'turnom pljuralizma* [*Let them leave... Essay on nationalism, racism and cultural pluralism*], Moscow: NLO, 2007, p.200.

69 Martin, T., *op. cit.*

70 Hirsch, F., *op. cit.*

71 Rodionov K, 'Pochemu stoit vvesti vizy dlja zhitelej srednej azii' ['Why it is worth introducing visas for Central Asians'], *Forbes.ru*, 2 February 2013 (http://www.forbes.ru/mneniya-column/konkurentsiya/234142-pochemu-stoit-vvesti-vizy-dlya-zhitelei-srednei-azii).

72 Interview, February 2009.

73 This is an important source for field researchers.

74 The head of the centre insists on the fact that he is also a deputy president of the Kyrgyz diaspora and was at the time of the interview (July 2010) creating the Society of Tajik Friendship.

75 Title of T. Martin's book, *op. cit.*

76 Bayart, J.F., Romain, B., *La problématique du legs colonial*, FASOPO report, 2005, pp. 68–9 http://www.fasopo.org/publications/legscolonial_jfrb_1205.pdf.

77 As suggested by Hibou, B., *Anatomie politique de la domination*, Paris: La Découverte, 2011.

PART 4

NEW GLOBAL DYNAMICS: STATES AND INTERNATIONAL ORGANIZATIONS STRATEGIES

CHAPTER 11

THE STATE AND THE DIASPORA: BUREAUCRATIC AND DISCURSIVE PRACTICES IN THE CONSTRUCTION OF A TRANSNATIONAL COMMUNITY

Sergei Rumyantsev
(Humboldt University, Germany)

*'When it comes to the state,
one never doubts enough'
Pierre Bourdieu*[1]

Introduction: From Spontaneity to State Diaspora-building

On 31 December 1989, the barriers on the border between the Nakhichevan Autonomous Region of the Azerbaijan SSR and the Islamic Republic of Iran were removed. This largely spontaneous action was directed by leaders of the anti-Soviet mass movement known as the Azerbaijani Popular Front (APF).[2] Participants in this action spoke of how this 'glorious day' would go down in history as the day of unity for all ethnic Azerbaijanis. Indeed, very soon after, on 16 December 1991, the anniversary was declared an official state holiday: 'Azerbaijani World Solidarity Day'. And so an incident on the border—a spontaneous act of mass protest against the leadership of the USSR, which had lost its last remnants of popularity—acquired the symbolic status of an official day of celebration. This symbolic event should be examined in the context of a state policy of diaspora-building which was still very much in its infancy in post-Soviet Azerbaijan.

The whole process of constructing the Azerbaijani diaspora is encapsulated by such examples of the ascription of a particular meaning to events. The uncoordinated, voluntary efforts of Azerbaijanis in emigration in the early 1990s to form ethnic ('diaspora') organizations rapidly came to naught. To begin with, this mere handful of unions and societies was founded in order, for example, to organize the collection and delivery of humanitarian aid (medicines, clothes etc.) into Azerbaijan, which had, following the collapse of the USSR, undergone an acute economic crisis, aggravated by the militarized political conflict with neighbouring Armenia.[3] Or, as was particularly the case for Russia, such organizations were created in order to arrange structures through which, in the new conditions of the USSR's collapse, the authorities in the receiving country could begin to establish relationships with different ethnic groups. It was specifically the collapse of the USSR that caused Azerbaijanis to be transformed from ordinary Soviet citizens, who happened to be living outside their national republic but still within the borders of a single Union, into a diaspora in Russia.[4]

These attempts to found emigré organizations were to a great extent chaotic and unco-ordinated; they were swiftly suborned to a state policy of diaspora building, which assumed its final shape at the start of the 21st century. Since that point, the 'Azerbaijani diaspora' has been deliberately constructed as a political project, brought into being by the regime governing the post-Soviet Republic of Azerbaijan (RoA). The nature of this governing regime, established in 1993 in the political homeland of 'All the World's Azerbaijanis' determines the content and the goals of the diaspora building project. This chapter attempts to analyse the content and the current results of this policy; it is based to a great degree on material gathered during a research project supported by Germany's Alexander von Humboldt Foundation.[5]

Research Methodology

Research methods included participant observation; life history interviews; problem-oriented semi-structured interviews; and critical discourse analysis of news media, speeches by and interviews with public figures and officials of different ranks, various official orders, etc.

The life history interviews were conducted in Georgia, in areas of compact settlement by ethnic Azerbaijanis (the Kvemo Kartli region); in St Petersburg, Russia; and in Germany (Berlin, Potsdam, Braunschweig and Cologne). In all, over the course of various projects, 140 interviews were performed. This set of interviews was carried out with Azerbaijanis who had settled permanently outside the borders of the Republic of Azerbaijan. Among the interviewees were activists who had founded and/or who were actively involved in the work of ethnic (diaspora) organizations.

The problem-oriented semi-structured interviews were held in Azerbaijan in 2008-09. These were interviews with officials and specialists of various descriptions, whose main task was to implement the official diaspora project, and also with activists of emigré organizations. In all, 20 such interviews were conducted. A further tranche of material was gathered by the participant observation method in various actions and events held as part of the implementation of diaspora policy, and also while staying with emigré families.

In addition, a very important research method was critical discourse analysis[6] of a significant corpus of narratives representing the official version of the reasoning process behind the diaspora building policy being enacted, and the results achieved. These included inter alia a large number of addresses and speeches (linked to various events) made by the Azerbaijani presidents Heidar Aliev (1993–2003) and Ilham Aliev (2003 to date) to Azerbaijanis in emigration; a great many interviews published in Azerbaijani mass media, in which both presidents, as well as officials of various ranks and activists in diaspora organizations, touch on issues of diaspora policy; speeches made by the Azerbaijani presidents, other officials, members of the intelligentsia, and activists in diaspora organizations at the three World Congresses of Azerbaijanis held in Baku; media news reports concerning the activities of Azerbaijanis in diaspora; and various documents revealing the diaspora policy of the Azerbaijani political regime.

Diaspora as Political Project

Prior to embarking on this analysis, it should be noted that the most widespread criteria for defining the phenomenon of the (ethno-national) diaspora do not appear relevant when describing the social networks and ethnic organizations of Azerbaijanis in emigration. Thus, one of the best-known researchers into diaspora communities, William Safran,[7] in identifying six major features that define a diaspora, pays great attention to the concept of the homeland.[8]

Robin Cohen expands the list of criteria which define a diaspora to nine. Among these he includes movement away from the homeland in search of work, in view of commercial interests or with colonial ambitions; a strong ethnic group consciousness, etc.[9] Based on these criteria, he puts forward his own typology of diaspora communities. In his opinion, it is possible to talk of the existence of victim, labour, imperial, trade and deterritorialized diasporas. However, Cohen himself emphasizes that, in this instance, he is, in the spirit of Weber, indicating ideal types of diaspora communities.[10] Cohen's cautious stipulation is undoubtedly important in the case under consideration here. If just the first type is excluded: the victim diaspora,[11] which Cohen labels as the classical type,[12] then many traits shared by the other four types and by the post-Soviet Azerbaijani diaspora can be found, as well as contrasts between them. For example, when dealing with Azerbaijani migration, there is value in talking of a possible nature which is determined within the contexts of both colonial and post-colonial (post-imperial) worlds.[13] This will be discussed in more detail below. At this point, it should be noted that the territory on which Azerbaijani Turks made their primary compact settlement was located at the point where two empires met: the Persian empire (and, latterly, its direct descendant the Islamic Republic of Iran) and the Russian/Soviet empire. The migration into which Azerbaijani Turks were drawn in the 20th century was undoubtedly determined both by their location in the composition of these empires and by the absence of an independent nation-state.

However, even if this chapter leaves to one side the justifiable mistrust aroused by an excessively elastic interpretation of the term diaspora,[14] it is nevertheless useful to approach the very possibility of applying the term to Azerbaijanis in emigration with great scepticism. At this point it is worth remembering yet another famous definition, offered by Gabriel Sheffer. Instead of criteria for describing diaspora communities or defining their types, he suggested his own version of the term:

> An ethno-national diaspora is a social-political formation, created as a result of either voluntary or forced migration, whose members regard themselves as of the same ethno-national origin and who permanently reside as minorities in one or several host countries. Members of such entities maintain regular or occasional contacts with what they regard as their homelands and with individuals and groups of the same background residing in other host countries, etc.[15]

The concept of homeland in this definition is of somewhat less importance. The more important features of this definition are the shared sense of ethno-national identity and also Sheffer's addition (albeit cautiously accentuated) of the preservation of group solidarity; i.e. in this case the diaspora is understood as a real, united group which, once formed, subsequently stays to a greater or lesser degree unchanged. This is an approach which Valerii Tishkov has rightly criticized:

> The main weakness in the interpretations in contemporary literature of the historical phenomenon of the diaspora lies in an

> essentialist reification of the diaspora as collective bodies ('stable populations'!); moreover, not only as statistical sets but also as culturally homogenous groups, which is almost impossible to sustain in a more sensitive analysis.[16]

Putting to one side the question of how it might be possible to measure degrees of group solidarity, in the definitions set forth so far there are no perceptible attempts to describe the diaspora phenomenon as a process; a process during which there may be rises and falls in the political, cultural and/or other activities of ethnic entrepreneurs in emigration. Or there may be varying degrees of intensity in implementing a policy of diaspora building that is supported or even directly sponsored by the country of origin (assuming any such policy exists). This was what happened when many Azerbaijani emigrés began to take an interest in the political situation in Azerbaijan in the early 1990s, for example, which interest rapidly declined towards the end of that decade and the start of the next. Or what happened in the case of the gradual rise in interest in the process of diaspora building within the political regime which took power in 1993 in Azerbaijan, which then adopted an energetic and determined state policy at the start of the new millennium.

And still, despite such a wide interpretation of the term, there is value in talking of a 'new' Azerbaijani diaspora.[17] According to Valerii Tishkov, who is very often sceptically inclined towards the relevance of the term diaspora in describing new emigrant communities:

> It is, of course, difficult to call the one million Azerbaijanis or the 500 thousand Georgians who circulate between Russia and Azerbaijan, or between Russia and Georgia (I do not include the long-standing populations of Azerbaijanis and Georgians in Russia) a diaspora; there is, however, indisputably a certain flavour of the diaspora in their culture and social practice, especially among those who have been residing in Russia for

> some considerable time. ... this is a diaspora very new in its nature, which, perhaps, deserves a new name.[18]

It should be emphasized that even if many of the criteria suggested by Safran, Cohen and Sheffer can indeed be applied to describe the social networks and structures of the ethnic organizations created by Azerbaijanis in emigration, none of these definitions are capable of assisting in explaining the diaspora-building policy being pursued by the political regime in the RoA. But it is specifically the content of this policy, along with the practices incorporated within it, that to a significant extent determines the exact nature of the social, political and cultural phenomenon that the authorities in Azerbaijan themselves label as the 'Azerbaijani diaspora'.

This chapter will attempt to argue the case that the main distinguishing feature of the Azerbaijani diaspora is the attitude of the Azerbaijani ruling regime towards its existence. To be precise, that it is the regime which in fact is creating the diaspora. In turn, the attitude of the majority of ethnic activists in emigration should be described as varying degrees of expectation aimed at the regime which rules the political homeland of all Azerbaijani Turks. These relationships between the state and the emigrés makes it possible to talk of a post-Soviet bureaucratic diaspora.

Key factors in the relatively rapid appearance of this diaspora were determined by the fact that the territory of present-day Azerbaijan was part of the Russian empire and the USSR. Both of these empires regarded what is now Azerbaijan as their Orient.[19] With varying degrees of intensity, they sought to modernize it (which was understood to mean making it more European), sponsoring a process of constructing a 'European' (i.e. in the context of imperial discourse, a 'modern') national elite.[20] The representatives of this new European elite in the Russian imperial era received their education in St Petersburg and Moscow, or in Paris and Berlin. Later on, of course, in Soviet times, to a large extent they did so only in Moscow, Leningrad, Kiev, and other Soviet cities. Frequently (and especially in the USSR years), once they had completed their studies, they ceased to return to the republic at all. Another route for emigration from the republic was offered by the development of the oil extraction industry in Siberia in the second half of the 20th century: many Azerbaijani oil workers, both novice and experienced, departed in this direction.

These were just the two most important exit routes from the republic. In reality, many Soviet institutions (for example, the army, or the appearance of an informal economy in the 'era of stagnation') provided the first steps up and out of the Azerbaijani Soviet Republic. In this way, as the result of a long-standing and deliberate policy, many ethnic Azerbaijanis were to be found outside Azerbaijan by the time of the Union's collapse.

But of yet more importance is the fact that, by the time the USSR collapsed, Azerbaijanis had had what Rogers Brubaker terms a 'quasi-nation-state'[21] for over 70 years – the Azerbaijani Soviet Republic, which very soon began to lay claim to the title of political homeland for all the world's Azerbaijanis.

Of course, active political emigration by Azerbaijani Turks[22] in the 20th century occurred for a whole host of other reasons as well. But these reasons were likewise determined by the nature of imperial influence on the region. During the period when Soviet power was being established in Azerbaijan (April 1920), many members of the anti-Bolshevik section of the elite were forced to leave the country. Prior to the Second World War, emigré organizations were active in a number of European countries (France, Poland, and certain others) and also in Turkey. Political parties had in some sense survived, and these united many emigrés, particularly the party *Musavat* (Equality).

During the Second World War, the ranks of the emigrés who had fled Sovietization were swollen by prisoners-of-war: Azerbaijani Turks who had collaborated with the Nazis and had served in the foreign legions of the SS. A few of these emigrés lived to see the collapse of the USSR. However, by this stage, the emigré organizations and, still more, the political parties in emigration had long since ceased to exist. In practice, they did not outlive their founding fathers. The potential interest of a few descendants of political emigrés in events in Soviet Azerbaijan did not provide sufficient stimulus for the preservation or formation of any sort of new diasporic structures,[23] as had been the case, for example, with the second or third generations of Russian or Georgian emigrés who were living abroad for the same reasons of enforced flight from the Bolsheviks.

The reasons why the first wave of Azerbaijani political emigrés was unable to found a long-lived diaspora community require further examination and research. Although even at this stage it is possible to cite the relatively low numbers of emigrés in the first wave as one such reason. Another reason is the fear and unwillingness of the majority of former Nazi foreign legionaries to engage in any form of active public life, considering that fascism had lost the war and deportation to the USSR might be awaiting many of their number. Finally, belief in the durability of the Soviet regime played no small role. However, it is more important to emphasize that, precisely as a result of this absence of any diaspora community prior to the collapse of the USSR and the appearance of the independent Azerbaijani Republic in 1991, it is necessary to talk in terms of a 'post-Soviet diaspora'.[24] Although this is only one of the reasons. Another, still more important reason for this label should be sought in the nature of the ruling regime in Azerbaijan. But this will be discussed later.

Here, it should be underlined that, in view of everything mentioned so far, when studying the phenomenon of the Azerbaijani post-Soviet bureaucratic diaspora it seems most constructive to proceed from the perspective offered by Rogers Brubaker:

> Rather than speak of 'a diaspora' or 'the diaspora' as an entity, a bounded group, an ethnodemographic or ethnocultural fact, it may be more fruitful, and certainly more precise, to speak of diasporic stances, projects, claims, idioms, practices, and so on.[25]

Proceeding from this position, this chapter takes the diaspora to be first and foremost the result of a political project. The results of this diaspora-building project should be analysed from the perspective of the practices and styles of its implementation, which shape the present condition of the Azerbaijani diaspora.[26] The diaspora itself—and this idea is lodged at the heart of the construction project—is represented as a community that unites all the ethnic Azerbaijanis who live outside the historical homeland. This chapter's central research question can be formulated thus: how, through which practices, does the political regime in Azerbaijan create this imagined vision of a united and populous diaspora? Furthermore, the practices and styles of the construction of this community owe much in terms of their design to the biographies of the people who began and are implementing the project. These practices and styles lend a further specific—bureaucratic—nature to the Azerbaijani diaspora.

Finally, it should be emphasized that the most important factor driving the interest of the Azerbaijani political regime in its policy of diaspora building is the Armenian–Azerbaijani conflict over Nagorno Karabakh. As often happens, the conflict led to the mobilization of many Azerbaijanis who had emigrated from what by this stage was already formerly Soviet Azerbaijan[27] and were living in Russia, Germany or the USA at the time of the USSR's collapse.[28] In the early 1990s[29] the regime that had established itself in the political homeland was already trying, with ever-increasing levels of intensity, to take advantage of this activity that had arisen spontaneously, thus supporting the thesis that 'the formation of diaspora is therefore an issue of social mobilization'.[30] Throughout the 1990s, the Azerbaijani political regime was acutely in need of international platforms and foreign actors in order to represent the Azerbaijani version of the conflict in EU countries, the USA and Russia.

The regime had particular hopes of the emigrés, and this was no coincidence. It had by now become commonly accepted that the existence of a large and influential Armenian diaspora had been of substantial help to the political regime established in post-Soviet Armenia in its victory in the information war that had unfolded in parallel with the military conflict. It seemed vital to create a diaspora 'of one's own' in order to overcome the adversary. If this perspective is adopted, it is necessary to acknowledge that the researchers who maintained that 'diaspora politics may be more a result of conflict than its cause'[31] were right. According to these authors, it was through these politics that the Azerbaijani diaspora was created in the first decade of the new century, from when its record of successful opposition to the Armenian diaspora can be measured.

However, this incentive to intensify the diaspora-building process was constantly being supplemented with others. Thus the widest possible publicity for the history, culture and economic achievements of Azerbaijan soon became publicity for the governing regime as well. Discourse about the need to strengthen the position of post-Soviet Azerbaijan in the international community ('They know us better and better') is likewise inextricable from the constant striving to reinforce the position of the ruling regime. In this context, the diaspora's real success on international platforms is not as important as the demonstration to Azerbaijani citizens of the achievements of the diaspora-building policy, or, put another way, of the successful policy of gathering Azerbaijanis scattered throughout the world into a single and united transnational community.

The politico-patriotic myth of the existence of such global unity is a major component of official ideology, which tells of the long, tragic, yet at the same time heroic struggle of the Azerbaijani people for independence. Like a fairy-tale with a happy ending, the result of this centuries-long struggle has been the appearance on the world map of an independent nation-state. The creator of this national happiness is held to be the, now late, former president, Heidar Aliev. Thanks specifically to his genius, if the official ideology is to be believed, the people were able to acquire (or restore) their independent nation-statehood.

Accordingly, this same Heidar Aliev became the main hero, the face of the global unity of the entire Azerbaijani people (the diaspora and the political homeland), their National Leader.[32] According to the official chronicle, at the most difficult moment in the twilight of the USSR's existence, it was none other than:

> Heidar Aliev [who] raised all the world's Azerbaijanis to their feet, embodying and declaring the political will of the people. This declaration gave impetus to the organization of the world's Azerbaijanis as a nation, and united our compatriots around a

> single politician, a national leader capable of bearing the historic responsibility of the people's fate.[33]

The transnational unity within the community and the success of the diaspora-building policy are gauged by the growing number of organizations, and also by their amalgamation into a single hierarchy. In this way, on the basis of everything so far discussed, it should be emphasized that the 'political homeland' is the key factor in the existence of a post-Soviet Azerbaijani diaspora.

The 'Political Homeland' as the Key Criterion in Describing a Diaspora

The modern Azerbaijani Republic is not the country of origin (homeland) for all emigrés. For Azerbaijanis, several countries, as opposed to just one, are the homelands from which emigration occurred. Apart from post-Soviet Azerbaijan, in fact, there are also Iran, Turkey and Georgia, where many groups of ethnic Azerbaijanis live in close proximity.[34] This means that any attempt to describe the Azerbaijani diaspora from a perspective that demands the presence of what Tishkov describes as a 'conditional category'– the homeland – acquires additional difficulty.

The criteria of belief in the inevitable return to the homeland and of the sense of a tie to it are not relevant, considering that there is not one such homeland, but several. Of course, Azerbaijani nationalists construe their imagined homeland to be a unified 'historical Azerbaijan' which includes a part of modern Georgia and some of North-Western Iran within its borders.[35] But even in the minds of nationalist emigrés this imaginary unified 'historical homeland' inevitably breaks up into unequal parts. i.e. this myth of a unified 'historical homeland' does not threaten the existence of borders between Iranian, Turkish, Georgian and former Soviet Azerbaijanis.

And now, after two decades of diaspora building, Iranian Azerbaijani activists in nationalist parties and other kinds of association are more concerned with events in Iran than in Azerbaijan. They proclaim their main aim to be the drive for cultural autonomy or for an exit from the composition of Iran (which is typical of the radicals' position). For Turkish Azerbaijanis, any kind of separatist ideas do not seem relevant in principle: the homeland for them is modern Turkey. Russian-speaking (or not) Azerbaijanis who grew up in Soviet Azerbaijan, of course, may be tempted by the idea of a big 'historical homeland', but the options for return or for 'loyalty' are always linked to post-Soviet Azerbaijan.

The majority of Iranian, Turkish and Georgian Azerbaijanis do not perceive the post-Soviet Republic of Azerbaijan to be a single homeland for all. However, at the same time, this circumstance does not prevent the majority of ethnic entrepreneurs in emigration from seeing modern Azerbaijan as their 'political homeland', i.e. they take the political regime ruling the RoA to be the single wielder of what Bourdieu termed the symbolic capital of recognized authority, and the sole sponsor, inspiration and manager of the diaspora-building project. Moreover, any group form of cross-border Azerbaijani solidarity only exists in the context of the authorities' diaspora discourse. Not that this prevents the ethnic entrepreneurs from either competing to receive support from the political homeland or from participating in joint actions and sundry other events organized under the patronage of, and with financial support from, the authorities in the political homeland.

Who Controls the Homeland, or the Nature of the Post-Soviet Political Regime?

The political project of diaspora construction assumed its current form towards the start of the new millennium. In November 2001, at Heidar Aliev's initiative, the first world congress of Azerbaijanis was held in Baku.[36] During the congress, final shape was given to the idea of creating an institution which would be charged with organizing and controlling the diaspora-building process—the State Committee for Liaison with Azerbaijanis Living Abroad. This committee was created in 2002, and has been headed ever since by Nazim Ibragimov ('The Diaspora minister'). The first world congress of Azerbaijanis also initiated the formation of a Co-ordinating Council of World

Azerbaijanis, headed by President Heidar Aliev. From that moment the success of the diaspora-building project has been measured by the growth in the numbers of organizations and their gradual inclusion into a subordinate hierarchy.

The chief author and inspiration behind the policy of constructing an Azerbaijani diaspora was the late president of Azerbaijan, Heidar Aliev. During his lifetime, so rich in events and state offices, he managed to spend time as the chairman of the Azerbaijani Soviet Republic KGB (1967–69), the First Secretary of the Communist Party of Azerbaijan (1969–82), a member of the USSR Communist Party Central Committee Politburo and the First Deputy Chairman of the USSR Council of Ministers (1982–87). In the years of the USSR's collapse, Aliev returned to Azerbaijan and from 1991 to 1993 he held the post of Chairman of the Upper *Medjlis* (Council) of the Nakhichevan Autonomous Republic.

Heidar Aliev returned to Baku in 1993 to lead the republic for the next ten years, now as the president (1993–2003) of an independent nation-state. After his death, Aliev also acquired the titles 'Great National Leader' and 'Father of the Nation'. The biography of this prominent member of the Soviet nomenklatura serves as an interesting example of the results of Soviet nationalities policies, and, in particular, of that part which has been labelled the 'indigenization' of the elite.[37] It is also an example of the way in which Soviet policies of constructing national elites have been able to affect the style of government to which many post-Soviet regimes resorted.[38]

Being beyond doubt a very successful politician and bureaucrat, when Aliev returned to power in 1993, he was able rapidly to reconstruct the system of state governance. Moreover, having been in government in the Soviet era, Heidar Aliev rebuilt the post-Soviet state apparatus and system of bureaucratic government using the familiar knowledge and experience he had gained during the USSR's existence. Naturally, by 1993, some years had passed since the Soviet authoritarian regime had existed. But did the downfall of what Stefan Kotkin termed 'uncivil society' lead to the appearance of a civil society? The answer has to be no. The collapse of the Soviet empire has yet to bring an end to the authoritarian style of government. Of course post-Soviet political regimes sometimes markedly parted ways with the system on the ruins of which they had established themselves and acquired power. But many of them are undeniably authoritarian, although they do not have sufficient resources to maintain previous levels of control over the public and, yet more, the private spheres of their citizens' lives.[39]

Not that the resources and potential of authoritarian post-Soviet regimes should be underestimated. Public space and the majority of the media are controlled with great success by post-Soviet authoritarian regimes. These regimes skilfully find a certain symbolic resource in both national-liberation and anti-colonial rhetoric. This rhetoric is also to be found in the discourse of diaspora building. In the context of the discourse of power, the (re)creation of transnational contacts and ties between all the world's Azerbaijanis is a result of the collapse of the USSR. More precisely, it is the result of the creation of independent nation-statehood i.e. the results of this acquisition of national independence are expressed not only in the appearance of a nation-state but in the legitimate right to construct a transnational community of Azerbaijani Turks as a single and indivisible nation.

This raises once again the idea that it is precisely the state which is a vital condition for the existence of a diaspora. Since the contemporary post-Soviet administration in Azerbaijan is so deeply oriented towards personalities, families and clans,[40] the very existence of statehood and, naturally, its cross-border (global) extension the ethno-national diaspora has been presented as the exclusive personal feat of the Great Leader Heidar Aliev. Although it should be acknowleged once again that the honours for the creation of the bureaucratic institutions and the diaspora discourse, within the bounds of which the Azerbaijani diaspora exists, do indeed belong to the late president.

It was precisely from the time he returned to power as president that processes were set in motion to establish contacts with ethnic Azerbaijani emigrés, not only from Azerbaijan, but also from Iran, Turkey and Georgia. The first visits made by Heidar Aliev to EU countries, the USA, Russia and other states were inevitably accompanied by meetings with emigrés (mostly businessmen, ethnic activists and intellectuals) to whom he would invariably make keynote speeches. It was none other than Heidar Aliev who laid down the mould in which the Azerbaijani diaspora would be formed as a bureaucratic structure he headed himself, in the role of pan-Azerbaijani president. To him also belongs the slogan 'One nation, two states' (meaning Turkey and Azerbaijan), from which it follows that Turks and Azerbaijanis should unite their efforts in the diaspora too.

Human rights or democratic freedoms have no place in the value system of such a state, a system which has spread into the diaspora, as well. Nor does the principle that the state exists for the good of the people. On the contrary, the people exist for the good of the state. The individual, the group, the people—in the eyes of the authorities, all these are just statistical categories subordinated to a single goal: the implementation of a range of activities aimed at strengthening the state. Sacrifices and losses are secondary; achieving the goal takes sole precedence in such a policy. Of course, the scattering of ethnic Azerbaijanis throughout the world was not caused by dramatic, large-scale events like, for example, genocide. But if such events had taken place during the formation of the diaspora, then the result achieved would have seemed fair recompense for such trials and suffering. Little human tragedies (and maybe even big ones), in this value system, are simply useful material for state- and nation-building. Very shortly after assuming the role of Azerbaijani president, Heidar Aliev made a speech to Azerbaijanis living in Switzerland in which he expounded this kind of approach clearly and precisely:

> Today, at lunch, I sat next to the President of Ireland, Mrs Mary Robinson. During our conversation she told me that Ireland had two distinctive features. The first was that Ireland had never been an empire, it had always been a colony. While the second feature was that, 150 years ago, there was the the potato famine in Ireland. As a result, around four million Irish people left their country and moved to different places. This is why,

> now, the number of Irish people living abroad is higher than the number of Irish people living in the country itself. Mrs Robinson mentioned that this year they would be marking the 150th anniversary of this event. I said to her that I could not imagine how they would be marking this date, but I considered that if, 150 years ago, this was a tragedy for you, at the same time this event was a great joy for your people. Because your people settled throughout the world and, in particular, in the USA and in various European countries. Now, the Irish have created a big lobby; such a small country like Ireland has a big lobby abroad.[41]

Heidar Aliev's son Ilham Aliev, the current president of the country, thus inherited the existing institutions and well-developed practices for the construction of the ethno-national diaspora. The sole novelty has been the renaming in 2008 of the committee mentioned above as the State Diaspora Liaison Committee. This change of name for an institution which itself wields the offical power to bestow appellations was a symbolic affirmation of the successful implementation of the diaspora-building programme. The authorities thereby asserted that the diaspora had been created, and that it was now necessary to develop and strengthen it, and also to focus on the formation of a political lobby. Ilham Aliev also inherited the post of leader of the Co-ordinating Council of World Azerbaijanis, just as Nazim Ibragimov inherited his post of head of the State Committee. In practice, the only important event, both for the country and for a slight change in the policy of diaspora building, was the death of Heidar Aliev in 2003. His idealized image (to be precise, his cult) as the Great National Leader took centre stage in the policy of memory in both Azerbaijan and in the diaspora.

The second world congress of Azerbaijanis that took place in 2006, again in Baku, began with a screening of a documentary film (*We are Azerbaijanis*) on the activities of the Great Leader. Each such congress is customarily launched with a speech by the president. At the third congress, in what is now a well-established tradition, Ilham Aliev once again devoted a significant portion of his president's speech to the activities of his own father, the National Leader.[42] In this speech he affirmed, perfectly precisely, that none other than Heidar Aliev was the author of and inspiration behind the policy of diaspora building.

In turn, the tradition has developed of holding all these congresses in Baku. Attendees are bound to include not only high-ranking officials but also members of the cultural and academic elite. For example, along with the presidential speech which opens these congresses, there will always be a speech given by the president of the Azerbaijani Academy of Sciences. The majority of congress delegates are long-standing partners of power: the ethnic entrepreneurs heading diaspora organizations who work with the Azerbaijani political regime.

An attempt at unification: the 'Charter of Solidarity of World Azerbaijanis'

In enacting its political project of diaspora building, the regime in turn takes account of a variety of boundaries between groups. Its understanding is reflected, for example, in the Charter of Solidarity of World Azerbaijanis. This refers to a document which has been created under the patronage of the RoA government, with the intention of presenting a certain programme of action (or some kind of a constitution). The charter does not just define the principles and goals of building a unified transnational community of world Azerbaijanis; the document has become one of the important discursive documents involved in the creation of the diaspora. The language of the charter determines the discursive framework of the Azerbaijani diaspora's existence. In it, to paraphrase Bourdieu somewhat, the state, which 'is the site par excellence of the concentration and exercise of symbolic power', puts forward the principles behind its vision of the diaspora.[43]

The working group drafting the charter is made up solely of experts in the humanities (19 people, in all) who work in various state-run higher education establishments and research institutes of the RoA Academy of Sciences, along with two officials from the State

Diaspora Liaison Committee. Recommendations and suggestions from a variety of of organizations, including in the diaspora, were considered while the charter was being drafted. These were not just ethnic Azerbaijani organizations such as the Azerbaijani Society of Lithuania, the Azerbaijani Council of America, the Azerbaijani Society of Mainz, the Azerbaijani Centre of Belgium, and others; recommendations and comments were also taken from such organizations as the Berlin Community of Turks. Not that it should be assumed that in such cases the political regime's control over the procedure of drafting the charter was anything other than absolute. Recommendations and comments also originated from the Socio-political Affairs Department of the Presidential Office, the country's ministry of Internal Affairs, the State Religious Organization Liaison Committee and, finally, the Research Institute of Philosophy, Sociology and Law of the Azerbaijani Academy of Sciences.

The document presents criteria for determining who should be counted as Azerbaijani (the ethno-social and philosophical concept of the 'Azerbaijani').[44] According to the charter's authors, 'Azerbaijanis ... are united by such ethnographic/cultural features as language, religion and spirituality.' The concept of the Azerbaijani is structured accordingly: firstly, in fact, Azerbaijanis (the charter's authors here, apparently, mean ethnic Azerbaijanis or, as it became customary in the post-Soviet period to consider them, Azerbaijani Turks). Secondly, 'the national minorities living in Azerbaijan and merging with Azerbaijanis of Turkish origin',[45] and finally, thirdly, any person considering him or herself to be Azerbaijani.

The content and the language used in the document leave no doubt that the approach taken to defining the nation is essentialist in nature. The charter reproduces to a great extent official diaspora discourse, which has already taken form in the law entitled 'On state policy concerning relations with Azerbaijanis living abroad'. This law was approved by President Heidar Aliev on 27 December 2002, i.e. a year after the first world congress of Azerbaijanis was held in Baku (in November 2001). In the spirit of this law, the charter's authors in turn indicate that former citizens of the Azerbaijani Soviet Republic or of independent Azerbaijan (or people who have not lost such citizenship) 'who consider themselves to be Azerbaijanis' are deemed to be Azerbaijanis living abroad. 'Also, people and their children not in the above categories [author's note: i.e. the categories of those who had at any time held Azerbaijani citizenship] but who consider themselves to be Azerbaijanis through ethnic, linguistic, cultural and/or historical ties.'

According to the authors of the charter, 'the fact that many Azerbaijanis are citizens of different states should not be an obstacle to their national unity'. The first (and most important) reason why dispersion should not be a hindrance to unity is the fact that an independent Republic of Azerbaijan exists. Other criteria are: 'a historical homeland etched in the ethnic memory of the people', followed by tradition, language, religion, an ethno-social worldview, an ethno-cultural system of rules, the ideology of 'Azerbajianism' (i.e. the idea of post-Soviet Azerbaijani nationalism, the author of which is held to be Heidar Aliev). Lastly, the existence of a National Leader, in the shape of Heidar Aliev: his catchphrase 'I have always been proud and I am proud today to be an Azerbaijani!' defines the ideal criteria of national identification.

The charter calls for precisely this manifestation of the particular meaning of ethnicity to be heeded. 'Dear Compatriot! Be proud that you are a child, a descendant of this ancient land, a member of a people with a glorious history! BE PROUD THAT YOU ARE AN AZERBAIJANI!' The final phrase of this call approaches a form of indoctrination. Based on these criteria for defining Azerbaijanis and on the modern ideology of Azerbaijani nationalism (Azerbaijanism), the charter's authors offer their own definition of the Azerbaijani diaspora, namely: 'a single and indivisible part of the Azerbaijani people living outside the borders of their historical homeland'. Overall, although in very different ways, Safran and the authors of the Charter give great importance to the homeland in their search for definitions of the diaspora. It only remains to be admitted that the presence of what Tishkov calls 'the conditional category' of the homeland is indeed vital when describing the substance of the (Azerbajiani) diaspora concept.

However, the most important criterion in the definition of the Azerbaijani diaspora is not the factor of the homeland, as the country of origin or the object on which the emotional attachment of the emigré is fixed, but the existence of that political referent which is the independent nation-state. From this viewpoint, the attitude of the emigré to the homeland or group solidarity in the diaspora should not be considered the most important criterion of ascription to the diaspora. On the contrary, the most important criterion is the fact that, in the context of diaspora building, the political homeland (or, to be precise, the governing regime in the political homeland) sees emigrés and constructs in its imagination a homogenous, united group: an ethno-national diaspora. Or, to put it another way, the fact that the criteria for ascription to the diaspora are determined in the context of a diaspora-building project inspired by the governing regime in the political homeland. There is also the way in which the symbolic capital of the acknowledged political regime allows the construction of a dominant diaspora discourse and a subordinated structure of organizations (which in some sense corresponds to the structure of the state itself), in the context of which the Azerbaijani diaspora in fact exists.[46]

In this way, an understanding of the nature of the post-Soviet political regime governing Azerbaijan becomes the key to understanding the nature, aims and tasks of the diaspora-building policy.

Diaspora as Discourse: Scientists and Statistics

The official diaspora discourse, through which the diaspora is constructed, is partially created by specialists in the social sciences and humanities working in state-run research institutes and universities. In this discourse, great importance is placed on statistics. Naturally, the bigger the diaspora, the more influential that particular community becomes. In the 1990s, it was still widely believed that mass emigration from Azerbaijan was proof of the economic problems that the corrupt and incompetent ruling administration was unable to overcome. Members of the latter seemingly came to the correct conclusion that it would be impossible to bring back hundreds of thousands of emigrants. Despite genuine growth in the economy, the present regime cannot guarantee employment to all migrants. For this reason, it is more preferable that they continue to work abroad. However, in the vein of triumphalist Soviet announcements, the ruling elite prefers to make public only success in economic growth, and to announce the creation of hundreds of thousands, if not millions, of new jobs.

The construction of a diaspora discourse allows this patent contradiction to be overcome. When the emigrés were transformed into a diaspora, discussions about the need for them to return gradually lost their urgency. They are now expected to stay in the receiving countries (preferably those which are perceived as serious geo-political players, i.e. the USA, Germany, the UK, Russia and others), and do their bit to help the political homeland flourish, while also helping in the fight against the 'historical enemy'–'World Armenianism'. Many emigrants visiting Azerbaijan on holiday find themselves faced by demands to answer questions posed by their relatives, their former neighbours or their present acquaintances as to what they personally have done to help the homeland thrive, and what personal contribution they have made in the struggle against this historical enemy. Ultimately, thanks to the successful imposition of the diaspora discourse as dominant, the government has acquired the opportunity to represent their country as attractive to foreign migrant workers. In turn, this attractiveness has become an important indicator of success in developments which were only made possible thanks to the ruling regime.

Academics and specialists in the humanities and social sciences have also played a role, by shaping this discourse. For example, Fatali Abdullayev, Chairman of the Legal Research Support Centre, devoted a section of his monograph to an analysis of migration policy in contemporary Azerbaijan. Abdullayev pointed to the most recent tendencies in migration to be reported:

> Since Azerbaijan occupies a leading position in economic development in the region and the world, while the policies

> pursued by the country's leadership have ensured an attractive environment for investment and an increase in public living standards ... Azerbaijan has transformed itself into an attractive country for migrants.[47]

It is these circumstances which formed the basis for the formation of a new concept for regulating labour migration into Azerbaijan. The official author of this concept is president Ilham Aliev; its main cornerstone is the assertion that over the last four years the balance of migration has changed in favour of Azerbaijan.

But the diaspora discourse does not only give life to an instrumental myth about the outstanding achievements of the government in the country's economic development. This discourse allows a 'single and indivisible' multi-million nation of Azerbaijani Turks to be imagined as really existing. There is no need at this point to expect any unification into Azerbaijan of territory in North-Western Iran or of the Eastern regions of Georgia, which have been settled by pockets of ethnic Azerbaijanis. But imagined national unity can be so imagined in the space of the diaspora discourse. As a result, even if the country's present rulers cannot chalk up 'the gathering of the historic lands' in their list of feats, they can claim 'the gathering of the people'.[48] Furthermore, the construction of this unity also allows the diaspora itself to be imagined as a big (which is equivalent to understanding it as strong), unified collective body.[49]

One of the most active authors is a researcher at the Institute of Philosophy, Sociology and Law in the Azerbaijani National Academy of Science (ANAS): Zaur Aliev. He is one of the specialists involved in drafting the Charter of Solidarity of World Azerbaijanis, and also the author of three extensive works on the diaspora. In his first monograph, *Dünya diasporları* [*The world's diasporas*], while the author does devote considerable time to a description of the major world diasporas (Jewish, Turkish, Armenian, Arab, Russian, and others), the Azerbaijani diaspora is at the centre of his attention. In his account, the diaspora acquires a history so ancient that it could easily compete with the Jewish diaspora. Separate sections of the work are devoted to the diaspora in ancient times, in the middle ages, and in the period up to the end of the 20th century.[50]

His next work was a reference book: *Diaspor* [*Diaspora*]. In it, he devoted a great deal of space to practical questions of the diaspora, which he understands as statistics about the numbers of emigrés and diaspora organizations. Aliev identifies 'the features inherent to a strong (successful) diaspora', or, to be precise, to that diaspora which the Azerbaijani political regime has constructed. In his opinion, this is, firstly: a clear 'conception (knowledge) of one's national roots, mastery of national riches and national property'. By this he apparently means a knowledge of tradition and custom, etc; secondly, 'Familiarity with one's historical homeland and agitation on its behalf abroad'.[51] In Appendix A of the reference work he even provides a list of 67 countries, showing the number of Azerbaijanis resident in each. He calculates the overall number of Azerbaijanis to be more than 50 million people (this is official discourse). The list was compiled in 2006; there is no reference to any source. (Aliev 2007: 343–45).

In his most recent work, published in 2009 with the support of the State Diaspora Liaison Committee, he turns to Turkish-speaking diasporas. In this publication, he talks of the influence exerted by diasporas on internal policy-making within Turkish-speaking states, and also of how the issues facing Turkish-speaking national communities are brought before the international community. Elsewhere, he describes the migration of 'Southern Azerbaijanis' or 'Southern compatriots' (i.e. Iranian Azerbaijanis).[52] In all the works listed here, the power of nomination (the symbolic capital of the academic) discursively creates a populous diaspora community spread out among 70 countries. Government representatives publicly reproduce these concepts and statistics, which are affirmed by the power of academics.[53]

Another method of maintaining the dominant status of diaspora discourse is documentary film-making. The State Committee for Liaison with Azerbaijanis Abroad prepared a documentary film with the significant title 'We are a People of Fifty Million' for the second world congress of Azerbaijanis (16 March 2006). Ever since, this title has been included on the list of films that must be screened at the various official events linked with the implementation of the diaspora project. And of course it is not the only such film. The important ideological value of these films to the ruling regime becomes clear if it is recalled that the launch of the second world congress of Azerbaijanis began with a showing of another such, entitled 'We are Azerbaijanis', which was intended as propaganda about the activities of Heidar Aliev for the diaspora. These films are very frequently shown at rallies of the various diaspora organizations (The European Congress of Azerbaijanis (ECA), the World Congress of Azerbaijanis (WCA) etc.).

Taking account of the special significance afforded to statistics as one of the 'institutions of power',[54] it is natural that the drafters of the Charter of Solidarity of World Azerbaijanis should have spent some time on the question of how many ethnic Azerbaijanis there are. The text of the charter states there are already over 50 million Azerbaijanis. According to their approximate calculations the charter's authors estimate that four out of five Azerbaijanis live in the 'historical homeland' while only one in five lives abroad. In the framework of the diaspora discourse, each individual in this official figure of ten million ethnic Azerbaijanis living outside the 'historic homeland' is part of a unified ethno-national diaspora.

At the same time, it seems impossible in reality to make any firm assertion at all as to the number of emigrants, whether they are RoA citizens or ethnic Azerbaijanis from Iran, or whether they are living permanently or temporarily beyond the borders of their country of origin. The aforementioned statistics only inspire confidence at the rallies and other collective events organized with the support of the regime in implementation of the diaspora project. In many other situations, the presidents themselves have often voiced highly contradictory figures regarding the numbers of emigrants, which are not supported at all by the official diaspora statistics.

Heidar Aliev often asserted in his speeches to Azerbaijanis living abroad that during the existence of the USSR, he single-mindedly 'wanted to disperse Azerbaijanis throughout the Soviet Union, not by means of tragedy, but by other means, and to build a buttress for

Azerbaijan. . . . the greater the number of Azerbaijanis living in each country, the better'.[55] He saw an opportunity to bring this about by sending Azerbaijani youth out of the republic to study. By the post-Soviet period, in a famous speech he gave to Azerbaijanis living in Russia, he admitted that 'it is difficult for me to say how many Azerbaijanis there are in Russia. Some say a million, others say two million. In my opinion, no-one has counted the exact number'.[56]

In all his time in power, Ilham Aliev has only once commented in detail on the issue of the real number of labour migrants from the country. This happened during an interview with the radio station Ekho Moskvy (The Moscow Echo) on 23 December 2006, when journalists expressed doubts over economic growth in Azerbaijan, pointing to mass emigration from the country as an indicator of real difficulties. In the words of the president:

> The number of Azerbaijanis of working age who are temporarily, or pretty much permanently, absent is in the order of 450 thousand people. . . . there are around 500 or 600 thousand[57] Azerbaijanis who are citizens of Russia. So figures of 2–3 million, you know, I think these do not correspond to reality.[58]

Exactly one year later, in December 2007, the head of the State Diaspora Liaison Committee's section dealing with Russia, Ukraine, Belarus, China and India, Shakir Salimov, gave an interview to a local newspaper in which he was already asserting that there were around two million of 'our co-citizens' living in Russia.[59] Naturally, information about ethnic Azerbaijani emigrants from Iran looks even more contradictory. However, the population of the diasporic communities in different countries only acquires meaning and the outline of reality in the context of the diaspora discourse.

Diaspora as Bureaucratic Structure

This discursive image of the diaspora is directly intertwined with the image of the diaspora as a system of organization. i.e. the political regime supports a process of continual increase in the number of organizations, 'including transnational ethnic and hometown associations'.[60] It is precisely as a subordinated structure of numerous organizations that the diaspora has, according to the discourse, become unified and successful. In its current form, various organizations representing cities and regions sit at the base of the bureaucratic pyramid of the Azerbaijani diaspora. Above them come organizations claiming to represent or co-ordinate the activities of all the Azerbaijanis in one or another country (such as the Co-ordinating Centre of Azerbaijanis in Germany, the All-Russian Azerbaijani Congress, etc.). Higher still can be found organizations claiming to lead Azerbaijani associations in several countries (such as the European Congress of Azerbaijanis, or the Benelux Congress of Azerbaijanis) or the whole world (e.g. The World Congress of Azerbaijanis (WCA)).

All of these organizations, which are multiplying year on year, collaborate closely with Azerbaijani embassies and the State Diaspora Liaison Committee. These state organizations co-ordinate and direct the activities of the diasporic organizations along the lines which are most useful at any particular time for the government in the political homeland. As mentioned earlier, at the head of this bureaucratic pyramid stands the Co-ordinating Council of World Azerbaijanis, which is elected at the Azerbaijani world congresses. The Council is headed by the president of the Republic of Azerbaijan.

An assessment of the effectiveness of the bureaucratic practice of diaspora building was given by the president himself at the most recent Congress:

> Over the period since the first Congress, that is, over the last ten years, much work has been done, and the number of organizations has risen. Whereas five years ago we had 336 diasporic organizations, we now have 416. This is very important. But at the same time, perhaps sheer numbers do not play a decisive role in this issue. I am very happy that our diaspora organizations are improving in quality, too; their activities have become more purposeful, and more effective.[61]

So it can be seen that this is a bureaucratic diaspora, which exists as a hierarchy (a pyramid) of interlinked organizations subordinated to the State Committee and the Co-ordinating Council. i.e. the regime in the political homeland has constructed the diaspora to be an organizational (bureaucratic) structure in which each of the newly-created organizations must demonstrate its loyalty to that political homeland regime. Only in such cases will the government enter into a partnership with that organization, and the latter find itself on the list of these ever-multiplying diasporic organizations.

Diaspora and the Potential for Democratization

And yet the regime is unable to exert complete control over the production of diasporic structures. In the post-Soviet years, many political emigrés who have no sympathies with the government in their country of origin have departed from that country. The activity of these political emigrés still goes relatively un-noticed, for now. However, they are gradually stepping up their activities. Such alternatives to the state-sponsored bureaucratic diaspora have become visible in the shape of groups and networks in Holland, Great Britain and the USA. But it seems that former undergraduate and post-graduate students who received their education in the EU and the USA, and who have remained in these countries to live and work, have greater potential to form networks and organizations that are independent from the regime in the political homeland. Their experience of integrating into these societies pushes them logically into supporting democratization in their country of origin. These hitherto little-noticed processes occurring in the diaspora make it possible to talk of the prospect of a possible gradual growth in influence for independent networks and organizations.

Conclusion

And so, as regards the political activities of Azerbaijani diasporic organizations, it is possible to talk in terms of, if not a commanding role, then certainly a regulating and co-ordinating role emanating from the political homeland. This co-ordination is not always managed directly through the embassies and the State Committee. In Germany, the Co-ordinating Centre for the Azerbaijani Diaspora in Germany has existed for several years now; it was created by the RoA embassy in that country, and is financed from state sources. The Centre exists as a nominally independent organization. This means that the RoA Ministry of Foreign Affairs and the State Committee can officially distance themselves from the activities of emigré organizations. All the political actions organized–pickets, protests

Figure 11.1 Heydar Aliyev 85th Anniversary. St Petersburg, May 2008 (S. Rumyantsev)

and the like–are represented as voluntary activity undertaken independently from the government in the political homeland.

The policy of memory and the ideology of post-Soviet nationalism (or 'Azerbaijanism') is also re-transmitted to the diaspora. Such events as the genocide of the Azerbaijanis, which is commemorated on 31 March each year in the diaspora, too, only appeared on the calendar in the post-Soviet period. Exactly the same applies to the holiday celebrated on 15 June as the 'Azerbaijani People's Day of National Salvation', which is linked to the commemoration of Heidar Aliev. In fact these commemorative dates are observed in the diaspora as well, including those of its members who emigrated from Azerbaijan long before these dates appeared on the calendar. The first holiday to be officially accepted by Heidar Aliev—the 'Day of World Azerbaijani Solidarity' (31 December)—has also taken root in the diaspora. These dates and holidays were introduced by the regime into the diaspora's festive activity, which had previously only

Figure 11.2 Picket held in Berlin on the occasion of Khodjali massacre anniversary. February 2011 (S. Rumyantsev)

revolved around celebrating *Novruz Bairama* (the coming of Spring) or the Muslim-wide *Kurban Bairami* (Greater Eid).

These (and certain other) goals of diaspora building are suborned to the most important—the fight in the diaspora to have the Nagorno Karabakh conflict resolved in favour of Azerbaijan. A variety of exhibitions, concerts, Azerbaijani cultural days, and also pickets and protests, are organized with the aim of realizing these goals. As a rule, a small number of activists, businessmen and intellectuals take real part in these collective actions. Their ability to influence the expansion of EU and US citizens' viewpoints appears doubtful. It is more likely to concern attempts to find new means of influencing the popularity of the regime in the country which it governs.

In Azerbaijan itself, the political regime, in the context of diaspora policy, has tried to encompass all Azerbaijanis. In a populist spirit, the regime also represents itself both as taking care of the problems

Figure 11.3 Subbotnik in Nizami Gandjevi (Azerbaijani poet, 12th century) park in St Petersburg. April 2008 (S. Rumyantsev)

Figure 11.4 The opening ceremony of the monument dedicated to the Khodjali victims. Berlin, May 2011 (S. Rumyantsev)

and needs of all Azerbaijanis, and as a successful opponent of 'World Armenianism'. The construction of the diaspora and a cross-border Azerbaijani unity has become the great triumph of Heidar Aliev, which everyone should remember. And in order that no-one in the country does forget about it, the media constantly report on news from the diaspora and on the successes of diaspora building.

Notes

1 Bourdieu, P., 'Rethinking the State: Genesis and Structure of the Bureaucratic Field', *Sociological Theory*, 1994, vol. 12/1, p. 1.

2 de Waal, T., *Black Garden: Armenia and Azerbaijan through Peace and War*, New York & London: New York University Press, 2003, pp. 86–9.

3 Cornell, S., *Small Nations and Great Powers: A Study of Ethnopolitical Conflict in the Caucasus*, Richmond: Curzon, 2001, pp. 61–137; de Waal, T., *op. cit.*; de Waal, T., *The Karabakh Trap: Dangers and Dilemmas of the Nagorny Karabakh Conflict*, London: Conciliations Resources, 2009.

4 In the case of those Azerbaijanis who were living permanently outside the borders of their national republic at the time of the USSR's collapse, there is merit in talking of that type of community which Rogers Brubaker designates as an 'accidental diaspora'. Brubaker very precisely labels post-imperial (i.e. those that arose towards the start of the 20 century after the collapse of the Russian, Hapsburg and Ottoman empires, and towards its end after the collapse of the Soviet Union and Yugoslavia) socio-political spaces as 'post-multinational'. In this case, he differentiates between diasporas which are the product of the post-modern, global or 'post-national' world and those which came into being on the ruins of the USSR. 'These great reconfigurations of political space along national lines represented the apotheosis, not the repudiation, of the principle of the nation state. They marked the triumph, not the transcendence, of the idea that national and state boundaries should coincide' (Brubaker, R., 'Accidental Diasporas and External "Homelands" in Central and Eastern Europe: Past and Present', *HIS Political Science Series*, 2000, vol. 71, pp. 1–2). Specifically, Brubaker discusses Germans and Russians in his work, whose homelands (Weimar Germany and post-Soviet Russia, respectively) actively sought to bring influence to bear on their positions. However, it seems indisputable that the Azerbaijani diaspora is one more result of the 'post-multinational' world. Of course, in some aspects, the position of Azerbaijanis may differ greatly from the situations faced by those Russians (or, more widely, Russian speakers) who found themselves in the former Soviet republics at the moment of the USSR's collapse (see Laitin, D., *Identity in Formation: The Russian-Speaking Population in the Near Abroad*, Ithaca: Cornell University Press, 1998; Kosmarskaia, N., *'Deti imperii' v postsovetskoi Tsentral'noi Azii: adaptivnye praktiki i mental'nye sdvigi (Russkie v Kirgizii, 1992–2002)* [*'Children of the Empire' in post-Soviet Central Asia: adaptive practices and mental shifts (Russians in Kyrgyzstan, 1992–2002)*], Moscow: Natalis, 2006). However, the specifics of the change in status of the homeland, and its striving to actively influence the position of their fellow countrymen in the diasporas, were also clearly displayed in this case. In fact, it is these specifics, the tools and aims invoked by a political homeland (i.e. the Republic of Azerbaijan) to exert influence on 'its' diasporas, that will be the focus of this chapter.

5 The author has, since September 2010, been an Alexander Von Humboldt Foundation Post-Doctoral Research Fellow in the Institute for European Ethnology, Humboldt University (Berlin). In addition, this chapter is also based on material gathered during fieldwork performed for a number of different research projects. The politics of memory in a diaspora, in the context of the Nagorno Karabakh conflict, were researched in Paris in Spring 2010, with the support of *La Fondation Maison des Sciences de L'Homme* (FMSH, Paris). Research into diaspora politics in Azerbaijan in 2009–10 was supported by the Caucasus Resource Research Center (CRRC, Baku). Further, the analysis here of the way in which state diaspora policy influences residents of the host country is likewise based on a range of projects conducted over a period of four years by the author with the support of various foundations in Georgia, Russia and Germany. A

project researching Azerbaijanis in Georgia was made possible by the support of CRRC in 2005–06. Some of the interviews were conducted as part of a research summer school that was held in Georgia in August 2007, with the support of CRRC and the Heinrich Boell Foundation (Germany). In Russia, research was conducted over several stages in St Petersburg: as part of training undertaken in April 2006 at the Centre for Independent Sociological Research (CISR, St Petersburg), supported by the South Caucasus Regional Office of the Heinrich Boell Foundation; in February–May 2007, during a project supported by the Smolny Collegium, St Petersburg (an Andrew Gagarin Fellowship); and likewise during independent trips to the city in April–May and October, 2008. In Germany, the first research project took place in October–December 2006, with support from the Heinrich Boell Foundation. The author would like to express his gratitude to all these foundations and to his colleagues for taking interest in his research and for providing him with invaluable support.

6 Fairclough, N., *Critical Discourse Analysis: The critical Study of Language*, Edinburgh: Pearson Education Limited, 2010.

7 Safran, W., 'Diasporas in modern societies: myths of homeland and return', *Diaspora*, vol. 1/1, pp. 83–4.

8 Both the term 'diaspora' and the concept of 'homeland' have recently been subjected to serious revision. 'In the older vocabulary, "homeland" was commonly depicted as a sacred place filled with memories of past glory and bathed in visions of nobility and renaissance. Paradoxically, in the new discourse "homelands" sometimes fade out of view entirely, or ... they become nation-states that by definition repress minorities and place limits upon their cultural and other freedoms' (Weingrod, A., Levy, A. (eds), *Homelands and Diasporas: Holy Lands and Other Places*, Stanford: Stanford University Press, 2005, pp. 4–5).

9 Cohen, R., *Global Diasporas: An Introduction*, London & New-York: Routledge, 2008, p. 17.

10 *Ibid*., p. 16.

11 This concept concerns, first and foremost, the Jewish diaspora. Safran notes that 'for many generations, the phenomenon of diaspora was dealt with only in connection with the Jews'. However, in his opinion, this ideal type could also be held to include Greek, Armenian, Chinese, Indian and certain other diasporas. Although the Jewish diaspora is distinctive due to its traumatic experience – 'conditions of minority status and of powerlessness' (Safran, W., 'The Jewish Diaspora in a Comparative and Theoretical Perspective', *Israel Studies*, 2005, vol. 10/1, pp. 36–8). However, as Cohen justly remarks, traumatic experience may be a distinctive feature of other such communities as well. For example, the Irish diaspora (Cohen, R., *op. cit.*, p. 3). Moreover, he rightly underlines the fact that the phenomenon of the Jewish diaspora, when examined more closely, appears much more complex than is generally thought. 'All scholars of diaspora recognize that the dominant Jewish tradition is at the heart of any definition of the concept. Yet, if it is necessary to take full account of this tradition it is also necessary to transcend it. ... Jewish diasporic experiences are much more

complex and varied than many assume. The Jews are not a single people; they have a multi-faceted, multi-located history with a genetically complex set of roots. ... Like other ethnics groups, their history is socially constructed and selectively interpreted' (*ibid.*, pp. 34–5). James Clifford justly emphasizes that 'we should be able to recognize the strong entailment of Jewish history on the language of diaspora without making that history a definitive model. Jewish (and Greek and Armenian) diasporas can be taken as non-normative starting points for a discourse that is traveling or hybridizing in new global conditions. For better or worse, diaspora discourse is being widely appropriated.' (Clifford, J., 'Diasporas', *Cultural Anthropology* 1994, vol. 9/3, p. 306).

12 Cohen, R., *op. cit.*, p. 2.

13 Even if it is acknowledged that the concept of post-coloniality is poorly suited to describing the networks and communities created by Azerbaijanis in, for example, post-Soviet Russia, looking at the contrasts from this perspective allows them to be better understood. This means it allows the phenomenon of the post-Soviet Azerbaijani diaspora to be more accurately described (on post-colonial diasporas, see e.g. Keown, M., Murphy, D., Procter, J. (eds), *Comparing Post-colonial Diasporas*, Palgrave: Macmillan, 2009, pp. 1–15).

14 Rogers Brubaker argues, that 'if everyone is Diasporic, then no one is distinctively so. The term loses its discriminating power–its ability to pick out phenomena, to make distinctions. The universalization of diaspora, paradoxically, means the disappearance of diaspora' (Brubaker, R., 'The "diaspora' diaspora', *Ethnic and Racial Studies*, 2005, vol. 28/1, p. 3).

15 Sheffer, G., *Diaspora Politics: At Home Abroad*, Cambridge: Cambridge University Press, 2003, pp. 9–10.

16 Tishkov, V., *Rekviem po etnosu: Issledovanie po sotsial'no-kul'turnoi antropologii* [*Requiem for Ethnos. Research in Social and Cultural Anthropology*], Moscow: Nauka, 2003, p. 440.

17 In this context, 'new' seems to act as a counterpoint to 'old', 'classical' diasporas. As Alex Weingrod and Andre Levy put it, 'today's new diasporas are considerably different. Depending upon the particular definition and usage, there are likely to be many more of them, and they are scattered about as a result of the global trends that shape the contemporary world. As we know these new diasporas have emerged from the world-wide movement of millions of persons, which in turn has been caused by global inequalities, modern information and production technologies, powerful multi-national corporations that frequently shift production across the world, as well as the more familiar "old-fashioned" reasons of famine and war.' (Weingrod, A., Levy, A., 'On Homelands and Diasporas: An Introduction', in Weingrod, A., Levy, A. (eds), *Homelands and Diasporas: Holy Lands and Other Places*, Stanford: Stanford University Press, 2005, p. 4).

18 Tishkov, V., *op. cit.*, p. 464.

19 The Tsarist Empire and the Soviet authorities undoubtedly differed in their judgement of the importance of the Transcaucasian region to them. For tsarist

Russia, this importance had arisen in the context of its strategic location on the border with the competing Persian and, especially, Ottoman empires. Nor did the title of 'Defenders of the Christian Faith' play an insignificant role for the Russian emperors, particularly as it was their protectorate over the Georgians and Armenians which bestowed this honorific upon them. The economic importance of the region only began to grow as the oil boom took off in the second half of the nineteenth century. For the Bolsheviks, in contrast, Azerbaijan had become 'a stronghold of socialism in the East', while its capital Baku was perceived as a city which showcased the achievements of the Soviet authorities to the whole of the Near East (Bretanitskii, L., *Baku*, Leningrad-Moscow: Iskusstvo, 1970, pp. 117–18; Baberowski, J., *Der Feiend ist Überal: Stalinismus im Kaukasus* [*The enemy is everywhere: Stalinism in the Caucasus*], München: Deutsche Verlags-Anstalt, 2003, pp. 217–394).

20 Altstadt, A., *The Azerbaijani Turks: Power and Identity under Russian Rule*, Stanford, California: Hoover Institution Press, 1992, pp. 50–73; Swietochowski, T., *Russian Azerbaijan, 1905–1920. The Shaping of National Identity in a Muslim Community*, Cambridge: Cambridge University Press, 1985, pp. 23–36; Baberowski, J., *op. cit.*, pp. 316–48).

21 Brubaker, R., *Nationalism Reframed: Nationhood and the National Question in the New Europe*, Cambridge: Cambridge University Press, 2000, pp. 41–2.

22 Discussions about what to call the nation began at the end of the 19th century and have continued, with the occasional pause, to the present day (Shnirelman, V., *The Value of the Past: Myths, Identity and Politics in Transcaucasia*, Osaka: National Museum of Ethnology, 2001, pp. 94–6; Swietochowski, T., *op. cit.*, p. 33). Taking the most common features, it can be stated that a proportion of nationalists (and particularly, to a greater or lesser degree, of radical pan-Turkists) consider the correct name to be Azerbaijani Turks [translator's note: in Russian, this may be spelt *turk* or *tiurk*] (Azəri-Türklər). The official version, established during Heidar Aliev's presidency, prefers the name accepted in the USSR from the end of the 1930s: Azerbaijanis (Azərbaycanlılar). In general, both in daily life and in academic studies, both names are used in parallel.

23 It is striking that Azerbaijani historians studying this first wave of emigration as a rule avoid the label diaspora, talking instead of political emigration (Balaev, A., *Mamed Emin Rasulzade*, Moscow: Flinta, 2009, pp. 207–77; Guliev, V., *Iz Naslediia Politicheskoi Emigratsii Azerbaidzhana v Pol'she (30-e gody XX veka)* [*From the Legacy of Political Emigration from Azerbaijan into Poland (the 1930s)*], Baku: Ozan, 2011, pp. 4–10). Meanwhile, specialists involved in the policy of diaspora building describe the history of this wave of emigration as one of the stages in the formation of the Azerbaijani diaspora, the roots of which are now being sought in the middle ages, if not even earlier (Rizvan, N., *Azərbaijan Diasporasi Tarixindən* [*From the history of the Azerbaijani diaspora*], Bakı: Borçalı HPM, 2002; Aliyev (Əliyev), Z., *Türkdilli xalqların diasporları* [*The Turkic-speaking peoples' diaporas*], Bakı: Adiloğlu, 2009, pp. 14–46).

24 This chapter does not consider the organizations formed by Iranian Azerbaijanis in emigration. These few organizations had no links with Soviet Azerbaijan; they are, effectively, part of the Iranian diaspora. The only exception is emigrants who were representatives of the Democratic party. This party, which headed the nationalists seeking autonomy for Azerbaijanis in Iran, was created in line with a Soviet policy aimed at increasing Soviet influence in Iran during the Second World War, at a time when the USSR was counting on being involved in the extraction of Iranian oil. However, following the departure of Soviet forces from Iran, the party and the regional government founded by its activists soon ceased to exist. Incidentally, some of these Azerbaijanis who left Iran in 1946 continued work in emigré structures that were created and operated under the patronage of Soviet security services (for more on these events, see Hasanli, J., *SSSR-Iran: Azerbaidzhanskii Krizis i Nachalo Kholodnoi Voiny (1941–1946 gg.)* [*USSR-Iran: the Azerbaijani Crisis and the Start of the Cold War (1941–1946)*], Moscow: Geroi Otechestva, 2006).

25 Brubaker, R., 2005, *op. cit*, p. 13.

26 In a wider sense, this chapter shares the position that Weingrod and Levy set up in contrast to the approaches of Cohen, Safran and Tölölyan, who prefer to begin by a definition of diaspora or by a catalogue of its types. 'In contrast, Clifford, Appadurai, Bhabha, Hall, and many others tend to use the term in a looser, more metaphoric sense and consequently they may discover 'diasporic features' among a wider range of migrating groups. For these scholars certain historical moments, social contexts, and political-cultural processes are more important than whether a specific community neatly fits the type.' (Weingrod, A., Levy, A., *op. cit.*, p. 7).

27 It should not be forgotten that this specifically concerns emigrés from the Republic of Azerbaijan. And now that many years of diaspora building have passed, ethnic activists frequently complain in interviews that the majority of Iranian Azerbaijanis lack any genuine interest in the problem of the Nagorno Karabakh conflict, that they know nothing of the basic facts and events of the Armenian–Azerbaijani confrontation, etc.

28 Demmers, J., 'Nationalism from Without. Theorizing the Role of Diasporas in Contemporary Conflict', in Atabaki, T., Mehendale, S. (eds), *Central Asia and the Caucasus: Transnationalism and Diaspora*, New-York: Routledge, 2005, pp. 11–12)

29 To be precise, from the moment when Heidar Aliev returned to power in 1993. More on this below.

30 Sökefeld, M., 'Mobilizing in Transnational Space: A Social Movement Approach to the Formation of Diaspora', *Global Networks*, July 2006, vol. 6 (3), p. 268.

31 King, C., Melvin, J. N., 'Diaspora Politics: Ethnic Linkages, Foreign Policy, and Security in Eurasia', *International Security*, Winter 1999–2000, vol. 24/3, p. 137.

32 This title of 'National Leader' was established while he was still in power. For example, among an array of official holidays. every 15 June since 1998 has been celebrated as 'Azerbaijani National Salvation Day'. This was the date of Heidar

Aliev's return to power in 1993. Since 2000, while he was still alive, 'Flower Day' has been celebrated, the date coinciding with the president's birthday. Every year on 12 December, the anniversary of the death of the 'Great Leader' is widely commemorated, although this date is not on the official list of days of mourning.

33 The Azerbaijani Diaspora (http://www.azerbaijan.az/portal/Society/Diaspora/diaspora_r.html).

34 Swiettochowski, T., *Russia and Azerbaijan: A Borderland in Transition*, New York: Columbia University Press, 1995; Shaffer, B., *Borders and Brethren: Iran and the Challenge of Azerbaijani Identity*, London: MIT Press, 2002; Nodia, G., 'Polietnichnost' Gruzii: Fakt, Otnoshenie k Nemu i Politicheskaia Strategiia' ['Georgian Polyethnicity: Facts, Attitudes to it and Political Strategies'], in *Odno Obshchestvo, Mnogo Etnosov: Etnicheskoe Mnogoobrazie i Grazhdanskaia Integratsiia v Gruzii* [*One society, Many Ethnoses: Ethnic Diversity and Civil Integration in Georgia*], Tbilisi: Kavkazskii Institut Mira, Demokratii i Razvitiia, 2003, pp. 59–93.

35 For a more detailed account, see Rumyantsev, S,. 'Natsionalizm i konstruirovanie kart 'istoricheskikh territorii': obuchenie natsional'nym istoriiam v stranakh Iuzhnogo Kavkaza' ['Nationalism and the Construction of Maps of "Historical Territories": Teaching National Histories in the Countries of South Caucasus'], *Ab Imperio*, 2010, vol. 4, pp. 415–61.

36 It should be said that an attempt to hold the first world congress or assembly of Azerbaijanis had been made earlier. At the end of December 1989, several dozen emigré intellectuals gathered in Istanbul through the mediation of the Turkish authorities. However, this gathering did not gain wide publicity, and it had no serious influence on the diaspora-building process.

37 Slezkine, Y., 'The USSR as a Communal Apartment, or How a Socialist State Promoted Ethnic Particularism', in Geoff, E., Suny, R.G. (eds), *Becoming National. A Reader*, New York and Oxford: Oxford University Press, 1996, pp. 203–4; Martin, T., *The Affirmative Action Empire: Nations and Nationalism in the Soviet Union 1923–1939*, Ithaca & London: Cornell University Press, 2001, pp. 10–13.

38 The character study of Heidar Aliev found in the book by the journalist Goltz is not without interest (Goltz, T., *Azerbaijan Diary: A Rogue Reporter's Adventures in an Oil-Rich, War-Torn, post-Soviet Republic*, New York & London: M. E. Sharpe, 1999).

39 Kotkin, contemplating the nature of the societies comprising the Eastern Bloc, rightly remarked that 'totalitarian or would-be totalitarian states did not eliminate society–they created their own societies. . . . the term "uncivil society" refers to these formidable bonds and forms of social organization that accompanied an illiberal state, particularly an illiberal state without private property' (Kotkin, S., *Uncivil Society: 1989 and the Implosion of the Communist Establishment*, New York: The Modern Library, 2009, p. 12). However, it is more important to emphasize the fact of the structural continuity of power. In the

post-Soviet period, rule by elected presidents was established, a Parliament was created, a multi-party system was arranged, the post of ombudsman appeared, a network of NGOs and independent mass media arose, and so on. But all of these institutions have a deeply imitative nature. Post-Soviet regimes, as many commentators have observed, imitate democracy (Ottaway, M., *Democracy Challenged: The Rise of Semi-Authoritarianism*, Washington D.C.: Carnegie Endowment for International Peace, 2003, pp. 51–70), yet their assessment seems too limited. It is modern statehood itself which is being imitated. In fact, not one of the institutions listed is performing its allotted functions. They were all created to imitate the institutionalized state structures familiar in those countries which are described as developed and democratic. And in this sense the regime is post-Soviet. After all, the Soviet authorities had no need of such large-scale imitations.

40 In the words of Yuri Slezkine, 'Clannishness is loyalty to a limited and well-defined circle of kin (real or fictitious)' (Slezkine, Y., *The Jewish Century*, Princeton & Oxford: Princeton University Press, 2004, p. 26). However, it should be added that Azerbaijani political clans are seemingly built not only on ties of kinship and friendship, but also on compatriotic and regional ties. Unfortunately, such phenomena in the organization of power as nepotism and clannishness still remain under-researched. Nevertheless, it can be stated that this does not concern some kind of traditional pre-Soviet forms of wielding power. The clans and the nepotism in their current form were born in the Soviet system. The practices of creating nepotism, or 'mutually protective "family circles"', in the milieu of Communist bureaucracy were illuminated by Sheila Fitzpatrick (Fitzpatrick, S., *Tear of the Masks: Identity and Imposture in Twentieth-Century Russia*, Princeton & Oxford: Princeton University Press, 2005, pp. 104, 110–11), while the spread of the system of personal inter-relations as an informal source of power prior to the Great Terror (1937–38) was examined by Gerald M. Easter (Easter, M.G., *Nationalist Mobilization and the Collapse of the Soviet State*, Cambridge: Cambridge University Press, 2002). In the case of Azerbaijan in those same years, Jorg Baberowski says that indigenization 'meant the tribalization and traditionalization of apparatuses' (Baberowski, J., *op. cit.*, p. 498). As regards the later period, when managers such as Heidar Aliev had come to power in the USSR, Adeeb Khalid has an array of valuable observations and remarks. He correctly emphasizes that 'at the political level, certainly, the "clans" were the creation of the Soviet period' (Khalid, A., *Islam after Communism: Religion and Politics in Central Asia*, Los Angeles: University of California Press, 2007, pp. 89–91).

41 Speech by the President of the Republic of Azerbaijan, Heidar Aliev, in a meeting with compatriots living in Switzerland. Berne, 29 January 1995 (http://library.aliyev-heritage.org/ru/9389127.html).

42 The image of Heidar Aliev as the National Leader had undoubtedly begun to form back in the years of the USSR. As noted by Adeeb Khalid, 'the party secretaries emerged as legitimate national leaders in the eyes of the population.

They wielded their power locally and mediated with central authorities for access to resources.' (Khalid, A., *op. cit.*, p. 91) Furthermore, if such rules were only established firmly in the Central Asian republics under Brejnev, this had happened in Azerbaijan much earlier. For this reason, assertions like this one of Mark Beissinger may be thought surprising: 'That the once loyal Soviet nomenklatura–the Heidar Alievs, Leonid Kravchuks, Mintimer Shaimievs, and Saparmurad Niiazovs of the Soviet world – could become 'fathers' of their respective nations was not a plausible outcome before the onset of the *glasnost'* tide of nationalism' (Beissinger, R.M., *Nationalist Mobilization and the Collapse of the Soviet State*, Cambridge: Cambridge University Press, 2002, pp. 36–7).

43 Bourdieu, P., *op. cit.*, p. 9.

44 Here, a provisional draft of the charter will be examined, since at the time of writing work was continuing on the final draft. This text was kindly provided by the Information and Analysis Department of the State Diaspora Liaison Committee.

45 This refers to members of a range of ethnic groups who, alongside Azerbaijanis, are regarded as native inhabitants of the country. These are Tats, Talysh, Lezgins, and certain other ethnic groups identified by statistics.

46 In this way, the article adopts a position closer to that outlined by Valerii Tishkov than those of Safran or Sheffer: Tishkov states that 'rather than the ethnic community, the so-called nation state is the key factor in diaspora formation' (Tishkov, V., *op. cit.*, p. 451).

47 Abdullayev, F., *Müasir Azərbaycanda miqrasiya siyasəti və beynəlxalq əməkdaşlıq* [*The migration policy and international cooperation in contemporary Azerbaijan*], Bakı: Elm və Təhsil, 2009, pp. 310–11.

48 It should be emphasized here that this refers to the 'gathering of the people' dispersed beyond the borders of the imagined "historical homeland," i.e. those ethnic Azerbijanis living in Iran or Georgia are not a part of the diaspora, according to the official discourse, but are living in their 'historical homeland.'

49 The government has been so successful in promoting its diaspora discourse into a dominant position that even specialists known to be opponents of the governing regime have started writing about the diaspora. For example, Arif Iunusov, who for a long time was head of the Departments of Conflict and Migration Studies of the non-governmental Institute of Peace and Democracy, became quite carried away during a discussion of the ancient history of the diaspora in one of his monographs. At the same time, he demonstrated the difficulty of avoiding adoption of the language of the official discourse. For example, while analysing processes in the formation of the Azerbaijani diaspora in the 'countries of Western civilization', he himself works on the basis of the concept of the 'compatriot' which is so common in populist patriotic discourse (Yunusov, A., *Migration processes in Azerbaijan*, Baku: Adiloglu, 2009, p. 152).

50 Aliyev (Əliyev), Z., *Dünya diasporları* [*The world's diasporas*], Bakı: Qismət, 2005.

51 Aliyev (Əliyev), Z., *Diaspor. İzahlı Sözlük və Məlumat Kitabı* [*Diaspora. Explanatory dictionary and reference book*], Bakı: Yurd, 2007, p. 67).

52 Əliyev, Z., *Türkdilli Xalqların Diasporları* [*The Turkic-Speaking Peoples' Diasporas*], Bakı: 'Adiloğlu', 2009, p. 63.

53 One of the largest-scale works (800 pages) among those devoted to the Azerbaijani diaspora might be mentioned as another interesting example of this kind. Its author is a professor, a doctor of philological science, and a senior researcher at the ANAS Nizami Institute of Literature, Vaqif Arzumanlı. He was previously the director of the ANAS Insitute of International Relations. His monograph addresses contemporary issues facing the Azerbaijani diaspora. The author describes the political and socio-cultural 'life of our diaspora in different countries, examining its interesting and valuable pages'. In the spirit of the ideology of 'Azerbaijanism', the second part of his work is devoted to his thoughts on the 'unity of world Azerbaijanis at a new stage' in the context of the activities of the World Congress of Azerbaijanis, the Federation of Azerbaijani Communities in Germany, the All-Russian Congress of Azerbaijanis and also the Ukrainian Congress of Azerbaijanis (Arzumanlı, V., *Azərbaycan Diasporu (Reallıqlar, Qayğılar, Problemlər)* [*The Azerbaijani Diaspora (Reality, Concerns, Challenges)*], Bakı: Qartal, 2001, pp. 226–394). See also: (Həbiboglu, V., *Heidar Əliev və Azərbaican diasporu* [*Heidar Aliev and the Azerbaijani Diaspora*], Bakı: Qartal, 1999; Həbiboglu, V., *Azərbaican diasporu yeni mərhələdə* [*The Azerbaijani Diaspora at the New Stage*], Bakı: Elm, 2006; İsmayilov, Z., *Dünya Azərbaicanlıları 20 Əsrdə* [*The World's Azerbaijanis in the 20th Century*], Bakı: Azərbaican DNA Mətbəsi, 1997; Məmmədov, R., *Azərbaycan diasporu və milli mətbuat* [*The Azerbaijani Diaspora and the National Press*], Bakı: Gartal, 2004.).

54 Anderson, B., *Imagined Communities: Reflections on the Origin and Spread of Nationalism*, London: Verso, 1998, p. 163.

55 Speech by the President of the Republic of Azerbaijan, Heidar Aliev, 1995, *op. cit.*

56 Speech by the President of the Republic of Azerbaijan, Heidar Aliev, given at the constituent assembly of the All Russian Congress of Azerbaijanis, in Moscow, 22 June 2000 (http://library.aliyev-heritage.org/ru/141697.html).

57 According to data from the All-Russian population census in 2002, the number of Azerbaijanis who were citizens of the Russian Federation at that point was 621,840.

58 Interview with the President of Azerbaijan Ilham Aliev by the radio station Ekho Moskvy (http://www.echo.msk.ru/programs/beseda/48358/).

59 In Russia, the Azerbaijani diaspora carries enormous weight and enjoys great respect – Shakir Salimov (http://www.newsazerbaijan.ru/exclusive/20071228/42088563-print.html).

60 Henry, L., Mohan, G., Yanacopulos, H., 'Networks as transnational agents of development', *Third World Quarterly*, 2004, vol. 25/5, p. 841.

61 Ilham Aliev's speech at the Third World Congress of Azerbaijanis, 5 July 2011 (http://ru.president.az/articles/2717).

CHAPTER 12

POLITICAL AND CULTURAL TOOLS OF TURKEY'S PRESENCE IN CENTRAL ASIA: THE AMBIGUITIES OF A NATIONALIST MODERNIZATION MODEL

Stéphane De Tapia
(CNRS and Department of Turkish Studies, University of Strasbourg)

With a growth rate to make all EU economies blush (9 per cent in 2010, 8.5 per cent in 2011), a GDP in 2010 of $1,105 billion in normal parity ($1,118 billion in PPA – Purchasing Power Parity) and a GDP rate per capita of $15,340, Turkey recently joined the club of the top 20 global economies (G20), ranking number 15. A candidate for EU membership, seemingly with little chance of succeeding despite the fact that the EU is its most significant economic partner representing over 50 per cent of foreign trade, Turkey is getting impatient and sees itself as a model for the Middle East. With all its recent successes, could Turkey be considered a country of the 'North' taking the lead among the Turkic-speaking countries previously belonging to the 'North' with the USSR, currently in search of their own stability?

Except for the Turkish-speaking minorities of the Balkans, Turkey is the most Westernized element of what is referred to by certain intellectual and ideological groups as the Turkic world (*Türk Dünyası*). From 1923 to 1991–92, Turkey was the only sovereign and independent state of this vast group of cultural and linguistic countries, and thus of Turkishness (*türklük*), but with very cautious leaders. They never really followed Pan-Turkism (*türkçülük*) as it emerged in Russia and Central Asia at the end of the 19th century, except using it internally as an ideological argument for building nationalism and the Nation-state. Two notable exceptions are the annexing of Sanjak of Alexandretta in 1939, and the intervention in Cyprus, now a territory of the Turkish Republic of Northern Cyprus, in 1974.

The political upheaval that followed perestroïka and led to the disintegration of the USSR saw the 'rebirth' of several independent states and sovereign entities,[1] all officially using an Altaic language of the Turkic group,[2] sometimes alongside Russian, an unexpected outcome that gave rise to great hopes in Turkey, going beyond traditional Pan-Turkist circles. Ankara was one of the first capitals to officially recognize Azerbaijan, Kazakhstan, Uzbekistan, Kyrgyzstan and Turkmenistan, to open embassies (sometimes providing temporary offices within their premisses and defending the interests of these new independent states at international level), to operate direct and regular airlines, to organize numerous congresses and cultural activities and to receive official and academic delegations.

These actions gave rise to incomprehension and suspicion, particularly in Russia, as they also touched non-independent entities such as Tatarstan. Official institutions were created or reinforced and communication satellites (*Türksat*) were launched in the same vein, with the creation of a specific television channel (*TRT-Avrasya*).

Although the economic outcome of this wave of recognition has had little impact on a global level, the effect in Turkey has been significant. The construction and public works sector opened several sites in the USSR with the arrival of perestroika,[3] investors and enterprises set up in Central Asia and the Caucasus, naturally followed by a large number of migrant workers. This activity led to the creation of numerous private and partly state-controlled institutions, professional associations and think tanks, both Turkish and bilateral. This chapter aims to describe and analyse this phenomenon and draw conclusions that go beyond the existing ideological assumptions for and against this new presence in Turkic-speaking Central Asia, a reinvented Turkic world, often fantasised about by Turkey and its neighbours. Understandably for areas that endured a long and bitter Ottoman presence (the Balkans, Armenia, Cyprus, Arab countries) or have experienced recurring conflicts (Russia, Iran), this is more surprisingly in Western countries, who on the whole are less concerned as conflicts with the Ottomans are not so recent (Austria) or more sporadic (France).

The question arises as to the role of Turkey in the Great Game, the term referred to by Rudyard Kipling and used at the end of the 19th and beginning of the 20th centuries, when the Russian and British Empires indirectly competed in Central Asia (Turkestan, Afghanistan) and in High Asia (Mongolia, Tibet, Xinjiang). Can Turkey be a real player at this level? Can it erase over a century of Russian presence at a time when it has made only meagre attempts to re-visit its 'ancestral' Central Asian lands? This territory has since been inhabited by other Turkic speakers, certainly linked linguistically and culturally, but who have never lived under the same roof. It would be a mistake to refer to 'poor Turkey', an expression used by Hélène Carrère d'Encausse during a television debate some time ago. A visit to the capitals (Tashkent, Bishkek, Almaty, Baku) reveals similarities in the day-to-day lives of Anatolians and Central Asians, despite a significant Russian presence in the latter. On examination, and in the light of recent tragic events,[4] both Turk and Turkic societies see themselves as unique and are not looking for contact, except from a business perspective. Azerbaijan is a different scenario.[5] Turks are discreetly present in the capitals and blend in with the local population.

A nation-state in the making, Turkey suffers significant recurrent problems including the Kurdish and Cypriot questions, the consequences of the refusal to acknowledge the Armenian genocide, swings from Kemalist secularism and Islamic modernism in the face of a deeply embedded Muslim culture, itself particularly complex, and finds itself torn between Europe and its Asian roots. The question of 'roots'–either Central Asian, Eurasian, or Turkic–and their effect on society must be raised. In Turkish, *Türk* can be used for a Turk from Turkey but also for a Turkic-speaker from Central Asia or elsewhere. To make a distinction and appear more politically correct, one can translate Turkic by *Türki*. *'Türk' Cumhuriyetleri* (Turkish republics) is, however, used more often than *'Türkî' Cumhuriyetler* (Turkic republics). Could this be a show of a Pan-Turkist ideology being overtaken by a lack of substance, a defiant stance against Europe, whereby the Turks would go along with the Russian definitions of Eurasianism,[6] or are these real alternatives to an increasingly unlikely European integration?

Turkish Approaches to Central Asia: A Confusing State Role and Contradictions of a Nationalist Position

This chapter provides a summary, and not an exhaustive list, of the steps intended to be taken by Turkey to maintain and develop certain links (political, cultural, university, economic, religious, etc.). Prior works, such as Landau,[7] an Israeli historian specializing in the forms of the quest for political identity in Turkey (Islamism, nationalism, Turkism, Pan-Turkism) or Copeaux,[8] a historian of Turkish nationalism, demonstrate that it is essential to separate recognized, and at times forcefully asserted, historical Central Asian roots, from unblended nationalism linked to the construction of a nation-state, vast at European level (over 780,000 km^2) but smaller than the Ottoman Empire (over 4 million km^2) or the even larger Turkic world, deeply Russified from 1931 to 1992.[9] Copeaux talks of schizophrenia with regards to school maps which opposes a national identity centred on 'Turkish Asia', with varying geometry, against political positioning that places European membership at the centre and openly criticizes Arab and Iranian neighbours, despite being Muslim. Another dimension to the argument distinguishes Turkish Islam from other forms of Islam on the basis of being *Türk* by birth, thus from Central Asia. Leaders, the army, schools and the press have for decades insisted on Turkishness, the last bastion of an identity aggressed by all, bemoaning foreign Turks (*Dış Türkler*), sometimes referred to as 'imprisoned Turks' (i.e. of communism *Esir Türkler, esaretteki Türkler*). The *soydaş* (literally, kin) have often been welcomed with open arms on the condition that they do not interfere with the external politics of the new republic, as Bezanis highlights with refugees from the Caucasus, the Volga and Central Asia.[10] From 1920 to 1950, the latter played an important role in the academic and cultural world (linguistics, Turkology, ethnography, history, media) but were carefully watched and prevented from making any move which might deviate from the position of the USSR. Despite this, their political role is not without significance. It could be argued, as does Georgeon,[11] that Turkish nationalism came to life on the banks of the Volga as Gasprinski (indirectly) or Akçura, Togan and others like Ağaoğlu (deputies, authors) were active and that one should refer to a Tatar model for the new Turkish nationalism.[12] The immigration of refugees from lost countries or allies of the Empire is a key element to understanding the ideological evolution of Turkish society.

Numerous public and partly state-controlled institutions were created to establish and maintain the symbolic link with Ankara, first and foremost, the Kemalist capital of Turkey, opposing Istanbul, the imperial and cosmopolitan Ottoman capital. Large numbers of refugees arrived and were settled in all regions, repopulating areas devastated between 1915 and 1922 and tipping back the balance in regions with significant non-Turkic speaking populations. This mechanism worked well while Turkey was the sole champion of the Turkishness cause. How have things changed since the independence of Turkic republics, each of which trying to find a place in this new evolving world?

Faced with an agreed state position (and cautious with regard to the outside world) and the difficulties associated with an often chaotic growth, public opinion did not take much interest in the matter, leaving the 'brothers' and other 'cousins' of Central Asia with their ultranationalist Pan-Turkish positions, for internal more than international use, until the break-up of the USSR. This brought with it new Turkish interest in Central Asia, albeit limited to specific pan-Turkist and Islamist groups with a clear tendency towards proselytism and a small number of investors in search of new markets without necessarily sharing the same political vision. In power since 2002–03, the AKP–*Adalet ve Kalkınma Partisi* (Party of Justice and Development) sees the world very differently to its predecessors, with a Turkic-speaking and Muslim Central Asia playing a lesser role. It is telling that in his publication *Stratejik Derinlik*, the current minister of Foreign Affairs Ahmet Davutoğlu, despite dedicating 50 out of 540 pages to Central Asia, paints a diluted and unrealistic picture of the situation. This has not prevented the creation of new institutions such as the Yunus Emre Institute and the recent Presidency of Expatriate Turks and Parent Communities.

The Ministries

A parliamentary republic, Turkey is represented by a President of the republic, who is elected by deputies and guarantees the respect of the constitution, and a Prime Minister from the party or coalition in power with executive powers, aided by sector competent public authorities.

The prime minister is the guardian of decision-making tools in various domains (planning, management of religious bodies, international cooperation) that can be employed at any given time and several reports have been written on the current or potential strategies with regards to Turkic-speaking countries. Two of these tools should be given further consideration:

- *TİCA* is the acronym for *Türk İşbirliği Kalkınma Ajansı* (Turkish International Cooperation and Development Agency), which as of today is the Presidency of the Turkish Administration of Cooperation and Development. This change in name comes with the change of affiliation from the Ministry of Foreign Affairs to the office of the Prime Minister, confirmed by the construction of a dedicated building in Ulus. TİCA implements an array of development projects with varying levels of public finances covering cultural, administrative, economic, touristic as well as practical areas (technological transfers, health and public amenities, school construction, irrigation, refugee accommodation). The agency has 21 overseas coordination offices (sub-Saharan Africa, the Balkans, Ukraine, the Caucasus, Central Asia and Mongolia). Three elements have appeared over time: Turkish Asia and the ex-Soviet Caucasus (including Mongolia as the cradle of Turkish literature and historiography), the former Ottoman area (including Palestine) and, more recently, African Islam (Mali, Senegal, Sudan). It produces general and specific reports (for Turkish investors), so-called 'prestigious' cultural works and reviews edited in several languages (generally Turkish, English and Russian, but also bilingual Turkish–Kazak, Turkish–Kyrgyz) for the benefit of an informed public.

- *DPT–Devlet Planlama Teşkilâtı*, or SPO (State Planning Organization), is an important public planning office that produces five-yearly sector reports. Of particular interest here are documents covering Turkic–Turkish relations or the culture and outreach of Turkey in the world, international transportation, trade, international relations and cooperation, such as the Report of the Special Commission on Turkey and Regional Integration in Globalization, the Report on Relations Between Turkey and the Turkish Republics (1995), the Report of the Special Commission on the Turkish Language for the 8th Plan 2000, coordinated by A. B. Ercilasun, President of the Academy of Turkish Language, the Report on Relations Between Turkey and the Turkish Republics (2000) (see footnote for original titles[13]). The aim of the SPO is to propose actions and take stock of the programmes undertaken by the government within its areas of competence. Reports on Turkic–Turkish relations are often very critical, highlighting strategic failures and a lack of means.

In addition to its embassies and consulates, the offices of the Ministry of Foreign Affairs produce reports and studies on the place and role of the country in the world. *SAM* (*Stratejik Araştırmalar Merkezi* /Centre for Strategic Studies), a specialized office working with Turkish and foreign political scientists and diplomats, sometimes considered as a think tank,[14] proposes two collections in English, *SAM Papers* and *Perceptions-Journal of International Affairs*. The former generally stems from conferences (e.g. Turkey and the question of Cyprus, Turkey and oil supplies, Turkey and the fight against terrorism) whereas the latter is a regular review. They both benefit from prestigious contributors including G. Winrow, R. Friedman, S. E. Wimbush, H. Kramer, H. Kissinger or Z. Brezjinsky, alongside renowned names in Turkey such as N. Devlet or M. Aydın.[15]

Tourism and culture are closely linked in Turkey and are generally grouped together under the auspices of the joint Ministry of Tourism and Culture. Depending on their ideology, successive governments have highlighted different priorities and programmes. For the purposes of this chapter, important trends should, however, be mentioned and discussed. The ministry edits statistics and documents, various reviews which concern us directly, including *Millî Kültür Dergisi* (National Culture Review, first appearing in 1980), and has specialized collections, as well as publishing houses, bookshops and boutiques.

The ministry publishes collections of works from writers, intellectuals and politicians who influence Turkish culture in a broad sense. Once again, Turkish and Turkic are not separated. The collection *Türk Büyükleri* (*Elders of Turkey*) includes old and more recent historical personalities: Ismail Gasprinski,[16] Z. Velidi Togan[17] as well as Genghis Khan,[18] who was certainly not a Turk in the eyes of the Mongols. The collections *Kaynak Eserler* (original works) or *Tercüme Eserler* (translated works) include classics and studies of the intellectual world, Ottoman as well as Muslim (Ibn Khaldun) or Western (Emmanuel Mounier), with few references to Central Asia. Lastly, in 1981, the more limited collection *Türk Dünyası Eserleri* (*Works of the Turkish World*) edited the work of Halife Altay entitled *Anayurttan Anadolu'ya* (*From Homeland to Anatolia*), an account of the Kazaks exodus from Xinjiang to Kashmir and then to Turkey (1930 to 1969).[19] These collections circulate internally and are of interest to Turkish readers from an informed public (teachers, students, researchers, journalists). It is not uncommon to find these books in modest homes due to their affordable price. The ministry also has other channels for information (or research):

- *HAGEM*–Directorate General for Development and Research on Popular Cultures. Since 1982, this service has edited a cultural review *Anayurttan Atayurda Türk Dünyası* (*Atauyurda Homeland of the Turkish World*), available in ministry-run boutiques and bookshops. It highlights the similarities of the cultures of the Turkic world, as does TÜRKSOY (see below).
- The Silk Road Programme details a number of heritage restoration projects with regard to medieval sites, in particular ancient Seljuk or Ottoman Caravanserai on the Anatolian parts of this famous route.
- The Turkic Speaking People Programme, supported by the historian Doğan Kuban and the photographer Ergun Çağatay, has led to the publication of works on ancient Central Asia (in Turkish, Russian and English) and on the state of Turkology (English and Turkish).[20] The programme status is unclear as it appears to have benefitted from the support of the Ministry of Culture as well as the prime minister for over 12 years. The most recent book is comparable to works edited by *TİCA*,[21] aimed at a foreign public and includes great names of global Turkology.
- An *Anthology of Literature on Turks outside Turkey* was published as a panorama of Turkic literature, including minority languages such as Nogai (vol. 21) or Karachay-Balkarca (vol. 22). This vast literary cooperation project is based on a review of literature in the Turkish language associated with other projects: *History of literature from the Turkish World* (13 volumes, 600 p.), *Encyclopaedia of literary personalities of the Turkish World* (5 volumes, 600 p.), *Encyclopaedic Dictionary of the concepts and terms of Turkish World literature* (4 volumes, 600 p.), *Anthology of ideas and styles of Turkish World literature* (8 volumes, 600 p.).
- On a different theme, the Ankara State Turkish Music Ensemble was created by decision of the Council of Ministers in April 2000, guided by İstemihan Talay, the Minister of Culture. Today it is supported by various institutions such as TİCA and TÜRKSOY.

- *TÜRKSOY*, which could simply be translated as the 'Turkish family', is the acronym for *Türk Kültür ve Sanatlar Ortak Yönetimi* (Joint Administration of Turkic Arts and Culture). The agency edits the review *TÜRKSOY Dergisi* as well as arts and literature works, often multilingual (Turkish, Russian, English, Kyrgyz, Kazak). Initially run by an Azerbaijani diplomat, Polad Bülbüloğlu, it is today presided over by the Kazak Dusen Küseynov, and his deputy, a young Turkish academic Fırat Pürtaş, specializing in Russian demographics. Like TİCA, it too has recently set up offices in a new building, organizing conferences and exhibitions, concerts and cultural events, and has shown itself to be open, particularly towards Russia, publishing and inviting Russian authors and artists to participate in its activities.

The Ministry of Transport and Communications has various missions. As land planner, it is obliged to serve the country and aid the development of external relations (ports, airports, international routes). It proposed that Turkmenistan open a free port on the Black Sea at Trabzon but this project never saw the light due to Iranian hostility. Responsible for the technological and logistical development of communication policies, it plays a major role in the international image of the country. TRT–*Türkiye Radyo-Televizyon* (Turkish Radio-Television) created a channel specifically for international programmes and provides capital cities with satellite receivers. The classic 5th channel (TRT International) transmits via TürkSat or other satellites (Hotbird). Known as TRT Int in Europe and Avrasya in Central Asia, programmes can vary according to the transmission system and, to a certain extent, content is adapted to the relevant audience.[22] At the other end of the spectrum, TRT5 and other channels transmit reports, musical programmes (including the Turkish-vision song contest in 2008 in Bishkek, presented in Turkish and Kyrgyz), debates and food shows emphasizing Turkic–Turkish relations and common cultural ground. Choices have evolved with TRT-Türk, TRT-Avaz, TRT-Anadolu, TMB-Türk Müzik Birliği, cultural channels drawing attention to Turkic and Turkish cultures, probably more internally than internationally. At the same time, some media groups, in particular those adhering to the Gülen Movement have created channels such as *Həzər* in Azerbaijan. Türk Telekom has launched Türksat satellites covering three zones, the territory of Turkey, Turkish expatriate migration areas and Central Asia.

The Ministry for Employment and Social Security (TİK–*Türkiye İş Kurumu*) publishes annual statistics on the number of employees working abroad and their professional characteristics (categories, recruitment channels, etc.) as well as bilateral agreements between Turkey and countries of immigration or large-scale construction sites. The most interesting document is probably the Annual Report of the Direction of International Relations and Expatriate Workers (DİYİH, 1983 to 2010)[23] that has, for some years now, included chapters on Azerbaijan and Kazakhstan, which are among the first 14 countries concerned by Turkish migration. Tables on the official departure of workers abroad show both Azerbaijan and Kazakhstan as main target countries, alongside Iraq and Afghanistan. Turkish enterprises are implicated in public works (hospitals, schools), reconstruction of infrastructures, trade and services through the spontaneous migration of small investors, craftsmen and traders opening small businesses in Azerbaijan, large-scale construction sites in Kazakhstan, and reconstruction in Iraq and Afghanistan under American authority.[24]

Schooling and Higher Education: A Stance for Internal as Opposed to External Use

Universities are key players in the transmission of historical and cultural heritage, teaching ancient and contemporary languages, educating in Turkish, Turkic and an array of other languages. However, an official report on the Turkish language,[25] that includes 'Turkish dialects'[26] strongly criticizes a lack of state support in the area with insufficient university positions to cover the language, literature, cultural and civilization aspects of the Turkish world. 105 specialists have been noted, whereas 500 additional ones are necessary to cover estimated Turkish-speaking needs (teaching, research) at university level by the year 2005. This report was to an extent followed up on with the creation of the Yunus Emre Institute, responsible for diffusing Turkish language and culture abroad (see below).

Institutes of Turkish Studies (*Türkiyat*, both linguistics and the history of civilisation) are present within the language faculties of many universities. Departments of contemporary Turkic Literature and Language exist in universities with an active policy of editing works on the history, linguistics, sociology and ethnology of 'Turks from the outside', be it partially or completely. Founded in 1935, the Ankara Faculty of Languages, History and Geography (DTCF) edits *DTCF Dergisi* (*DTCF Review*), *Türkoloji Dergisi* (*Turkology Review*) and an electronic review *Modern Türklük Araştırmaları Dergisi* (*Review of Research on Modern Turkishness*). The University of Hacettepe in Ankara and its Department of Turkish Language and Literature, run by Şükrü Elçin, which is involved in the TKAE as well as the Atatürk Cultural Centre, created a *Millî Folklor Dergisi* (*Review of National Folklore*) with students, a folklorist review from an historical, literary and anthropological viewpoint developing the Turkish-Islamic Synthesis. Other periodicals are also of interest: the Ankara Department of Turkish for Foreigners (TÖMER) edits three reviews, the *Türk Lehçeleri ve Edebiyatlar Dergisi* (*Review of Turkish Dialects and Literature*) is of direct relevance. Erzurum-Atatürk edits two literary reviews, one of which covers Turkology (*Türkiyat Enstitüsü Dergisi*). Izmir-Ege works in the same way with the review *Türk Dünyası Dergisi* (*Review of the Turkish world*). Istanbul also edits a review dedicated to Turkology *Türkiyat Mecmuası* (*Review of Turkology*), as does Istanbul-Marmara *Türklük Araştırmaları Dergisi* (*Research on Turkishness*) with contributions from the respected Nadir Devlet who appears in numerous publications.[27]

Given that language forges identity, more so than any communal history (ancient history is shared among individual nations with a divide occurring in the 11th century, as the Seljuks moved into the Mediterranean area) or religion (in majority Sunnite Islam, although Shiism, heterodoxies, Christian enclaves, Buddhists, Shamanists are still present and treated with caution even by the most nationalistic elements, outside their country), it is all but logical that literary figures and linguists play an important role.

History faculties can go beyond their main study area, i.e. Turkey of Anatolia and the former Ottoman area, and look at ancestors (*atalar*), lands of origin (*Anayurt*) and Turkic-speaking cousins (*soydaşlar*). They offer publications such as the University of Istanbul's *Institute of History Review*. The reviews *Belleten* (published by the Turkish Institute of History since 1937) and *Erdem* (published by the Atatürk Cultural Centre since 1985) present the works of historians with a nationalistic vision of Turkish history. They represent important scientific sources on Anatolia or the ancient Balkans but minimize, or do not even mention, non-Turkish (what of the role of the Kurds?) and non-Islamic (Christians generally, Armenians in particular) contributions. Copeaux[28] analyses this further for a better understanding of the importance of historical thesis in political life and the definition of the parameters of identity of Turkish society since the 1920s. A contradiction appears between a vision of the Turkish world destined for internal use (images and iconography, stereotypes, political slogans often exclusive and superficial) and the realities of this same world that has evolved differently depending on Soviet, Chinese or Balkan influence. This contradiction was heightened with the independence of ex-Soviet republics, which largely explains the shortcomings and inappropriate Turkish attitude to these newly accessible regions.

Political Science and International Relations faculties also study Central Asia, albeit differently. Until 1989–92, research and teaching was centred on the position of Turkey between the West (USA, NATO, the European construction of Europe) and the USSR. Turkist authors and those specialized in geopolitics contributed mainly to works on Central Asia, although references were mainly American (Henze, Wimbush, Schoeberlein), sometimes with close ties to the CIA, and European (Bennigsen, Akiner, Kramer, Steinbach). The 1990s witnessed the publication of works by Russian and ex-Soviet writers in *Avrasya Dosyası, SAM Papers, Perceptions*, linked to the

Ministry of Foreign Affairs or centred on new think tanks formed by academics.

These intellectuals see political commitment (Turkism, Pan-Turkism, Turko-Islamic Synthesis) as a necessity, as is allying with a university closely monitored by public authorities (in particular the control of the YÖK-*Yüksek Öğretim Kurumu*, Council for Higher Education, set up by Kenan Evren and his government after the 1980 putsch). They play an important role in the foundations and centres described as think tanks, more than present in Ankara. There is an obvious difference between the former perception, (pan-)Turkist and confined to a double logic of cold war and the inaccessibility of Central Asian areas, and the new perception, the discovery of other partial Turkic-speaking nation-states, accessible and where Russian influence resounds (with the arrival of Chinese influence): on the one hand, national protectionism and on the other, new geopolitical and economic opportunities. Turkey thus continues to oscillate between these two poles to the dismay of State Planning Organization reporters who are overtly critical of such blatant hesitation.

Muslim Theological Faculties, specific to Turkey and almost unique in the Muslim world, under the authority of the Presidency of Religious Affairs itself governed by the office of the Prime Minister, an institution which oversees places of worship and religious figures, are trained in these public faculties and are civil servants. Information circulated by the Presidency (news and newsletters) often covers current affairs in the Turkish-Muslim world (from the former Ottoman Balkans to Central Asia, via Arabic countries). A Eurasian Islamic Council was also created and meets in several cities (Ankara 1994, Istanbul 1996, Istanbul and Sarajevo 2000). This state trustee of Islam, acting within an officially secular framework, can thus act outside of Turkey and does not hesitate to do so, offering copies of the Koran and grants to Kazaks of Mongolia, participating in the construction of new mosques (Ashgabat-Ertuğrul Gazi in Turkmenistan, Koshkor Ata in Kyrgyzstan, Talgar in Kazakhstan) and restoring historical monuments (mausoleum of Ahmet Yesevî at Türkistan in Kazakhstan, headquarters of a Turkish-Kazak University or the mausoleum of Sultan Sandjar in Turkmenistan).

It has also helped create theology faculties based on the Turkish model in Osh (Kyrgyzstan), Ashgabat-Makhtumkuli (Turkmenistan) and Shymkent (Kazakhstan).

Turkish Universities of Central Asia

One of the most representative actions of the Turko-Central Asian cooperation is the creation of new universities, with various statuses and partners. Although already discussed by Balcı[29] and in official reports,[30] the issue should be considered in detail. The following universities have been created: Ahmet Yesevî (Türkistan 1991) and Süleyman Demirel (Almaty 1996) in Kazakhstan, Manas Kırgız-Türk (1995) and Atatürk-Alatoo (Bishkek 1996) in Kyrgyzstan, Uluslararası Türk-Türkmen (Ashgabat) in Turkmenistan, Qafqaz (Baku 1993) in Azerbaijan. These establishments enrol Central Asian and Turkish students, employ local teachers, both Turkish and foreign, and are a long-term investment alongside the numerous Turkish schools and high schools.[31]

National Institutes

The status of these institutions is ambiguous. For example, TDK or TTK are public services whereas the very productive Atatürk Institute Cultural Centre or TKAE have a mixed and not altogether clear status and as such are much criticized by supporters of Kemalism and/or the democratization of Turkish politics.[32] TDK *Türk Dil Kurumu* (Academy for the Turkish Language) edits official dictionaries and reviews and its contribution to renewing the Turkic language of Turkey is undeniable. Ancient or dialect Turkish, conserving original ancient terms or terms with extremely ancient roots, occasionally Chinese, and Turkic languages, including Mongol, have all played a significant role in this 'linguistic revolution' (*dil devrimi*). Since 1937, TTK–*Türk Tarih Kurumu* (Institute of Turkish History) has edited an historical review *Belleten* that covers all aspects of Anatolian history since antiquity but also publishes Turkish studies, in particular on the role of Central Asia in Turkish history. The Institute has played a role comparable to that of the TDK from a language viewpoint with its promotion of national historiography.

Although much of the research is now outdated, TTK remains a prestigious institution. *Atatürk Kültür, Dil ve Tarih Yüksek Kurumu* (Atatürk Higher Institute for Culture, Language and History), created by the constitution of 1982, publishes a quarterly newsletter and review (*Erdem*).[33] This publication is a clear attempt to gain control over *TDK* and *TTK* by officializing the 'Turkish-Islamic Synthesis', an ensemble of ideas put forward by right wing intellectuals with the hope of reconciling Asia, Turkey and Islam, an openly Turkish-Muslim stance aimed at defending the country – and its youth – from socialist and communist influence. The government of Kenan Evren, the principal author of the putsch, puts forward this idea. His government has also made religious studies once again obligatory in schools for the very same reason. Many believe that this idea of 'synthesis' and 'national', in the form of *millî/millet* and not *ulus*,[34] is the starting point for political currents such as Eurasianism, the collusion between the national left wing (*milliyetçi sol*) and the extreme right rapidly becoming more Islamist. The success enjoyed by 'moderate Islamism' currently advocated by the AKP should also be noted. TKAE–*Türk Kültürünü Araştırma Enstitüsü* (Institute for Turkish Research and Culture), probably the oldest functioning group, edits several clearly Pan-Turkist reviews, including *Türk Kültürü* (*Turkish Culture*) since 1961, *Cultura Turcica* and *Türk Kültürü Araştırmaları* (*Research on Turkish Culture*) since 1964. A private organization supported by the state, the Institute is mainly interested in history, Turkology and nationalism, particularly Turks from the Outside.[35] The Institute greatly influenced the Turkish-Islamist Synthesis that took form in the 1980s and 1990s and which was promoted by the daily *Türkiye*, the Nationalist Movement Party (MHP) with its European migrant networks, the TEDEV Foundation (*Türk Edebiyatı Vakfı*) or the Club of Intellectuals (*Aydınlar Ocağı*).

The latter two institutions play a role in the construction of an internal identity.[36] They accentuate Central Asia in order to affirm (without great risk, until 1989–92) that Turkey is the only possible leader of the Turkish world. This idea is deeply rooted in nationalist groups and its use in reality weakens Turkish policy in the new Turkic republics, not on the lookout for a 'new big brother'. Two new entities have recently appeared, the first a foundation and the second a public establishment under the supervision of the office of the prime minister.

The Yunus Emre Institute is run by a foundation whose principal members are Prime Minister Erdoğan, the President of the Republic Abdullah Gül, the Minister for Foreign Affairs, Ahmet Davutoğlu, the Minister for Culture and Tourism, Ertuğrul Günay, among other senior government officials. This speaks clearly of the importance accorded to this Institute with a declared mission to transmit Turkish language and culture throughout the world. Created in 2007, by 2011 it had centres in Cairo, Astana, Tirana, Damas, Skopje, Sarajevo, Bucharest, Pristina, Prizren, London and Brussels, and intends to open further centres in Tokyo, Beirut, Tehran and Paris. Although Astana was one of the first centres, Central Asia otherwise seems to have been overlooked, the focus being on Europe and the Middle East.

The Overseas Turks Agency (YTB) was created in 2010 to deal with problems faced by expatriates, develop relations with related communities in social, cultural and economic areas, teach and train youths abroad, especially in the EU, and facilitate the arrival of migrant youngsters to Turkey for training. Initial activities targeted children of European emigrants (the starting block being the 50th anniversary of the Turkish presence in Germany) although YTB is now working with Eurasia, commencing with Azerbaijan.

Think Tanks and Foundations: New Expressions of Turkism and Pan-Turkism

Close to the American model, Turkish think tanks are often foundations (*vakıf*, from the Arabic *waqf*), with a more solid base than associations, a curious reminder of Muslim law in Kemalist Turkey. In theory selected for devout reasons, foundations are in reality chosen by those seeking to avoid administrative and police harassment.[37] It is fashionable to create Strategic Study Centres under the auspices of either private foundations, universities or, in at least two cases, the state (SAM, Ministry of Foreign Affairs and

Table 12.1 Centres and Foundations Studying Central Asia

Name	Website	Publications	Other activities
TDAV Türk Dünyası Araştırmalar Vakfı Turkish World Research Foundation	http://turan.org	Reviews	Scholarship for students in Central Asia
AVSAM / ASAM Avrasya Bir Vakfı-Avrasya Stratejik Araştırmalar Merkezi; First Eurasian Foundation; Centre for Eurasian Strategic Studies	http://www.avsam.org.tr	Reviews, publications	
TASAM TürkAsya Stratejik Araştırmalar Merkezi; TürkAsya Centre for Strategic Studies	http://www.tasam.org	Publications, reports, newsletters, reviews	Thoughts on multivector policies
TÜRKSAM Uluslararası İlişkiler ve Stratejik Analizler Merkezi; Centre for Strategic Analysis and International Relations	http://www.turksam.org.tr		Two sections: 'Institute of the Turkish World' and 'Turkestan'
TÜSAM Türk Ulusal Güvenlik Stratejileri Araştırma Merkezi, Centre for Research on National Security Strategies		The supplement *Strateji* for the daily *Cumhuriyet*	

KÖK *KÖK* Sosyal ve Stratejik Araştırmalar Vakfı; Kök Foundation for Social and Strategic Research	http://www.koksav.org.tr	E-Newsletter	Bureau of 'Turkish, Tajik and Mongol republics', members of the University of Ankara
Altinmiras 'Golden Heritage', in Turkish: Özbekistan Uluslararası Altın Miras Vakfı; in Uzbek: O'zbekiston Respublikası Xalqaro Oltin Meros Xayriya Jamg'arması	http://www.altinmiras.com		Turkish-Uzbek Cultural Cooperation

SAREM, Turkish General Staff's Strategic Research and Study Centre). These bodies are more or less interested in Central Asia and produce works on specialized areas in reviews, articles and interviews in the media, internet sites and seminars, participating in or organizing national and international conferences.[38] Some of these centres and foundations study Central Asia more systematically (Table 12.1).

Some of the more established foundations with closer ties to right wing intellectual groups of pan-Turkism and the Turkish-Islamist synthesis, via their editors, have edited noteworthy encyclopaedias. Between 1998 and 2002, TKAE edited a *Guide to the Turkish World (Türk Dünyası El Kitabı)* in four volumes (2,600 p.). Editors are generally speaking historians or linguists close to TDK and TTK, well known for their conservative or nationalist opinions. Also from 1998 to 2002, the TKHV-*Türk Kültürüne Hizmet Vakfı* (Turkish Cultural Foundation) edited a bilingual English-Turkish atlas in 12 volumes (6,000 p.) called *Türk Dünyası Kültür Atlası/Atlas of the Turkish World.* The editors E. Gürsoy Naskalı and A. Taşağıl are also members of related networks.[39] Finally, the publication in 2002 of two encyclopaedias, entitled *Türkler (The Turks)* (19,391 p. in 21 volumes), under the direction of H. C. Güzel, a politician closely linked to Turgut Özal, K. Çiçek and S. Koca,[40] and, in English, *The Turks*, in 10 volumes, again under the direction of H. Güzel and C. C. Oğuz and O. Karatay.[41]

These works span across the entire Turkish world and place Turkey at the forefront, understandably so in the light of the potential readership. They adopt a common stance based on nationalism and a superiority complex over other Turkish-speaking entities with regards to Turkish culture and historicity. The latter work is, however, particularly amateurish, illustration sources are badly referenced, or not referenced at all, with some surprising confusions. The authors, particularly those writing on emigration to Europe, are relatively unknown outside their political circles (no foreign contributions, none or few internationally recognized specialists). Consequently, these publications remain on the whole internal to

Turkey and do not go far beyond the groups that produce them, despite a certain quality, such as with the THKV atlas.

It is sometimes difficult to navigate through such an abundance of initiatives. The significant role of the state and the various relations between public services and political groups on the notions of pan-Turkism, Turkish-Islamic synthesis, Turkish-Islamic union is, however, evident. The intellectuals comprising these public or private institutions are geographically widespread, from the USA to Central Asia, and career-wise (a review of Turkish sources reveals all) stem from universities, private foundations, public establishments, ministries and senior administrations. The overlapping of competences between foundations and public organizations, sometimes even between state agencies (for example TİCA, Yunus Emre and YTB), make it somewhat complicated to decipher cooperation policies. Governmental oscillations as to the use of one or other tool at a given time are also criticized by analytical observers of these policies, such as Parlak,[42] published by TİCA, or more modest but critical articles highlighting errors.[43]

Civil Society and Associations: Marginal or Influential Pressure Groups?

Contrary to European opinion, there is a rich associative sector in Turkey, admittedly not always easy to work in. Two legal forms co-exist: the association and the foundation (*vakıf*). The latter, derived from Muslim religious foundations, has the advantage of being more stable due to the relative protection of the law. It is thus not uncommon to see the foundation form selected by groups of refugees, intellectuals or other economic actors with no religious affinity. This chapter considers associations of emigres originating from the two Turkestans, Muslim proselyte and missionary associations and professional associations or consular bodies.

Associations of Emigres from the two Turkestans, the Caucasus, or Russia (Crimea and Volga-Ural) are numerous. Their story is well-known and was published in the Central Asian Survey.[44] Although many pan-Turkist publications exist, and despite support from

Turkish nationalist intellectuals, they face difficulties surviving due to stringent controls by the authorities. Examples include *Azerbaycan Yurt Bilgisi, Doğu Türkistan Sesi/Şarkî Türkistan Avazı (The East Turkestan Voice), Kardaş Edebiyatlar, Millî Kültür, Orhun, Türk Dilleri Araştırmaları, Türklük (Turkishness)*. M. E. Batur, a journalist of Uighur origin runs from Kayseri an internet site and several local papers with Turkish nationalist and pan-Turkish leanings (*Erciyes, Satır Arası, Istiklâl*), while at the same time highlighting the specific case of Xinjiang. The most important Eastern Turkestani actor is the Eastern Turkestan Foundation created by M. E. Buğra and Y. İ. Alptekin. Today presided over by H. Göktürk, for a long time general secretary and loyal deputy to General M. Rıza Bekin, President from 1986 to 2010 (whose brother, an academic at Ankara University, is a sinologist, both being nephews of M. E. Buğra). The Foundation edits a bilingual Turkish-Uighur review *Doğu Türkistan Sesi / Şarkî Türkistan Avazı (The East Turkestan Voice)* and numerous works on the history of this group of refugees, today isolated from other larger and now independent Turkic populations.

Several private sites, physical persons and legal entities, often with close ties to existing nationalist or immigrant groups, reproduce university texts or publish their own vision of the Turkish world online, for example, a site on the minority Turkic populations which produces texts on the Nogays or Kazakhs of Turkey. Political parties such as the MHP or BBP,[45] a splinter group of the former, animate and edit reviews and newsletters referring to Central Asian origins. However, they too have been left behind by the realities of the Turkish world largely based on mythology or folklore to suit internal, electoral and militant politics.

Muslim Proselyte and Missionary Associations

A secular republic pursuant to its constitution, like the Central Asian republics and Azerbaijan, Turkey nevertheless strictly controls the majority religion through a specific administrative department, Diyanet, ignoring minority confessions, including Alevism, despite their demographic importance. Proselyte and missionary activities are as such difficult to carry out. An exception to this rule are the

American evangelist movements, working under the auspices of humanitarian organizations and protected by American diplomacy and the military. Although views can easily be expressed through the educational sector, they remain tame from a religious viewpoint.[46] The main and most efficient movement is Feth'ullah Gülen, of Nurcu origin, a recent branch of the Naqshbandi order, itself originating from Central Asia. Although it is not the only activist, it benefits from real power (intellectual, media, economic and social) in Turkey. It has succeeded in partially transferring this power to the Balkans, Central Asia and different countries of migration. The movement rapidly implanted itself in Central Asia through businesses and private foundations, even creating private universities. Some governments have since become wary, in particular in Uzbekistan, where these Turkic enclaves are prohibited.

The Press and Media

The independence of the Turkic republics awakened interest in Central Asian countries within the media and informed groups, often working together to produce editorials, articles, televised programmes, debates and concerts. Once again however, the majority remain close to nationalist groups, including those referred to in Turkey as 'left wing nationalist' (*milliyetçi sol*) with Eurasian and anti-imperialist leanings, as they sometimes define themselves.

The group İhlâs holding, owner of the daily *Türkiye*, with frequent pan-Turkish ideas, conveys the conservative Islamic-nationalist tendency of the Turkish-Islamic synthesis. With the publication of articles, maps and atlases of the *Türk Dünyası*, editorials and reports seek to reveal the *soydaş* to a maximum number of readers. *Tarih ve Medeniyet* (History and Civilization), an historical review belonging to the same group, from the outset showed great interest in the Ottoman period and Turks from the outside. *Zaman*, a daily of the Fethullah Gülen group, has also published articles on the region. The group owns schools, colleges and private universities in Central Asia, as well as publications (*Dyalog Avrasya*), and satellite television channels (Samanyolu, Həzər TV). The group was to a large extent revealed by the works of Balcı.[47] The republican and Kemalist daily

Cumhuriyet, associated with the aforementioned TÜSAM Foundation, edits the supplement *Strateji*, also associated with the television channel Avrasya. This supplement, more so than the television channel, regularly covers Eurasian geopolitics and geostrategic policies of Turkey, often criticizing the lack of interest of Turkish politicians in this area. The authors of *Strateji* are the principal presenters of *TÜSAM,* B. Adıbelli, author of numerous works on China and Xinjiang, A. Külebi, A. Somuncuoğlu, C. Veliyev and A. Nogayeva. *Atlas* and *National Geographic-Türkiye*, *Tourism* and discovery monthlies for the wider public have a different viewpoint and as such could be argued to be more informative on Central Asia and contemporary Turkish-speaking communities. Based on articles with quality photos, the presentation is largely devoid of ideological references or when reference is made, it is subtle and allusive. Despite its links with the Doğan media Group, *Atlas* proposes original Turkic articles whereas *National Geographic* is based more on translations of foreign articles. It would be interesting to study readers' letters to understand the apprehension of articles on the Caucasus, Armenia, Kurdistan, Buddhism or Turkish Orthodox Christianity in Siberia, the Urals and the Balkans, and form an idea of their impact on the pre-conceived ideas that essentially make up pan-Turkism.

Particular mention should be made of the unclear position of the Gülen enterprises, well documented by Balcı,[48] and their aforementioned media influence: on the one hand supportive and objectively allied enterprises, and on the other hand enterprises that are direct members of the Gülen holding particularly interested in education and private schools and universities. Among others, the daily *Zaman* with publications in Turkmenistan, Kazakhstan and Kyrgyzstan, the publishers DA Dyalog Avrasya (also present in St Petersburg and Moscow) and Ufuk linked to the Foundation of Turkish Journalists and Writers (*Türk Gazeteciler ve Yazarlar Birliği*), management companies of private schools Feza, Şelale, Eflak, Sebat, Başkent Eğitim and Silm in the same countries, the company Ulug'bek International School in Tashkent, and additional private players active on all fronts, from the USA to Kazakhstan, via European migration paths. The business world should be covered in a separate article detailing the actions of companies and the outcome 20 years after the opening up of Central Asia.[49]

A 'Tentative' Conclusion

This rather incomplete inventory shows the many facets of a society largely obsessed with the question of identity and origins. Although the Turks can lay claim to nine centuries of presence on what is today the territory of the nation-state, though the Kurds would deny them this autochthony in their own search for a nation-state, the need to declare roots in this disputed territory is apparent. The move towards the original Turkish world, practical, useful and easy when the Republic of Turkey was the only country in the world to legitimately claim this identity, today faces the problem of other actors who argue, mainly internally, for a legitimate and undisputed presence on this territory.

Questioning the age-old imperial principle of *divide ut imperare*, in its Stalinist version here, is all too easy in the face of emerging nation-states seeking to anchor their identity in what is sacred territory. The contradiction is significant for societies whose origins are largely nomadic, for a long time heterogeneous and to a large extent remaining so. Despite the energy and tools used by Turkey to affirm the existence of a Turkish world, it remains knotted with paradoxes, differences, tensions and centrifugal tendencies. Language on the other hand, much more alive and connected than one could imagine, could reinforce cooperation on the basis of complementary elements, failing true unity which pan-Germanism, pan-Slavism or pan-Arabism (or other pan-isms) have never succeeded in creating. Is this Turkish world in reality just a myth for romantic nationalists – somewhat late in the day – preoccupied with internal affairs as opposed to a political project? An objective and forward-looking connection should be made between Turkish and Central Asian, Russian, Chinese, American and European researchers. Françoise Aubin[50] insisted that in order to truly understand Central Asian societies one needed to speak Turkish, Turkic, Russian, Chinese, Tibetan, and Mongol and not just rely on unilateral sources.

It remains difficult to provide a definitive response to the question of Turkey's position as a country of the South, hitherto referred to as developing countries, just as it is difficult to classify Azerbaijan and Kazakhstan, great oil nations, in the same vein. Turks have always considered themselves a great power, whether it is actually the case or in theory. Atatürk never ceased pushing his country into the league of the great and it is paradoxical that an Islamic government, staunchly opposed to Kemalist policies, has succeeded in getting the closest. The opening to Turkish interests in Central Asia would have been an ideal opportunity that appears to be fading, maybe more due to the actions of the Turks themselves than to regional players, whether made up of Chinese, Russian or local interests.

Notes

1 Declarations of sovereignty that did not lead to independence: these legal entities are members of the Russian Federation (for example Tatarstan or the Republic of Sakha-Yakutia).

2 Altaic group: this family includes Turkic, Mongolic and Tungusic languages. The scientific debate continues as to the association of languages such as Korean or the genetic relationship between Turks and Mongols.

3 Tayanç, T., *İnşaatçıların Coğrafyası. Türk İnşaat Sektörünün Yurtdışı Müteahhitlik Hizmetleri Serüveni {Geography of Contractors [The Adventure of the Services of expatriate Contractors of the Turkish Construction Sector]*, Istanbul: Türkiye Müteahhitler Birliği-Tarih Vakfı, 2011.

4 As was the case with the Meskhetian Turks (1989) or in 1989 and 2010 between Kyrgyz and Uzbeks in the Ferghana Valley.

5 Two initial visits of the author to Azerbaijan were made in spring and autumn of 2011. Being a Turkish speaker helped develop immediate contact with the population across the board. The same cannot be said for Central Asia.

6 Laruelle, M., *Russo-Turkish Rapprochement through the Idea of Eurasia: Alexander Dugin's Networks in Turkey,* Occasional Paper, The Jamestown Foundation, 2008, (http://www.jamestown.org); Tapia, S. de, 'Avrasya: les versions turques de l'Eurasie', in Dressler, W. (ed.), *Eurasie. Espace mythique ou réalité en construction?*, Bruxelles: Bruylant, 2008, pp. 321–45.

7 Landau, J.M., *Pan-Turkism in Turkey. A Study in Irredentism*, London: C. Hurst & Co, 1981; Landau, J.M., *The Politics of Pan-Islam. Ideology and Organization*, Oxford: Clarendon, 1990; Landau, J.M., *Pan Turkism. From Irredentism to Cooperation*, Indiana University, 1995.

8 Copeaux, E., *Espace et temps de la nation turque*, Paris: CNRS Editions, 1997; Copeaux, E., *Une vision turque du monde à travers les cartes de 1931 à nos jours*, Paris: CNRS Editions, 2000.

9 Kazakhstan: 2,717,000 km^2, Turkmenistan: 488,000 km^2, Uzbekistan: 447,000 km^2, Kyrgyzstan: 198,000 km^2, Azerbaijan: 86,000 km^2, Xinjiang-Uygur: 1,653,000 km^2, not including the sovereign entities of the Russian Federation (Tatarstan, Bashkiria, Sakha-Yakutia) or predominately Turkic-speaking provinces such as Iranian Azerbaijan.

10 Bezanis, L., 'Volga-Ural Tatars in Emigration', *Central Asian Survey*, 1992, vol. 11/4, pp. 29–74; Bezanis, L., 'Soviet Muslim Emigrés in the Republic of Turkey', *Central Asian Survey*, 1994, vol. 13/1, pp. 59–180.

11 Georgeon, F., *Aux origines du nationalisme turc. Yusuf Akçura (1876–1935)*, Paris: Editions de l'ADPF, Institut d'Etudes Anatoliennes, 1980; Georgeon, F., 'Des Ottomans aux Turcs. Naissance d'une nation', *Analecta Isisiana*, vol. 16, 1995.

12 Georgeon, F., 'Le "modèle tatar" dans l'Empire Ottoman et la Turquie républicaine', in Dudoignon, S., Is'haqov, D., Möhämmätshin, R., *L'Islam de Russie; conscience communautaire et autonomie politique chez les Tatars de la Volga et de l'Oural depuis le XVIII° siècle*, Paris: IFEAC/Maisonneuve et Larose, 1997, pp. 249–57.

13 DPT, *Dünyada Küreselleşme ve Bölgesel Entegrasyonlar (AT, NAFTA, Pasifik) ve Türkiye (AT, EFTA, KEİ, Türk Cumhuriyetleri, İslam Ülkeleri, ECO) İlişkileri Özel İhtisas Komisyonu. Türkiye-Türk Cumhuriyetleri İlişkileri Raporu Özeti* [*Abstract of the Report about Turkish and Turkic Republics. Special Commission about the Globalisation and Regional Integration (European Union, NAFTA, Pacific Area) face to Turkey (EU, EFTA, Black Sea Community, Turkic Republics, Islamic Countries, ECO*], Ankara: Kitap 5, DPT 2410, ÖİK 471, 1995; DTP, *Sekizinci 5 Yıllık Kalkınma Planı Türk Dili Özel İhtisas Komisyonu Raporu* [*Report of the Special Commission about the Turkish Language, 8th Quinquennal Development Plan*], Ankara: DPT 2526, ÖIK 542, 2000a; DTP, *Sekizinci 5 Yıllık Kalkınma Planı Türkiye-Türk Cumhuriyetleri İlişkileri Raporu* [*Report about the Relations between Turkey and Turkic Republics, 8th Quinquennal Development Plan*], Ankara: DPT 2511, ÖİK 528, 2000b.

14 Yılmaz, S., 'Sistematik ulusal bilgi üretilmeli' ['We must produce systematic national intelligence'], *Cumhuriyet Strateji*, 2007, Year 3, n°133, pp. 6–7.

15 Devlet, N., 'Ethnicity and Power: Relations Between the Central Asian States', *Perceptions*, 1997, vol. 2; Aydin, M., 'New Geopolitics of Central Asia and Caucasus. Causes of Instability and Predicaments', *SAM Papers*, (http://www.sam.gov.tr/perceptions/sampapers/NewGeopoliticsofCentralAsiaandCaucasus.pdf).

16 Devlet, N., 'İsmail Bey (Gaspiralı)', *Kültür ve Turizm Bakanlığı* (*Türk Büyükleri Dizisi*), 1988, vol. 962/99.

17 Baykara, T., 'Zeki Velidi Togan', *Kültür ve Turizm Bakanlığı* (*Türk Büyükleri Dizisi*), 1989, vol. 1042/110.

18 Temir, A., *Cengiz Han* [*Genghis Khan*], Ankara: Kültür Bakanlığı, 1989.

19 Altay, H., *Anayurt'tan Anadolu'ya* {*From the Motherland to Anatolia*}, 1991, vol. 354.
20 Çağatay, E., *Bir Zamanlar Orta Asya* {*Once Upon a Time Central Asia*}, Istanbul: Tetragon İletişim, 1996; Çağatay, E., Kuban, D. (eds), *The Turkic Speaking Peoples: 2000 Years of Art and Culture from Inner Asia to the Balkans*, Munich: Prestel Verlag & The Hague: Prince Claus Fund Library, 2006.
21 Lawton, J., *The Turks of Eurasia*, Ankara: TİCA, 1996.
22 Tapia, S. de, 'Türksat et les Républiques Turcophones de l'ex-URSS', *Cahiers d'études sur la Méditerranée orientale et le monde turco-iranien,* 1995, vol. 20, pp. 399–413; Pahlavi, P. C., 'La diplomatie culturelle à l'ère de l'interdépendance globale. La Turquie à la recherche des éléments fédérateurs de l'identité panturque', *Etudes Internationales*, 2002, vol. 33/2, pp. 247–74 (http://www.diploweb.com/asie/pahlavi1.htm).
23 *DİYİH–Dış İlişkiler ve Yurtdışı İşçiler Hizmetleri Genel Müdürlüğü, 2000–2007. Yılı Raporu. Yurtdışındaki Vatandaşlarımıza İlişkin Gelişmeler ve Sayısal Bilgiler* {*Statistical Informs and Development tied to our Expatriate Citizens, Annual Reports of the General Directorate of Public Relations and the Services for Expatriate Workers, 2000–2007*}, Ankara: TC Çalışma ve Sosyal Güvenlik Bakanlığı {Ministry of Labour and Social Security}, yearly from 1982 to 1999. The name was changed in 2000, from YİHGM to DİYİH.
24 Tayanç, T., *op. cit.*
25 DPT, 2000a, *op. cit.*, p. 16.
26 Referring to Turkic languages as 'Turkish dialects' is contested by the countries concerned.
27 Several universities edit Social Science reviews, including the Turkish-Kyrgyz Manas University of Bishkek, bilingual, *Sosyal Bilimler Dergisi / Koomluk İlimler Jurnalı*, or *Bilig-Türk Dünyası Sosyal Bilimler Dergisi* (*Social Sciences Review of the Turkish World*) edited by the President of the Delegation of Directors of the University of Ahmet Yesevî (*Ahmet Yesevî Üniversitesi Mütevelli Heyet Başkanlığı*). For this last review, the words used are eloquent, a *mütevelli* is the custodian of an asset *waqf*.
28 Copeaux, E., 1997 and 2000, *op. cit.*
29 Balci, B., *Missionnaires de l'islam en Asie Centrale. Les écoles turques de Fethullah Gülen*, Paris: Maisonneuve & Larose, Istanbul: IFEA, 2003.
30 DPT, 2000a, *op. cit.*, pp. 293–4.
31 Balci, B., *op. cit.;* Balci, B., 'Education, Nationalism, and Hidden Da'wa: Turkish Missionary Movements in Central Asia and the Caucasus', in Hacket, R. (ed.), *Proselytization Revisited: Right Talks, Free Markets and Culture Wars*, London: Equinox, 2009, pp. 367–89.
32 Copeaux, E., 1997, *op. cit.*, pp. 81–101.
33 Entitled Virtue.
34 The notion of *millet* is particularly ambiguous. It is an Ottoman term of Arabic origin meaning nation in the most general sense–*öztürkçe* would more readily use *ulus*, borrowed from ancient Turkish-Mongol but still used today–but can also

be understood within its Ottoman meaning of a confessional nation, that is to say a Turkish-Muslim Sunnite population that would exclude Armenians, Jews, Christians and even Kurds or Alevis. It should be noted that the programme of Necmettin Erbakan, founder and long serving leader of the National Salvation Party (Millî Selamet Partisi) is entitled Millî Görüş (National Vision), like Islamist immigrants in Europe, and that the members of the Synthesis published a report on *National Culture* (*Millî Kültür*) in favour of a re-Islamization of Turkish society.

35 *Ibid.*, pp. 95–101; Güvenç, B., Şaylan, G., Tekeli, İ., Turan, Ş., *Türk-Islam Sentezi* [*Turkish-Islam Synthesis*], Istanbul: Sarmal, 1991.

36 Copeaux, E., 1997, *op. cit.*, pp. 94–5.

37 Bilici, F., 'Acteurs de développement des relations entre la Turquie et le monde turc: les *vakıf*', *Cahiers d'études sur la Méditerranée orientale et le monde turco-iranien*, 1992, vol. 14, pp. 17–30.

38 Yılmaz,; S., *op. cit.*

39 Gürsoy Naskali, E., Taşağıl, A. (eds), *Türk Dünyası Kültür Atlası* [*Atlas of the Turkish World*], Istanbul: TKHV–Türk Kültürüne Hizmet Vakfı, İlke Kitap, 1998–2002, 12 volumes.

40 Güzel, H.C., Çiçek, K., Koca, S. (eds), *Türkler* [*The Turks*], Adana: Kültür, 2002, 21 volumes.

41 Güzel, H.C., Oğuz, C.C., Karatay, O. (eds), *The Turks*, Ankara: Yeni Türkiye, 2002, 10 volumes.

42 Parlak, N., *Orta Asya-Kafkasya-Balkan Ülkeleriyle İlişkiler ve Türk Dış Yardımları, 1992–2003* [*Turkish Aids and Relations with the Central Asia, Caucasus and Balkan Countries, 1992–2003*], vol. 91, Ankara: TİCA, 2007.

43 Yorulmaz, O., 'Türkiye-Türk Dünyası İlişkilerinde Türkiye'nin Hataları ve Eksikleri' ['Errors and Failings of Turkey in the Relations between Turkey and Turkish World'], in Öztürk, N., Satan, A. (eds), *Türk Dünyasının Problemleri ve Çözüm Önerileri* [*Recommendations to Solve the Problems of the Turkish World*], vol. 241/199, Istanbul: IQ Kültür Sanat (Araştırma-İnceleme), 2007, pp. 483–94.; Yazgan, T., 'Türkiye'nin Türk Dünyasına Yönelik Siyasetine Eleştirel Bir Bakış', in Öztürk, N., Satan, A. (eds), *op. cit.*, pp. 475–82.

44 Bezanis, L., 1992 and 1994, *op. cit.*

45 MHP–Milliyetçi Hareket Partisi or Nationalist Movement Party created by Alpaslan Türkeş, today run by Devlet Bahçeli, its young militants are known as the Grey Wolves. BBP–Büyük Birlik Partisi or Great Union Party, created by Muhsin Yazıcıoğlu, former senior member of the *MHP*.

46 Balcı, B., 2003, *op. cit.*; Balcı, B., Motika, R. (eds), *Religion et politique dans le Caucase post-soviétique (Les traditions réinventées à l'épreuve des influences extérieures)*, Paris: Maisonneuve & Larose, Istanbul: IFEA, 2007; Ateş, T., Karakaş, E., Ortaylı, I. (eds), *Barış Köprüleri. Dünyaya Açılan Türk Okulları* [*Bridges of Peace. Turkish Schools are opening to the World*], vol. 60/8, Istanbul: DA Yayıncılık (Ufuk Kitapları/Güncel Kitaplar), 2005.

47 Mainly Balci, B., 2003, *op. cit.*

48 Balci, B., 2003 and 2008, *Op. cit.*

49 Uludağ, I., Memmedov S., *Sovyetler Birliği Sonrası Bağımsız Türk Cumhuriyetleri ve Türk Gruplarının Sosyo-ekonomik Analizi, Türkiye ile İlişkileri* [*The Independent Turkic Republics After the Soviet Union. Socio-Economic Analysis of the Turkic Groups and their Relations with Turkey*], Ankara: TOBB, 1992; Güler, M., *Orta Asya ve Kafkaslara Türk Bakışı* [*A Turkish Look on Central Asia and the Caucasus*], Istanbul: İlgi Kültür Sanat (İnceleme-Araştırma), 2007, vol. 34/14.; Tayanç, T., *op. cit.*

50 Aubin, F., 'Donneurs ou preneurs, quelques réflexions sur le jeu des transferts culturels entre Chinois, Turcs et Mongols', in Dor, R. (ed.), *L'Asie Centrale et ses voisins; influences réciproques*, Paris: INALCO, 1990, pp. 165–80.

CHAPTER 13

PARADOX OF THE 'GOOD GOVERNANCE AGENDA': GEOPOLITICAL EXTERNALITIES AND DEVELOPMENT PRACTICE IN TAJIKISTAN

Mana Farooghi
(SOAS, UK)

Since Tajikistan was created as a Soviet republic less than a century ago, it has been under great outside political influence and heavily dependent upon external assistance. Created in 1929 out of the Soviet Nationalities policy, the structure of its relationship with other republics within the USSR as well as internal structures of power and socio-economic dynamics posed critical challenges to Tajikistan's autonomous status. A combination of insufficient exploitable resources and lack of infrastructure, arbitrary ethnic repartition, resettlements and unequal distribution of power led to a civil war in 1992 that opposed clans, regions and political and ideological groups in a contest for access to resources.

The settling of the war revealed Russia's control over the military, security and political powers in the region. The control of Moscow over the peace process and its conditions, through its military presence and its political influence, created a pro-Russian outcome for what had begun as a post-independence conflict. The political submission of Tajikistan to Russia continued through the 1990s while the 'new world order' and the country's critical need for economic assistance introduced the dynamics of the North–South divide.

Unable to rely on the USSR economy and energy grid and dismantled by a post-independence civil war, the country sank into poverty and food and energy shortages became commonplace. As for all post-Soviet countries, international organizations swiftly took charge of Tajikistan's 'development and democratization', while International Financial Institutions (IFIs) managed its economic liberalization and provided financial assistance.

After a few years these organizations' economic credo evolved and as a result a new development framework materialized that began to reshape the conditionality of the financial assistance provided. Also known as the 'good governance agenda', this paradigm permitted the IFIs to condition grants and loans on important reforms in every sphere of national policy-making. In a country heavily in need of external resources, this implied surrendering significant aspects of national sovereignty and autonomy over political and economic policy-making.

This chapter argues that in recent years the Tajik leadership has however taken quite daring and dissenting decisions that herald a newfound confidence and autonomy. From the War on Terror to the rise of China as a regional and global power, new geopolitical developments have changed the power relations and opportunities for the Tajik ruling clan. They increasingly provide this small landlocked country with a 'geopolitical rent', a capacity to gain political and economic advantage from regional and international actors interested in its geostrategic position, used by the government to resist exogenous constraints to its autonomy. But they also fuel internal rivalries that had been superficially contained by international efforts politically to stabilize the country.

This chapter argues that the downsizing of international actors' sway over the state-building process liberates a space for the expression of the real nature of Tajikistani statehood and of its informal structure. The ruling clan's increased control over the country's resources and policy-making space raises new challenges and increases the weight of patron–client networks. While this competition is described by international observers as hindering economic development and posing new threats to the stability of the state, this chapter suggests an alternative reading of recent developments. It argues that this newfound autonomy forces the ruling clan into negotiating the terms of its power with internal forces in Tajikistan and infers it might represent a chance for economic development and for independent post-colonial state-building.

The first section of this chapter describes the introduction of Tajikistan into the global market through liberal reforms, the gradual shift in status from a 'transition country' to a 'developing country' in the IFIs, rhetoric and how this shift was accompanied by an extension of IFIs, prescriptions to wider spheres of state responsibility. It further suggests that the increasing convergence of Western countries' assistance channel is responsible for considerably shrinking the policy-space of the Tajik Government. Section two assesses the new economic and political opportunities which Tajikistan was gradually granted thanks to changed dynamics in the region's geopolitical balance with the arrival of the US in Russia's near neighborhood, followed by China's rise as a regional and global economic power. An account of the Tajik government's ambition for autonomous development is given through the example of the Roghun industrial project. Section three exposes the impact of this new found autonomy on internal politics and the importance of resources to access power in the Tajik political landscape. Applying to the Tajik context Mushtaq Khan's analysis of patron–client relationships, it argues that the supposed relationship between good governance and economic development cannot be treated as a given, nor is it supported by strong evidence in developing countries. In the latter context, case studies show that not only can corruption be inherent to the transition process but it can even have desirable outcomes for economic development just as for stability. This rests crucially on the proviso that the type of patron–client politics is one that enables long-run growth, and sufficient space for negotiation in the 'political marketplace'.

The chapter argues that rather than rejecting current developments as 'failure' or 'poor performance' of the Tajik state, international actors should engage through a more nuanced and reflective analysis. It will particularly underline the importance of such a context-sensitive approach to development practice with regards to engagement with civil society.

Global Market, Institutional Reform, and Shrinking Policy-Space

Tajikistan was one of the last post-Soviet countries to begin its economic transition. In the first years, due to the civil war, IFIs experts had difficulty finding a stable interlocutor. Only from 1996 onwards, once the first agreement establishing the Commission on National Reconciliation was signed in December, did the main Transition Assistance credits begin to link the country to the structures and rules of the global market. As Hoen expresses, 'the transition to a market economy embedded in a democratic order for the 7 million Tajiks could begin'.[1]

The International Monetary Fund (IMF) and the World Bank (WB) launched their programme together in May 1996 followed by other regional financial institutions. Although destroyed by war and in urgent need of social and productive infrastructure, all the IFIs present offered grants and loans for the rebuilding of the financial structure of the country, with a focus on the banking system.[2]

In a country deprived of infrastructure and skilled labour,[3] one can wonder why a focus on financial reform was chosen. But in the 1990s, despite the emerging critic of the IFIs' policies, the economic theory and policies governing IFIs' loans were still focused on macroeconomic and fiscal reforms.

Only at the very end of the millennium did the IFIs start to concede that the policies had failed to achieve development and growth in most countries. In the late 1990s IFIs' economic policies, also known as 'Structural Adjustments' though sometimes referred to as 'shock therapy' in the post-Soviet context, became subject to increasing criticism. The main critic of these ultra-liberal reforms imposed on developing countries appeared to be the Vice President and Chief Economist of the World Bank himself, Joseph Stiglitz.[4] However, Stiglitz's critique would not question the neoliberal ideology *per se*. It would rather help to usher in a new development paradigm, or 'Comprehensive Development Framework' developed in 1999 by then President of the World Bank, James Wolfensohn.[5] Blaming the failure of markets on corrupt institutions in recipient countries, this 'new' theory states that poverty is created due to mismanagement by governments, a consequence of bad governance. It contends that poverty-alleviation and growth have to be linked to institution-building and governance reform, that 'good and clean governments' will in turn guarantee the success of the markets and ensure a trickle-down effect of economic growth to 'the poor'. This new theory would allow the IFIs to expand their involvement beyond economic reform, to social, legal, financial and institutional policy and increasingly to democracy governance and even human rights. This 'holistic approach to the structural, social and human aspects of development'[6] would become known as the 'good governance agenda' and frame the new narrative of the IFIs and the United Nations (through the Millennium Development Goals) from year 2000 onwards.

Tajikistan was among the first countries to be subjected to the new development paradigm. This 'repackaging' of economic policies of the IFIs into an all-inclusive socio-political reform package accompanied another shift in Tajikistan's dependency-type. The East–West division being obsolete, Tajikistan shifted from a 'transition' country to the IFIs' category of 'developing country' in need of policy advice to develop its economy.

There were only a few months between the July 1999 Enhanced Structural Adjustment Facility (ESAF) loan, that did not mention the word 'poverty', and the December 1999 Letter of Intent[7] that introduced the same loan as a Poverty Reduction Growth Facility (PRGF) with some confusion between one and the other. This 'overnight relabeling'[8] of the same economic policies now glazed with poverty-reduction buzzwords became the new IMF and World Bank rhetoric, mainstreamed by the *World Development Report 2000/2001, Attacking Poverty*. The new rhetoric came with a new instrument, or action plan, to implement this 'novel' vision: the Poverty Reduction Strategy Papers (PRSP).

Tajikistan was among the first countries to draft the interim PRSP, 'assisted in the design of the programme by staffs of the World Bank and the IMF and other international supporters of the Tajik development process'.[9] As Stiglitz expressed, in this new paradigm 'participation and ownership are crucial',[10] both to ensure efficiency and legitimize the action plan: 'countries must be in the driver's seat and set the course'.[11]

But the degree of ownership of recipient countries over the PRS process was soon to be evaluated as insufficient by many observers, including the Independent Evaluation Office (IEO) of the IMF, which in 2004, observed 'tensions between ownership and the [IMF and World Bank's] own judgments on what policies are good for growth and poverty reduction'. The IEO report noted that 'on a few issues [the discussion appeared to be] overprescriptive, [and that] the policy papers establishing the [Poverty Reduction Strategy] approach never explicitly address [the tensions that show up in] the question of how far the "policy space" should be broadened . . . to be acceptable to [the IMF and the WB]'.[12]

Subsequently, in 2005, the United Nations 'called on countries to prepare national development strategies [to help them] take advantage of and expand their policy space–their effective room for manoeuvre in formulating and integrating national economic, social, and environmental policies'.

Thus, three years after the adoption of the first Tajik Poverty Reduction Strategy Paper, the IFIs offered their support to the Tajik Government again in drafting a National Development Strategy (NDS),[13] described as 'a long-term socioeconomic programme developed to regulate the development process of the country, taking into account long-term perspective and compliance with the Millennium Development Goals, currently implemented through medium-term Poverty Reduction Strategies'.[14] In other words, the goals and the vision were set for Tajikistan before it even drafted its 'national strategy'.

According to Aminjanov, the NDS is 'intended to define the priorities and direction for the long-range strategic outlook while the PRS is an action plan that outlines the implementation of the NDS over a three-year period'.[15] But in effect the NDS was created after the PRSP, and duplicates the latter's priorities, or as the IMF itself puts it 'the National Development Strategy of Tajikistan mainly complements future renewals, ensures implementation of development process of the country'.[16] Yet, development practice in Tajikistan is today centered on this double-document i.e. Poverty Reduction Strategy Papers/National Development Strategy. Considering the NDS as a 'vision document from the state', all development partners working in Tajikistan 'focus their programmes and plans on these priorities'.[17] Recently a new coordination mechanism, the Joint Country Partnership Strategy, comprising all the major multilateral donors, including the OECD Donor Assistance Committee (DAC), institutionalized their alignment around One Strategy (i.e. the NDS/PRS-3).[18]

Despite the efforts to give an appearance of ownership to the endorsed policies, the inverse effect of this development framework is obvious. As Abrahamsen (2004:184) shows, the Poverty Reduction Strategy Papers has become the main conditional procedure for the disbursement of development aid and new loans under HIPC (the Highly Indebted Poor Country Programme).[19] Furthermore the World Bank and the IMF 'retain the power to veto' a country's PRSP.

In order to avoid disagreement and potentially refusal of assistance, the 'Bank undertook to develop a "PRSP Sourcebook"[20] offering guidance on best practices and to organize outreach and learning events'.[21] A look at the PRSP Sourcebook's chapters demonstrates the extent of the inclusiveness of this new strategy. Each aspect of economic, fiscal, governance and social policy is mentioned and guidelines are offered to help the country apply the 'right' methodology and fill the boxes. The space for developing a national strategy is obviously limited by the need to see the PRSP accepted in order to receive any assistance or debt relief. As

Abrahamsen notes 'not surprisingly, to date, no country's poverty reduction strategy has rejected the economic philosophy of the international financial institutions'.[22]

The PRSP gives directions for every aspect of a country's national policy, from economy and finances to institutions, social protection, labour, education, local governance and environment. As Craig and Porter argue 'it is a way to bind country debt management into global macro- economic, governance and social policies'.[23] The new methods of management and channeling of the assistance through budget support, sector wide approaches, earmarked assistance and convergence towards the PRSP priorities increasingly shrunk the Tajik government's capacity to design its own policies and left little room for the state to invest in sectors not covered and endorsed by the PRSP.

The institutional reforms directly controlled both the organization of the Government and the way it manages its resources. As Craig and Porter express: 'the scope of this convergence in "good governance", especially through its macro-planning mechanisms, represents ... an attempt to generate a level of global to local integration, discipline and technical management of marginal economies, governance and populations unprecedented since colonial times'.[24]

Furthermore, control over countries' national policy has taken on a new dimension in recent years. A series of high-level harmonization forums took place from 2003 to 2005, resulting in the Paris Declaration on Aid Effectiveness and the Accra Agenda,[25] which call for greater coordination of all OECD/DAC aid, which means a major part of the Official Development Assistance. Although the discourse emphasizes the importance of harmonization for countries' ownership, in practice it has the opposite effect. The PRSP is once again the strategy around which harmonization will take place through the Joint Country Partnership Strategy. The increasing convergence of economic assistance towards the IFI-led development model is increasingly shrinking the autonomous policy-space of recipient governments.

Although international transitional aid helped the Tajik ruling clan secure its assets and reinforce its increasingly authoritarian rule during and after the peace process,[26] the 'new' development paradigm increasingly limits its capacity to extend and consolidate its advantage. The 'good governance agenda' and its emphasis on institutional reform democracy and decentralization and especially on the fight against corruption, increasingly interfere with the ruling clan's means of securing its advantage on the internal political stage.

As Craig and Porter express, the 'good governance agenda' does not give voice or ownership to the recipient country but rather 'it narrows local politics around service delivery mandates, while realpolitik interests continue to operate with impunity'.[27] And, indeed, understanding the 'real politics' is key to appreciate the new directions development is likely to take in Tajikistan.

Geopolitical changes, opening of policy-space and access to resources

In the 1990s Tajikistan was a small landlocked country coming out of Soviet rule, and of limited interest to the Western world. Moscow had greatly influenced the outcome of the civil war in a pro-Russian direction and was politically and militarily very present in the country that it never ceased considering as its zone of influence.[28]

Since the beginning of the War on Terror, the situation started to change. Developments in the regional geopolitical context provided Tajikistan with a geostrategic advantage that it has used gradually to extend its sovereignty and policy-making autonomy.

With the involvement of the United States in Afghanistan, Tajikistan became a staging ground for operations. Stabilizing Tajikistan hence became a priority and the United States deployed important military as well as humanitarian and development assistance, through a large number of NGOs, to help stabilize and secure the country. The IFIs scaled up their assistance budget and, following the money, a myriad of international NGOs discovered the poorest country of Central Asia, shifting the direction of aid from humanitarian to development assistance, and began to implement the newly-conceived 'good governance agenda'.

With these flows of global assistance and the engagement of the United States, the Tajik government saw the opportunity to downplay the influence of its former Russian 'metropolis'. The president Emomali Rahmon was guaranteed flows of external assistance, border protection as well as support for his authoritarian regime by the United States and the IFIs. The Tajik government used this new geopolitical strategic position amidst the War on Terror to push for its own agenda: securing autonomy from Moscow.

This new geopolitical rent was double-edged; if it permitted the strengthening of the president and his clan's power to gain some degree of autonomy from Moscow, it also tied the ruling clan into a bargaining game that had limited scope for autonomous policy-making.[29]

Nevertheless recent years have seen a new trend in global economics and politics as well as regional dynamics that have created new opportunities for the Tajik government to start making autonomous policies amid signs of true 'ownership'. Building on its bargaining experience, the Tajik government has now made good use of the rise of China as a global power on its doorstep. China's exceptional economic boom had a positive outcome for Tajikistan, both in terms of economic opportunity and political momentum.

Because China needed to expand its markets through Tajikistan to reach Central Asian economies, the giant neighbour has been very interested in building infrastructure in Tajikistan, from roads to electricity lines and power stations, to transport its products.[30] The two countries signed a $2 billion contract in 2009 to build major infrastructure in the country. China also boosted its trade agreements, becoming the leading investor in the country: the volume of bilateral trade was of $1.5 billion in 2009.

Apart from financial assistance and loans,[31] and investment in infrastructure much needed in a country where the little existing was destroyed by the civil war, the importance of the relationship with China lies in the Chinese assistance model. Subject to much controversy currently,[32] Chinese assistance has a similar structure in

Tajikistan as it does in Africa: China sends its own manpower to build infrastructure with no political or economic policy conditions attached. China's development model is based on 'non-interference in internal affairs' and the aid is channeled into 'apolitical infrastructure projects'.[33]

Although some significant concessions are already appearing, as with the recent ceding of 1,000 square kilometres of Tajik land to China,[34] and in spite of many legitimate questions relative to the repayment of Chinese loans in the future through political or financial concessions, the economic partnership is currently beneficial and crucial for the Tajik government in terms of tangible economic outcome. While IFIs offer assistance in exchange for strict economic reforms supposed to attract foreign investment into the country (the total FDI by Western donors in 2010 was of $46 million), non-DAC donors like China, Russia and Iran invest directly in infrastructure, providing $124.7 million in 2010.[35]

As expressed by the US Ambassador to Tajikistan in 2005:

> From the West, Rahmonov receives painful and long-drawn-out economic restructuring and seemingly endless and inconclusive feasibility studies. From Russia (and Iran and perhaps China), he receives promises of large-scale investment that could potentially lift the entire economy. He has no extensive experience in the West and no deep understanding of the complexities and realities of the global economy. He wants Tajik economic growth, and he wants it now.[36]

The economic partnership with China provided the Tajik ruling clan with increasing economic resources and investment in infrastructure, which is a priority for the stability of the regime. But another advantage is the development model that the rise of China offers as an alternative to the mainstream IFI-led model.

Chinese development is indeed iconoclastic. Based on a state capitalism not averse to corruption or patronage, it is far from the model of a liberal-democratic state that IFIs prescribe as the precondition to achieve economic development and growth. The success of China not only in achieving growth but also in reducing poverty[37] to an extent that no PRSP-equipped country was able to match, offers a credible alternative to the economic reforms proposed by the IFIs. It also gives way to new discourses on 'knowledge' and norms of development, directly through the example of its success and because the Chinese government's voice is more present on the international scene, directly challenging the universal values mainstreamed by Western countries for half a century.

The rise of China therefore does not offer simply operational freedom through its economic partnership and support; it provides rhetorical flexibility in a changing world. China also provides a more convenient and less intrusive economic partner, and a possibility for integration in a regional cooperation framework where Tajikistan could have a role to play. The Shanghai Cooperation Organization (SCO) is gaining regional importance and membership could make Tajikistan less reliant on Official Development Assistance for its economic development and in the future perhaps less in need of the United States for maintaining control of its borders and hence less dependent on the dynamics of the War on Terror. Moreover Tajikistan has a critical role to play in relation to 'anti-drug trafficking', 'restraining terrorism and separatism', all major priorities of the SCO. The latter is particularly critical to Beijing, due to its anxiety over the separatist movements in its border region Xianjiang, where political support from Dushanbe would be welcome. Through such cooperation, Tajikistan becomes more than a recipient country offering strategic advantages. It becomes an interlocutor and a partner that can to some extent set its own rules, within bounds. Decreasingly dependent on the United States and Russia's rivalry as well as on the IFIs' financial support, the Tajik government increasingly undertakes more autonomous policies. This also gives room for manoeuvre to the Tajik ruling clan to negotiate bilaterally with Western actors, especially with the United States, revealing the limits of harmonization and multilateral convergence when particular security interests are at stake.

This 'new geopolitical deal' is likely to increasingly impact on the government's policy-making. We can already observe some examples of how the Tajik ruling clan uses its newly granted economic and political room for manoeuvre. Recent policies of the Tajik Government appear to translate its priorities for the country's economic development into the objective of ensuring the Government clan's ability to keep power by (i) ensuring the country's capacity to create economic resources and dispel a popular uprising which might be used by influential groups as inequality and poverty grow and (ii) developing its economy such that its own clan is able to benefit from the resources.

For many years the Tajik government has tried and to a certain extent succeeded in enriching itself through corruption of the financial assistance,[38] and from direct capture of national income through state-owned enterprises such as Barki-Tojik (electricity) or cotton and aluminium enterprises, which consume part of the country's energy. But as Heathershaw argues, the integration of these state enterprises in 'global assemblages' limits the capacity of the ruling clan to capture their economic output.[39]

The government needs to secure additional assets both to ensure its rule and to fund its vision of an independent Tajikistan. Electricity seems to be currently the most crucial field where the guarantee of autonomous resources is at stake. Dependent on other countries for electricity supplies the priority of the government is to develop independent sources of energy, both to ensure its income and the development of the country. This is well illustrated by the Roghun hydroelectric dam project.

After years of failed deals with Russia, the Tajik president did not find any investors apart from Iran for a construction project evaluated at more than $2 billion. Building on a narrative of national pride and independence the government launched a campaign to raise money through popular participation in the construction of the dam. The Tajik people were invited to buy shares in the Roghun enterprise. Campaigns plastered the streets and the media. Monuments were built to the glory of this 'national pride'; national channels would transmit repeated broadcasts of patriotic songs about Roghun followed by interviews with people queuing to buy shares.

It soon appeared that buying shares was not optional. Human Rights organizations reported that people were forced into buying shares through different means. A top-down pressure would force each Tajik to buy a share, from public administration workers to schoolteachers, businesses, NGOs. Unemployed and poor people would be denied access to social benefits if they didn't provide a receipt of a Roghun share. People even reported being paid with Roghun shares in place of their salaries.[40] Confronted with these obvious violations of economic rights, international organizations criticized the campaign. The IMF even declared that forcing poor people to spend such amounts would 'undermine macroeconomic stability'.

Yet no member of the international community took any real step or measure to condemn the policy. Nor did they offer to participate financially to help build the dam, most likely because Roghun created important tensions with Uzbekistan. Resting downstream, Uzbekistan asserted that a dam would substantially reduce its water supply and denounced the environmental impact of the project. The real concern of Uzbekistan was not only environmental but political as the control of the Amu Darya river would give substantial leverage to Tajikistan as well as strengthening its economy and autonomy. As a result the international community refused to invest in this infrastructure project that would solve not only Tajikistan's water issues but also the power supply problems, representing substantial potential for economic development.

However the prospect of seeing such a high-scale project that might have a considerable economic weight in the region be monopolized by China, Iran or Russia, pushed the World Bank into breaking the stasis of the international community at the risk of alienating Uzbekistan, and ordering an environmental study of the project.[41] One can speculate that given the economic importance of Roghun and the export potential it holds for Tajikistan, the study will strive to create the conditions for a consensus. As Sodiqov shows, the World Bank declared that 'if the project proves financially and environmentally sustainable, [it will] assist the Tajik government to create an international consortium to build it'.[42]

In support of this analysis Grimm argued that 'some more recent reoccurrences of issues on the Western aid agenda might have to do with practice (or perceptions) of Chinese policies. On their agendas for development cooperation, Western donors have rediscovered infrastructure, for instance'.[43]

Roghun appears to be a first victory for the Tajik Government in navigating between rivalries within the regional powers and the world market to develop access and control over crucial resources. It reveals the bargaining power of the government in respect to IFIs and the international community and heralds greater ownership over infrastructure and economic development. This ownership was granted neither by a PRSP nor by the Paris Declaration for Harmonization, but rather by the opposite: the decreasing capacity of IFIs to prescribe national policies through conditional assistance.

The Roghun case also communicates the importance of resources for the exercise of power. Autonomy comes at a price for the ruling clan: the loss of protection and of the stability deal brokered by the international community through the peace process.[44] As the superficial political and economic system created by international donors fades, revealed is a particular form of statehood where politics do not happen through competitive elections but through the political negotiation of the access to resources.

Corruption, Development and Political Marketplace: An Alternative Analysis of Tajik Statehood

The rise of China and its 'developmental state' model has fuelled recent academic debate. Inspired by the Chinese model and strengthened by its new economic opportunities, the Tajik Government seems to be seeking its own version of the developmental state model. As the Roghun example shows, the Tajik government is determined to secure its access to hydroelectric resources, key to exercising a power that is not constrained by external pressures and is dominant on the internal scene. But Tajikistan is no China and the prospects for its 'developmental' path are unclear. The current academic literature offers different lenses to read the political and economic situation in Tajikistan and its future as a developmental state.

Following one strand of the current debate, Tajikistan can be considered as a 'hybrid regime', i.e. a regime where formal transition to democracy has taken place but where 'democratic structures are not consolidating'. This analysis foresees that state-led development will be 'captured by narrow interests more concerned with building clientelist networks than with fostering a transformation of the country's economy ... condemning any developmental initiative to failure'.[45]

Indeed, if judging by Tajikistan's ranking by international corruption watchdogs[46] or by the recommendations of international organizations such as the UNDP, the OSCE, or the International Crisis Group, in recent years, the level of corruption in Tajikistan has been increasing and represents the main impediment to its development.

But the link between 'clientelist networks', 'narrow interests' and economic development failure has not been proven by evidence so far. Mushtaq Khan's analysis of the relationship between corruption, economic development and democracy offers a useful framework to assess the trends of development in Tajikistan. According to this approach, 'good governance' reform and democracy, although desirable 'goals', are not necessarily the adequate 'means' to achieve development. The direction of causality between prosperity and good governance is not a given and 'there is not a single example in History of a poor country that first achieved high levels of democracy, transparency and rule of law and then became a developed country'.[47] Evidence shows that rapidly growing developing countries like China, India, Malaysia, Thailand etc. have the same 'inefficient' governance characteristics as low-income countries. Although none of them is a good performer in terms of good governance, the role of the state in these countries is crucial to understand their rapid growth.

Khan gives an evidenced account of how the good governance agenda is doubly-problematic as in 'it sets developing countries goals they cannot achieve [democratic accountability, anti-corruption, rule of law], and in addition, even if they could have been achieved, these goals are not sufficient to ensure sustainable growth, that must rely on state capacity to promote necessary technological, social and political conditions'.[48]

The question of 'state capacity' is crucial. The amount of taxation that society can raise is extremely small in poor countries because the productive sectors are small. Therefore there are no resources in the state budget and no money to spend on redistribution of different sorts to achieve political stability. As Khan argues, because there are many powerful groups of interests that need to be accommodated by the government and given access to resources, developing countries have significant amounts of political corruption. The principal tenet of Khan's approach is to describe the 'good governance' agenda as based on a neo-Weberian vision of the state, wedded to the belief that political stability can be achieved by controlling the fiscal space.[49] But such processes would require significant fiscal resources to be viable. In the Tajik case, as in many other low-income countries, these resources, which depend on tax collection, are simply not available.

So far, inclusion in the global market and liberalization accompanied by poverty-reduction strategies based on institutional reforms seem to have failed to create the conditions of economic development in Tajikistan. Poverty is 'widespread and persistent' and the 'overall productivity and demand for labor remains quite low'.[50] Economic growth is highly dependent on professional migration to Russia and remittances (41 per cent of GDP in 2011, the highest in the world in terms of GDP share), which are not a reliable source of budget revenue.

In this context, political stability needs therefore to be gained through other channels. The most important politics according to Khan 'take place off-budget, with off-budget resources being raised for redistribution down patron-client networks'.[51] All the evidence of democratization in developing countries shows that competition, transparency and electoral contest 'do very little to undermine the dominance of patron-client politics'.[52] As we will argue later in this chapter, the Tajik ruling clan seemingly has started to distribute a growing share of the political pie and to negotiate to achieve internal power stability outside of the 'elections politics' sphere.

In this context, one might consider the critique of the good governance agenda suggested by Mushtaq Khan and others to show that Tajikistan merits a place in the debate over the developmental state, alongside analyses of successful state-led development characterized by high levels of patronage, like China. However, identifying patron–client politics as inherent and structural is insufficient to fully understand Tajikistan's context and prospects. Using the Chinese example to assume they are necessarily conducive to economic development would likewise be deceptive. Corruption can be equally damaging for growth. As Khan shows in the case of Asian countries, the type of patron–client networks within which their corruption is located create differential economic performances.[53] Academic debate and prolific research on state building in Tajikistan have extensively analysed and exposed the nature of the Tajik state, its localist, factionalist and neo-patrimonial nature, in reference to nation-building, security and legitimacy. To have descriptive power, these empirically-driven analyses will need to be more systematically linked to the question of economic development. The type of patron–client network particular to Tajikistan must be analysed in regards to political accumulation and stabilization to provide a better understanding of how the particular nature of the corruption is likely to impede or foster economic growth and redistribution. A rigid disapproval of any kind of clientelism and strenuous fight against corruption as the one prescribed by the 'good governance' rhetoric[54] is therefore problematic in the Tajik case.

As De Waal argues in reference to Nigeria, those likely to be targeted in a war on corruption are not the most corrupt ones, but rather those who have demanded too high a price and have fallen from the ruler's favour ... An anti-corruption campaign, ostensibly aimed at institution-building, becomes an instrument for manipulating patronage and, by extension, an exercise in corruption itself. Within a political marketplace, the only way a member of the elite can respond cogently to an anti-corruption effort is to offer a pay-off to the political master of the anti-corruption tsar. Abdicating from the patronage system is a short cut to political oblivion'.[55]

Alex De Waal's concept of 'political marketplace' offers us a helpful tool to understand the nature of statehood in Tajikistan. De Waal's account of patron–client networks shows that 'in places where formal state institutions do not provide stability and services, patron-client systems may function as a repository of trust and security and patronage mechanisms can dispense resources, sometimes in a way that is recognizably fair'. Patronage is thus the 'circulatory system of real politics [and] the heartbeat of the system is possession of the symbols of sovereignty, which allows a ruler to allocate aid funds or mineral revenues'.[56]

The political marketplace conception is particularly problematic for Western-led policy-making approaches. As De Waal argues 'state-builders ignore vernacular politics, to the detriment of the countries they leave at the end of their contracts ... forces such as kinship and patron-client networks are readily denigrated as "tribalism" or "corruption". While Western policymakers uncritically judge patronage as a character of "fragile states," it can alternatively be seen as a sign of resilience. A state that is negotiating with different forces in the country shows on the opposite, signs of sovereignty, itself a "commodity to be bartered"'[57] and is likely to be a bigger political player than a government whose legitimacy depends only on external support. This system of allocation creates a competition that works as a political marketplace where allegiance is bought or sold in exchange for access to resources.

The competition is sometimes expressed through direct confrontation when an 'insurgent uses targeted violence against the government to get himself noticed and command a good price for his allegiance ... The government uses violence against the insurgent, or his community, in order to weaken his asset base and drive down the price'.[58]

The Rasht insurgency is one example of 'direct competition' in the political marketplace that has been misinterpreted by many observers. In 2011, a report by the International Crisis Group (ICG) entitled 'Tajikistan: the changing insurgent threats' reveals a significant misunderstanding of the Tajik political situation. Opening with an assessment of the insurgency in Rasht and the incapacity of the government to deal with the attack, the 2011 ICG report swiftly goes on to link the growing threat of the Islamic Movement of Uzbekistan (IMU) and its vision of an 'Islamic caliphate' to the cronyism of the government and the popular discontent, the emergence of new Islamic guerrillas to the inadequate response of the government and finally the growing threat of Jihad to the protection of drug routes by senior officials. The report quotes the US Director of National Intelligence as stating that:

> In 2010, Tajikistan's President Rahmon was forced to negotiate with regional warlords after failing to defeat them militarily, an indicator that Dushanbe is potentially more vulnerable to an Islamic Movement of Uzbekistan with renewed interests in Central Asia.[59]

The *mujohed* insurgency that took place in September 2010 in the Kamarob Gorge resulted in heavy losses on the government side. As Roche and Heathershaw found out in Rasht during the fighting, 'if it is highly unlikely that the conflict in Kamarob is part of a regional Islamist struggle it is just as improbable that it is part of a national uprising against the state. The evidence indicates that local commanders in Rasht acted autonomously against the government as they felt threatened by the further incursion of the Dushanbe government into their region'.[60]

After a few months of armed conflict and loss on both sides, fighters involved in the attacks, including Mirzokhuja Akhmadov, former opposition fighter during the civil war and head of a local militia unit in Gharm, have been offered employment in the Ministry of Interior in order to dismantle armed guerrillas networks. While many observers read Rasht events as the demise of the Tajik state and signs of its high instability, one can interpret it as a more nuanced rise in prices of allegiance in the political marketplace, according to which the government will have to further negotiate the terms of its stability, allocating additional resources to new groups. The recommendation to fight against corruption to tackle insurgent threats therefore denotes a misunderstanding of the nature of the Tajik state.

Within the same conceptual approach, rather than embracing an alarmist reaction to the increasing islamicization of Tajik society and to the inadequate response of the Tajik government, one can instead perceive yet more potential for negotiation by groups at a very modest social level where few other levers of influence are available. This is echoed by Olimova, who argues that the 'deterioration of the socio–economic situation, unmet expectations and disregard for the vital interests of large segments of the population have boosted political Islamic movements that offer alternatives in the political marketplace and display a marked social slant'.[61]

Under the Soviet regime the predominantly rural Tajik population maintained its traditional social organization, kinship and *mahalla* ties were transferred into the *kolkhoz* organization through forced collectivization. Local family, clan and kinship relations resurfaced during the war and after the peace process under the rule of Rahmon they became the only way of survival in a collapsed economy deprived of any social protection. For years the majority of the country strengthened its local sociability and nourished resentment towards the government that was unable to provide for basic needs. More importantly, in this new *mahalla* sociability, the religious leaders became the first recourse in the absence of a response from the government.[62]

The religious field must be seen in light of wider political–economic context, a view consistent for example with Epkenhans who describes the division of the religious field and of its relations with the government as well as the intricate links between local business men, local elites and religious leaders. He argues that in local communities, patronage networks provide alternative forms of social order, access to business opportunities and a certain norm for the practice of Islam.[63] All of these represent forces that the government will have to negotiate with to secure stability and access to local resources. On the religious front, Epkenhans' account of the work and influence of a leading religious authority, Hoji Akbar Turajonzoda, on the country's religious life as well as of its political profile shows that the government does negotiate, even with religious circles, when it is considered strategic. As for the recent anti-Islamic measures[64] and the ruling clan's use of its state power, they offer different possible interpretations: they may lead to a radicalization of Islamic groups but they might also encourage local religious leaders to 'sell' their allegiance and that of their communities in exchange for resources.

A critical aspect of the Western-led development paradigm imposed upon Tajikistan is a flawed conception of the nature of the Tajikistan state and polity. As Heathershaw has recently argued many officials, aid workers, academics and concerned citizens in Western countries observe the developments in Tajikistan through the lens of 'policy priorities and imaginations of the international community'.[65] In 2009, commenting on another ICG report that qualifies Tajikistan as a 'failed state',[66] Heathershaw argued that this analysis relies on a 'simplistic neo-Weberian account of the modern state' adding that in the ICG report, as in many others, 'the ideal-type liberal democratic state provides the normative foundation against which stateness is assessed'.[67]

Two years later, after simplistically associating the Rasht insurgency with a regional Islamic threat and the 'failure' of the Tajik state, the 2011 ICG report concludes with recommendations to the international community, calling for a 'reconfiguration of the strategy and philosophy of aid'. It suggests that they 'make conditionality the norm to reward reform and new approaches and penalize corruption or incompetence'.

The report also concludes rather patronizingly that:

> Aid should be used to encourage and reward behaviour ... If the leadership refuses to cooperate – which in this case may well be tantamount to opening the way to the Islamic Movement of Uzbekistan or other armed insurgent groups – the international community may have to reach for a more painful weapon. It should deploy forensic accountants and

lawyers and investigate the widely reputed leadership bank accounts in places like the British Virgin Islands.[68]

As Heathershaw expressed in reference to the 2009 ICG report:

> The prescription that a modern republic should be first and foremost responsive to the demands of external actors for international and human security and must adhere to a certain model of governance ... is more likely to exacerbate, rather than attenuate state weakness.[69]

Moreover, the Tajik government is unlikely to abide by these prescriptions or recommendations as conditionality of aid is increasingly losing its efficiency, as alternative resources appear at its door. There is therefore an alternative way of interpreting the policy choices of the Tajik government that points to an increasingly resilient state. According to Matveeva, the regime provides 'short term stability at the cost of substantive reform ... the weakness of the current state is not in its tendency towards crisis and failure, but in its inability to act as a developmental engine in the long-term interests of the country'.[70]

Before condemning the long-term perspectives of the country, one has to analyze the conditions for successful economic development and Tajikistan's assets and shortcomings, as well as the extent to which development depends on the ruling clan's moral commitment to development or on structural political and economic mechanisms, which, if accurately comprehended and engaged with, might foster the development process.

Conclusion

By critically questioning the efficiency and accuracy of institution-building as it is theorized and implemented in Tajikistan by mainstream development practitioners and policy-makers, this chapter proposed to use alternative theoretical frameworks to analyze recent developments in the Tajik government's policy-making.

Examples of the Tajik Government's policy, such as Roghun, or reaction to 'threats', such as to the Rasht insurgency, highlight the need for both reflection upon the (in)adequacy of orthodox development conceptual frameworks and introduction of concepts otherwise ignored in analysis of Tajikistan's development. This chapter's modest aim is therefore to stimulate debate and encourage further research to support or invalidate the hypothesis that patron–clients politics in Tajikistan is not necessarily ill-fated and that institutional and political responses to the presence of corruption should be better informed and take into account different dimensions of this phenomenon.

As the country distances itself from Western blueprints of development, the possible permutations of its future become increasingly difficult to forecast. Tajikistan is at a watershed. It has many opportunities for a genuine post-colonial national transformation that could include different components of society in a political negotiation for the country's progress and development. Although beyond the scope of this chapter, the role of society will be crucial to ensure real ownership in the future. Western policy-makers and development practitioners in particular should rethink their engagement with civil society in Tajikistan. As this chapter argues, society is a constituent part of the patron–client networks and engaging with it requires a far deeper understanding than the simplistic opposition between state and civil society promoted by most foreign organizations. By mediating depoliticized relations of society with the state, a superficial barrier is created of a liberal bureaucratic elite that is detached from the reality of the country, unable to negotiate its share in the real political arena.

While insisting, perversely, on the questionable goal of increasingly irrelevant and context-insensitive convergence and harmonization strategies, the international community must reassess its role in these processes as the wishful thinking that underpins IFIs' continued adherence to the 'good governance agenda' represents, in the Tajik case, an ongoing triumph of hope over experience.

Notes

1 Hoen, H., 'Transition strategies in Central Asia: is there such a thing as shock-versus-gradualism?' *Economic and Environmental Studies*, 2010, vol. 10/2, pp. 229–45.
2 On this subject see the list of projects of IMF and EBRD between 1996 and 1999 on their website: (http://www.ebrd.com/pages/country/tajikistan.shtml;) (http://www.imf.org/external/country/TJK/index.htm).
3 World Bank, *Tajikistan Country Assistance Strategy*, 24 May 1996 (http://www-wds.worldbank.org/external/default/WDSContentServer/WDSP/IB/2000/03/03/000009265_3961019214916/Rendered/PDF/multi_page.pdf).
4 Stiglitz, J., 'Towards a New Paradigm for Development', address at the 9th Raul Prebisch Lecture UNCTAD, October 1998 (http://unctad.org/en/docs/prebisch9th.en.pdf).
5 Wolfensohn, J., 'Proposal for a Comprehensive Development Framework', 21st January 1999 (http://web.worldbank.org/archive/website01013/WEB/0__CO-87.HTM).
6 Stiglitz, J., *op. cit.*, p. 10.
7 IMF, Tajikistan Letter of intent, 30 December 1999
8 Craig, D., Porter, D., *Development Beyond Neoliberalism? Governance, Poverty Reduction and Political Economy 1997–2005*, Routledge: 2006, p. 4.
9 IMF, *op. cit.*
10 Stiglitz, J., *op. cit.*, p. 12.
11 Wolfensohn, J., *op. cit.*, p. 9.
12 IEO–Independent Evaluation Office, 'Evaluation of the IMF's Role in Poverty Reduction Strategy Papers and the Poverty Reduction and Growth Facility', 2004, p. 60 (http://www.imf.org/external/np/ieo/2004/prspprgf/eng/index.htm).
13 Republic of Tajikistan, 'National Development Strategy of the Republic of Tajikistan For The Period to 2015', Regional Conference on MDG based NDS and PRSP, 15–17 March 2007, Dushanbe, 2010 ([http://www.gki.tj/img/NDS%20till%202015_Eng.pdf).
14 IMF, 'Country report n°12/33, Republic of Tajikistan: Poverty Reduction strategy Paper-Progress Report', 2012, p. 3.
15 Aminjanov, R., *Case study on Aid Effectiveness in Tajikistan*, Wolfensohn Center for Development Working Paper n°13, October 2009, p. 7.
16 IMF, 2012, *op. cit.*, p. 3.
17 Aminjanov, R., *op. cit.*, p. 7.
18 JCPS–Joint Country Partnership Strategy, Dushanbe, November 2009, p. 16 (http://www.undp.tj/files/JCPS_November_2009_signed_eng.pdf).
19 Abrahamsen, R., 'Poverty Reduction or Adjustment by another name?', *Review of African Political Economy*, 2004, vol. 31/99, p. 184.
20 The PRSP Sourcebook is available on the World Bank's website (http://go.worldbank.org/35ICHSR3M0).

21 Cammack, P., 'What the World Bank Means by Poverty Reduction, and Why it Matters', *New Political Economy*, 2004, vol. 9/2, pp. 189–211.

22 Abrahamsen, R., *op. cit.*, p. 185.

23 Craig, D., Porter, D., 'Poverty Reduction Strategy Papers: A New Convergence', *World Development*, 2003, vol. 31/1, p. 60.

24 *Ibid.*, p. 55.

25 Paris Declaration and Accra Agenda for Action are available on OECD website (http://www.oecd.org/document/18/0,3746,en_2649_3236398_35401554_1_1_1_1,00.html).

26 Nakaya, S., 'Politics of Resource Distributions in Post-Conflict State Building', IUCSHA, 2006 (http://web.gc.cuny.edu/dept/rbins/IUCSHA/fellows/Nakaya-memo-final.pdf).

27 Craig, D., Porter, D., 2006, *op. cit.*, p. 252.

28 The outcome of the civil war is by far more complex and nuanced of course. Peace negotiations were not purely Russian-influenced as the UN and Iran and even Afghanistan were involved and had a common interest in ending the conflict. However the evolution after the 1997 General Agreement saw the Moscow-backed 'Rahmon clan' increase its hold on the government against other parties to the conflict and to the peace agreement, thereby strengthening Russia's position in Tajikistan. On the Tajik peace process, see Abdullaev, K., Barnes, C. (eds), *Politics of Compromise: The Tajikistan Peace Process*, London: Conciliation Resources Accord, 2001.

29 American officials acknowledge the rivalry and competition with Moscow for influence on Tajikistan and the gradual ousting of Russian military, political and cultural assets from the country, in a series of Wikileaks cables from November 2005 onwards (Wikileaks, 'US Embassy Cables: Russia Targeting Tajikistan to Reduce Western Influence, says US, November 14 2005', *The Guardian*, 12 December 2010).

30 On China–Tajikistan economic relations, see Korniyenko, Y., Sakatsume, T., 'Chinese investment in the transition countries', *EBRD Working Paper n°107*, January 2009 (http://www.ebrd.com/downloads/research/economics/workingpapers/wp0107.pdf); Roque, J., 'China invests in Central Asia stability through Tajikistan', *China Briefing*, 22 May 2008 (http://www.china-briefing.com/news/2008/05/22/china-reconnects-with-tajikistan.html); Sodiqov, A., 'China boosts investment in Tajikistan', *CACI Analyst*, 7 January 2009.

31 In 2007 Tajikistan was granted a $200 million loan and a $172 million loan by China through the SCO.

32 In spite of a spectacular economic growth, there is intensive debate over China's own model of development as well as its assistance to other countries. The main critics address the lack of democracy and of labour and human rights in China as well as the question of the long-term benefits to local capacity-building and economic productive capacity in countries where China is an investor.

33 Kassenova, N., 'China as an emerging donor in Tajikistan and Kyrgyztan', *Russie.Nei.Visions* (IFRI Russia/CIS Center), 2009, n°36, p. 8.

34 BBC News, 'Tajikistan cedes land to China', 13 January 2011 (http://www.bbc.co.uk/news/world-asia-pacific-12180567).

35 US Department of State, '2011 Investment Climate Statement', Bureau of Economic, Energy and Business Affairs, March 2011 (http://www.state.gov/e/eb/rls/othr/ics/2011/157368.htm).

36 Wikileaks, *op. cit.*

37 As the World Bank 2007 report shows, China's economic development has significantly contributed to poverty-reduction and 'the drop in the world's extreme poverty over the past two decades is entirely due to the rapid extension of China and India'. The Report states that the drop in the number of people living on less than a dollar a day is more than accounted for by the $300 million taken out of extreme poverty in China. It further states that excluding China, there has actually been no improvement (World Bank Annual Report 2007).

38 In 2008 IMF revealed that the National Bank of Tajikistan and the Finance ministry had been 'fiddling the country's accounts for several years, falsifying the flow of funds and concealing the disappearance of uncounted millions of dollars of international loan funds' (Helmer, J., 'IMF Blows Whistle on Tajik Corruption', *Asia Times Online*, 26 March 2008 (http://www.atimes.com/atimes/Central_Asia/JC26Ag01.html)).

39 Heathershaw, J., 'Tajikistan Amidst Globalization: State Failure or State Transformation?' *Central Asian Survey*, 2011, vol. 30/1, p. 147.

40 Based on interviews with NGO workers, Dushanbe 2010.

41 Bank Information Center, 'Tajikistan's Roghun Hydro: Social and Environmental Aspects', Brief note, 21 March 2011.

42 Sodiqov, A., 'World Bank to Assess Roghun Hydropower Project in Tajikistan', *Central Asia-Caucasus Analyst*, 2010, vol. 12/8.

43 Grimm, S., 'China as Africa's Ambiguous Ally. Why China has a responsibility for Africa's development', CCS Discussion Paper n°1, 2011, p. 20.

44 Although the 'Rahmon clan' didn't respect the conditions of the 1997 Peace agreement in the exercise of its rule, the international community backed his rule, especially after 2001, as security concerns over the War on Terror made stability a higher priority than some democracy standard of the 'good governance agenda'.

45 Fritz, V., Roche Menocal, A., '(Re)building Developmental States: From Theory to Practice', ODI Working Paper n°274, September 2006.

46 Tajikistan was ranked 152nd out of 183 countries on its corruption rate (Transparency International, Corruption Perceptions Index, 2011).

47 Khan, M., 'Lecture on Governance Reform and Economic Growth', Governance in Africa lecture Series, 2009 (http://governanceinafrica.wordpress.com/).

48 Khan, M., 'Governance and Development', Workshop on Governance and Development organized by the World Bank and DFID, 11–12 November 2006, Dhaka, Bangladesh, p. 3.

49 *Ibid.*, p. 30.

50 Babajanian, B., 'The Social Exclusion Framework and Poverty Reduction Strategy in Tajikistan', *Central Asian Survey*, 2006, vol. 25/4, pp. 403–18.
51 Khan, M., 2006, *op. cit.*, p. 52.
52 Khan, M., 'Markets, States and Democracy: Patron-Client Networks and the Case for Democracy in Developing Countries', *Democratization*, 2005, vol. 12/5, pp. 714.
53 Khan, M., 'Patron-Client Networks and the Economic Effects of Corruption', *The European Journal of Development Research*, 1998, vol. 10/1, p. 15
54 Already in 1999, James Wolfensohn identified corruption as the 'most corrosive aspect of development', one that 'must be fought systematically at all levels'. And called on a 'vigorous commitment from the leadership to fight corruption at all levels' (Wolfensohn's, J., *op. cit.*).
55 De Waal, A., 'Dollarised', *London Review of Books*, 2010, vol. 32/12, p. 7.
56 *Ibid.*, p. 2.
57 *Ibid.*, p. 3.
58 *Ibid.*, p. 3.
59 International Crisis Group, 'Tajikistan: the Changing Insurgent Threats', *Asia Report*, n°205, 24 May 2011.
60 Roche, S., Heathershaw, J., 'Conflict in Tajikistan. Not Really about Radical Islam' and 'Tajikistan's Marginalised Youth', *Open Democracy.net*, 19–20 October 2010.
61 Olimova, S., 'Islam in Central Asia: Today and Tomorrow', *Human Security and Peace in Central Asia*, 2006, Academy OSCE in Bishkek, p. 99.
62 Freizer, S., 'Neo-liberal and communal civil society in Tajikistan: merging or dividing in the post war period?', *Central Asian Survey*, 2005, vol. 24/3.
63 Epkenhans, T., 'Defining Normative Islam: Some Remarks on Contemporary Islamic Thought in Tajikistan. Hoji Akbar Turajonzoda's Sharia and Society', *Central Asian Survey*, 2011, vol. 30/1, p. 84.
64 The government recently passed a law banning children (under 18) from mosques, adding to previous anti-beard campaigns, the closing down of unregistered mosques and religious schools and repatriating religious students from Islamic countries.
65 Heathershaw, J., 2011, *op. cit.*, p. 149.
66 International Crisis Group, 'Tajikistan: On the Road to Failure', *Asia Report*, n°162, 12 Feb 2009.
67 Heathershaw, J., 2011, *op. cit.*, p. 151.
68 International Crisis Group, 2011, *op. cit.*
69 Heathershaw, J., 2011, *op. cit.*, p. 147.
70 Matveeva, A., 'Tajikistan: "Revolutionary Situation" or a Resilient State?', *EUCAM Policy Brief*, n°12, 19 December 2009, p. 4 (http://ssrn.com/abstract=1604028).

INDEX